In Search of Cool Ground

War, Flight & Homecoming
in Northeast Africa

Edited by TIM ALLEN

Africa World Press, Inc.

P.O. Box 1892

Trenton, NJ 08607

P.O. Box 48

Asmara, ERITREA

Africa World Press, Inc.

P.O. Box 1892
Trenton, NJ 08607

P.O. Box 48
Asmara, ERITREA

Copyright © 1996 UNRISD
First Africa World Press, Inc. Edition 1996

Library of Congress Cataloging-in-Publication Data

In search of cool ground : war, flight & homecoming in northeast
    Africa / edited by Tim Allen. -- 1st Africa World Press ed.
        p.   cm.
    Includes bibliographical references and index.
    ISBN 0-86543-524-3 (cloth : alk. paper). -- ISBN 0-86543-525-1
(pbk. : alk. paper)
        1. Refugees, Political--Africa, Northeast. 2. Disaster relief-
    -Africa, Northeast. 3. War relief--Africa, Northeast.
    4. Repatriation--Africa, Northeast. 5. Return migration--Africa,
    Northeast. 6. fh.   I. Allen, Tim
    HV640.4.A355I5   1996
    362.87'0961--dc20   96-16119
                                                                        CIP

Published in England by:

James Currey Ltd.
54b Thornhill Square
Islington, London N1 1BE

... she nervously peered
Into the tarmac of our makeshift
Borders, her wind-blown babe suckling
The bitter sweat of her dry breasts,

Her teeth (tarred by wild fruit
on flight) exposing embittered memories
Of yet another home charred, ...

JACK MAPANJE,
from 'These Straggling Mudhuts of Kirk Range',
published in the *London Magazine*,
February/March, 1993: 45

'*kalamo ba lalini*'
'We are [a people who are] looking for cool ground'.

A MURSI SAYING

Note on
UNRISD

The United Nations Research Instititute for Social Development (UNRISD) is an autonomous agency that engages in multi-disciplinary research on the social dimensions of contemporary problems affecting development. Its work is guided by the conviction that, for effective development policies to be formulated, an understanding of the social and political context is crucial. The Institute attempts to provide governments, development agencies, grassroots organizations and scholars with a better understanding of how development policies and processes of economic, social and environmental change affect different social groups. Working through an extensive network of national research centres, UNRISD aims to promote original research and strengthen research capacity in developing countries.

Its research themes include Crisis, Adjustment and Social Change; Socio-Economic and Political Consequences of the International Trade in Illicit Drugs; Environment, Sustainable Development and Social Change; Ethnic Conflict and Development; Integrating Gender into Development Policy; Participation and Changes in Property Relations in Communist and Post-Communist Societies; Refugees, Returnees and Local Society; and Political Violence and Social Movements. UNRISD research projects focused on the 1995 World Summit for Social Development included Rethinking Social Development in the 1990s; Economic Restructuring and New Social Policies; Ethnic Diversity and Public Policies; and the War-torn Societies Project.

Contents

List of Tables,
Maps & Figures

List of
Abbreviations

CC	Central Committees
CERA	Commission for Eritrean Refugee Affairs
COR	Sudanese Commissioner for Refugees
DP	Democratic Party (of Uganda)
EDLM	Eritrean Democratic Liberation Movement
ELF	Eritrean Liberation Front
ENPA	Eritrean National Pact Alliance
EPLF	Eritrean People's Liberation Front
EPRDF	Ethiopian People's Revolutionary Democratic Front
ERC	Eritrean Referendum Commission
ERCS	Ethiopian Red Cross and Red Crescent Society
FAO	Food and Agriculture Organization
FY	financial year
GOE	Government of Eritrea
ICARA II	Second International Conference on Assistance to Refugees in Africa
ICOLD	International Commission on Large Dams
ICRC	International Committee of the Red Cross
ICVA	International Council of Voluntary Agencies
IDA	International Development Association
IFRC	International Federation of Red Cross and Red Crescent Societies
IGAAD	Inter-Governmental Authority on Drought and Development
IIHL	International Institute of Humanitarian Law
ILO	International Labour Organization
JMC	Joint Ministerial Committee
KY	Kabaka Yekka
MDM	Médecins du Monde
MDTM	Multi-Donor Technical Mission
MSF	Médecins Sans Frontières
NCA	Norwegian Church Aid
NGO	Non-Governmental Organization
NRA	National Resistance Army
NRM	National Resistance Movement
NURP	Northern Uganda Reconstruction Programme
ODA	Overseas Development Administration
OECD	Organization for Economic Co-operation and Development
OLF	Oromo Liberation Front
OLS	Operation Lifeline Sudan
PFDJ	People's Front for Democracy and Justice

PGE	Provisional Government of Eritrea
PROFERI	Programme for the Reintegration and Rehabilitation of Resettlement Areas in Eritrea
PTSD	Post-Traumatic Stress Disorder
QIPs	Quick Impact Projects
RASS	Relief Association of Southern Sudan (formerly SRRA)
RCs	Resistance Councils
REST	Relief Society of Tigray
RRPE	Relief and Rehabilitation Programme for Eritrea
SCF UK	Save the Children Fund UK
SERP	South-East Rangelands Project
SIM	Society of International Missionaries (formerly Sudan Interior Mission)
SNM	Somali National Movement
SPLA	Sudan Peoples' Liberation Army
SPLM	Sudan Peoples' Liberation Movement
SRRA	Sudan Relief and Rehabilitation Association
TGE	Transitional Government of Ethiopia
TPLF	Tigray People's Liberation Front
UPC	Uganda People's Congress
UPDA	Uganda People's Democratic Army
UNDHA	United Nations Department of Humanitarian Affairs
UNDP	United Nations Development Programme
UNLA	Uganda National Liberation Army
UNHCR	United Nations High Commissioner for Refugees
UNICEF	United Nations Children's Fund (formerly UN International Children's Emergency Fund)
UNOVER	United Nations Observer Mission to Verify the Referendum in Eritrea
UNRISD	United Nations Research Institute for Social Development
USAID	United States Government Aid Programme
USC	United Somali Congress
USCR	United States Committee for Refugees
WFP	World Food Programme

Editor's
Acknowledgments

This book has been made possible by the work of many people. In addition to the chapter authors, several of whom have taken the trouble to help me find photographs and drawings to illustrate their texts, I would like to thank Alula Pankhurst of the University of Addis Ababa, Josephine Grin-Yates and other staff at UNRISD, staff at South Bank University, Annelisse Hollmann of the UNHCR photograph library, Geoff Sayer of the Oxfam photograph library, Paddy Donnelly of the Cafod photograph library, and staff at James Currey Ltd particularly Lynn Taylor. I should also mention Paul Baxter and Melissa Parker, who have been constant sources of encouragement and support.

Finally I would like to take this opportunity to acknowledge the work of Hubert Morsink, who conceived, initiated, developed and co-ordinated the UNRISD programme of research on the return of refugees. Without his efforts the Addis Ababa symposium, and the other meetings held in Harare and N'Djamena, would never have happened.

On the evening of 31 March 1992, Lourenço Mutaca, the head of the UNHCR's field office at Dire Dawa in Ethiopia, was gunned down and killed. Lourenço was a Mozambican who had played an active role in his country's struggle for independence. Before taking up his post in Ethiopia, he had run the UNHCR field office in Moyo, northwest Uganda. I came to know him well while working among returned Ugandan refugees, and counted him a good friend. He did everything he could to encourage my research, whatever criticisms I made of UNHCR activities. On one occasion when he visited me in the village where I lived, he endeared himself to my neighbours by trying to eat a meal of gathered 'famine' food, including porridge made with water-lily seeds. He had a reputation for being willing to listen, and for sympathizing with displaced peoples' concerns. His tragic death highlights the personal risks often taken by those attempting to deliver humanitarian assistance. During the previous seven months, another fourteen relief workers had been killed in Ethiopia alone. Others had died in Somalia, Sudan and Uganda, and several more have been killed subsequently. This book is dedicated in memory of Lourenço, and in memory of all the relief workers who have lost their lives in northeast Africa during the 1990s.

The title of the book, *In search of cool ground*, has previously been used as the title of a Granada Television 'Disappearing World' documentary about the Mursi of southwest Ethiopia.

Tim Allen

Preface

Hubert Morsink
Senior Adviser & Programme Co-ordinator
for Refugee Research
UNRISD

The United Nations Research Institute for Social Development (UNRISD) was established to complement the work of other United Nations agencies by promoting in-depth, policy orientated, social research. The aim was both to provide new insights into the complex processes of development and to draw together existing research findings, in order to make them more accessible to government officials, development planners, and those engaged in humanitarian interventions. UNRISD's activities over the years have been inspired by the conviction that, in order to formulate effective development strategies, a thorough understanding of the context in which events occur is crucial. Indeed, several UNRISD studies have demonstrated that it may be highly counter-productive to implement well-meant programmes without comprehending how social groups, or social categories within those groups, are being affected. Occasionally UNRISD publications have made severe criticisms of what has been done in the name of aid, particularly when the evidence indicated that the plight of the marginalized and impoverished had actually worsened as a consequence. Some such criticisms are also made in the following pages.

UNRISD has been conducting research on refugees since the 1970s, but this book is a product of a larger scale project, set up in the late 1980s to pioneer studies of the curiously neglected topic of mass voluntary return. Although repatriation to the country of origin had long been recognized as one of the possible durable solutions to the global refugee problem, very little information was at that time available about what had happened when refugees had gone home in the past.

The project has focussed particular attention on Africa. This was partly because large-scale repatriations of displaced Africans had occurred in the past (e.g. to Algeria in 1962, to Sudan in the mid-1970s, to Zimbabwe in 1980 and to Uganda after 1986), but it was also a response to the appalling upheavals which have been occurring in several African regions during the 1990s. Fieldwork was sponsored in Zimbabwe, Chad and Uganda, and papers were commissioned from researchers with first-hand experience among returned populations in several other countries, including Ethiopia, Mozambique, Namibia, Sudan and Eritrea. Findings were discussed at international symposia organized in Harare, N'Djamena and Addis Ababa, attended by the researchers themselves, as well as policy makers and staff of national and international agencies.

A book based on the discussions in Harare has already been published (Allen and Morsink (eds), 1994). The present book is intended as a companion volume, although in several respects it takes arguments a stage further. It concentrates attention on the situation in northeast Africa, where dealing with ongoing social trauma appears to have become a way of life for thousands of people. Most of the chapters are revised and updated versions of papers originally presented in draft form in September 1992 at the Addis Ababa symposium. They take into account discussions which took place at that meeting which involved a questioning of the basic suppositions behind both the conventional ways of looking at mass population displacement and the underlying assumptions of most assistance operations.

Research findings made it clear that, in northeast Africa, formal distinctions between internally displaced persons, returnees and stayees violate the realities of circumstances on the ground. The very notion of repatriation is ambiguous or even meaningless where international boundaries nominally divide closely related groups, many of which have traditionally migrated with their herds, and may conceptualize their own collective identity more out of shared patterns of movement than a relationship with a specific territory. Moreover, the fact that wars have been waged for years within neighbouring countries means that flight often involves shifting from one war zone into another, and a situation which outsiders may view as a return to a homeland may be locally experienced as one more attempt to escape the fighting. Similarly, the widespread idea of displaced people as completely dependent on assistance is a misconception. They may seem to be so, or may present themselves as such, but they are rarely so in practice. Most of the relief programmes discussed in Addis Ababa had manifestly failed, nevertheless populations had survived through their own efforts and ingenuity.

Obviously such findings have many important implications for national and international agencies. It often makes no sense, for example, to try to separate out returnees or refugees from other war-damaged communities, or to try to maintain a division between emergency and development assistance. Unfortunately, existing mandates and policies encourage such responses among both national and international organizations, often undermining humanitarian interventions. Furthermore, there are crucial issues which have been largely ignored, and which must become key aspects of assistance programmes in war-torn areas. The rapid provision of food, shelter and medicines may be helpful, but the more hidden effects of social upheaval need to be better understood in order to promote peace and more acceptable levels of wellbeing. Mental suffering, the destruction of customary institutions, the forced abandoning of established modes of livelihood, and the collapse of social networks, all pose formidable challenges. But unless serious efforts are made to alleviate the effects of these problems, and to help create new ways of sustaining relatively stable societies, things can only become worse.

This book confronts such issues. While it can offer no easy answers, it emphasizes that there are certain things that should not be done, and indicates some possible ways forward. The reader is likely to find parts of the book depressing, perhaps even shocking, but the extraordinary capacity of the peoples of northeast Africa to make the most of extreme conditions also comes through. In addition, it is worth noting that, while specific criticisms are made of particular agencies, staff from many of those agencies have participated fully in the UNRISD symposia themselves. They have often been remarkably open about the errors that have been made, seeing this as a necessary step towards trying to avoid them in the future. Moreover, without the financial contributions and logistical support of some of these agencies, the fieldwork on which this book is based could not have taken place.

Apart from the participants at the Addis Ababa symposium, who made the discussions there so lively and insightful, I would like to express particular gratitude to the Netherlands Government, which has provided the bulk of the funds for the UNRISD refugee programme since the late 1980s. Additional finance for the Addis Ababa symposium and for the research supported by UNRISD which led up to it was provided by the UNHCR, Danida, the World Bank, and FAO. Valuable logistical support in Ethiopia was provided by the UNDP office. Thanks are also due to the University of Addis Ababa for co-sponsoring the meeting and to H.E. Minister Abdul Meijid Hussein, Minister for External Economic Co-operation, who gave the opening address.

Notes on Contributors

Tim Allen is an anthropologist who teaches development studies at South Bank University, London. He has worked as a consultant to UNRISD since 1990, writing reports on refugee repatriation and on the rebuilding of war-torn societies, and is a member of the team at the Open University which produces a distance-learning course on 'Third World' development. Among recent publications, he has co-edited the books *Poverty and world development in the 1990s* and *When refugees go home*.

Johnathan Bascom is a geographer at East Carolina University. He has conducted long-term field work in eastern Sudan as well as archival work in the UK with financial assistance from the American Philosophical Society, the National Science Foundation, and two Fulbright-Hays Fellowships. His recent publications focus on the relationships of agrarian change and rural transformation to refugee settlement and repatriation.

A. Brett is a social worker with many years experience of working with abused children. She is currently working with refugees in London, many of whom have undergone torture and other extremely traumatic experiences. She lived in Uganda during the 1960s and early 1970s, returning in 1991, after a gap of 16 years. During the early 1990s she carried out research among traumatized Ugandans with the help of a grant from the London School of Hygiene and Tropical Medicine.

E.A. Brett is Reader in development studies at the London School of Economics. He lived and worked in Uganda during the 1960s and early 1970s, returning again in 1987. Subsequently he has visited the country for a period each year, and has written numerous reports and articles about developments under the National Resistance Movement government, including *Providing for the rural poor: institutional decay and transformation in Uganda*.

Michael Cernea is Senior Adviser for Social Policy and Sociology in the Environment Department of the World Bank. He is the editor of *Putting people first: sociological variables in rural development*.

Yonas Endale is a medical doctor, based at the department of psychiatry, Armed Forces General Hospital, Addis Ababa. He is working with soldiers from all sides of the Ethiopian conflicts who have been traumatized by their experiences.

Ahmed Yusuf Farah is a social anthropologist based at the department of sociology,

Addis Ababa University. He has spent several years working among pastoral groups of Ethiopia, and has written numerous articles and consultancy reports, many of which have focussed on the priority needs of displaced and distressed groups.

K.N. Getachew is an Ethiopian social anthropologist who is currently writing up his Ph.D, based on field research among the Afar, at the School of Oriental and African Studies, London University. During the 1980s and early 1990s he researched among the pastoral groups of southern Ethiopia, writing several articles and consultancy reports.

Elias Habte-Selassie is a lawyer and an Eritrean activist, based in The Hague. He has written several articles about the problems associated with repatriation of refugees to Eritrea, and the difficulties associated with post-war reconstruction.

Barbara Hendrie is a social anthropologist based in the department of Anthropology at University College, London. Formerly she was the deputy director of the Emergency Relief Desk, an NGO consortium that acted as a channel for relief assistance to non-government controlled areas of Eritrea and Ethiopia, She was resident in Sudan from 1984–8, and was witness to many of the events described in her chapter. She is presently conducting research on famine-coping strategies in northern Ethiopia, including two years' residence in a highland peasant community.

Julius Holt is a consultant on aid issues who has spent many years living and working in northeast Africa. During the 1990s he has been based in Ethiopia, working for Save the Children Fund. Among other projects he has been involved in a pioneering survey of the population of the Ogaden and Somaliland. He has written several articles and reports on these areas, with particular reference to food supply and the needs of pastoralists.

Richard Hogg has spent many years in Ethiopia and other parts of northeast Africa among pastoralist groups, both carrying out field research and working for aid agencies. During the early 1990s he has been socio-economic adviser to the Ethiopian Ministry of Agriculture, South-East Rangelands Project. He has written extensively on issues related to the lives of African pastoralists, and is acknowledged as a leading authority on the subject. Recent publications include the co-edited book *Property, poverty and people: changing rights in property and problems of pastoral development*.

Wendy James teaches at the Institute of Social and Cultural Anthropology, University of Oxford. She has been researching on Sudan since the 1960s. Among her publications are two books about the Uduk: *'Kwanim Pa: the making of the Uduk people*, and *The listening ebony: moral knowledge, religion and power among the Uduk of Sudan*. In recent years she has written consultancy reports for the UNHCR on assistance programmes among Sudanese refugees in western Ethiopia.

Douglas Johnson is a research fellow at St Antony's College, University of Oxford. He is a leading authority on Sudan. Among his recent publications are *Nuer prophets: a history of prophecy from the Upper Nile in the nineteenth and twentieth centuries,* and the co-edited book *Revealing prophets: prophecy in Eastern African history*. In the early 1990s he spent periods working as a consultant for the World Food Programme in Operation Lifeline Sudan.

Gaim Kibreab is associate professor in the department of economic history, Uppsala University, Sweden. He has carried out long-term field research among Eritrean refugees in Sudan, and has written numerous articles and several books on refugee issues.

Recent publications include *Refugees and development in Africa: the case of Eritrea*, and *The state of the art review of refugee studies in Africa*. Two further books are in press: *People on the edge: displacement, land use and the environment in the Gedaref state, Sudan*, and *Ready and willing ... but still waiting: factors influencing the decision of Eritrean refugees in Sudan to return home*.

Enoch O. Opondo is a lecturer in the department of Government and Public Administration, at Moi University, Kenya. He is also the Deputy Director of the Centre for Refugee Studies at the same institution. His current research is on the state and refugee policies in Eastern Africa.

Melissa Parker is a medical anthropologist, currently based at Imperial College of Science, Technology and Medicine and at Goldsmiths' College, London University. She has spent many years researching in Africa, including a period of long-term fieldwork in Sudan. She has an interest in mental health issues, particularly in situations of social stress, and has published several influential articles on tropical diseases.

Terence Ranger is Professor of Race Relations at St Antony's College, University of Oxford. He has published several books on Africa, including *Peasant consciousness and guerrilla war in Zimbabwe* and *Are we not also men: the Samkange family and African politics in Zimbabwe, 1920–64*. He is also co-editor of *Soldiers in Zimbabwe's liberation war* and *Society in Zimbabwe's Liberation War*.

M.A. Mohamed Salih is senior research fellow in the Scandinavian Institute of African Studies, Sweden, where he runs a research programme on 'Human life in African arid lands'. He has published widely on Sudan, Arab politics and on issues associated with pastoralism, including the co-edited book *Social science and conflict analysis*.

David Styan writes on the Horn of Africa for the Economist Intelligence Unit. He teaches economics at South Bank University, London.

David Turton is a social anthropologist, based at the University of Manchester. He has written articles and reports about the Mursi of southwestern Ethiopia, and acted as consultant for five Granada Television documentaries about them. He has been editor of the *Journal of the Royal Anthropological Institute* and *Disasters*, and is Director-elect of the Refugee Studies Programme at the University of Oxford.

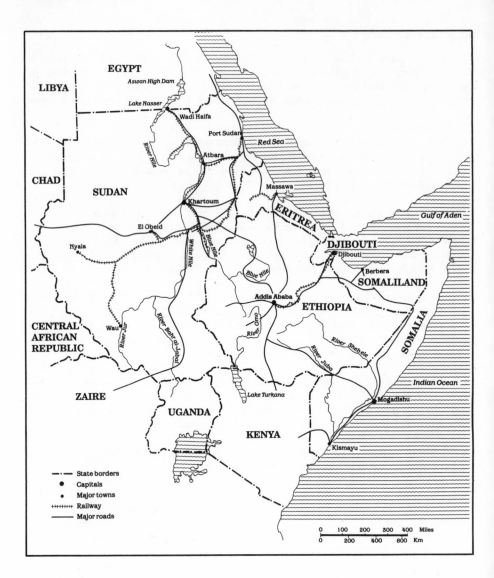

Northeast Africa

1

TIM ALLEN & DAVID TURTON
Introduction

In Search of Cool Ground

It seems reasonable to assume that the return of forcibly displaced populations to their homes will often have very significant socio-economic implications. It is also known that large migrations of this kind have occurred quite frequently. In Africa alone, it has been estimated that around 3.5 million refugees repatriated between 1971 and 1990 (Rogge, 1994: 16–17). During the same years, millions more Africans went home after periods of exile within their own countries. Following the National Resistance Army's (NRA's) victory in Uganda in January 1986, for example, perhaps as many as 750,000 displaced people returned to their devastated villages in the 'Luwero Triangle' (Kabera and Muyanja, 1994: 96). Until recently, however, little effort has been made to find out what happened to returnees after they arrived in their places of origin, or to assess the impact of mass return movements on local and national developments (Allen and Morsink, 1994: 1–13).

There have been several reasons for the neglect. There are difficulties, for example, in studying population groups which are generally less geographically concentrated than refugees, and it can take years before some of the effects of homecoming can be adequately assessed. Governments, furthermore, have commonly resented any interest shown in their internally displaced populations by human rights organizations, humanitarian agencies, and foreign states, maintaining that it is an infringement of national sovereignty. A similar tendency has sometimes been evident with respect to repatriated refugees. From the late 1940s until the 1980s, the very idea of refugee repatriation was a controversial issue at international meetings, due either to Cold War politics or allegations that, in certain parts of the world, refugees were being made to go home against their will. Not surprisingly, the consequence was that facilities to undertake inquiries about returnees were not always forthcoming, and attention was usually focussed on other responses to refugee movements, such as third-country asylum.

There may also have been a tendency to overlook returnees because of the way in which forced displacement has been conceptualized in politico-legal terms. New regimes have commonly asserted a capacity to end social upheavals, and they have normally encouraged the recongregation of 'their' people, ostensibly to enable the nation state to emerge (or re-emerge) as an integrated social unit. Such nationalist ideology influenced the framing of UN resolutions, which persistently mention voluntary repatriation as the 'most desirable' solution to the refugee problem. The possible implication is that return to the country of origin is unproblematic and will in itself resolve matters. As a consequence, mass repatriation has not generally been viewed as a disaster or as a 'complex emergency', but as an indication that a resolution to

1

1.1 *Until recently, little effort has been made to find out what happened to returnees after they have arrived in their places of origin: a Ugandan returnee in Moyo District, 1991. (Tim Allen)*

suffering is at hand – a perception, incidently, which has sometimes made it difficult to raise funds for humanitarian assistance.

The lack of knowledge and understanding about returned populations became increasingly apparent during the 1980s. Partly due to the requirement that the UNHCR should be seen to be doing everything possible to keep its rapidly growing budget under control, pressures were brought to bear on the organization actively to promote repatriation. Although the issue remained politically sensitive for much of the decade, the result was an important change of policy. In 1984, the Second International Conference on Assistance to Refugees in Africa (ICARA II) recommended that returnees be provided with assistance to help them reintegrate in their home countries and, while the internationally recognized mandate of UNHCR to protect refugees was not formally extended to include returnees, in 1985 the Executive Committee affirmed that UNHCR had a legitimate interest in the consequences of return and should have access to returned populations.

With the decline of Cold War constraints and alliances the UNHCR and other UN agencies began following interventionist precedents already set by several international non-governmental organizations (notably by the French NGOs Médecins sans Frontières (MSF) and Médecins du Monde (MDM)). In some places, especially in Africa, UNHCR worked together with other agencies in negotiating access to war-affected populations in ways that set aside national sovereignty, funding or running operations across borders and in rebel-controlled territory in order to provide a kind of welfare 'safety-net' (Duffield, 1994; Styan, 1994; Benthall, 1993: 123–72; UNRISD, 1993b). An important early example of these arrangements was Operation Rainbow in southern Sudan, set up in 1986, while a significant turning point in formal terms was the UN's Resolution 43/131 of 8 December 1988, which legitimized the crossing of national boundaries in order to provide humanitarian assistance.

This approach brought aid agency staff face to face with the acute hardships experienced by homecoming populations in economically poor and war-damaged areas. At the same time, the few social researchers who had begun to examine situations of return were showing that homecomings of the past were associated with difficulties which had not been effectively dealt with. In some instances, such as in Sudan during the 1970s, repatriation and recongregation had caused serious local tensions, and eventually led to renewed warfare and further population displacements (Crisp, 1987; Coles, 1985, 1989; Akol, 1987, 1994; Allen, 1989; see also the chapter by Mohamed Salih in this volume). Far from being a straightforward and optimal solution, it became clear that mass voluntary return could have adverse consequences and tended to compound other problems of post-war reconstruction. Indeed, in some instances, returns were found to be not voluntary at all. They were a response to political upheavals spreading into places of exile, rather than to the end of fighting and oppression in the displaced population's homeland.

In the 1990s, the negotiated access operations of the late 1980s have been superseded in several of the world's trouble spots by high-profile peace-keeping and peace-making, associated with the threat of armed force. In spite of much publicized failures in Somalia and Bosnia, militarized humanitarianism has become acceptable in a way that would have been hard to predict a few years ago. The development has had worrying implications for the rights of refugees in that the international community has appeared to guarantee personal safety to war-affected populations within their own countries, making it harder for people to argue that they cannot return 'owing to a well-founded fear of persecution' (the phrase used in the 1951 Convention Relating to the Status of Refugees). Recently there have been reported cases of groups being refused refugee status, or effectively having it taken away (examples include some of the Somalis in Kenya, Kurds in Turkey, Haitians in the USA and Bosnians in Europe). However, the resort to militarized humanitarianism can also be viewed as a reflection of a new realism in international approaches to forced displacement, including an acceptance that monitoring is often necessary to prevent homecoming from exposing populations to serious abuse.

This new realism is evident in recent UNHCR thinking. During the 1990s, the organization has persisted in promoting voluntary repatriation of refugees and the return of internally displaced groups to their own areas as the way forward. Indeed, the High Commissioner herself declared that 1992 should be the start of a decade of voluntary repatriation and, in the course of that year, an average of 46,000 people were estimated to have returned to their own countries each week (UNHCR, 1993: 103). But UNHCR officials have also emphasized that returnees can expect to encounter hardship and possible danger, and have highlighted the need to ensure that returned groups have a viable and sustainable livelihood. The recognition that return can be a very fraught and painful process and that international agencies often do little to assist displaced populations has led to a healthy crisis of confidence in some quarters.

Given the speed of political change and the scale of upheavals in the 1990s, it is understandable that the activities of the UNHCR and other humanitarian organizations on the ground have not followed a consistent line. This has particularly been so in the matter of protection and in attempts to establish links between *ad hoc* relief and long-term assistance. In practice, international responses to mass displacement are constrained by the attitudes and capacities of agency staff in the field, the political and economic priorities of the major aid donors and the nature of news coverage by the international media.

Nevertheless, the current willingness of some aid workers and policy-makers to question what they have been doing has led to some potentially helpful developments. In northeast Africa, for example, the repeated failures of assistance operations have prompted pioneering attempts at collaboration between UNHCR, other UN agencies, NGOs and governments in a so-called 'cross-mandate approach'. The aim is to assist all those in need, regardless of whether they are local or displaced people, and to provide relief, rehabilitation and small-scale development aid, as well as repatriation assistance. The experiment is discussed further below, as well as in several other chapters of this book.

It is also encouraging to find frank and perceptive chapters on 'Protection in Times of Armed Conflict' and 'Going Home' in such a significant document as the UNHCR's *The State of the World's Refugees* (UNHCR, 1993: 103–16). Among other issues, this report comments on the setting aside of national sovereignty by the international community, on the manner in which humanitarian assistance can be used as a weapon or a means of fuelling hostilities, and on the incapacities of development agencies in dealing with the longer term requirements of war-damaged regions. Furthermore, it points out that the majority of those who repatriate do so 'spontaneously' (that is, without the help of international organizations in planning or in the provision of relief), and that many

1.2 *One of the most chronically unstable parts of the world: EPLF fighter overlooking the war front, 1989. (Julian Summers/Cafod)*

people have little choice about return, being effectively expelled from places of exile and forced to move back into war zones.

Such a discussion of sensitive topics in the UNHCR's most important and widely circulated publication indicates an unprecedented openness within the international community, as well as a growing awareness of the political and social dilemmas associated with homecomings. This in turn reflects a concern with the apparent proliferation of violent ethnic conflicts and civil wars in the post-Cold War era and with the prospects for their resolution in some form of peaceful social integration. In this context, insights gleaned by researchers and aid agency field staff since the mid-1980s seem to be having an influence on organizations which have, in the past, been notoriously weak in terms of institutional learning.

Some of the research findings which are informing current debates are the results of projects set up a few years ago, in response to the need to know more about what happens to people following return. Most notably, comparative studies of repatriation during conflict have been carried out by a group of mainly North American researchers (Larkin, Cuny and Stein, 1991; Cuny, Stein and Reed, 1992), and studies of the broader consequences of homecoming in Africa have been made under the auspices of the United Nations Research Institute for Social Development (Crisp, 1987; Morsink, 1990; UNRISD, 1993a, 1993b; Allen and Morsink, 1994). Most of the chapters presented here were written as part of the UNRISD project.

During the late 1980s and early 1990s, UNRISD sponsored in-depth field research in African countries in which large-scale returns had occurred in the past, and commissioned papers from individuals with specialist knowledge of particular areas. Three regional symposia were organized to present the findings and to try to draw out lessons and comparative insights. These were held in Harare (March 1991) and N'Djamena (February 1992) and Addis Ababa (September 1992). Participants at these gatherings included African governmental and non-governmental policy-makers, administrators and practitioners; representatives of international organizations and donor countries; as well as scholars and researchers from Africa and elsewhere.

Although those giving papers were invited to address operational issues, much of the discussion was in fact dominated by the understandable need of several participants to bear witness to the appalling situations they had observed or lived through and by a questioning of conventional wisdom and of normally unexamined assumptions. This was particularly so at the Addis symposium, which was concerned with northeast Africa, one of the most chronically unstable parts of the world. There were two main thrusts to the questioning.

First, there was a call to rethink organizational and bureaucratic structures. The main incentive here was the scale, duration and apparently unending nature of the refugee crisis. In northeast Africa it had become a 'permanent emergency' with which the

UNHCR was neither equipped nor mandated to deal. A further incentive was the impact of the ending of the Cold War on political and economic relations between North and South, on the global political 'order', on the United Nations system and on the very survival of nation states.

Secondly, there was a call to rethink certain basic assumptions of a more conceptual kind. This arose first of all from some close-grained studies of particular cases of population movements based on local-level fieldwork. These showed, for example, that local experience, because complex and particular, was resistant to the imposition of blanket 'solutions'; that 'refugees' were not, in reality, the passive 'victims' they were so often seen (and expected to behave) as; that geographical mobility and wide-ranging support networks are a normal rather than pathological aspect of life; that the distinction between 'refugees' and 'returnees' may have no meaning for the people themselves (except as identities to be assumed in order to obtain access to relief); and that ethnic boundaries are fluid and often very recent.

Another source of this concern with questioning basic assumptions was the desire to get away from the 'us-doing-things-to-them' model of development and refugee assistance. It is part of current development orthodoxy that 'sustainable development' requires 'grass-roots participation'. To convert this from aspiration into practice, however, requires not only detailed empirical knowledge of the local situation but also the ability to re-assess, in the light of this knowledge, the assumptions one started out with. Organizational rethinking is necessary but not sufficient to produce change. Unless accompanied by the questioning of basic assumptions, it is liable to lead to the proliferation of purely bureaucratic solutions, which look good on paper but fail to produce an impact on practice and performance in the field. By giving an *impression* of change, furthermore, they may actually prevent it from occurring.

Such themes are touched on repeatedly by the contributors to this book. The majority of chapters are revised, expanded and updated versions of presentations made in Addis or of papers written for the meeting by people who were unable to attend. (The rhetorical style of the final chapter, by the historian Terence Ranger, is explained by the fact that it was his personal summing up of the symposium, given in a closing address.) The title of the book is a translation of a phrase often used by the Mursi of southwestern Ethiopia, encapsulating their view of themselves as a people whose very identity has been formed by movements and migration (see the chapter by Turton). It is an appropriate title for two reasons. First, it reflects a local perspective of most displaced and impoverished groups of the northeast African region – groups whose primary concern is to find a relatively secure place in which to begin working towards a better life, often irrespective of the country in which that place is located. Secondly, it directs attention towards the links between migration and collective identity and helps undermine simplistic conceptions of refugee and returnee livelihoods. A summary of the chapters could not do justice to the emphasis most authors place on the details of local circumstances. In the remainder of this introduction, therefore, we focus on what turned out to be the major topics of discussion at the Addis symposium and attempt to draw out and reflect on points which may be of particular relevance for assessing and planning future relief and development strategies.

The Tyranny of Labels

In attempting to deal with the huge numbers of displaced people in northeast Africa over the past few years, the UNHCR has been forced by its mandate to make anomalous and sometimes spurious distinctions between 'refugees' and 'returnees'. The chapter by Opondo examines legal and administrative reasons why international agencies have persisted with the conventional labels, while many of the chapters provide examples of their inadequacies, pointing out: (1) that refugee flows in the region have taken place across international boundaries which are more or less irrelevant to the cultural and economic relations of local populations, and (2) that they are not single events but part of a long-term process.

The international borders of northeast Africa were established through the nineteenth-century partitioning of Africa by the colonial powers and bear hardly any relation to the subsistence activities, migratory movements and the trade, exchange and support networks of the local people. In these circumstances, deciding where (in which country) a person 'belongs' can be an arbitrary and (for the person him- or herself) meaningless exercise. This is clearly seen in the case of Somali 'refugees' and 'returnees' in the Ogaden where, the more one knows about the past and present social relations and economic activities of an individual, the more difficult it becomes to place him or her unambiguously in one of these two categories. As the chapters by Getachew, Hogg, Holt and Farah indicate, the division of the present population of the Ogaden and northern Somalia into refugees and returnees is more a requirement imposed by agency mandates than a reflection of the living conditions, motivations and objectives of the people themselves.

The Ogaden, although administratively part of Ethiopia, is economically and culturally tied to Somalia. With its low and erratic rainfall and generally poor soils, it is best suited to nomadic pastoralism, although agriculture is practised in better-watered areas. It is inhabited mainly by Somali-speaking pastoralists who are divided into clan groups, each with its own clan territory. Since many clan territories stretch across the international border, it is common for pastoralists to make use of watering points and grazing areas belonging to their clan on both sides of the border. There is much cross-border toing and froing by friends and relatives, and wealthy merchants own shops and houses in both countries. Many of those who moved into Somalia to escape fighting in Ethiopia during the 1970s and 1980s, and many of those who fled in the opposite direction in the 1980s and early 1990s, were from the Ogaden originally, had relatives and clansmen living in the area and/or were living in their own clan territories. There is no doubt that these people suffered terribly from the effects of war and famine, but their conception of themselves as 'refugees' and 'returnees' was largely a response to the activities of government officials and aid workers.

Not only is the distinction more or less meaningless for many local people in the Ogaden and Somalia, but it also diverts the attention of outsiders from the economic and cultural continuities which underpin their survival strategies. It is precisely these strategies which need to be supported and strengthened, through the provision of assistance to the population as a whole and, where necessary, by treating both sides of the international border as one economic zone. International boundaries are no respecters of the regional networks of trade, economic co-operation and kinship/clan relations which are the basis of subsistence and, in times of crisis, survival for most peoples of the region. If these networks are to be strengthened it will be necessary to find ways of encouraging rather than inhibiting cross-border economic links and migratory movements, even after 'repatriation' has taken place.

Most of today's refugee populations in northeast Africa are the direct result of circumstances which, like those in the Ogaden, go back more than 10, and in some cases, more than 30 years. Some members of these populations have spent years almost continuously on the move. Others have spent their formative years, 'in exile', had to flee as 'returnees' to their 'country of origin' and then moved back as 'refugees' to their former 'host country'. One example is provided by James, who recounts how the Uduk have remained a relatively cohesive group since 1987, in spite of the fact that they have been forced to travel over 1,000 km in the border region between Sudan and Ethiopia looking for somewhere safe to live, and have crossed the international frontier five times.

Another, somewhat different, case is that described in the chapter by Allen. The area along the border between Uganda and Sudan has been in an intermittent state of 'crisis' for the past 40 years, and the flow of refugees back to northern Uganda from southern Sudan which began in 1986 was just one of a series of movements across the same border over this period. To focus, in such a case, on a single movement of people, in one direction and at a particular point in time, would be to give a false, if comforting, impression that one is dealing with a simple and well circumscribed event rather than with an untidy process, involving multiple, and sometimes overlapping migrations in both directions, and considerable flexibility with respect to nationality and ethnicity.

1.3 *'Fleeing from Uganda and fleeing from Sudan!!!': a drawing by L. Itsara of Logoba, Pacehwi, Moyo District, Uganda, 1988.*

The continued application to these kinds of movements of labels which had their legal origin in the 1951 United Nations Convention Relating to the Status of Refugees and in the political realities of post-war Europe, has led to a contradiction between the bureaucratic needs of the UNHCR and its humanitarian objectives. Legally speaking, only refugees come under its mandate but, as noted earlier, it has been encouraged by various resolutions of the United Nations General Assembly to 'promote' repatriation and to assist in the 'rehabilitation' of 'returnees'. As funds tend to be earmarked for particular groups, it is necessary to distinguish not only between refugees and returnees, but also between the latter and 'stayees' and the 'internally displaced'. Examples given in this book indicate that it can be a very time consuming, resource-expensive and ineffective approach. It is often impossible, moreover, to register war-affected and displaced people in ways that relate to their own ideas about collective identity, or to their livelihood strategies and migration patterns. Once terms like 'returnee' begin to be employed by officials and aid workers, they may of course take on a local currency, and people may aspire to a particular designation, particularly if it is a way of obtaining relief commodities or avoiding military conscription and taxation. But care needs to be taken in using such labels for purposes of analysis. They can easily obscure much of what is really going on.

The Eritrean case, discussed in the chapters by Habte-Selassie, Kibreab, Bascom and Styan, is perhaps the exception here, as it seems to be in so many other ways. The half a million Eritrean refugees in Sudan have been in exile over a long period, some of them since the late 1960s, but most seem to have retained (or gained) a distinctive 'national' identity, irrespective of their other ethnic and religious affiliations. They perceive themselves as Eritrean nationals, and it appears to be partly for this reason that they have been unwilling to return home until their country has been liberated and facilities have been arranged for their formal repatriation by the international community in co-operation with their government. In the event, relatively little aid has been forthcoming for repatriation, rehabilitation and development following the Eritrean People's Liberation Front (EPLF) victory against Ethiopian government forces in 1991, and there has been a stalemate in negotiations between the UNHCR and the Eritrean leadership. The refugees have mostly remained in exile, where they were registered and enabled to

1.4 *In spite of the defeats suffered by Ethiopian government forces in the late 1980s and early 1990s, the refugees have mostly remained in exile: EPLF soldiers talking to captured Ethiopian troops, 1990. (Stephen King/CAFOD)*

vote in the 1993 Eritrean independence referendum. At the time of writing in 1995 most of them have still not returned.

All this is in striking contrast to the responses of other displaced populations of the northeast African region, including the Tigrayans, whose repatriation to Ethiopia is discussed in the chapter by Hendrie. The great majority of displaced people ignore, avoid or subvert governmental and aid agency imposed controls and regulations. On reflection, however, the Eritreans might be viewed as the exception that proves the rule. Their behaviour has certain similarities with that of Zimbabwean refugees in the 1970s and Namibians in the 1980s (see Makanya, 1994; Tapscott, 1994, and Preston, 1994). As in these southern African examples, responses have been powerfully influenced by the political ideology and discipline of the liberation movement. Unlike most of the other armed factions and governments of northeast Africa, the EPLF has been remarkably successful in promoting the notion of a nationalist struggle, which should subsume or incorporate all other loyalties. In so doing it has drawn upon the same tradition of nation-statehood and citizenship as those who have framed UN resolutions, and it seems that many Eritrean refugees have come to think about themselves in ways that correspond to the criteria of formalized classifications, notably those enshrined in the 1951 Convention on refugee status. In so doing they have taken on an identity which, combined with the insulation and regimentation of camp life, has the effect of making them adamant that the decision to repatriate must be a communal one, made with the approval of traditional leaders and the Eritrean political elite. It also prompts them to expect certain responses from government officers and international organizations. Sadly, many of these responses have not been forthcoming and as Kibreab puts it, the Eritreans in Sudan have been 'left in limbo'. There are surely other factors at work too, such as concerns about the degree of devastation in Eritrea and the reluctance of young men to return to obligatory national service, but the Eritrean case reminds us that we use labels to 'make' the world as well as to describe it.

The legal language of refugee status, the humanitarian language of refugee assistance and the academic language of refugee studies have helped to create, unintentionally, an image of the refugee as 'victim'. Professionals working within all these institutionalized discourses, the legal, the humanitarian and the academic, 'need' refugees as a condition of their own survival and this has resulted in an inevitable process of objectification. Refugees are conceptualized essentially as recipients of action – our action – rather than as actors. They are seen, and may come to see themselves, as populations whose lot it is to be counted, registered, studied, surveyed and, in due course, hopefully 'returned', at which point they become 'ordinary people' once again. Too often, resort to the terms 'refugee' and 'returnee' is an extreme example of imposing stereotypes upon the poor, making them appear (and possibly even become) mere 'recipients' of well-meaning interventions. All that has been said in recent years about the need for 'participation' and 'empowerment' in development work applies also to refugees – only more so. This is the topic of the next section.

The Myth of Dependency

Any displaced people in northeast Africa who become genuinely dependent on relief agencies are unlikely to survive long. The majority of forced migrants have either received no assistance from humanitarian agencies or, where they have, this assistance has been an additional bonus rather than the basis of their livelihood.

Because most groups on the move never go through a camp registration process and are never, therefore, given the 'official' status of refugee or returnee, they tend to be invisible to outsiders. In late 1992, there were nearly three times as many 'self-settled' as officially registered Somali returnees in the Ogaden, but this figure was only arrived at by a unique helicopter survey described in the chapter by Holt. Other populations do receive formal recognition, but usually fare little better in terms of aid. As Kibreab emphasizes, dependence was not even a viable prospect for the UNHCR-assisted Eritrean refugees living in settlements in Sudan. Their reluctance to go back to Eritrea without adequate international help has not been a result of either over-generous aid provision in the past or a local lack of initiative.

Similar points are made in most of the other chapters of the book. For example, the Ugandans who returned from southern Sudan in 1986–7, discussed in the chapter by Allen, found themselves thrown back on their own devices. This was in spite of the fact that their repatriation was recognized as a returnee emergency, with the UNHCR becoming an operational agency in the area and funding several international NGOs. The relief effort was hampered by continuing insecurity, administrative inefficiencies and lack of co-operation (even outright antagonism) between the staff of different agencies. Food distributions in the early months of the return were consequently far below requirements. It is true that relatively small amounts of food aid may have been very valuable for some families but, for the most part, the returnees had to find their own means of winning a livelihood in difficult circumstances.

There is plenty of evidence that such observations might be applied to most displaced populations, and not only in northeast Africa. It has, moreover, become an orthodoxy of aid organizations to claim their purpose is to 'empower' the poor, and to emphasise that the knowledge, capacities and coping strategies of the people themselves are their chief means of survival and hope for the future. Why then has the idea that displaced populations are particularly prone to dependency also retained a wide currency?

In 1985, a joint international council made up of voluntary agencies and UNHCR staff held a workshop on 'Development Approaches to Refugee Situations', at Puidoux, Switzerland. The recommendations included advice on 'how to put newly arrived refugees to productive work at a very early stage so as to avoid a dependency syndrome developing' and how to achieve the 'transition from relief to development'. To avoid dependency it is suggested that the refugees 'be employed early on in camp construction and other infrastructural building activities' and that they 'be allowed to build their own houses'. The document recognized that, to achieve the transition to development, refugees must be involved in the planning of projects but the contribution envisaged for them is primarily one of making their needs known: 'projects should include needs assessment in which refugees play a central role' (cited in Cuénod, 1990: 233–4). There is no mention of the knowledge, strengths and resources of the refugees, only of their needs.

The assumption here, as in so many other reports and publications on refugees, seems to be that people are made dependent merely by the fact of being given relief – an assumption that is also evident in the concern shown by politicians in affluent countries to avoid the 'dependency syndrome' among social welfare 'malingerers'. In both cases, there is an apparent contradiction within the popular image of the welfare recipient: on the one hand passive, lethargic and indolent but on the other adept at 'playing the system' and at finding ways to take 'unfair' advantage of it. The symptoms that are described here as 'dependency' are the result, not of receiving relief *per se* (we are all dependent, in one way or another, on state hand-outs and subsidies), but of losing, and attempting to regain, a sense of being in control of one's own life.

In these circumstances people will attempt to carve out some area of personal autonomy, however trivial, in which to exercise independent choice. The more rigid and impersonal the structure within which they are forced to live, the more likely it is that they will exercise this choice in ways which challenge the structure. Thus, when refugees buy and sell ration cards, register their children several times over, split their families between a relief camp and external economic activities and set up markets around camps to trade in relief grain and other commodities, they are demonstrating qualities of resourcefulness and ingenuity which are their only defence against dependency, given the situation in which they find themselves. And yet these very strategies, by which they seek to maintain some degree of control over their own lives, are likely to be classified by 'the system' as inappropriate and undesirable.

Thus, interpreting the behaviour of displaced groups as a consequence of 'dependency' is something of a misconception. Sometimes it is hard to avoid the conclusion that it is a deliberate attempt to obscure what is happening. The way forward must be to maximize the area within which people are able to make decisions for themselves. This means emphasizing their strengths rather than their needs. It means, for a refugee population, giving them as much control as possible over the allocation of scarce resources, including food, rather than 'putting them to productive work' and asking them what they would like others to do for, or to, them.

The 'Problem' of Movement

As noted earlier, the idea that return is the 'most desirable' solution to refugee movements contains the implicit assumption that a given population has its own proper place, territory or homeland. This assumption is deeply embedded in the European political theory of nationalism, according to which there is a natural identity between people and place, and the world is naturally made up of clearly bounded politico-territorial entities

– sovereign states. From this point of view, while 'sedentarism' (staying in one place) is the taken-for-granted condition of human existence, movement is problematic – both for researchers who want to 'explain' it and governments who often want to stop it.

Anthropologists, for example, have given much thought to the causes and consequences of the nomadic movements of pastoralists, discovering that they cannot by any means be solely attributed to environmental pressure, but have virtually ignored the causes and consequences of sedentarism. They have, until recently, written about territorially based 'tribes', 'societies' or 'ethnic groups' as though they were given in nature. The issue here is not whether such groups exist, but how they are conceptualized. Because, in sedentarist thinking, they are conceptualized as natural, so also is the identity people derive from association with a

1.5 *'In search of cool ground': a young Mursi man, one of the migrants to the Mago valley, 1986. (David Turton)*

particular territory. From the vantage point of northeast Africa, however, this seems an exceptional point of view. First, movement has historically been an integral part of survival for the peoples of the region. Secondly, these movements were not *necessarily* undertaken by people who considered they were thereby losing their ethnic identity. Today's population movements may be seen, therefore, as a resumption, albeit on a larger scale, of a state of affairs that was 'normal' before the colonial period.

For many groups, such as those discussed by Allen, Farah, Getachew, Turton and James, oral traditions are predominantly about movement and flight from various invaders. During the nineteenth century, the violent activities of the armed retinues of slave and ivory traders, Turco-Egyptian, Ethiopian, Belgian and British forces, as well as locally powerful chiefs allied to these outsiders, had a devastating impact. So did the bovine and human diseases that were introduced at the same time. Thousands died and thousands more moved around in search of relatively secure locations. One consequence was that, in a region in which ethnic identities had long been flexible, people speaking different languages mixed together and intermarried, and the international boundaries, established in the early years of this century, divided closely related populations. It was only under colonial rule that so-called 'tribal' identities were formalized and regulated for the sake of administrative convenience. Despite this, and despite the existence of enmities between neighbouring populations, these identities can still sometimes be switched, merged or otherwise set aside, opportunistically, by individuals and families.

Movement does not necessarily involve a denial of collective identity. It can reinforce it. As Turton shows for the Mursi, movement is both an aspect of survival and an integral part of historical tradition: the Mursi see themselves as a people who are permanently 'in search of cool ground'. In this respect, it is most revealing that those Mursi who migrated away from the Mursi homeland in the Lower Omo Valley in response to severe drought in 1979 asserted they they were being 'true' Mursi. They likened their occupation of an uninhabited part of the Mago Valley to a similar move into unoccupied territory made by members of their parents' generation in the 1930s. They saw themselves, like those earlier pioneers (and no doubt as the latter saw themselves in relation to yet earlier ones), as domesticating the wilderness, clearing the forests for cultivation and making the grasslands fit for cattle herding.

The assumption that it is natural for an ethnic group to be 'rooted' in a particular place may lead to the conclusion that voluntary return is the 'natural' resolution of displacement. But many of the cases described in this book warn us to treat this view with some scepticism, on two counts. First, 'going home' may not be the 'natural' outcome of population displacement for the people displaced. Making a new home in a new area may be perfectly consistent with their history and with their view of themselves as a distinct group. Attachment to territory, in other words, is not the only source of group identity. Secondly, they may see their ethnic identity not as given in nature but as more or less problematic and fragile. In which case, simply 'going home', in the sense of taking up residence in one's former territory after a forced exile, will not automatically recreate a sense of belonging and of moral obligation to neighbours and kin. This is especially so if the original dispersal took the form of a mass exodus, accompanied by horrific experiences of violence and death, and if the return is to an area with an infrastructure and economy devastated by war. In such areas, and after such experiences, communities may have to reconstruct themselves, as it were, from scratch.

The Reconstruction of Communities

It has become a commonplace of the literature on famine in Africa to point out that saving individual lives, which is the chief priority of aid workers, may not be the chief priority of the people themselves. There is an obvious logic here which explains why people are reluctant to dispose of assets which are necessary for long-term survival even if this means going hungry in the short term. This is not surprising, but it is sometimes made to seem so by being presented as a deliberate choice between saving a 'way of life' and saving 'lives'. In fact, it shows a concern to put off that choice for as long as possible and, it is to be hoped, to avoid it altogether; to avoid, that is, a situation in which these two objectives become incompatible and saving lives means taking action that undermines the viability of a 'way of life'. The phrase 'way of life' should, in any case, be understood in more than an economic sense. It comprises not just economic and material necessities but also the basic value premises which make an orderly and co-operative social life possible in the first place. It is literally what makes 'life', meaning the social existence of an individual, 'worth living'. It creates, furthermore, at least for many African peoples, not just the social world but the world: the order, whether natural or human, beyond the local community is seen as depending on the order within it. For a people with such a 'socio-centric' cosmology, being forced to flee their homes because of war or famine, or both, is an indication that something is wrong, not in the stars (as the etymology of the English word 'disaster', implies) but in society.

Such people suffer not only from the immediate physical upheaval but also from a loss of confidence in the formerly taken-for-granted norms and moral codes governing, among other things, economic co-operation and exchange, marriage, links with the spirit world and public decision-making. There is likely to be fierce competition and conflict within populations, as well as outbreaks of religiosity. Among the people Allen lived with in Uganda during the late 1980s, for example, the emergence of a new possession cult seemed to play an important part in allowing people to come to terms with what had happened, and there was a constant preoccupation with distinguishing between trustworthy relatives and suspect 'outsiders', as well as a generally accepted understanding that the community needed to be 'healed'. The main form this healing took was the eradication of sorcery, which resulted in a number of particularly brutal killings of accused individuals. Similar incidents of extreme violence for purposes of

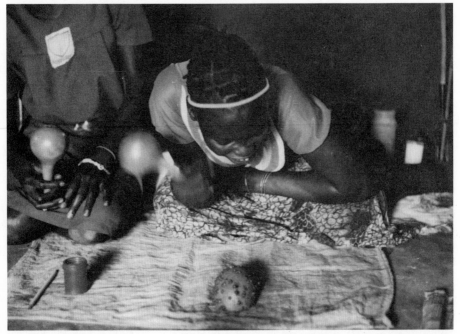

1.6 *Following the repatriation to northern Uganda in the late 1980s, a cult of spirit possession seemed to play an important part in helping people come to terms with what had happened: a spirit medium talking to ghosts, whose voices appear to come from the upturned calabash in front of her, Moyo district, 1990. (Tim Allen)*

social cleansing are alluded to among other Ugandan groups in the harrowing testimonies recorded by Amelia Brett.

Seeing the problem of reconstructing a community as one of healing raises the question of how to diagnose and treat symptoms which have come to be known in the language of Western psychology and psychiatry as 'survivor syndrome' and 'post-traumatic stress disorder' respectively. This is an issue raised in several chapters, most notably those by Parker, Amelia Brett and Endale. It is only relatively recently that the effects of war and other terrible experiences on individuals have come to be recognized in the developed countries as requiring investigation and treatment in their own right. As yet virtually no research has been carried out on the psychological consequences of war and upheaval in Africa and it is not clear, therefore, whether psychoanalytic and psychiatric approaches to the study of trauma will shed light on the problems faced by African refugees and returnees. Cultural factors in the definition of what constitutes 'health' and what constitutes a 'traumatic' experience will clearly need to be allowed for, but those involved in assisting people, of any culture, who have been through terrible experiences should at least be aware of the symptoms of post-traumatic stress, as these have been identified by Western clinicians.

Another way of understanding the problem faced by returnees in rebuilding a stable and predictable community life is to see it as one of allocating accountability. It is usually the least visible costs of war and upheaval that are most difficult to repair. If the resources and political will are forthcoming, roads and shops can be rebuilt relatively quickly, seeds and commodities can be distributed by humanitarian agencies, and fields can be cleared of secondary forest. But those things which really make social life viable are harder to pin down: little gifts, the sharing of knowledge about soils and plants, the acceptance of hierarchies and moral codes, the recognition of avoidance customs, a sense of duty, a network of debts, consensus about how to settle squabbles, understanding where the distinction lies between flirting and harassing, or between teasing and abusing, a common experience of the spirit world – all these aspects of interaction are part of the continual process of inventing and reinventing society. When they have been set aside or destroyed they may be exceedingly difficult to establish again. They are likely to take on new forms, and may be a focus of competition and conflict.

On the one hand, locally resident individuals have to establish relationships of trust among themselves so that neighbours can feel accountable to each other for their actions. On the other hand, they have to restore confidence in their ability to make sense of, and thereby predict and control, the malign forces which created so much death, pain and misfortune. When there seems to be nowhere else to point the finger of blame than within, this can necessitate identifying and dealing with those held responsible for anti-social behaviour. Usually the scapegoats are marginal individuals: poor men who are not living near their brothers, or wives for whom no bridewealth has been paid, or women who had taken advantage of new opportunities in exile and resist the imposition of controls on their behaviour by their menfolk (those who are accused of having been prostitutes may be particularly vulnerable).

The struggles to allocate local accountability may additionally make it impossible for a residential community to act as a unit. There is likely to be a great deal of dissent over who should take decisions on behalf of others and in what context. Most old people may have died, and those who remain may have lost much of their ritual and political authority, particularly if this depended on a level of relative affluence or on alliances outside of the community. There may be no individuals who are generally accepted as representatives or 'decision-makers'. In some cases, the apparent incapacity of particular groups to respond to community development initiatives may have nothing to do with a lack of interest, let alone with the 'dependency syndrome', but may reflect a fundamental crisis of mutuality.

Reference to alliances outside of the community draws attention to wider spheres, going beyond the neighbourhood, within which accountability can be viewed as equally problematic. Most displaced and impoverished groups in northeast Africa have at some point looked to government officials, aid workers and international organizations for direction, and many people in the region have had access to some public services, such as basic health or veterinary care, buses running on state-maintained roads and district-level courts. Also, thousands of refugees have spent years in official camps where life may have been regulated by strangers and foreigners. Others have avoided many aspects of the aid regime but have nevertheless become used to some kind of relationship with aid workers. All these various linkages are unlikely to have become the basis of physical survival. They may have played an important part, however, in shaping the institutions of social organization and their sudden withdrawal may create a vacuum which is not easy to fill.

Many of the region's basic categories of ethnic differentiation have evolved out of relatively recent events. Thus, Allen argues that the collective 'way of life' of the Ugandan Madi until the 1970s depended upon the existence of a relatively efficient local government system, district and county courts and the state purchasing of cotton. When they fled into Sudan, the role of local government was replaced by Sudanese officials and aid agency staff in the special refugee settlements in which most of them chose to live. On their return to Uganda, they found that the local administration was inadequate and the acute difficulties they faced were partly the result of struggling to allocate social accountability without recourse to state institutions. Efforts to resolve matters involved the new Resistance Councils (RCs) set up by the National Resistance Movement (NRM) government, and discussed in the chapter by E.A. Brett.

Looked at in this light, the problem of rebuilding communities becomes the problem of rebuilding 'civil society' and, specifically, the problem of how to create an administrative system which is genuinely representative of local interests and from which no section of the population feels excluded. The 'natural' way of attempting to solve this problem may seem to be through defining the politically significant local units in ethnic terms, on the grounds that ethnicity is the 'given' that 'breaks through' when state structures collapse. As is clearly shown, however, in several chapters of this book, ethnicity is not static or natural, and is as much a product as a cause of social upheaval and flight. To use ethnic units as building blocks of the state political system – as is currently being attempted in Ethiopia – is therefore likely to be counter-productive, leading to domination of the system by one or other ethnically defined group and further demands for secession. As E.A. Brett shows, the integrative institution building in Uganda since 1986 would appear to be a more appropriate model for emulation.

Voluntary Return – Who Decides?

Although the case for return is often made on the grounds that it is the best solution for displaced people themselves, the strongest argument in favour of it, at least where African refugees are concerned, appears to be pragmatic. The chances of substantial resettlement outside Africa are so remote, for political reasons, as to be hardly worth considering, while African countries of asylum have been reluctant to encourage the permanent integration of large numbers of refugees within their borders by offering them full citizenship. Host governments and 'refugee-based' guerrilla movements have both learned that by keeping refugees visible and accessible to humanitarian agencies they can become a useful means of attracting international funding. The result is that hundreds of thousands of refugees remain on the assistance list, together with their children and grandchildren, until such time as they avail themselves of the only politically acceptable ('most desirable') solution to their problem, repatriation.

UNHCR sets out four conditions which must be satisfied before it is prepared to involve itself in assisting refugees to repatriate. First, there must have taken place a 'substantial and permanent' change in the conditions which led to the original refugee flow; secondly, the decision to return must be made freely by the refugees; thirdly, the country of origin and the host country must formally agree to the repatriation; and fourthly, the refugees must be able to return safely, and with dignity. These conditions clearly flow from the protection mandate of the UNHCR and are based on the assumption that refugee flows take place between sovereign states with recognized borders and legitimate governments. Praiseworthy as the conditions are in theory, the recent history of repatriation in northeast Africa suggests that they represent an ideal which is virtually unattainable in the conditions of intra-state conflict which have characterized the region for 20 years or more.

There has been little that is either voluntary or safe about the returns discussed in this book. Most of them have been a consequence of a deteriorating situation in areas of exile including, in some cases, military action against the displaced groups. Sometimes this appears to have been officially ignored by the UNHCR. Allen, Johnson, James, Getachew and Farah all give examples of circumstances in which displaced groups have been forced to flee from their places of refuge and have returned to war zones. UN agencies have nonetheless been active in running or funding assistance operations, as if the four conditions mentioned earlier had been fulfilled. On other occasions, the UNHCR has shown considerable reluctance to participate at all, a case in point being the return movement of Tigrayans from the Sudan in 1985, discussed by Hendrie.

Between October 1984 and May 1985 around 200,000 people from Tigray Province of Ethiopia crossed into the Sudan because of impending famine. They were mainly from areas controlled by the Tigray People's Liberation Front (TPLF) which, together with its associated relief organization, the Relief Society of Tigray (REST), set up a series of transit stops with food and medical supplies, to assist the refugees on their four to six week walk. Facilities on arrival were wholly inadequate, however, and there was an unprecedented death rate among the new arrivals. Even while refugees were still arriving in the Sudanese camps, the earlier arrivals were beginning to head back for their home areas, despite heightened military activity, in order to take advantage of the rainy season. By April the trickle had become a flood and 54,000 had returned by the end of May. The UNHCR found it impossible to assist the repatriation, beyond making a 50-day food ration available from its stock. Although this food allowed the returnees to remain reasonably fit on the journey home, it is likely that their lack of seed, tools and oxen was a major contributor to continued food insecurity in the region and the recurrence of famine in 1987–8. The UNHCR was reluctant to assist the refugees because they were returning to rebel-held areas in the midst of military conflict. The concern not to step outside – or to be seen to step outside – the statutory framework in this particular instance was at least partly dictated by the foreign policy objectives of its major donors. Essentially, the problem was that it had no legal authority to co-operate with the TPLF, a 'non-recognized entity' which was fighting a war against the country of origin of the refugees, Ethiopia. Without such authority the UNHCR literally could not afford to take action that would be seen by its donors as against their short-term political interests.

This case illustrates the potential that exists not only for the interests of refugees to be subordinated to those of political leaders in the donor countries but also for refugees to become pawns in the fight between government forces and 'refugee-based' guerrilla movements. It was clearly in the interests of the TPLF that famine-threatened Tigrayans should have moved to the Sudan in 1984–5 rather than to areas controlled by the Ethiopian government. The government, on the other hand, was using food aid to attract people from rebel-held rural areas to the towns, from where they could be sent on to resettlement sites in western Ethiopia. One wonders how much pressure was needed to persuade families to make the arduous and, for many, disastrous six-week trek into the Sudan rather than the much shorter (for some only three-hour) walk to a government-held town. Whose interests came first – those of the people who were threatened with starvation, or those of their would-be political leaders who were not?

Equally, one wonders what part the Sudanese People's Liberation Army (SPLA) played in persuading Sudanese refugees to make for the camps on the Ethiopian side of the border which the Mengistu government allowed it to use as bases for its activities inside the Sudan. And when these camps emptied after the fall of Mengistu, how far was this the result of pressure from the SPLA, which now saw the need to set up similar camps, to attract relief food and other resources, on the Sudanese side of the border? (see the chapters by James and Johnson). Also, who has benefited from the EPLF's approach to the return of Eritrean refugees from Sudan? Here is a case in which the four conditions for return appear to have been met, but the refugees continue to stay in the camps, and the UNHCR has been unable to assist their repatriation. As Kibreab and Habte Selassie assert, this is partly due to a lack of donor support, but the Eritrean leadership must take some of the responsibility. Irrespective of their own wishes, the refugees have been used for purposes of political bargaining.

If refugees are unable or unwilling to act independently and avoid formal registration, it seems that the means do not yet exist to enable their choices to play a decisive part in determining their own future. The UNHCR is rightly concerned with the protection of refugees but this is a concept that can be interpreted very broadly. The sense it had in the minds of those who drafted the 1951 Convention was, quite specifically, the protection of individuals from persecution by the authorities in their countries of origin. The extension of the protection mandate to cover mass movements of people in the developing countries, people who are not fleeing from persecution but removing themselves from a generalized source of danger such as military conflict or famine, has been accompanied by a tendency to emphasize the needs of refugees and returnees, seen as homogeneous categories.

Divisions within these groups in specific locations is commonly set aside as an issue, and the different priorities of first and second generation refugees, of the young and the elderly, of the formally educated and the traders, of pastoralists and farmers, of recently married women and politically active men are often ignored. Amorphous and externally generated collective labels are invoked at the expense of individual capacities – in particular, the capacity of people to make informed and rational decisions about matters affecting their own and their children's' futures.

'Who decides?', then, is a question that deserves empirical investigation from at least three angles. First, who decides what is in the best interests of the refugees? Where return is encouraged (or discouraged) by agencies, governments and guerrilla movements, is this because it serves (or does not serve) the interests of these powerful outside organizations rather than of the refugees? This is undoubtedly a much too simplistic formulation but to go beyond it we need more information about the factors which, in particular cases, have influenced and constrained decision-making within international agencies, government offices and liberation movements. Secondly, who has responsibility, among the refugees, for making decisions about return and/or the power to influence them – household heads, whether male or female, older people in general, traditional leaders ...? Thirdly, which families decide to return and which decide to stay? Or, in other words, what are the factors that influence some refugees to favour, and others not to favour, return?

It is symptomatic of our failure to take these questions seriously that we tend to treat 'the Ugandan refugees' or 'the Tigrayan refugees' or even simply 'refugees' as homogeneous categories, as though all the people so designated shared the same interests and the same objectives. This is another unfortunate and, unless deliberately guarded against, inevitable effect of labelling. It is not something which is completely avoided in some of the chapters of this book, or indeed in this introductary chapter. To overcome it we need to learn much more about the way particular displaced populations are internally differentiated and about how these differences affect preferences for and against, and decisions about homecoming and homemaking. The result will be an untidy picture, but it is only by understanding the choices, preferences and decision-making procedures of the people themselves that it will be possible to give substance to the much repeated objective of 'empowering' them. It is also a necessary precondition of another much repeated objective: making aid to refugees and returnees 'development oriented'.

This is the subject of our next section, which discusses the issue with respect to assistance in circumstances of refugee and returnee migration. However, as Cernea points out, it is also important to recognize that certain forms of development may actually cause population displacement. In his chapter, Cernea notes that comparative analyses of refugee and returnee groups usually ignore studies made of other kinds of involuntary displacements, such as those caused by dam construction. This is another example of how the use of amorphous collective labels may be unhelpful. Cernea also draws attention to the Ethiopian government's huge population resettlement scheme in the 1980s. Hundreds of thousands of people were forcibly moved under the Mengistu regime, and many experienced situations similar to those associated with refugees (see Pankhurst, 1992). That experiment has been generally condemned for violating human rights, but Turton observes in the postscript of his chapter that there are proposals for further displacements in the name of development in the southwest of the country. It is planned to remove hundreds of people from the Omo and Mago valleys in order to promote wildlife conservation and tourism. If the project goes ahead, Mursi families may end up dispossessed as well as impoverished, and it may make little sense to distinguish them as a category from other displaced populations of the region.

From Giving Relief to Developing Institutions

The desirability of moving refugee assistance in developing countries away from the provision of temporary or 'care and maintenance' relief, specifically targeted at refugees and returnees, to a more development-orientated approach has been accepted in principle by governments and humanitarian agencies for at least a decade. Several chapters draw attention to this point. Kibreab, for example, notes that in 1984 the Declaration and Programme of Action of ICARA II stated that: 'assistance ... should be development-orientated as soon as possible and, in least developed countries, it should take into account the needs of local people as well'. The case for responding along these lines to situations of return in northeast Africa is unquestionable, for at least two reasons.

First, most returnees are not officially registered and are therefore invisible to outside agencies. During the 1990s, in the Ogaden and in northern Somalia, there have been hundreds of thousands of impoverished migrants, who might be defined as unregistered returnees (see the chapters by Getachew, Farah, Hogg and Holt). They comprised a significant proportion of the population (about 20 per cent in northern Somalia in mid-1992), and most of them have been living with relatives and friends at a time of general food shortage. Targeting help on returnees in such circumstances, by providing individual families with 'reintegration packages', may encourage them to leave the camps but may also prolong the 'relief syndrome' by failing to address the underlying problems of poverty and vulnerability in their home areas. Such preferential treatment may also be resented by 'stayees' who are expected to welcome the returnees home but who are themselves at least as economically vulnerable.

Secondly, the end of conflict in the refugees' country of origin may not be enough to attract them home if, as is likely, the infrastructure and economy of their home areas have been devastated. Eritreans and Ugandans in Sudan, for example, have been reluctant to return to war-damaged areas. It seems that the crucial factor in northeast Africa is not so much the allure of home (as Kibreab and Habte-Selassie maintain) but the circumstances in exile. As has already been discussed, many people return because they have been attacked. They are in fact refugees from refuge.

In the northeast African region, it is clearly not enough to focus help on a group classified as returnees. Such people are almost invariably going back to places in which the resident population is at least as impoverished as themselves. The implementation of 'beneficiary-blind' development programmes in refugee/returnee areas has been as elusive, however, as the arguments in favour of it are convincing. Aside from the operational problem that 'low intensity' conflict may persist in areas which are supposedly under the control of a sovereign government, there is a legal and a political problem. The legal problem is that development assistance does not fall within the mandate of the UNHCR. The political problem is that long-term development programmes are not only more expensive than humanitarian assistance, but funding for them is even more dependent on the perceived political self-interest of donors.

In response to the problem of mandate boundaries, the UNHCR in Ethiopia has initiated a cross-mandate/community-based approach which deserves close and sympathetic attention. 'Cross-mandate' implies that the United Nations agencies operating in a particular area are prepared to go beyond the boundaries of their traditional mandates in order to meet the needs of the people of that area, regardless of whether they are, or can be categorized as, refugees, returnees, drought victims, or internally displaced. A cross-mandate approach is therefore community-based by definition. It is development-orientated because, by channelling assistance in ways that benefit the community as a whole, the normal coping mechanisms of the community are strengthened.

The realization that such a change in direction was needed arose specifically from the experience of the UNHCR in the Ogaden, where the traditional pattern of providing assistance to refugees and returnees as special categories of the population had led to what seemed like an open-ended commitment to the support of permanent refugee/returnee camps. In essence, repatriation by the traditional means of providing individual families with reintegration packages simply was not working. Camps had become 'honey pots' to which needy people were attracted, whether or not they were officially classifiable as refugees/returnees, while for many pastoral families, keeping some of their

1.7 *In northeast Africa, people are almost invariably going back to places in which the resident population is at least as impoverished as themselves: 'shoe-shine boys' on the streets of Addis Ababa, 1992. (Tim Allen)*

members in camps to receive regular rations had become an integral part of their subsistence calculations. Switching available funds from the care and maintenance costs of refugee camps and from the provision of reintegration packages for returnee families to community-based projects would have the double advantage of reducing the population dependent on UNHCR support while reducing the vulnerability of entire communities.

The cross-mandate approach will clearly be welcomed by donors as an attempt to address the problem of unnecessary duplication between different United Nations agencies working towards the same overall objective. But, however successful it is in bringing about effective inter-agency co-operation in the short term – and the mechanisms by which this will be achieved are not yet clear – the real test of the approach will lie in the effectiveness of the community-based projects to which it leads. It will be judged, in other words, not by its immediate impact on organizational efficiency (e.g., the sharing of transport facilities and of office premises by different agencies) but by its long-term impact on the underlying problems of poverty and vulnerability in refugee and returnee areas.

The kinds of projects envisaged remain a matter of discussion, but early initiatives seem to have been modelled on the programme of Quick Impact Projects (QIPs) developed by the UNHCR in Nicaragua. This is a community-based programme of micro-projects, funded by the UNHCR but carried out by NGOs and self-help groups, which has the aim of 'anchoring repatriation as a durable solution by maximising returnees' chances of significant reintegration into their communities' (UNHCR, 1992: 2). They can consist in the provision of tools and on-the-job technical training (presumably to the community as a whole), and in the repairing of bridges and roads. By setting up these projects in 'integrated circuits', it is hoped to bring about 'the economic and social reactivation of communities, towns and even entire regions serving as the basis on which national development plans can be built'. Whatever the likely and actual achievements of the QIP programme in Nicaragua, the general level of poverty and infrastructural devastation in northeast Africa gives grounds for some scepticism that an effective dash for development could be mobilized on a similar basis there. This is not to say that such projects would not be beneficial but that they are unlikely to make possible, in the short term, the phasing out of relief assistance, especially food aid.

The Save the Children Fund (SCF UK) surveys of nutrition and economic conditions in the Ogaden and northern Somalia, discussed in the chapter by Holt, found that the chief source of grain in the region as a whole, but especially northern Somalia, was food-aid wheat from the Ogaden camps. Even before the emergency of the early 1990s, grain accounted for at least half the food calories consumed by most rural people in the area, including pastoralists. The chief means available for the purchase of grain was the sale of livestock. The key to survival for most people, therefore, lay in the terms of trade between grain and livestock. If the camps were closed and hundreds of thousands of people repatriated, grain would still have to come into the region at prices which would allow people to survive without reducing their herds below a viable level. This could be achieved by free distribution of grain or cash or by a subsidized marketing arrangement, such as the food 'monetization' programme already under way. In any event, food aid should not be seen as a way of targeting individuals, identified anthropometrically as malnourished, but as a form of economic redistribution to the poor.

Among the advantages given by the UNHCR for embracing a cross-mandate approach are that it will be a way of getting better value from its existing financial resources. That is, funds which would have been available for returnee family reintegration grants will be used instead for community-based projects. In fact, there are indications that considerable savings are envisaged in costs per returnee. The QIP Primer states that 'in most repatriation operations, returning refugees are provided with a basic package of rehabilitation assistance including foodstuffs (usually for a three to six month period) shelter materials, seeds, other agricultural inputs and cash grants (approximately US$50 per person)' (UNHCR, 1992: 3). A Quick Impact Project Proposal Format prepared by the UNHCR office in Addis Ababa suggests that projects will be funded to a maximum of 80 Ethiopian birr per returnee – or approximately US$38 at the then official rate of exchange. It is possible, therefore, that the main advantage of 'community-based quick impact projects', from an organizational point of view, is not that they are community-based, nor that they are quick, but that they are cheap. In this case, and in the context of northeast Africa, there is a danger that they will be seen as 'quick-fix' solutions, helping the organization to solve its problem – how to get large numbers of refugees and returnees off its hands at minimal cost – while failing to solve *their* problem – how to revitalize the economies of their home areas. (For a recent critical assessment of the cross-mandate approach in the Ogaden, see Brabant, 1994).

If the apparent gap between relief and development aid is to be bridged, this will require the investment of considerable resources in the revitalization of devastated and poverty-stricken areas. It needs to be emphasized that the relative success of the NRM in reconstructing Ugandan state institutions has been very dependent on foreign aid. According to E.A. Brett, donors have provided more than half of the resources required to sustain imports and finance the budget, and to deliver services in many parts of the country (particularly those affected by civil war). This raises the major political problem of funding. UNHCR and other United Nations agencies are required to adopt a non-political stance in their relations with states and yet their funding is so organized (annual discretionary grants, earmarking of funds, etc.) that they can be used as instruments for advancing the national interests of the major donor countries. For a variety of historical reasons, there has been both considerable sympathy for Uganda in the international community, and a willingness to work with and support the NRM. Such a combination of sympathy and willingness is not always present elsewhere.

If the necessary levels of funding and support are to be more universally available, a new kind of national self-interest will need to be developed among the richer nations, one that is based not on calculations of short-term political and economic advantage but on the realization that the future well-being of all nations depends upon a redistribution of resources from North to South, based upon established principles, and the constructing of viable social institutions in those parts of the world in which existing state structures (often supported in the past by Cold War alliances) are disintegrating.

The primary responsibility given to the United Nations by its charter is 'the maintenance of international peace and security'. Threats to international peace were defined exclusively in terms of aggression between sovereign states. Conflict within national boundaries, leading to human rights abuses, is thus not covered by this definition. It follows that the United Nations has no right under its charter to intervene in the affairs of a state to protect the human rights of its citizens. This was reiterated in 1992 in the Secretary-General's document, 'An Agenda for Peace':

> In … situations of internal crisis the United Nations will need to respect the sovereignty of the State; to do otherwise would not be in accordance with the understanding of Member States in accepting the principles of the Charter.' (UN, 1992: 9)

In the same document, however, it is noted that:

> the time of absolute and exclusive sovereignty has passed … It is the task of leaders of States today to understand this and to find a balance between the needs of good internal governance and the requirements of an ever more interdependent world. (UN, 1992: 5)

One way in which political leaders could accept 'the requirements of an ever more interdependent world' is by resisting the temptation to earmark funds donated to United Nations agencies in line with their own political priorities, thereby providing these agencies with secure budgets. This would amount to a voluntary limitation on their own autonomy as sovereign states.

Since the end of the 1980s, we have witnessed the collapse, as complete as it was unexpected, of a principle of international political order based on a balanced opposition between opposing segments. A 'new world order' has not emerged painlessly out of this process. A range of *ad hoc* arrangements have been made by the major powers and the UN in an effort to keep matters in hand. In northeast Africa (and in eastern Europe), the evidence indicates that this militarized international crisis management has had muddled objectives and has repeatedly ended up institutionalizing violence (UNRISD, 1993b; Duffield, 1994). A new world order will, nevertheless, have to be built, either on a different arrangement of opposing segments or by limiting the autonomy and independence of individual segments (i.e., sovereign states) through a kind of international social contract. This will require states, voluntarily and out of self-interest, to give up some of their freedoms in exchange for greater overall security, making themselves thereby subject to a central authority, or world government.

We have suggested many ways in which the displaced peoples of northeast Africa might be helped and many other ways are suggested in the chapters which follow. In the long run, however, greater centralization of the global political system, based on consensus but with the limitations on national sovereignty that this would entail, is likely to offer the only 'durable solution' to the problem of refugee flows, whether in northeast Africa or elsewhere in the world.

References

Akol, J.O. (1987) 'Southern Sudanese refugees: their repatriation and resettlement after the Addis Ababa Agreement', in J. Rogge (ed.) *Refugees: a third world dilemma*, Rowman and Littlefield, Totowa, NJ.

—— (1994) 'A crisis of expectations: returning to Southern Sudan in the 1970s' in T. Allen and H. Morsink (eds) *When refugees go home*, UNRISD, Geneva, and James Currey, London.

Allen, T. (1989) 'Full circle?: an overview of Sudan's "Southern problem" since independence', *Northeast Africa Studies*, Vol. 11, No. 2: 41–6.

Allen, T. and Morsink, H. (eds) (1994) *When refugees go home*, UNRISD, Geneva, and James Currey, London.

Benthall, J. (1993), *Disasters, relief and the media*, I.B. Tauris, London: 123–72.

van Brabant, K. (1994) *Bad borders make bad neighbours: the political economy of relief and rehabilitation in the Somali Region 5, eastern Ethiopia*, Network paper No. 4, Relief and Rehabilitation Network, Overseas Development Institute.

Coles, G. (1985) 'Voluntary repatriation: a background study'. Report for UNHCR's Round Table on Voluntary Repatriation, International Institute of Humanitarian Law, San Remo, and the UNHCR, Geneva.

Crisp, J. (1987) 'Voluntary repatriation for refugees in developing countries: a bibliographical survey', UNRISD, Geneva.

Cuénod, J. (1990) 'Refugees, development or relief?' in G. Loescher and L. Monahan (eds) *Refugees and international relations*, Clarendon Press, Oxford: 233–4.

Cuny, F. Stein, B. and Reed, P. (eds) (1992) *Repatriation during conflict in Africa and Asia*, Centre for the Study of Societies in Crisis, Dallas.

Duffield, M. (1994) *Complex political emergencies: an exploratory report for UNICEF*, University of Birmingham.

Kabera, J.B. amd Muyanja, C. (1994) 'Homecoming in the Luwero Triangle', in Allen, T. and Morsink, H. (eds) *When refugees go home*, UNRISD, Geneva, and James Currey, London.

Larkin, M. Cuny, F. and Stein, B. (eds) (1991) *Repatriation under conflict in Central America*, Centre for Immigration Policy and Refugee Assistance, Georgetown University, Washington DC.

Makanya, S.T. (1994) 'The desire to return', in Allen, T. and Morsink, H. (eds) *When refugees go home*, UNRISD, Geneva, and James Currey, London.

Morsink, H. (1990) *UNRISD and its research into social and economic aspects of mass voluntary return of refugees from one African country to another*, UNRISD, Geneva.

Pankhurst, A. (1992) *Resettlement and famine in Ethiopia: the villagers' experience*, Manchester University Press, Manchester.

Preston, R. (1994) 'Returning exiles in Namibia since independence', in Allen, T. and Morsink, H. (eds) *When refugees go home*, UNRISD Geneva, and James Currey, London.

Rogge, J. (1994) 'Repatriation of refugees' in Allen, T. and Morsink, H. (eds) *When refugees go home*, UNRISD, Geneva and James Currey, London.

Styan, D. (1994) 'The origins of "*le droit d'ingérence*" and its contradictory relationship with French African policy', unpublished, South Bank University, London.

Tapscott, C. (1994) 'A tale of two homecomings' in Allen, T. and Morsink, H. (eds) *When refugees go home*, UNRISD, Geneva and James Currey, London.

UN (1992) 'An agenda for peace', Document No. A/47/277, New York: 9.

UNHCR (1992) 'A primer on Quick Impact Projects', Managua: 2.

—— (1993) *The state of the world's refugees*, Penguin Books, Harmondsworth: 103–16.

UNRISD (1993a) 'Refugees returning home', report of the Symposium on the Horn of Africa on the Social and Economic Aspects of Mass Voluntary Return Movements of Refugees, Geneva.

—— (1993b) 'Rebuilding wartorn societies', report of the workshop on The Challenge of Rebuilding Wartorn Societies and the Social Consequences of the Peace Process in Cambodia, Geneva.

2

ENOCH O. OPONDO
Refugee Repatriation
in the Horn of Africa

A Contextual Overview
of some Socio-Economic,
Legal & Administrative Constraints

In a world where most refugees are confined to over-crowded, makeshift camps in conditions as dismal – if not more dismal – than the situation they have fled, the right to return to one's homeland must be given as much recognition as the right to seek asylum abroad.

(Mrs Ogata, the UN High Commissioner for Refugees, in her opening statement to the 42nd session of the Executive Committee Meeting, Geneva, 7–11 October 1991.)

Introduction

Voluntary repatriation is recognizably the most desirable solution to the refugee phenomenon, in that it has the potential of turning a refugee into an ordinary person once more enjoying the protection of his/her state of origin. A recognition of this by the international community led the UN General Assembly – when establishing UNHCR – to call upon governments to assist in the promotion of voluntary repatriation, which was declared to be one of UNHCR's principal functions (UN, 1950; Goodwin-Gill 1983: 219; Hathaway, 1991: 191).

This being the case, the UN High Commissioner for Refugees' description – coming 41 years on – of 1992 as 'the year for voluntary repatriation' (UNHCR, 1991: 22) inevitably attracted a lot of international attention. It came as a culmination of a decade or so of increased mass return of refugees to their home countries, with voluntary repatriation emerging as a solution most favoured by donors (Harrell-Bond, 1989: 42; Larkin, Cuny and Stein, 1991: ix; Wilson 1992: 20–1; Cuny and Stein, 1992: 7).

Whereas voluntary repatriation is in keeping with the right to return to one's homeland, a basic human right under international law (see the African Charter of Human and Peoples Rights, 1981, Art. 12, par. 3; the Universal Declaration of Human Rights, Art. 13, par. 2; International Convention on Civil and Political Rights, Art. 12, par. 4), its resurgence has been explained as a function of the failure of the other two classic 'durable' solutions, integration and resettlement. 'In any given year, less than one per cent of the world's refugees escape the limbo of refugee status either by resettling in third countries or by obtaining citizenship in the country of asylum' (Larkin, Cuny and Stein, 1991: 2). Apart from failing to become integrated members of the host societies, the refugees are in many instances surviving in conditions of squalor often worse than the situations they fled (see opening quotation; Harrell-Bond, 1986: 187).

The poignant manifestation of the inability of the international refugee regime to find a solution to the crisis is the refugees' own reaction, in what amounts to resigning to fate:

2.1 *Ugandan refugees in Sudan were attacked in 1986, and were forced to flee back to Uganda: returnees at the UNHCR reception centre, Pakelle, Moyo District, Uganda, May 1986. (UNHCR/M. Barton)*

refugees' decision to return to their homelands usually in the midst of the crises that forced them to become refugees in the first place (Cuny and Stein, 1992: 5). 'Voluntary repatriation' consequently becomes, not the expected happy resolution of the refugee phenomenon envisaged by the 1950 Statute of the Office of 'the UNHCR, but a *de facto* continuation of 'refugeeism' even when the refugees are back in their home countries, where they join the mass of internally displaced persons, or, as one writer calls them, the internal refugees (Clark, 1988: 19).

This tragic drama has been going on for some time in the Horn of Africa with Somalia, Sudan, Ethiopia/Eritrea and Uganda as the principal actors. Djibouti and Kenya have generally been in the wing playing supporting roles. For the past 30 years the Horn has been in a state of turmoil, devastated by drought and famine, torn apart by civil and regional wars and uncontrolled banditry (Hutchinson, 1991: 13).

The consequence has been extensive forced migration in the area, earning it the dubious name of 'a land of refugees' (US Committee for Refugees, 1988: 2). December 1991 estimates indicated a refugee population in excess of 1.5 million (US Committee for Refugees, 1992a: 32). These are conservative estimates given the increasing complexity of the Horn's crisis, and therefore do not reflect the extent of displacement and forced migration in the region.

Part of the complexity is that the process of flight has largely become indistinguishable from the process of return. The High Commissioner for Refugees (UNHCR, 1991: 22), for example, reported that Ethiopian refugees fleeing back into Ethiopia to escape the fighting in Somalia have had to contend with hunger and homelessness upon return. The net effect is that the same organizations end up dealing simultaneously and within the same region with those fleeing and those returning, with flight and return taking place within the context of famine, political instability, and social cleavages (Loescher, 1991: 4).

This analysis is based on the argument that the ongoing and contemplated mass

voluntary return movements of refugees in the Horn of Africa are basically a consequence of: (i) the continuation of socio-economic and political problems in the region
which often make conditions in host societies as bad as, if not worse than, the situation
the refugees had escaped from; and (ii) the inability of the international humanitarian and
refugee assistance regime to live up to the bold objectives of protecting refugees,
improving their situation, reducing the number requiring protection (by addressing
causal factors), promoting voluntary refugee repatriation, or resettlement and assimilation elsewhere (UN, 1950). This is not to say that the various non-governmental
organizations (NGOs), governments, and inter-governmental agencies operating in the
region have not worked to alleviate the problems of returnees and refugees. On the
contrary, the Horn has attracted considerable activity by these organizations.
Nevertheless, assistance has fallen short of what is needed, thereby necessitating the
return of refugees, sometimes in massive numbers, without sufficient preparation on
their part and/or on the part of the home state or the international community.

Below is an attempt to identify weaknesses in the existing refugee assistance regime
and to give some suggestions as to why these need to be guarded against in the Horn's
repatriation processes. The experiences gained during and after mass return movements
in Africa and elsewhere have also been pointed out, with a further attempt being made
to apply these to the situation in the Horn today.

From 'Refugees' to 'Returnees' – Labelling and its Implications

One analysis of how and with what consequences people become labelled as *refugees* has
concluded that it is a process of stereotyping, and that it is a vehicle for promoting non-
participation and control (Zetter, 1991: 44–5). Similarly, restrictive and legalistic
conceptions of the term 'refugee' have been used to deny countless people international
protection – and thus making refugee status a privileged position which accesses
individuals to international assistance, including material relief, asylum, and even
permanent resettlement (Shacknove, 1985: 276). This means that those in refugee-like
situations, but who have not been labelled as refugees, miss out on assistance marked 'for
refugees'.

It is true that labelling could be positive in the sense that it 'at least provides a way of
recognising the existence of a class of people, of identifying their special needs, and of
mandating responsibility for meeting these needs' (Clark, 1988: 19). Nevertheless, it can
be manipulated to the detriment of those it is intended to benefit and also jeopardizes the
resolution of their problems in the context of the society in which such persons find
themselves.

In some of the recent literature on repatriation (e.g. Larkin, Cuny and Stein, 1991: 3),
there have been references to those who have repatriated as 'returnees'. Innocent as this
term may be, it is a label which has the potential of isolating the returning refugees from
the rest of their home societies and thereby setting them apart for special treatment even
though some of the 'stayees' may be in similar, if not worse predicaments.

One aspect of labelling which has characterized assistance to those repatriating is
stereotyping, in which the repatriants are viewed by humanitarian organizations and
donors as helpless individuals who need outsiders to plan for them (Kabera and Muyanja,
1991: 10). This misjudges the situation. It has been documented, for example, that
Ugandan refugees in southern Sudan had their own schemes for returning to their
homes as soon as it was safe, and for using the food they had grown in the Sudan to
sustain a few members of their households while they re-established fields in Uganda

(Harrell-Bond, 1986: 191). In the Tigrayan case, the heads of households and other able adults preceded the rest of the family members (Hendrie, 1990). The logical thing to do in cases such as these would be for assistance agencies to facilitate the initiatives instead of simply supplying relief or developing parallel arrangements.

The consequences of poor co-ordination of agency and refugees' own repatriation plans (a function of labelling) have been demonstrated at the Mayukwayukwa settlement for Angolan refugees in Kaoma, Zambia (Geloo, 1992). The UNHCR's plans to repatriate could not immediately be implemented because of a late realization that the safety of the returning refugees would be jeopardized by the land-mines strewn in the Angolan countryside. Meanwhile, the refugees had been told to prepare for repatriation and this included selling their crops, animals and possessions because there would be no room for these on the trucks. Eight months later, they were still at Mayukwayukwa and on the verge of starvation. The Christian Council which distributed food to refugee centres had stopped its programme because as far as it was concerned, the refugees were on their way home.

Voluntary Repatriation or Refoulement – an Interplay between Labelling and Safety Considerations

The lack of sensitivity to the need to give refugees more leeway in charting their destinies spills over into the determination of whether the situation back home is secure enough for return. The Mayukwayukwa case also points to the fact that initial agency assessments of the security situation in the home country are not always correct. After declaring that the refugees would shortly return home, the Lusaka UNHCR representative reversed his decision, arguing eight months later that the delay had been caused by his organization's 'emphasis on safety and dignity when repatriating' (Geloo 1992:19). Ironically, the refugees were not keen on going back home in the first place, citing insecurity. It had taken a lot of persuasion by UNHCR and government officials before they unwillingly agreed to repatriate (Geloo, 1992).

Refugees usually have their own mechanisms for testing the security situation in their home countries. These include, as in the case of Ugandans in southern Sudan, sending individuals back home to investigate how safe it is for all to return (Harrell-Bond, 1986: 190–1). A conflictual situation usually arises in the event of differing perceptions of security between the UNHCR and governments, on the one hand, and the refugees on the other. In a situation where the refugees perceive that the security conditions at home are better than those in the country of refuge, and where the aid agencies think that the security situation at home is worse, the refugees will inevitably choose to defy the latter's warnings and go back with or without assistance (Cuny and Stein, 1992: 5).

Alternatively, when the aid agencies perceive that there is sufficient security at home but refugees think otherwise, the entire process of return may amount to forced repatriation. This was the situation regarding a repatriation planned for refugees from Sudan in 1981. Not only were they unwilling to embark on the trip, but by the time the lorry transporting them reached the border with Uganda, less than a half of those who had started off were still continuing with the journey (Harrell-Bond, 1986: 190).

The repatriation of Ethiopian refugees in Djibouti in the 1980s is a further vivid illustration of how what starts off as persuading refugees to go back home can easily become forced repatriation. In response to pressure exerted on limited resources of Djibouti, the refugees were coerced to volunteer to repatriate using threats of imprison-ment, cutting off of assistance and being bundled into a 'human shield' refugee camp (MIPT, 1986; Horekens, 1985; Crisp, 1984; Phillips, 1983; Clark, 1987: 37-41).

Whereas voluntary repatriation may be the durable solution of first choice, the questions asked with respect to whether most of the ongoing repatriation programmes are really voluntary are in essence questions relating to violation of the principle of *non-refoulement* which prohibits the return of refugees to places where their lives or freedom would be threatened (US Committee for Refugees, 1992b: 2). The Lawyers' Committee for Human Rights has argued that 'return cannot be considered truly *voluntary* if the conditions in a refugee camp are so dangerous, dire or dehumanizing that the refugee may be choosing to return to prosecution as the preferable alternative' (Lawyers Committee for Human Rights, 1992: 6–7).

The fluid situation pertaining in some parts of the Horn of Africa necessitates that all those concerned pay more attention to the degree to which active promotion of mass repatriation is not tantamount to *refoulement*. In this respect, the Lawyers' Committee for Human Rights' (1992) 'General Principles Relating to the Promotion of Refugee Repatriation' are quite handy as a checklist, pointing out that:

1. repatriation should not be promoted unless all countries involved can ensure the protection and respect of the fundamental human rights of the refugees;

2. refugees must not be returned to any country where they would face persecution;

3. refugee repatriation must be voluntary;

4. repatriation should be promoted only if it can be accomplished in a manner that ensures safety and dignity upon return;

5. the UNHCR should be involved in a meaningful way from the inception of the repatriation plan to its conclusion;

6. NGOs, in addition to the UNHCR, should have independent access to the refugees both before and after their return;

7. any repatriation plan should establish that the conflict has abated and its attendant risks eliminated before promoting return;

8. repatriation should be promoted only if there is no longer a likelihood of recurrence of the human rights abuses that precipitated the flight;

9. particular emphasis must be placed on the unique protection needs of returning women and children, who are a high risk group within an already vulnerable population; and

10. these principles and considerations may apply as well to unassisted repatriation.

These principles underscore the need for caution when handling cases of repatriation in places like the Horn of Africa where conflict has not abated, and in which agency-instigated repatriation processes may not be easily distinguishable from *refoulement*.

Towards a Developmental Approach to Assistance to Repatriants in the Horn

The effects of droughts which regularly ravage eastern and southern Africa, coupled with political uncertainty in some parts of the Horn, create the need for safeguards if the repatriation process is to be successful. The key concern is how to provide emergency assistance that meets immediate needs of the repatriants and which, at the same time, contributes to and supports settlement at home in such a way that a return to exile is not contemplated. In essence, therefore, the central issue is how to make repatriation assistance contribute not only to the welfare of the repatriants, but to also facilitate improvements in living conditions, infrastructure and development opportunity for the larger communities to which they belong (Anderson and Woodrow, 1989: 2; Larkin, Cuny and Stein, 1991: 210).

Since the Second International Conference on Assistance to Refugees in Africa (ICARA II) of 1984, the need to focus on development-orientated assistance, as opposed to purely emergency relief assistance, has found acceptance among most refugee assistance circles. The former means working towards empowering refugees by securing their productivity and self-reliance. It also leads to a recognition of the importance of facilitating empowerment by creating an enabling environment in the surrounding community. In any case, 'for social, psychological, and political reasons' development assistance must be targeted to both the refugees and the local population (Clark and Stein, 1985: 37).

There is little doubt that circumstances in the Horn of Africa call for a reaction to repatriation in a manner similar to the one which emerged from ICARA II with respect to Africa's refugees. An influx of repatriants can create acute conditions for both the repatriants themselves and to the population of the home country, thereby accentuating poverty and insecurity. The experience of dealing with refugees shows that rarely are their needs sufficiently met by the welfare model of refugee assistance. For example, relief rations handed out to refugees in many cases do not meet their actual nutritional needs. Consequently, enabling refugees to produce their own food is surely a better way of ensuring that their nutritional requirements are met through revival of traditional feeding habits (Harrell-Bond, 1986: 234–44).

An attempt by the International Council of Voluntary Agencies (ICVA) and the UNHCR to translate the ICARA II 'philosophy' into concrete recommendations for action established that developmental assistance in this context would mean: (i) avoiding encampment; (ii) encouraging settlement in small groups close to work possibilities, and providing employment opportunities to the migrants in such forms as in the building of their own shelters; and (iii) starting development activities which are linked to national development plans, and thus facilitating elimination of artificial distinction between categories such as 'returnees' and 'stayees' (Harrell-Bond, 1992: 11).

Whereas the actual implementation of these principles in the refugee situation has not fared well, due to ICARA II's failure 'to take sufficient account of political interests in earmarking of funds for refugees and of the need to re-define the mandates of the agencies with the UNHCR system' (Harrell-Bond, 1992: 11), this does not negate their validity as concrete starting points for meaningful assistance to the returning refugees. Ways must be sought to surmount the financial difficulties by raising sufficient international interest. There are indications from the repatriation processes going on in Afghanistan, Cambodia, and in many other places that the political will to facilitate the process already exists. The next steps would be, first, to direct international attention towards resolving the wider socio-economic and political issues leading to crises in places such as the Horn, followed by a sensitization to the vitality of adopting a developmental approach to assisting refugees who go back home.

Role Determination in the Repatriation Process

Another practical difficulty faced in repatriation is determining the roles of agencies and concerned governments in the repatriation process, and the nature of refugees' own involvement. Two factors should provide the foundation for deciding who is to do what. First, according to the 1950 Statute of the Office of the UNHCR, governments and the UNHCR have roles to play that should support each other in the repatriation Process (UN, 1950). Secondly, studies in Africa, Asia and in Central and Latin America have provided evidence that many repatriation processes are initiated, organized, and implemented by the refugees themselves outside of formal assistance, and often occur in the face of official opposition (Wilson, 1992: 21; Larkin, Cuny and Stein, 1991, Hendrie, 1990). These two factors at least provide a lead: refugees should decide on repatriation and UNHCR and governments should help them to return and settle.

An important contribution of governments and agencies would be to enable refugees to make informed decisions by providing the necessary information. This excludes 'counselling' and other persuasion techniques which in the final analysis may amount to coercion (Lawyers' Committee for Human Rights, 1992: 5–77). By the same token, those who have returned should be allowed to determine what types of assistance they would rather have within the limits of the available resources. The need to adopt this approach has been recognized in part in the repatriation of Cambodian refugees from Thailand. The idea is to allow the refugees to decide which part of the country they could resettle in. Under a housing settlement option, the refugee is to be provided with transport, food, a household plot and building materials. A third option is the cash grant per individual, transport and food. A refugee can also opt for a tool kit, such as that needed by mechanics, tailors or artisans to become gainfully employed (UNHCR, 1992).

Baloro's (1992: 41–5) discussion of the UNHCR's involvement in the repatriation to South Africa bears out the contention that the agency's mandate and relation to other agencies in the UN system with respect to repatriation needs re-definition (Harrell-Bond, 1992: 11), because at the moment it is in a state of some legal confusion (Wilson, 1992: 21). One area which needs sorting out is the UNHCR relation to UNDP regarding the nature of their collaboration in the 'development-not-relief' approach adopted by ICARA II for refugee assistance. In Zambia, UNDP funded two projects from the ICARA II Reserve Fund in refugee-affected areas and implemented them with no advance consultation with UNHCR (Harrell-Bond, 1992: 11). It is such lack of a clear definition of who does what, where, and when, which – carried into the process of repatriation – can be responsible for unco-ordinated use of resources, and, consequently, to very limited results in enabling those who return to adjust adequately.

The determination of when, in the repatriation process, a refugee ceases to be one can probably assist in identifying where the jurisdiction of UNHCR ends. Simply put, the logic would be that because the agency is concerned essentially with refugees – unless otherwise legislated by the UN General Assembly – it will hand assistance programmes for those who have ceased to be refugees over to other agencies and bodies charged with the execution of development programmes in Africa. Mrs Ogata has acknowledged that 'UNHCR is not a development agency' (UNHCR, 1991: 23).

The scourge of war, civil unrest and drought in the Horn of Africa has created a situation in which a smooth co-ordination of the activities of various agencies, NGOs and other humanitarian organizations is clearly called for if a resolution of the problem of population displacement and a return to normalcy in civil life is to be realized. Such co-ordination is difficult to achieve if the roles are not clearly defined, and the areas requiring joint efforts spelt out. Currently, there is unnecessary duplication and waste in the use of resources (Kabera and Muyanja, 1991: 10).

Governments' Role in the Repatriation Process

Coupled with the need to re-define the roles of UNHCR and other UN agencies is the need to place the role of governments in perspective. One central responsibility of governments – host and home – is to create an enabling environment for the repatriation process. A way in which this has been taking place is in the 'Tripartite Commissions' involving host and home governments, and the UNHCR which have become the 'hallmark of organized (as opposed to spontaneous) repatriation processes. Two points can be made regarding this. First, as Stein (1992: 7) has stated, most repatriation processes are in fact spontaneous rather than organized. The challenge facing governments in this respect is how to cope. Cases have been reported in which governments turned a blind eye to the problems associated with the influx of returning refugees for political or other reasons (The Relief Society of Tigray, 1985: 2). Given, for example, that the country of origin must accept responsibility for its own citizens – both in terms of conditions which avert forced exile and also which promote voluntary return (UNHCR 1991:2), decisions not to act when refugees take the initiative to return amount to abdication of responsibility.

Secondly, there are fears that tripartite agreements do forget that whereas a community of refugees may wish to return, there may be individuals within that refugee community who may wish to remain behind (Opondo, 1992a: 8). A study conducted under the auspices of the Harvard Program in Refugee Trauma, and the World Federation for Mental Health, for example, established that 18 per cent of adult Khmer residents of Site II were not sure that they wanted to return to their communities and provinces of origin (Mollica et al., 1992: 4). Sufficient provisions must be made by governments to enable those who (temporarily or permanently) do not want to go back – for reasons ranging from fear, to marriages and business interests, and simple preference to continue living in a host country – to remain behind. An indication that this is feasible is Somalia's decision in 1983 to allow refugees who did not wish to repatriate to Ethiopia to be integrated locally in rural settlement schemes (Barton, 1984: 21).

There is also the problem of preparing the receiving community. It is usually assumed that returning refugees will automatically be accepted in their home countries. This is not always the case, given the dynamic nature of society as well as of individual personality (Harrell-Bond, 1989: 42). The reintegration of those who return may be as complicated as the experience of adjusting to a new culture while a person is outside his or her country. Thus, in 1990, when Tanzania expelled some Kenyans who had settled in Tanzania, some were rejected by their extended families. The main reason was that during their stay in Tanzania, family lands had been demarcated and sub-divided among individual family members. These people were, therefore, a threat to individual possessions. Other reasons for rejection included importation of 'alien' cultural practices such as witchcraft (Opondo 1992a: 3–4).

It is imperative that clear provisions should be made to deal with such social realities, and the government of the country of origin has a responsibility in this respect. As Ayok-Chol (1992: 22) has indicated, one of the thorny issues which must be addressed in order to 'end the refugee tale' for returning refugees is that of land ownership. One cannot simply assume that refugees will be able to go back to their former land. Governments must address this problem. Indeed, the wider question of property ownership must be addressed. Otherwise, efforts, such as the current attempts by Ugandan authorities to facilitate the return of Asians (expelled by Amin in 1972) by making it possible for them to reclaim their property, will lead to additional conflict between the government, the returning owners and the de facto owners or occupiers of the property.

Kabera and Muyanja (1991: 10–11) have noted the assumption in international circles that the governments and institutions in the developing world are insufficiently prepared to deal with refugee assistance programmes due to weaknesses emanating from poorly trained personnel and corruption. Their discussion of the organization of assistance to returning refugees in Uganda's Luwero Triangle, however, shows a level of preparedness on the part of the Ugandan authorities. Since 1986, provision of relief and general rehabilitation has been vested in the Prime Minister's Office which co-ordinates

2.2 *In some countries in eastern Africa one can find structures which can facilitate the co-operation between governments and agencies involved in relief programmes: grain distribution for returnees to Luwero, 1986. (Ben Male/Oxfam)*

activities from the national to the grass-roots levels. This suggests that in some countries in eastern Africa one can find structures which can facilitate the co-operation between governments and agencies involved in relief programmes for returning refugees. Otherwise, in the process of trying to assist returning refugees, international agencies can contribute to what Harrell-Bond (1986: 67–70) calls 'institutional destruction' of the administrative machinery in the home country. She cites developments in the administration of relief in the Sudan in 1982 which undermined the local Sudanese administration's power of decision-making.

Close co-operation between humanitarian agencies and governments is necessary in tackling conditions which lead people once again to contemplate fleeing their homes. For the Horn, these include mitigating the consequences of drought which lead to famine and flight. It is axiomatic that drought does not necessarily lead to famine. In his analysis of the 1972–4 Ethiopian famine Sen (1981: 86–112), has shown how other factors intervene to make a drought situation lead to famine. A co-ordinated assistance programme by agencies working in close co-operation with the government could have prevented the famine which led to the displacement of people in Ethiopia.

There are, of course, other issues which precipitate flight and which governments also need to address. In the Horn of Africa, these are mainly in the domain of social cleavages that create political problems. There is little doubt that getting international assistance – especially from the UNHCR – for those returning to areas controlled by 'unofficial governments' is often difficult. Habte-Selassie (1992: 23) has mentioned the case of Eritrean refugees – repatriating from the Sudan to the areas held by the Eritrean People's Liberation Front (EPLF) – who could not be assisted by UNHCR because the EPLF 'government' lacked official international recognition.

The result is that even though refugees may identify 'space for return' (Larkin, 1992:

7) in areas where conflict is still going on and move into it in desperation to escape the often degrading conditions in refugee camps, very little can be done short of antagonizing the recognized governments by seeming to side with liberation/rebel movements. Similarly, if the return of refugees is pegged to granting refugees 'amnesty' some refugees may argue that they were not criminals in the first place. It behoves the governments in the region and the international community at large to address these issues if the various repatriation processes are to succeed.

Conclusions

The objective has been to give an overview of some of the main social, economic, legal and assistance co-ordination constraints on the repatriation processes in the Horn of Africa, drawing from experiences in the Horn and elsewhere. It has been noted that the failure of the other durable solutions to the refugee crisis has led to the present preoccupation with repatriation. For the Horn of Africa, mass repatriation movements have also been instigated by the problems in some of the countries in the region hosting refugees, and the inability of the international community to address the refugee issue adequately. There is, therefore, need to avoid existing weaknesses in the refugee assistance regime when handling the affairs of repatriating refugees and of those who have ceased to be refugees in the legal usage of the term. Four areas of weaknesses have been discussed.

First is labelling, which is a persistent danger in assistance programmes. It has been argued that labelling leads to stereotyping and, subsequently, to trying to solve the problems of the beneficiaries of assistance programmes outside the context in which they find themselves. For the Horn of Africa, it has been emphasized that people who avoided exile also face problems similar to those of the returning refugees. For example, very many people have been internally displaced. It has, therefore, been suggested that a developmental approach be adopted to the repatriation process in the Horn. Such an approach would be in the spirit of the ICARA II philosophy which recommends a 'development-not-relief' approach to solving Africa's refugee problem.

On the strength of the argument that the economic, social and political situation in the Horn is rather fluid, it has been suggested that care be taken to make provision for those who do not wish to repatriate. It is, therefore, critical that the repatriation process in the region be absolutely voluntary.

2.3 *It is critical that the repatriation process in the region be absolutely voluntary: refugee from Somalia in Kenya, 1992. (UNHCR/22045/P. Moumtzis)*

The roles of agencies, governments and the repatriants themselves have also been discussed. It has been emphasized that the

UNHCR definitely has an important role to play in the repatriation process in the Horn of Africa. It has been noted, however, that there is need to address the wider issue of the organization's mandate and the co-ordination between it and the other UN agencies. Similarly, the primacy of the role of host and home governments has been emphasized, especially with regard to creating an enabling environment for the repatriation process, and taking up more co-ordination responsibilities. In all these, it is necessary to recognize that it is the refugees who are at the centre. Ideally, therefore, they should play a central role in the determination of when to repatriate and how to go about it.

Finally, it has been noted that the refugee crisis in the Horn is a function of wider social, economic and political problems in the region. Because repatriation is an attempt at providing a lasting solution, it is imperative that, for it to be meaningful, these wider issues are addressed squarely by the governments in the region and by the international community at large. It is a truism that individuals and families will not find it necessary to contemplate seeking refuge elsewhere if there is social, economic and political stability at home.

In conclusion, it must be pointed out that there are no easy answers to the refugee crisis in the Horn of Africa, given that it is only a symptom of wider regional and international issues. The Horn has been one of the Cold War theatres. Regimes have collapsed and some parts are awash with sophisticated weaponry. The search for a meaningful resolution of the refugee crisis therefore goes beyond repatriating refugees. The task calls for the participation not only of humanitarian agencies, but also other actors in the international system. Together with this, the significance of researchers' input cannot be over-emphasized. Research findings provide a sound basis for policy formulation. As Kibreab (1991: 61) has suggested, there is need to have more research on the situation of African refugees to 'enable us to test the existing myriad of theoretical assumptions and to develop alternative concepts based on empirical investigation of the specific situation of African refugees'. This, followed by an exchange of ideas between researchers and those working on the ground, establishes a good basis for providing the decision-makers with more reliable assessment of the situation.

References

Anderson, M. B. and Woodrow, P. J. (1989), *Rising from the ashes: development strategies in times of disaster,* Westview Press, Boulder and San Francisco.

Ayok-Chol, A. (1992), 'Paper on the endless tale of the Mozambican Refugees', paper for 'First Country of Asylum and Development Aid' Conference, 8–12 June 1992, Malawi.

Baloro, J. (1992), 'The law and pattern of the repatriation of Namibian and South African refugees', paper for 'First Country of Asylum and Development Aid' Conference, 8–12 June, 1992, Malawi.

Barton, M. S. (1984), 'Repatriation and resettlement in the Horn', Africa Report, January–February: 20–22.

Clark, L. (1984), *Key issues in post-emergency refugee assistance in eastern and southern Africa,* Refugee Policy Group, Washington, DC.

— (1988), 'International refugees: the hidden half', in *World Refugee Survey – 1988 in Review,* American Council for Nationalities Service, Washington.

Clark, L. and Stein, B. N. (1985), 'ICARA II and refugee aid and development', *Migration Today,* Vol. XIII, No. 1: 33–38.

Crisp, J. (1984), 'The politics of repatriation: Ethiopian refugees in Djibouti, 1977–1983', *Review of African Political Economy,* No. 30, : 73–82.

Cuny, F. C. and Stein, B. N. (1991), Repatriation Under Conflict in Central America, CIDRA and Intertect, Dallas.

— (1992), *Repatriation during conflict: a guide for NGOs,* (Draft) Intertect Institute, Dallas.

Geloo, Z. (1992), 'Angolans in dilemma: Mayukwayukwa no longer a haven of peace', *Search,* Vol. 2, No. 5, July: 19–20.

Goodwin-Gill, G. S. (1983), *The refugee in international law,* Clarendon Press, Oxford.

Habte-Selassie, E. (1992), 'Eritrean refugees in the Sudan: a preliminary analysis of voluntary repatriation' in Martin Doornbos *et al.* (eds) (1992) *Beyond conflict in the Horn: prospects for peace, recovery, and development in Ethiopia, Somalia and the Sudan,* James Currey, London.

Harrell-Bond, B. E. (1986), *Imposing aid: emergency assistance to refugees,* Oxford University Press, Oxford.

— (1989), 'Repatriation: under what conditions is it the most desirable solution for refugees? An agenda for research', *African Studies Review*, Vol. 32, No. 1: 41–69.

— (1992), 'Refugees and the reformulation of international aid policy: what can Britain and Japan do?', background paper for UK–Japan 2000 Group, March 1992.

Hathaway, J. C. (1991), *The law of refugee status*, Butterworths, Toronto.

Hendrie, B. (1990) 'The Tigrean refugee repatriation: Sudan to Ethiopia, 1985–1987' a study prepared for Intertect Institute, Dallas.

Horekens, J. (1985) 'Voluntary repatriation of Ethiopian refugees in Djibouti', report issued by Deputy Representative, UNHCR office, Djibouti.

Hutchinson, R. A., (ed.) (1991), *Fighting for survival: insecurity, people and the environment in the Horn of Africa*, IVCN, Gland, Switzerland.

Kabera, J. B. and Muyanja, C. (1991), 'A review of reintegration of returnees to the Luwero Triangle, Uganda', paper presented at Symposium on Social and Economic Aspects of Mass Voluntary Return of Refugees from One African Country to Another, Harare, Zimbabwe, 14–19 March 1991.

Kibreab, G. (1991), *The state of the art review of refugee studies in Africa*, Research Report No. 26, Universitet Reprocentraten HSC, Uppsala.

Larkin, M. A. (1992), 'Research findings on Central American repatriation', Paper presented at "Repatriation During Conflict: the Need for a New 'Conventional Wisdom' Regarding Repatriation" Seminar, Oslo, Norway, 21 May 1992.

Larkin, M.A., Cuny, F.C. and Stein, B.N. (1991), *Repatriation under Conflict in Central America*, Center for Immigration Policy and Refugee Assistance, Georgetown University, Washington DC.

Lawyers' Committee for Human Rights (1992), 'General principles relating to the promotion of refugee repatriation', Briefing Paper.

Loescher, G. (1991), 'Mass migration and the "New International Order"', *The Oxford International Review*, Vol. III, Winter.

MIPT (Ministry of Interior, Post and Telecommunication, Djibouti) (1986), 'Circular for all refugees in the Republic of Djibouti', issued on 29 July 1986.

Mollica, R. F. *et al.* (1992), *Repatriation and disability: community study of health, mental health, and social functioning of the Khmer residents of Site Two, Volume 1 – Khmer adults*, (working document, Harvard Program in Refugee Trauma, Harvard School of Public Health and the World Federation of Mental Health).

Opondo, E. O. (1992a), 'Refugee repatriation during conflicts: some reflections from the International Study of Spontaneous Voluntary Repatriation Day-Workshop held on 23 May 1992 under the Auspices of the Refugee Studies Programme (QEH), University of Oxford', unpublished paper, Refugee Studies Programme, Oxford University.

— (1992b), 'Refugee repatriation during conflict: grounds for scepticism', paper submitted to *Disasters*, Vol. 16, No. 4: 359–362.

Phillips, A. (1983) 'Djibouti – A voluntary repatriation programme?', Report for British Refugee Council, April 1983.

Relief Society of Tigray (1985), 'The repatriation of refugees from Tigre', report commissioned by the Refugee Studies Programme (RSP) for Independent Commission of International Humanitarian Issues, mimeo, Oxford.

Sen, A. (1981), *Poverty and famines: an essay on entitlement and deprivation*, Clarendon Press, Oxford.

Shacknove, A. E. (1985), 'Who is a refugee?', *Ethics*, Vol. 95, No. 2, January, 1985.

Stein, B. N. (1992), 'Policy challenges regarding repatriation in the 1990s: Is 1992 the year for voluntary repatriation?', paper commissioned by the Programme on International and US Refugee Policy, the Fletcher School of Law and Diplomacy, Tufts University, Medford, Massachusetts.

UN (1950), General Assembly Resolution 428(v) of 14 December 1950, par. 2(d); Annexe, paras 1, 8, 9.

UNHCR (1991), 'Report of the 42nd Session of the Executive Committee of the High Commissioner's Programme, Geneva, 7–11 October 1991' (UN General Assembly A/AC.96/783 21 October 1991).

— (1992), 'Repatriation operation – Cambodia', *Information Bulletin*, No. 6, 3 August.

US Committee for Refugees (1988), *Beyond the headlines: refugees in the Horn of Africa*, American Council for Nationalities Service, Washington.

— (1992a), *World Refugee Survey 1992*, American Council for Nationalities Service, Washington, DC.

— (1992b), *Refugee Reports*, Vol. XIII, no. 6.

Wilson, K. B. (1992), *A state of the art review of research on internally displaced, refugees and returnees from and in Mozambique*, report prepared for the Swedish International Development Authority (SIDA/ÅSDI), July 1992.

Zetter, R. (1991), 'Labelling refugees: forming and transforming a bureaucratic identity', *Journal of Refugee Studies*, Vol. 4, No. 1: 39–62.

3 BARBARA HENDRIE
Assisting Refugees
in the Context of Warfare

Some Issues Arising
from the Tigrayan Refugee Repatriation,
Sudan to Ethiopia 1985–7

This paper considers the question of appropriate forms of assistance to voluntary refugee returns in a specific context – that of returns which occur to areas under the administrative control of an armed insurgency movement, in the midst of military conflict. The argument put forward here is that internal warfare, usually between central governments and guerrilla forces, creates distinct practical and especially political circumstances that render 'normal' channels of refugee assistance problematic. This is also true since nearly all international refugee protocols discuss repatriation in terms of government-to-government agreements, and do not address forms of co-operation with so-called 'non-recognized' entities such as liberation fronts. Consequently, new thinking is needed that accounts for those cases which fall outside established protocols, and that considers alternatives in both the type of inputs provided and the mechanisms through which they are made available to refugees.

The material presented here is drawn from a case study of the voluntary return of some 154,000 Tigrayans from eastern Sudan to northern Elthiopia, spanning the years 1985–7, but with particular focus on 1985.[1] During that year, nearly one-third of the original influx of 200,000 refugees opted to return home to their villages in Tigray to cultivate. However, due to the sensitivity of major donors in assisting refugees returning to areas controlled by the Tigray People's Liberation Front (TPLF), virtually no external assistance was provided for the movement. In this case, the failure of the international community to respond had significant implications, since the refugees in question were poor farming households who fled the devastating famine in northern Ethiopia beginning in late 1984. To recover agricultural productivity, and survive the four-week walk from the Sudanese lowlands to the Ethiopian highlands, refugees required substantial inputs. Instead of mounting a co-ordinated assistance programme, however, major donors created a series of obstacles to repatriation, which was considered 'irregular' by the Khartoum Branch Office of the United Nations High Commissioner for Refugees (UNHCR).

The main events in the Tigrayan case, and their implications for short-term food security and future livelihood of the refugee population, are presented below.

Background

Tigray province has a population of approximately 4.5 million people, the great majority

---

[1] The case study was conducted by the author in 1988–9 for the Intertect Institute Study on Spontaneous Voluntary Repatriation, supported by the Ford Foundation (Hendrie, 1992). See also Hendrie, 1991.

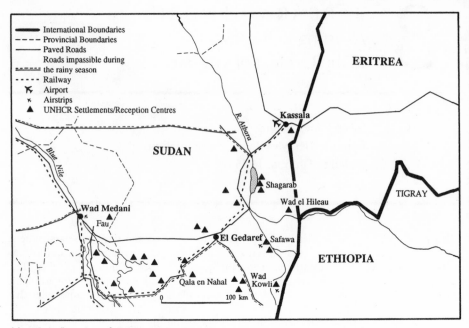

Map 3.1 *Location of COR/UNHCR refugee settlements and emergency reception centres, Eastern Sudan, 1990.*

of whom are subsistence peasants living in an extremely marginal environment. Drought and famine are not new phenomena to the region, and as a consequence Tigrayan farmers have adopted a wide variety of strategies to cope with chronic food shortages. Among these are the sale of household assets such as oxen, and migration from the densely populated central highland plateau to the surplus-producing western lowlands (see de Waal, 1990; Rahmato, 1987).

Unlike previous 'bad' years in Tigray, however, the drought and famine of 1985 occurred in the context of an internal war between the former Ethiopian government, known as the Dergue, and the TPLF, which had each carved out distinct regions of military and administrative control. While TPLF forces operated throughout the countryside, government forces were confined to towns and villages along the main roads (Smith, 1987). This division in military control was mirrored by a division in the provision of humanitarian assistance to the region, into two parallel but separate operations: the 'official' programme based in Addis Ababa, and an 'unofficial' cross-border programme channelling relief aid to TPLF zones from a logistics base in eastern Sudan. The cross-border operation was managed by the indigenous Relief Society of Tigray (REST), and supported by only a handful of international non-government organizations. Due to the reluctance of major donors to support REST, the amount of aid provided through cross-border channels was only approximately 10 per cent of the total resources committed by the international community to the Ethiopia famine (Smith, 1987). Hence, very little relief assistance was available in the heart of the famine zone during the autumn of 1984, when lack of rain caused crops to fail for the third consecutive year.

At the end of 1984, when it became clear that crops would fail not only in the central highlands, but also in the normally productive western lowlands, the TPLF made a decision to enable as many people as possible to evacuate the famine by setting up a migration route westward to the border of Sudan.[2] REST organized the emergency 'pipeline' by establishing a series of 40 transit stops where food and medical services were available. Between October 1984 and May 1985, some 200,000 rural Tigrayans used this support system to cross the border (UNHCR, 1985a). The majority of these people were from TPLF-controlled areas, who preferred to seek assistance as refugees in Sudan rather than risk crossing military lines and enter government-controlled towns (Hendrie, 1985). The government's use of food aid to attract rural families to the towns for its controversial resettlement programme was an important factor in these decisions (see Clay, and Holcomb, 1985). In some cases, farmers living only three to four hours' walk from the towns chose instead to make the four to six week walk to Sudan (Hendrie, 1985a). In this respect, the Tigrayan refugee influx to Sudan was only indirectly a consequence of the war, and more directly a result of the politicization of humanitarian aid to the war zones.

Unfortunately, Tigrayans crossed the border at a time when Sudan itself was in the midst of a famine disaster in both eastern and western regions; moreover, a simultaneous influx of some 200,000 refugees from Eritrea was occurring. Facilities along the border in Kassala province were wholly inadequate, and the situation rapidly escalated into a second refugee 'disaster'. Overcrowding, lack of regular food supplies, disease epidemics and poor water and sanitation led to unprecedented death rates among the new arrivals (Toole and Nieburg, 1988). It is likely that a significant proportion of the deaths associated with the Tigray famine in fact occurred during the first critical months of the refugee emergency. This would later prove a key factor in refugee decisions to return home. In addition, migrants en route to Sudan became a target for bombing attacks by the Ethiopian airforce, despite their movement by night, as did migrant transit centres established in the western region (*The Times*, 1984).

The fact that refugees originated from TPLF-controlled areas had profound implications for subsequent events in the camps, once rains returned to Tigray in 1985. In March, small numbers of refugees, mainly men, began returning home from Wad Kowli reception centre on the border, to prepare their land for cultivation. In April, the number of refugees returning from Wad Kowli escalated dramatically; meanwhile, refugees who had been relocated to the inland camps were pressing for transport to move them to the border in order to begin the long walk home to the central highlands in time to take advantage of the rainy season.

The bodies responsible for managing the emergency programme for refugees were the Sudanese Commissioner's Office for Refugees (COR) and UNHCR. Initially, UNHCR was not convinced that a major repatriation would occur. On 8 March the office in Khartoum informed Geneva that a large-scale return did not seem likely within the next few months. However, this position represented an error of judgement on the part of UNHCR, which assumed that as long as refugees were continuing to enter Sudan, it must indicate that food supplies inside Tigray were insufficient to support the existing population. In this respect, UNHCR failed to comprehend the complicated migration pattern Tigrayan farmers were utilizing in response to food shortages. Shortly thereafter, when it became apparent a large-scale movement would occur, UNHCR reformulated its position; in early April, it sent a message to headquarters in Geneva laying out a policy framework for the organization:

> Given these persons have neither the intention of fulfilling normal formalities with the Ethiopian government, nor placing themselves under its authority, it seems to us their return to Ethiopia cannot be considered in the context of a voluntary repatriation under UNHCR

---

[2] The decision was in part a response to the lack of adequate relief assistance available in TPLF-controlled areas in late 1984. Subsequent to the establishment of the route, TPLF and REST were overwhelmed with pressure to accomodate large numbers of out-migrants. Food-aid stocks only enabled REST to support approximately 60,000 people in the 'pipeline' at any given time, however, leading to a system of triage among villages (see Hendrie, 1990).

auspices ... To the extent that refugees deliberately and in spite of the risks really wish to go home, we consider UNHCR cannot oppose this ... UNHCR, while ensuring the voluntary character of the departure, should not sanction nor be associated with the return to Ethiopia, a return which could be considered irregular by the Ethiopian authorities' (UNHCR, 1985b).

The end result of this position was that Tigrayan refugees returned across the border without formal assistance from UNHCR; further, given UNHCR's central position as the co-ordinating body for refugee assistance, its failure to engage in the operational aspects of the return meant that no other major donors, and only those NGOs already working in camps along the border, were mobilized to provide assistance. The bulk of responsibility for supporting returnees fell instead on REST and COR.

By early April, REST had become increasingly alarmed at the prospects for a full-scale return. They had relocated part of their administration to Sudan, in order to provide refugees with various services and act as a liaison with international NGOs. When the number of people returning from Wad Kowli began to escalate, REST attempted to slow down the movement by asking people to sign registration forms, stating that they understood they would not be receiving support from REST once they reached their home villages. This was intended to discourage large numbers from returning, who might overwhelm REST's already limited support capacity inside Ethiopia. At the same time, COR was becoming increasingly concerned at the lack of operational initiatives coming from UNHCR. Since it appeared that some portion of the refugee population was determined to repatriate, regardless of the level of assistance provided, COR wanted to ensure that Tigrayans were well enough supported to prevent them from returning immediately to Sudan. Further, a spontaneous movement of refugees directly across the border was clearly in COR's interest, since it would lessen the burden of refugees crowding into the Eastern Region. Subsequently, COR drafted an operational plan which was presented to UNHCR Branch Office at the end of April 1985.

UNHCR's response to the plan was immediately negative with respect to those aspects that entailed the use of UNHCR-donated trucks to move refugees from inland camps to the border,[3] and the distribution of a 50-day food ration from its stocks. Further, UNHCR rejected the possibility of rehabilitation inputs, considering these to be outside its mandate (see Hendrie, 1990). Meanwhile, refugees at the inland camps were growing restless as trucks failed to materialize. On the morning of 7 May, REST informed UNHCR that it could no longer convince refugees to wait for transport to Wad Kowli. Later the same day, some 2,000 refugees in Safawa took matters into their own hands and simply walked out of the camp. The following day, a further 2,500 left for the border. The event was highly dramatic; some NGO medical staff tried, in tears, to argue with the refugees not to leave (Heiden,1988).

The Safawa walk-out galvanized aid agencies working in the east, who had previously doubted the wisdom of a refugee return to a war zone, and led COR to procure commercial vehicles for transport of families to the border. A transit facility was quickly established at Wad Kowli to provide medical screening and high-energy biscuits prior to departure. Further, COR decided unilaterally to go ahead with plans for the distribution of a 50-day food ration from UNHCR stocks, which was handed over to REST for onward transport.

After 7 May, events accelerated rapidly. By 10 May, groups of up to 7,000 people were departing nightly from Wad Kowli (UNHCR, 1985a). In total, approximately 54,000 Tigrayans returned home prior to June, at which time the flooding of the Atbara river along the border effectively marked the end of the 1985 repatriation. In 1986 and 1987 respectively, a further 100,000 people left the Sudan. None of these returns was

---

[3] One of the reasons put forward for this was that the trucks were painted with UNHCR logos on their sides; thus, they could be construed as a visible sign of UNHCR sanctioning of the return (Cuny, 1988).

3.1 *None of these returns was formally assisted by UNHCR: Tigrayans on the move from Wad Kowli towards Safawa, 1986. (UNHCR/16037/J.-M. Goudstikker)*

formally assisted by UNHCR, although in the years after 1985, informal support was provided by major donors, in the form of food supplies and transport to the border. Despite predictions by some donors,[4] there are no reported cases of Tigrayans changing their minds and returning to Sudan, except to retrieve family members and return home again to their villages.

Issues to Consider – The Effects of Minimal Support

Tigrayans returned home with a minimum of external support, aside from the 50-day food ration provided from UNHCR stocks, and medical services en route inside Tigray provided by the International Committee of the Red Cross (ICRC) which had been discreetly supporting cross-border operations since mid-1984. Although this aid probably enabled people to remain reasonably fit during the four to six week walk to their villages, the lack of rehabilitation inputs, such as seed, tools, and oxen, had major implications for their ability to resume food production during the 1985 rainy season. According to REST, 1.2 million people in Tigray were in need of food-aid *after* the 1985 harvest, due to the lack of these inputs and consequent inability of many households to cultivate (REST, 1985). As a result, many people were forced to fall back on short-term strategies, such as disruptive internal migrations and additional sales of livestock, in order to make up food shortages. Hence it can be said that the failure to provide adequate assistance to the Tigrayan repatriation in 1985 was a contributing factor to the continued food insecurity in the region, and the recurrence of famine in 1987–8.

In addition, during the period of repatriation, no effort was made by either multilateral or major donors to bolster REST's cross-border operation in order to support

---

[4] For example, in 1985 the US Embassy in Khartoum estimated that mortality among returnees could be as high as 25 per cent (US Department of State, 1985); some embassy officials also considered that Tigrayans were on a 'death march' home (Heiden, 1988).

3.2 *No effort was made by either multilateral or major donors to bolster REST's cross-border operation in order to support returnees inside Tigray: helping a blind companion, Zelazele transit centre, 1985. (Mike Goldwater/Network/CAFOD)*

returnees inside Tigray. Rather, the political sensitivity among donors about co-operating with REST did not change during the course of the return movement. Consequently, the only channel for supporting refugees once they crossed the border was rendered non-viable, especially for UN bodies. In this respect, repatriation represented a significant 'window of opportunity' for multilateral institutions to assist the victims of the Ethiopian famine in Sudan, before they returned to the politically sensitive war zones. Such assistance would have enabled a portion of the famine-affected population to recoup their economic viability in a single season, thus reducing the total number vulnerable to new cycles of drought. It would also have achieved a knock-on effect, since households no longer at risk would be in a position to assist others in the community still vulnerable to decline.

The failure of multilateral institutions to take advantage of the opportunities offered by repatriation was also at odds with assets that existed for mounting an assistance programme from Sudan. These included a co-operative host government, a relatively well-established human and material infrastructure in camps along the border, and most important, the existence of an indigenous agency capable of mobilizing refugee communities. Nevertheless, the important role of REST, and the fact that a direct linkage existed between REST's activities in Sudan and in Tigray, was never properly understood or exploited by the international community; this was mainly a result of suspicions about its political affiliations with the TPLF. In situations of internal warfare, however, it is sometimes the case that opposition groups are able to establish direct relations with the local level that also function as an effective means for the targeting and distribution of aid resources, in this case through popularly elected village committees. Proper external monitoring can assure, to the extent possible, that such resources are used for civilian, rather than military purposes. This applies equally to aid provided through government channels. In this instance, however, there was a distinct lack of pragmatism in recognizing the potential of REST to provide continuity between emergency assistance to returning refugees, and longer-term rehabilitation aid to farming households inside Tigray. Hence, the Tigrayan case is illustrative of a context where concrete options did exist for appropriate and timely assistance to returnees, but where political obstacles severely delimited the actions major donors were willing to take.

In addition, the needs to which donors could have responded were relatively well-defined. These focussed on inputs that would enable farming households to return to production as soon as possible, after consecutive years of divestment of capital resources in response to drought. As mentioned above, they included seed, tools, and oxen for ploughing. Since REST's limited transport capacity was already taken up with moving food-aid across the border, and since refugee families would be unable to carry heavy burdens during the journey home, the most appropriate means of assistance in this case would have been the provision of cash. In two separate surveys of the refuge population carried out in 1985, cash was listed as the preferred form of assistance (see Clay and Holcomb, 1985; Hendrie, 1985b). Cash would have enabled people to purchase assets inside Tigray that were unavailable in Sudan, especially oxen. The lack of oxen during rainy season months is the most important factor limiting food production in rural Tigray. Cash would also have enabled people to purchase assets according to individual requirements. Several options existed for making cash available to repatriants, aside from straightforward distributions; these included buying back ration cards, expanding employment opportunities in the camps, and setting-up of cottage industries. None of these options was seriously considered during 1985, however.

Further Issues – Alternative Channels

In light of the failure of major donors and UNHCR to respond to the repatriation process, it is worth considering what other entities had sufficient flexibility and resources to fill the gaps. One potential candidate in this respect is the ICRC, especially given its role of operating in the midst of military conflict. In the Tigrayan case, ICRC did provide much-needed emergency medical services along the return migration route, as well as clean water supply from tanker trucks that followed returnees as far as the base of the central highlands. However, ICRC cannot replace UNHCR's important role as a co-ordinating and information body, due to the limitations of its mandate. In 1985, ICRC's extreme discretion about its cross-border activities meant that very little independent information about operational conditions on the other side of the border was available in aid forums. Moreover, ICRC's operations in TPLF-controlled zones were exceptional for the organization, which normally requires the consent of both parties to a conflict before it can implement a programme.

The second type of aid organization that could have provided assistance were those international NGOs which had established a presence in the Eastern Region of Sudan. There were a number of reasons why these entities failed to respond adequately to events in 1985. First, the disorganization of the emergency operation, and the continued influx of new refugees, collapsed the time-frame in which NGOs were operating to a day-to-day crisis management level. For medical agencies in particular, horizons were often narrowed to the saving of individual lives. In this context, strategic thinking to anticipate new developments was virtually impossible. Second, once repatriation was under way, aid agency personnel found it difficult to shift their conceptual framework from relief assistance to refugees in a camp, to recovery assistance to poor farmers returning home to cultivate. The tendency to view refugees almost solely in terms of their physical needs, to the exclusion of their broader economic requirements, was a key

3.3 *The Tigrayans effectively fell between the cracks: a church school, Wikro, Tigray, 1992.*
(Catherine Morgan/CAFOD)

aspect of the Tigrayan case. Finally, the continued arrival of undernourished people to Sudan led many aid workers to the impression of a Tigray 'that was completely eaten bare' (see Hendrie, 1990). Without a proper understanding of the economic strategies Tigrayans were employing, most aid workers found it difficult to comprehend why people were moving in two directions across the border at the same time. Consequently, a common reaction among NGOs was to question the wisdom of refugee decisions to return home.

Conclusion – The Role of UNHCR

The Tigrayan repatriation is an excellent example of a case that falls outside existing protocols on voluntary repatriation. Voluntary repatriation as expressed in UNHCR and OAU Conventions (Article V) implies the agreement of both the government of the country of origin and the host country. Hence, there is no authority for UNHCR to co-operate with non-recognized entities *in situations where the government of the country of origin does not also give its consent* (see Clark, 1988). In the case of Ethiopians in Sudan, the former Ethiopian government required that each refugee wishing to return obtain a laissez-passer for his/her departure.

Consequently, the Tigrayans effectively fell between the cracks for a donor-assisted repatriation programme In this context, the only alternative for UNHCR institutional support would have been a highly informal role at local level: to co-ordinate assistance provided through other entities, and engage in behind-the-scenes lobbying and informa-tion sharing. This is exactly what did happen in 1986 and 1987, with positive results. Repatriations in those years were supported with timely transport from inland camps, through a specific funding allocation to COR well in advance of the rainy season. In addition, inputs for the Tigray-side were pledged during informal meetings convened by a new UNHCR Representative in Khartoum.

However, the issue remains as to whether or not specific protocols are required to address circumstances such as the Tigrayan case, that will enable UNHCR to become involved. UNHCR's involvement, as a transnational entity capable of mobilizing significant resources, and as a powerful lobby on behalf of refugee interests, remains important in any repatriation process. In the absence of formal guidelines, however, UNHCR becomes vulnerable to the influence of member governments or its own major donors. In Sudan in 1985, the interest of the United States in discouraging repatriation, during a period when it was managing the secret evacuation of Ethiopian Jews, or Falasha, and negotiating sensitive agreements with the Ethiopian government, added to UNHCR's concern to be seen to be acting strictly within its statutory framework. In this climate, policy decisions appeared more as attempts to limit the political damage that might occur through association with an 'irregular' refugee return, than an attempt to address concrete operational issues. Such a damage-control perspective appears all too common among multilateral institutions during major emergencies. Its effect is to greatly limit the options decision-makers believe they have available to them; the apparent constraints on action appear more real than the potential opportunities. In 1985, UNHCR did not exploit opportunities for creative action that could have facilitated the return and recovery of Tigrayan refugees.

References

Clark, L. (1988) 'Key issues in post-emergency refugee assistance in eastern and southern Africa', *Migration News*, ICMC, 1 November.

Clay, J. and B. Holcomb (1985), *Politics and the Ethiopian Famine 1984–85*, Cultural Survival, Cambridge, MA.

Cuny, F. (1988) 'Constraints in mounting a prompt relief effort in the Sudan refugee crisis of 1984/85', Intertect, Dallas, unpublished.

de Waal, A. (1990) 'Famine survival strategies in Wollo, Tigray, and Eritrea: a review of the literature', Oxfam, Oxford.

Heiden, D. (1988) 'Famine Diary', personal notes on the 1985 refugees crisis in Eastern Sudan', unpublished.

Hendrie, B. (1985a) 'Report on a visit to Tigray, February 1985', Grassroots International, Khartoum, unpublished.

— (1985b) 'Survey conducted in Shagarab East 2 Refugee Camp, eastern Sudan, September 1985', Community Aid Abroad, Khartoum, unpublished.

— (1990) 'The Tigrayan Refugee Repatriation 1985–1987', Intertect Institute, Dallas, published.

— (1991) 'The politics of repatriation: the Tigrayan refugee repatriation 1985–1987', *Journal of Refugee Studies*, Vol. 4, No. 2.

— (1992) 'The Tigryan refugee repatriation: Sudan to Ethiopia 1985–1987' in F. Cuny, B. Stein and P. Reed (eds) *Repatriation during conflict in Africa and Asia*.

Rahmato, D. (1987) 'Famine and survival strategies: a case study from Northeast Ethiopia', *Food and Famine Monographs*, No. 1, Institute of Development Research, Addis Ababa University, Addis Ababa.

REST (1985) *Annual Report*, Relief Society of Tigray, Khartoum.

Smith, G. (1987) 'Ethiopia and the politics of famine relief', *Middle East Report*, March/April.

The Times (London) (1984) 'Refugees bombed by Ethiopians', Robert Fisk, reporter, 12 December.

Toole, M. and P. Nieburg (1988) 'The association between inadequate rations, undernutrition prevalence and mortality in refugee camps', *Journal of Tropical Pediatrics*, Vol. 34, October.

UNHCR (1985a) Situation Reports, (Various), Branch Office of the United Nations High Commissioner for Refugees, Khartoum.

— (1985b) Memorandum to the High Commissioner, Geneva, from UNHCR Branch Office, Khartoum. (Copy obtained by the author.)

US Department of State (1985) Telex communiqués from Khartoum Embassy to the Bureau of Refugee Affairs, Department of State. (Copies obtained by the author under the United States Government Freedom of Information Act.)

4

ELIAS HABTE SELASSIE
Homecoming in Eritrea

Challenges & Constraints

In early 1991 the resolution of the long war between Ethiopia and Eritrea still appeared remote to many concerned parties, but co-ordinated military offensives by the Eritrean People's Liberation Front (EPLF), Ethiopian People's Revolutionary Democratic Front (EPRDF) and the Oromo Liberation Front (OLF) proved to be rapidly and decisively effective. Eritrea was entirely liberated by 24 May, and three days later EPRDF forces entered Addis Ababa, ending Mengistu Haile Mariam's 17-year reign of terror. On 29 May, a provisional Eritrean government was formed, and was recognized by the new Ethiopian administration. In early July a peace conference was convened to lay down the foundations for a democratic transformation in Ethiopia and to find a permanent solution to the Eritrean conflict. The conference issued a charter which, among other things, resolved to recognize the Eritrean people's right to self-determination, to be ascertained through an internationally supervised referendum. However, legal status notwithstanding, Eritrea become, *de facto*, an independent country as soon as Ethiopian forces had been defeated.[1]

Since the establishment of the Provisional Government of Eritrea (PGE), the political situation in Eritrea has remained fairly stable (in marked contrast to developments in Ethiopia). There have been no significant opposition forces to obstruct the implementation of the PGE's political, social and economic policies. The major constraint has been financial, and this remains the case. Although United Nations specialized agencies (e.g. WFP, UNHCR, UNICEF) and several NGOs have established offices in Asmara, the United Nations has taken a foot-dragging attitude towards implementation of the referendum. As a result, whatever official economic assistance may now flow to Eritrea is usually expected to be lumped with assistance programmes to Ethiopia.

There are a few exceptions. An important one is the assistance provided by the Italian government (which has agreed to provide Eritrea with a total of US$82.5 million.[2] Another hopeful sign is that the WFP is expected to supply Eritrea with about 33,000 tons of relief food. But, significantly, none of the US$650 million earmarked for emergency aid to Ethiopia by the consortium co-ordinated by the World Bank has been specifically allocated to Eritrea (*Washington Post*, 2 February 1992). How much will be

---

[1] This chapter was written at the end of 1992, before the referendum on independence. Eritrea is now recognized as a fully fledged independent state. Events in Eritrea since 1992 are discussed in the following chapters by Kibreab and Styan.

[2] However, even this agreement is facing setbacks in implementation owing mainly to Italy's insistence on a number of conditions unacceptable to the Eritrean authorities. (Personal conversation with Eritrean authorities during my visit in September and October 1992) *Eritrea Update* (Feb 1992) Washington DC: PGE).

44

channelled to the country will depend on an accord to be reached between the PGE and the Transitional Government of Ethiopia (TGE). The same applies to the large USAID programme.

At the time of writing (late 1992), the PGE is struggling to provide food to a large proportion of the population (estimated at 3 million), to cope with the effects of severe drought and to rehabilitate and reconstruct the war-devastated economy. With little in the way of external support, there is nothing to fall back on but human resources. Close to 100,000 EPLF fighters continue to work in national reconstruction programmes without salary, and the PGE has now also enforced a 12–18 month national service obligation for all Eritrean nationals between the ages of 18 and 40 (PGE, Proclamation No. 11, 1991). Immediate priorities are seen to be water conservation and communications, and there are plans to construct 16 dams, 30 ponds and 150 miles of feeder roads on a food-for-work basis. Tremendous efforts are being made, but the tasks ahead are formidable indeed. Moreover, the PGE and the future government of independent Eritrea will soon have to live up to the challenge of finding land, employment, education and health facilities for perhaps half a million repatriating refugees and an equal number of internally displaced persons. This situation requires both urgent responses and effective planning for longer-term development. In the following sections I assess aspects of the situation that will face those returning home, and some of the challenges and options facing the Eritrean authorities.

The situation up until May 1991

There are no reliable figures of how many Eritreans have fled abroad, but it would not be unrealistic to estimate the current refugee population at between 600,000 and 750,000. Of these, around 500,000 reside in Sudan, mostly in official camps under the administration of COR (the Sudanese Commissioner's Office for Refugees) and UNHCR. Thousands of children have grown up in these camps, and many have never visited their homeland.

During much of the 1970s and 1980s, the Dergue's counter-insurgency policy of bombing civilian hamlets and economic targets had made large parts of Eritrea continuously insecure. However, this began to change after the liberation of Afabet in March 1988. The defeat of the Dergue's forces at Enda Selassie in Tigray followed in February 1989, and the capture of the port city of Massawa on 10 February 1990. These events extended enormously the areas under the effective control of the EPLF in Eritrea and the EPRDF in Ethiopia, encouraging refugees to contemplate returning.

Considerable numbers of Eritrean exiles in Sudan began urging CERA (Commission for Eritrean Refugees Affairs – an organization affiliated with the EPLF) to help them to repatriate. Indeed, so inspired were they by the taking of Massawa that many walked from the Sudanese settlements to such eastern border towns as Kassala, Laafa and Karora. They did so at a time of drought (one of the most severe in recent years) and against a background of the worsening social, political and economic situation in Sudan. Unfortunately there was a lack of sympathy and assistance from the international community, with both UNHCR and COR avoiding their responsibilities. COR authorities blamed UNHCR for failing to make funds available. Meanwhile the UNHCR blamed COR for not co-operating in determining the number of Eritrean refugees in the camps who desired to return home, and in establishing the voluntariness of each case through interviews by UNHCR's protection officers. Although COR did administer the refugee camps through its branch offices, there are reasons to believe that both UNHCR and COR were guilty for their concerted lack of action. In the end it was the refugees and the country of origin that bore the burden of their bureaucratic red tape.

4.1 *Around 500,000 Eritrean refugees settled in Sudan, mostly in official camps: Wad Sherife reception centre, 1989. (UNHCR/19075/S. Errington)*

To make matters worse neither UNHCR nor COR were prepared to work with the EPLF and its civilian departments because of mandate dilemmas (in particular their unwillingness to work with an 'unrecognized' liberation movement). As a consequence, in the pre-liberation repatriation process 'the entire burden of care, maintenance and resettlement of returnees [was] the responsibility of the EPLF and its affiliates' (Habte-Selassie, 1992: 27). Hopelessly overstretched, CERA was able to repatriate only 20,000 refugees between the end of 1989 and the total liberation of the country in May 1991. Not surprisingly, the period was one in which CERA was engaged in a persistently confrontational relationship with the UNHCR and officials of COR.

While these accusations and recriminations continued, events in the Horn of Africa took a dramatic turn. Many observers were taken by surprise at the apparently sudden collapse of Mengistu's regime. In fact, an accord was struck between the three major resistance armies ahead of the May talks, convened in London by the US undersecretary of state for Africa. This left the remnants of the Dergue government with no room to manoeuvre. When its delegation arrived in London, it was already bereft of any authority. If the talks have any historical significance, it is because arrangements were made for the July 1991 Addis Ababa Conference for Peace and Democracy between the EPRDF, the OLF and the EPLF, and the basic ideas of the Addis Ababa Charter were worked out. It was also agreed in London that the EPLF would defer implementation of the referendum for two years and make Assab a free port for Ethiopia. This was a gesture of solidarity with the new Addis Ababa government to enable it to stabilize the situation in Ethiopia for a peaceful transition to multi-party democratic rule.

The Addis Ababa Charter's official recognition of the Eritrean people's right to self-determination, and the Addis Ababa government's consent that the international community could deal seperately with the PGE, seemed to give the UNHCR and the Sudan government the opportunity to begin an organized and assisted programme of repatriation. The new Ethiopian government encouraged international organizations and governments to deal and work with the PGE directly. Several UN agencies (UNDP, UNICEF, WFP and UNHCR), USAID and some NGOs established offices in Asmara, and various countries (Eygypt, Yemen, Sudan, Italy) opened embassies or consular offices. Even the International Committee of the Red Cross (ICRC), which for years had been hostile towards the EPLF, formally recognized the PGE (see PGE *Eritrea Update*, Washington DC, January 1992). Nevertheless, until the referendum is carried out, Eritrea's status still falls short of full recognition as an independent UN member state, and large-scale repatriation has not yet commenced.

Planning for Repatriation

In the following subsections I comment on some of the socio-economic and demographic implications of the return of the refugees for independent Eritrea. As the vast majority presently remain in exile, my remarks are somewhat speculative. The issues I have selected do not in any sense comprise a complete list, but they are all matters of great and immediate concern.

Timing and funding

It seems likely that the current lack of action with respect to facilitating repatriation will soon change. At some point, before or after the referendum, the Sudan government, UNHCR and Eritrean authorities will negotiate a tripartite agreement. Indeed the Sudan government and UNHCR seem to be eager to actively promote the return of the refugees as soon as possible. The PGE, however, must be cautious and tough. There is no question about the desirability of repatriation as the most favoured solution. But what is of concern is its timing and the modality of its implementation. Repatriation must be voluntary; and the donor community must link it to the country's reconstruction and development needs.

One of the serious temptations which the PGE must avoid at all costs is accepting rushed repatriation for political motives (i.e., desiring Eritreans to return home before the referendum). It is disturbing to learn that the UNHCR and PGE are discussing repatriation of some 250,000 Eritrean refugees in 1992 (PGE, *Eritrea Update*, February 1992). This is inappropriate. Adequate research and planning has not been done. Moreover, the rights of the refugees must be seriously considered. Although it is an indisputable right of every refugee to return home, the exercise of that right should not be imposed by any party or authority; be it the PGE, the host government or UNHCR. What parties could and should do is to provide adequate and up-to-date information on the military, political, social and economic situations prevailing in the homeland. This is within the spirit and standard practice of international refugee law. The important matter here is the perception of the refugees themselves, not what others may perceive is good for them (see Habte-Selassie in Dornbos *et al*, 1992: 30). Without disregarding the socio-economic and political importance of repatriation after 30 years of war, the PGE must not trade off short-term gains for long-term detrimental consequences.

Foreseeably, the most acute pressure will come from the international donor community, especially the UK and USA, which are very critical of the present government in Sudan. Suspicious of the Sudanese government's track record of administering the refugee settlements, donors would like to end their refugee assistance programmes in the Sudan (even though much of the funding provided is by UN agencies with specific projects being implemented by a plethora of NGOs).

The end of the war between Ethiopia and Eritrea and the removal of the Mengistu

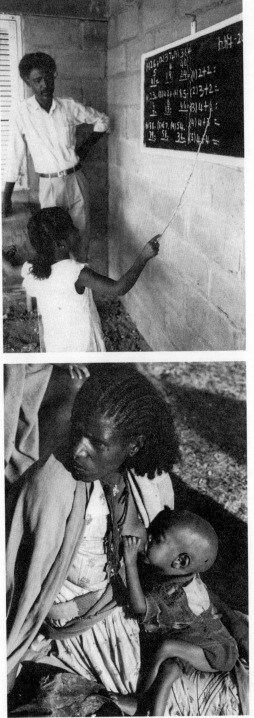

4.2 *Few Eritrean refugees in Sudan have received higher education: refugee girl attending primary school, near Port Sudan, 1989. (UNHCR/19091/ S. Errington)*

4.3 *The problems may appear insurmountable, but the Eritreans have shown extraordinary courage and determination during 30 years of warfare: mother and child in an EPLF controlled area of Eritrea, 1990. (Stephen King/CAFOD)* regime offer legitimate grounds to advocate repatriation and donors will argue that they are responding to the refugees' own stated preference.

The PGE must respond with proposals for rehabilitation and development funding. There is no rational reason why the United Nations should not be responsible in making the required funds available for this purpose. The PGE is charged with the duty of establishing stable and democratic political institutions, while at the same time coping with enormous problems. It deserves sympathy and concrete external assistance.

If precedents are required, the UN committed hundreds of millions of dollars to the Namibian repatriation operation of 1989 and is committed to nearly US$3 billion for similar operations in Cambodia (*The Guardian*, London, 30 March, 1992). However, given the expensive commitments of the international community in other parts of the world, the PGE will have to stand firm and put forward compelling arguments to ensure that it receives what is needed.

The requirement for international assistance

The costs of repatriation, rehabilitation and reconstruction are going to be exceedingly high. Even if we use CERA's rather conservative 1990 estimate of US$3,000 for a household of five persons, repatriating half a million Eritreans could easily cost US$300 million. This estimate does not include infrastructural development, provision of health and educational services, development of human capital through skills training programmes, environmental conservation, or long-term support for the most vulnerable groups. It also needs to be noted that the PGE and the future government of Eritrea will be obliged to allocate some of its scarce trained personnel to the administration and management of returnee related projects, something which will undoubtedly affect the already tight human resouce demands of other sectors of the national economy.

As economic resources within Eritrea are meagre, the success of returnee-related projects will largely depend on the amount and quality of external assistance. But is external assistance going to be accessible? So far the UN has shown unwarranted reluctance even in meeting the cost of the forthcoming referendum, and cannot be relied upon to extend the total amount required. As we have seen, other funders have also been slow to respond. It is hard to see how much progress can be made while this remains the case.

Patterns of migration and return

One argument that the PGE can make to donors is that the bulk of those who will return to Eritrea in the initial wave of repatriation will be impoverished. Few will have received higher education, and many will not have the necessary skills or material resouces to rapidly achieve self-sufficiency in their homeland. Unless some of their needs can be accomodated, there is likely to be a crisis of expectations and this may have serious political connotations. In the worst scenario, something which cannot be ruled out, there could be a major famine. The reason why most returnees will initially fall into this category of impoverishment is to do with the migration movements of Eritreans in the last two decades.

By and large, the urban elite, the most skilled, the professionals and the students moved to the Middle East, Europe and North America. This movement was partly induced by the need for skilled labour and professionals in the oil-producing Arab countries, by the desire among many Eritrean youth to go to secondary school and university, and since 1981 by the USA's resettlement programme (which took some 2,000 selected Eritreans and Ethiopians each year from the Sudan).

The return home of Eritreans from abroad will certainly be affected by this experience of migration. Eritreans in the Sudan, most of whom are languishing in the run-down and poorly serviced camps, will be the first group to want to repatriate. Given their rural and semi-urban socio-economic backgrounds, the lack of opportunities open to them in exile, as well as the predominance of women and school-age children, their resettlement and reintegration will be enormously difficult.

The second group to return will probably be those in the Arab countries. The labour market is becoming tighter in these places, and African migrant workers are being substituted by cheaper labour from Pakistan, Sri Lanka, Korea, the Philippines etc. This second group will bring many skills back with them, but the most educated and affluent group, the Eritreans living in Europe and North America, are likely to delay their repatriation for some time.

Since June 1991, many of this latter group have been visiting their country. There have been charter flights from several European countries and from various cities in the United States carrying hundreds of Eritreans to Asmara. However, despite these short visits, not many Eritreans in Europe and North America have decided to return home for good. For this category of people the decision to permanently return to Eritrea will depend on a number of factors: political stability and the institution of democratic values, economic opportunities, health and education facilities, transport services, public utilities (water and energy), housing etc. It will take several years for these needs to be met and only a small fraction of Eritreans based in the North can be expected to return in the immediate future.

Environmental considerations

That Eritrea has for decades suffered the effects of war and environmental neglect requires little elaboration. The Eritrean countryside today is characterized by severe land degradation, deforestation and in some areas expanding desertification.

In highland Eritrea especially, agricultural production has suffered grossly from over-cultivation, soil erosion and the fragmentation of land holding owing to the rate of population growth and the concentration of settlement. Highland Eritrea will have to be reforested and protected if its future productive potential is to be revived and sustained. However, concurrent with this recovery programme must be the creation of alternative income-earning possibilities for those sections of the highland population which will probably have to be displaced by these schemes (or at least prevented from farming for several years).

Lowland Eritrea presents a different set of problems and opportunities. Future economic activities of the eastern lowlands must be geared towards developing the fishing, tourism and trade sectors. The western lowlands, on the other hand, are inhabited by pastoral and agro-pastoral peoples. A significant percentage of the Eritrean refugee population in the Sudan originated from the Barka, Sahel and Gash-Setit areas and it will be important to consider carefully the future of this area.

The Eritrean liberation struggle was born in this region and long-drawn-out war has caused tremendous social disruption, dislocation, out-migration and devastation of the environment. Sahel province is perhaps the most environmentally degraded region in the western lowlands. Only in the upper Gash-Setit area are scant forest resources surviving. But even here, firewood cutting, felling of trees for building purposes and, in some instances, charcoal production as a source of income for many displaced house-holds has markedly diminished the population of trees. If a considerable number of those refugees to be repatriated are to be reintegrated into their respective pre-flight localities, then their energy and housing construction material needs have to be met from outside the area. If they are not, the people will further tax the local environment in order to provide for their needs, something which may have devastating consequences. There are, in addition, the issues of reserving land for pasture, and restocking herds and flocks. These are things which need to be analysed and planned very carefully.

The land question

In the quite recent past, the tenure system of lowland Eritrea, and in many highland village communities, was based on communal land ownership. Individuals had usufruct but not property rights. This customary land-tenure system was deliberately ignored by colonial governments in Eritrea. Large tracts of fertile land, both in the highlands and lowlands, were taken away from the rightful occupants and given as concessions to Italian settlers. Such land alienation also continued after Italian colonial rule ended. A good example was the Ali Gider cotton plantation (abandoned since early 1970 due to the war), which belonged to Barattolo, an Italian capitalist who received it from the Ethiopian government as a long-term concession.

Colonialist land expropriation for commercial agriculture introduced new forms of land use. As more and more land was seized from the local pastoral communities for expanding agriculture, conflict of interests became unavoidable between farmers and pastoralists. The colonial state invariably favoured agriculturalists, and therby placed the pastoral communities under increasing pressure. This continued until liberation. But what will the policy and practice of the Eritrean government be?

It might be too early to expect the present provisional government to come up with a well-thought-out policy with respect to pastoralists, but there are some indications of the direction of current trends which are grounds for concern. The PGE appears to be encouraging and favouring settlement of pastoralists as agricultural communities.

If this is the official policy of the PGE, then it is an alarming development. As is the case elsewhere in Africa, the ecosystems where many pastoral and agro-pastoral communities have survived for ages are not suitable for intensive cultivation. Although short-term gains from agricultural schemes exploiting these fragile soils may be high, in the long run they will result in costly environmental damage.

Probably the way forward is to link livestock production with agro-industrial projects and to create a demand for livestock products (milk, meat, hides and skins etc.).

Political accommodation and restraint

The PGE has in less than a year taken many bold and admirable steps in building the necessary institutional and administrative structures. Laws have been enacted, administrative structures have been set up at provincial, district and sub-district levels and the PGE has appointed administrators and allocated personnel. A restructuring took place (in May 1992) which involved the PGE establishing a 28-person Executive Council to act as the executive arm of the government, while the EPLF Central Committee as a whole assumes the legislative functions. Visitors to Eritrea have come away agreeing on at least one point: that both urban and rural Eritrea today is peaceful and that (in spite of a serious shortage of skilled and professional human resources) there is a well-functioning administrative and institutional structure.

However, much more is required to attract foreign private investment. It is not enough simply to proclaim an 'investment code'. How far the democratic process advances towards the promised target of multi-party rule and the holding of free and fair elections will be a testing ground. It seems likely that the Eritrean professional, intellectual and business classes will only return in significant numbers if it can be shown that concrete and verifiable steps have been taken towards the constitution of a viable democratic political system in Eritrea. It is highly questionable that the process of democratization (establishment of a free press, multi-party politics, public accountability, etc.) will move far enough to be satisfactorily attractive before the implementation of the referendum.

Other policy considerations

I have made it clear that the PGE must avoid falling into the temptation of agreeing to a rushed, ill-funded and unplanned repatriation operation, which may be the wish of the UN and donors. The PGE ought to form a high-level inter-departmental committee for repatriation to study policy options, identify viable and sustainable projects and submit them to diversified aid donors for funding. Although CERA will still retain the overall responsibility for implementing repatriation programmes, because once the refugees are home their needs will be multi-sectoral (health, education, water, energy, farming, livestock, etc), major policy issues should be entrusted to a committee such as the one I am proposing here.

In order to lessen the pressure of massive repatriation movements, the PGE could strike a deal with the Sudan to conclude a mutually advantageous agreement concerning the free and unhindered movements of border peoples. Western Eritrea and Eastern Sudan share a great deal of ethnic, cultural, religious and environmental similarities, for example, the Beni Amer, Hadendewa (Beja), Elit and Rashaida ethnic/national groups are found on both sides of the border. For these groups the existence of the border is artificial and, although it might have created inconveniences, it never actually stopped their cross-border movements. An agreement between the two states should officially acknowledge these traditional patterns of movement. The act might even constitute a first concrete step towards long-term regional co-operation, perhaps even the eventual integration of Northeast Africa.

Another point which needs serious consideration by the PGE is the establishment of a rural credit system as soon as possible. This will encourage rural entrepreneurs to establish themselves and enhance creative initiatives, badly needed in rural settings. Moreover, rural credit could diminish the 'dependency mentality' which affects many refugees after prolonged periods in refugee settlements.

Finally, rehabilitation programmes in Eritrea will have to give special attention to those who have been rendered particularly vulnerable by war and displacement. Thousands have been traumatized by the upheavals and suffer psychological consequences. There are also an estimated 10,000 disabled ex-combatants of the EPLF, 8,000 orphan children of fallen combatants and 50,000 disabled civilians, as well as 42,000 orphans of civilian families. (*Voice of the Masses*, 4 February 1992: 3)

Conclusion

I have highlighted some of the critical challenges currently facing the PGE and which will be inherited by the eventual government of independent Eritrea. The problems may appear insurmountable and without external assistance the aspirations of the Eritrean people will not be realized. But the Eritreans have shown extraordinary courage and determination during 30 years of warfare. They can be expected to do so again when confronted with the dilemmas, opportunities and possibilities which come with peace.

References

The Guardian (London) 30 March 1992.
Habte-Selassie, E. (1992) in Doornbos *et al*, *Beyond conflict in the Horn: the prospects for peace, recovery and development in Ethiopia, Somalia, Sudan and Eritrea*, ISS, The Hague and James Currey, London.
PGE, North American Mission, *Eritrea Update* (January 1992) PGE Representative in Washington, Washington DC.
— Proclamation No. 11, 1991 (Tigrigna); Investment Proclamation No. 18/1991; Eritrea Referendum Proclamation No. 22/1991; and Eritrean Nationality Proclamation No. 21/1991; Hadas Eritra (New Eritrea) 17 June 1992.
Voice of the Masses, No. 250 (4 February 1992).
Washington Post (2 February 1992).

5

GAIM KIBREAB
Left in Limbo

Prospects for Repatriation of Eritrean Refugees
from the Sudan & Responses
of the International Donor Community

In this chapter I reflect on the plight of Eritreans in Sudan following the Eritrean People's Liberation Front (EPLF) victory over Ethiopian forces in 1991. Many of my observations are based on field work I carried out among the refugees between October 1991 and April 1993 (in particular in the Qala en Nahal settlements, some 50 kms southwest of El Gedaref see map 3.1 on page 36). However, I also comment more generally on issues relating to refugee repatriation, and discuss the tensions which have arisen between Eritrean representatives and the international donor community. It is important to place the difficulties faced by the Eritreans in a wider context, because it then becomes apparent how they have been largely ignored, just as a solution to their suffering seemed to be at hand.

The Right to Return

In a background document on voluntary repatriation, prepared for the International Institute of Humanitarian Law, the following evocative statement is made.

> [F]undamental to the protection of human well-being is ensuring respect for the fact of belonging and for the necessary implications of this fact for human well-being generally ... Belonging relates not only to a community of people but, normally, also to a land (the 'motherland' or the 'fatherland' or the land of one's ancestors). Man is not an ethereal spirit living outside space or time but a terrestrial creature with roots in a land and its history. A people is formed by physical propinquity, a native soil and a shared history that has formed common beliefs and values (i.e., its culture or civilization) and conferred on it an identity. The link between a people and a land is a profound one (IIHL, 1985: 185–6).

Like ill health, the consequence of involuntary absence from home cannot be appreciated until it is experienced directly. Apart from the overwhelming sense of loss, citizenship is usually a prerequisite to the enjoyment of a host of civil, political and property rights. The entitlement of displaced people to return home in security and dignity has therefore been recognized as a basic principle of international law. Article 13 (2) of the 1948 Universal Declaration of Human Rights declared that '[E]veryone has the right to return to his country' (United Nations, 1948), and Article 12 (4) of the 1966 International Covention on Civil and Political Rights 1981 stated '[N]o one shall be arbitrarily deprived of the right to enter his own country'. In addition the right to return is also defined in several regional conventions. The African Charter of Human and People's Rights states (1981) that, '[E]very individual shall have the right ... to return to his country', and the guidelines to voluntary repatriation of refugees, and the responsibilities of the governments of countries of origin, is provided in detail in Article 5 of the 1969 OAU Convention Governing the Specific Aspects of Refugee Problems in Africa.

Such explicit acceptance of the right to return in official declarations is very important. However, in practice things are much more complicated. The circumstances that make the right operational are often multi-faceted and sometimes elusive. International instruments generally assert that the right to return becomes exercisable when the conditions in connection with which a person has been granted refugee status come to an end. This is normally taken to mean that there is no longer a well-founded fear of persecution in the country of origin. The assumption is made that when such a situation occurs, refugees will repatriate. But it does not always happen. The factors which prompted people to flee from Eritrea have ceased to exist since 1991, and all available evidence indicates that the majority of refugees in Sudan wish to go home. Nevertheless, at the time of writing (the end of 1983), fewer than 20 per cent have actually crossed the border. The problem is that while the displaced can be confident of relative political security in their country of origin, as yet most of them are unable to return home in dignity.

In economically poor regions, homecoming is not just a function of a cessation in the proximate causes (i.e. violations of human rights) that triggered flight. It is inextricably intertwined with livelihood security as a whole. No reasonable parent will voluntarily choose to take children out of school and move into an area where formal education is not available, or choose to leave behind health care facilities with no prospect of such needs being met in the homeland, or choose to abandon farms without an assurance that adequate land will be made available for cultivation. Conditions may be deplorable in refugee settlements, but after years of residence people will have found ways of managing. They will be reluctant to move until they are sure that life will not be worse elsewhere. Particularly in northeast Africa, the decision may also be affected by the weather. Recurrent droughts can literally make migration an issue of life and death. In such circumstances, a legal right to return may be rendered meaningless without concerted international humanitarian assistance.

In Eritrea, political change has made return a possibility. It seems reasonable to expect the international donor community to seize the opportunity, and rid itself of indefinite financial responsibilities for the refugees in Sudan by ensuring that the right to return is a practical option. As elsewhere in the world, this requires provision of development aid.

The Need for Development Aid

From the late 1940s, the refugee problem in Europe was largely dealt with in the context of exile. Cold War antagonisms made the issue of repatriation very sensitive, while unprecedented economic growth facilitated conditions for absorption of displaced populations. However, with the emergence of anti-colonial struggles in Asia and Africa, mass involuntary migration occurred in other parts of the world, and these displacements required new approaches (Kibreab, 1991a, 1991b, 1992).

Discussion about refugees within the OAU recognized that absorption in the country of exile was usually untenable, both because hosting regions were often very poor and because the refugees themselves were committed to liberation struggles in their homelands. In most instances, repatriation was accepted as the only viable option. This obviously required peace as a precondition, but it was also recognized that, in as much as the refugee movements were caused by an interplay between political, environmental and socio-economic factors, a solution also required coming to grips with all these factors simultaneously. By its very nature, the reintegration of returnees into their homeland required a developmental approach.

This point has been made repeatedly at international fora in which discussion of repatriation has occurred. It was reiterated again at the International Conference on Assistance to Refugees in Africa, convened by UNHCR in 1981 (ICARA I) and 1984 (ICARA II). The most important principles that underpinned debates in 1984 were the recommendations of the Meeting of Experts on Refugee Aid and Development. These had been endorsed by the Executive Committee of the UNHCR on 21 December 1983. It was emphasized that the solution to the refugee problem required reintegration in the country of origin after voluntary repatriation (United Nations General Assembly, 1984a: 3). It was further stated that:

> ... in the case of large-scale voluntary repartiation to a low-income country, an international commitment to help is needed to achieve successful reintegration, and that this may need to include, beyond UNHCR's programmes, developmental investments for the benefit of the returnees that would also benefit their compatriots in the areas concerned.

The argument was taken up at ICARA II, and reiterated in a Declaration and Programme of Action which delegates adopted. It was noted that:

> For solutions to last, assistance to refugees and returnees must aim at their participation, productivity and durable self-reliance; it should be development-orientated as soon as possible and, in least developed countries, it should take into account the needs of local people as well. (UNHCR, 1984b)

ICARA II was convened to circumvent the deteriorating asylum situation in Africa. Most of the national economies of the sending and receiving countries were on the verge of collapse. It was recognized that asylum seekers in Africa were not only people with well-founded fears of persecution who had fled their countries of origin in search of international protection. Many had fled because their survival was threatened by the interplay between political, economic, social and environmental factors. A developmental approach was perceptively considered to be essential. This was conceptualized as a process which, in the words of the then High Commissioner, had three interrelated objectives: to provide relief assistance for refugees and returnees in Africa; to help those refugees and returnees to find new lives for themselves and their families; and to help the countries that harbour the refugees or returnees (UNHCR, 1984a).

Such a developmental approach is exactly what economically poor African countries of asylum and return have been demanding. It has been the basis of the Eritrean leadership's position in negotiations with UNHCR, other international agencies and donor governments. But the response in Eritrea, as in several other parts of Africa, has been very unenthusiastic. A question that springs to mind is whether ICARA II has lost momentum or was ICARA II only another ploy to mollify African governments? It is certainly hard to avoid the conclusion that, in practice, priorities affecting international responses to the reintegration of returnees are not always based on the needs of the populations themselves, but rather on the political and strategic concerns of the major powers.

International Responses to Reintegration Programmes for Returnees

The record of international humanitarian assistance for repatriation programmes is not encouraging. Stein has drawn attention to both financial and organizational factors in accounting for the failures (Stein, 1991). However, it would seem that financial constraints are less of an issue than they sometimes appear. In Africa, the crux of the matter is a combination of organizational incapacity and a lack of political will. If funding was such a problem, why should reintegration programmes be more susceptible than programmes focussed on providing assistance to refugees, and why should donor responses vary so greatly from one part of the world to another?

The fact is, whatever concerns are voiced by UNHCR in official statements and publications, the organization's attempts to take responsibility for the welfare of returnees have often been inadequate or have been frustrated. Resolution 428(V) of the UN General Assembly declares that UNHCR's function is to provided 'international protection' to refugees, and makes clear under what conditions the High Commissioner's competence ceases to apply. One of the conditions is when the refugees concerned voluntarily re-avail themselves of the protection of their own state. This inevitably influences the responses of UNHCR staff in specific circumstances, and also means that donor funding tends to be discretionary. UNHCR cannot act forcefully to raise funds for repatriation programmes, particularly when such programmes do not coincide with the interests of the major donor governments. If UNHCR tries to be too high-handed, it will be criticised for exceeding its constitutional mandate, and for trying to become a developmental agency.

The theoretical rationale for donor governments' reluctance to give assistance to returnees emanates from the fact that states which force their citizens into external (or internal) displacement should themselves take the responsibility to meet the costs of re-integration. Donors may view the provision of development assistance to countries of origin as a reward for a bad human rights record. In effect, this presupposes that the refugees are returning to an unresolved conflict situation or that the government which is receiving the returnees is the one that previously caused their flight. In some circumstances it is widely accepted that a government may not be responsible for past displacement of civilians. Human rights abuses may have been perpetrated under a previous regime, or even by the armed forces of another country (as was the case in Eritrea). Yet even in these cases, a country which receives its citizens from exile does not have the same leverage on the international donor community as a country which receives refugees. A country hosting refugees can threaten to expel asylum seekers if its conditions are not met. No such option is open to a country of return.

It is important to recognize that a lack of support for programmes assisting returnees may have far-reaching implications. It may eventually force governments to refuse admission to their own nationals. Towards the end of the 1970s, the Rwandese government banned its citizens living as refugees in neighbouring countries from returning on the grounds of land shortage (Kibreab, forthcoming). According to principles of international law, such an act can be interpreted as a violation of human rights. But it has to be recognized that the sudden influx of hundreds of thousands of returnees to impoverished or war-damaged regions may constitute a threat to national security and political stability. Up to now, international and local pressures have discouraged other African governments from following the Rwandan example. However, it may well be only a matter of time before they do so.

The option is in fact enshrined in Article 12(2) of the African Charter on Human and People's Rights (1981). The charter states that:

[E]very individual shall have the right to leave any country including his own, and to return to his country. *This may only be subject to restrictions provided for by law for the protection of national security, law and order, public health or morality.* (emphasis added)

This suggests that the right to return is revocable provided the act of denial is lawful and conforms to customary procedures. In reality, however, these conditions are nothing more than legal niceties. Refugees, especially those of rural backgrounds are powerless and seldom challenge the decisions of their governments in a court of law. Thus, if a host government feels that a return of a large number of refugees unaccompanied by international assistance can destabilize the political or social order, the outcome is most likely to be outright restriction. Such a scenario is a real threat. It could rapidly undermine the viability of the institution of asylum, and all concerned parties should endeavour to ensure that it does not occur. This is likely to require some kind of clear extension of the UNHCR's mandate, enabling the organization to assist returnees.

In fact, the activities of the High Commissioner's Office have in practice sometimes expanded well beyond its initial mandate. As the High Commissioner put it in 1980, the UNHCR:

> ... has been increasingly called upon to engage in more far-reaching activities in the case of large-scale repatriations. Where a large-scale return of refugees is foreseen, the absence in the country of origin of the necessary facilities for the reception and reintegration of substantial numbers of returning refugees may constitute a major disincentive to repatriation. The idea has thus emerged that UNHCR should concern itself with the availability of adequate reception arrangements in the country of origin and in certain cases even with the implementation of assistance projects for the reintegration of returning refugees. UNHCR, 1980)

This extension of the Office's functions in regard to voluntary repatriation derives from a series of General Assembly resolutions which make use of the High Commissioner's 'good offices'. In 1962, such a resolution enabled UNHCR to assist returnees to Algeria from Morocco and Tunisia. In 1972, another resolution allowed for assistance to returning Sudanese, and during the following decades there have been several other instances. Provided there has been a political will among the main donor governments to assist particular populations, the issue of UNHCR not being a development agency has been set aside. However, the *ad hoc* nature of the approach has meant that UNHCR has not been able to operate autonomously, and when donors have lacked interest in a region, it has been extremely difficult to respond effectively.

There are many examples which illustrate the way that Western foreign policy interests have been linked to international assistance. A recent incidence is the lack of support provided to the 600,000 refugees from Croatia and Bosnia in Serbia and Montenegro. Despite the fact that these refugees have had nothing to do with the heinous crimes committed by the Serb nationalists, governments often specify that their donations to UN and other relief agencies should not be used to assist these refugees (USCR, 1993). With respect to repatriation, the ad hoc responses emanating from the United Nations General Assembly resolutions have frequently related to particular populations of strategic importance to the big donors. It is striking that, before the end of the Cold War, the expected repatriation of Afghan refugees was a focus of world attention but has subsequently been overlooked. The Afghans are no longer of much concern to the superpowers. They languish in hundreds of dusty camps and villages in Pakistan and Iran (*Refugees*, 1992: 16–17). In contrast, refugee crises in strategically important areas continue to attract attention and assistance. The Cambodian case is a good example.

The countries of Southeast Asia are still of political significance to the big donors and it is therefore no surprise that the Comprehensive Plan of Action for the refugees in the region is the highest per capita refugee programme in the world (Lyman, 1991). After the Cambodian peace agreement was signed in Paris in October 1991, UNHCR outlined the preconditions that had to be met to allow safe return of Cambodian refugees. In January 1992, following the completion of land and mine surveys and registration of the 370,000 refugees in Thai camps, UNHCR's repatriation plan was set under way. It provided the returning refugees with three options. One of these, which was considered by the refugees as the most attractive, offered each returning family wood for construction of a house, US$25 to purchase thatch and bamboo, houshold and farming tools, food for 400 days, $US50 per adult and $US25 per child under the age of 12 (USRC, 1993:80).

This package may not be enough to enable the repatrating Cambodians to re-establish themselves. Nevertheless, it was the best offer which has ever been made to returnees, and was remarkably generous when compared with what has been offered in Northeast Africa. The response of the donor community to the Eritrean situation should be understood in this context. One of the areas of contention that led to a stalemate over the issue of Eritrean repatriation was the question of UNHCR's mandate to engage in reintegration projects. Restrictions placed on UNHCR's role by donors were clearly inconsistent with programmes elsewhere but, in the post Cold-War era, countries like Eritrea have become marginalized. The refugees in Sudan counted on international assistance, and Eritrea certainly deserved the attention of the donor community in its bid to achieve peaceful reconstruction. But funds for this particular region are scarce. Donor priorities lie in other geographical locations.

Repatriation of Eritrean Refugees from Sudan

The history of the Eritrean people has been a history of struggle and displacement. Several decades of peaceful resistance and three decades of armed struggle have resulted in the birth of the 52nd independent African nation. International recognition had to wait until after the referendum of April 1993, but for the mass of the population this was just a legal nicety. The dream of an independent state had materialized on 24 May 1991, when the last Ethiopian troops were defeated at Asmara.

At that time there were 592,381 Eritrean refugees in Sudan (537,621 in the eastern State, 25,760 in Central State and 29,000 in Khartoum) (COR, 1993). In spite of their host's generous hospitality, most were living in poverty and longed to return to their homeland. Those who had the means to re-establish themselves in Eritrea without outside assistance seized the opportunity and returned immediately to start a new life. Indeed several thousand returned to EPLF-contolled areas of Eritrea before the final Ethiopian defeat (Habte Selassie, 1991). By August 1992, about 50,000 refugees had spontaneously repatriated, the vast majority without any international assistance. Those who lacked the means to do so waited eagerly for a repatriation programme to be established. The author carried out research in the Eritrean refugees settlements in Qala en Nahal in Sudan during November 1991. Refugees explained that after the Ethiopian forces had been thrown out of Eritrea in May 1991, many families were reluctant to plant crops. The temptation to just pack and make ready to leave was irresistible. After they harvested their crops in October/November, they waited impatiently for the formal repatriation programme to begin. Many of them sold their possessions and dismantled their houses. To their dismay, the response of the donor community to CERA's (Commission for Eritrean Refugee Affairs – the EPLF organization concerned with issues relating to refugees and to repatriation) appeal for financial support was sluggish.

Following the cessation of hostilities in Eritrea, CERA planned to repatriate 250,000 refugees from Sudan over a period of two years (starting in February 1992). This operation was expected to be completed by the spring of 1993 (Refugees, No.88, 10). The total budget for repatriation and re-establishment of the refugees in Eritrea was estimated by the then Provisional Government of Eritrea (PGE) in the range of US$200 million. This estimate was based on precedents of UNHCR involvement in other repatriation programmes. However, UNHCR's estimate for the Eritrean repatriation was only in the range of US$31 million. Even so, it proved difficult to mobilize donors. Far from being completed by the spring of 1993 as expected, the programme had not even started by the winter.

The question that comes to mind is why the refugees did not just follow the example of those who had returned to Eritrea of their own accord? Informants in the villages of Qala en Nahal provided a range of explanations.

One important factor was ease of movement back and forth across the border. Since the end of Ethiopian occupation refugees in the settlements had visited their home areas and witnessed the scale of destruction. In the absence of development aid, many of them recognized that reintegration was going to be hard. Another consideration which prompted caution was the loss of refugee status. Those refugees who had returned before the Ethiopian defeat could re-avail themselves of refugee status if the need arose. However, once the fighting stopped, repatriation became an irreversible decision. Those who officially returned would lose their land possessions in the settlements. Moreover, after years (sometimes decades) in refugee settlements provisioned by international agencies, the refugees considered it as their right to be helped. They were frustrated that assistance programmes were being delayed, but it did not occur to them that the international donor community, which had assisted them for nearly a quarter of a century, would hesitate to assist them to return home when a permanent solution to their problems was at hand.

Given the socio-economic reality prevailing in present-day Eritrea, development, national reconstruction and reintegration of the dislocated populations (including reintegration of returnees) should be conceptualized as constituting integral parts of the same continuum. The situation in both rural and urban Eritrea is such that few returnees would be able to re-establish themselves without the general economic reconstruction of the areas to which they return. In most places there is a need to create amenities from scratch. Most roads in the areas controlled by Ethiopia are unusable, bridges have been blown up, clinics, schools, mosques and churches have been destroyed. There is also an urgent requirement for training, for the clearing of landmines and for the provision of productive inputs, particularly agricultural implements and seeds. The country is faced with a dilemma. On the one hand it needs the human capital of the refugees. Over one third of the population is displaced (internally or externally), and many regions are seriously underpopulated. On the other hand, without international assistance, the sudden repatriation of refugees could be disastrous. If they cannot be integrated into the economy, they could become an unbearable burden and even a threat to national security.

In principle, the policy of the Eritrean government towards those refugees who have returned is to allow them freedom to choose their own destination. It has been recognized that inducing populations to relocate has failed elsewhere, and that people should not be settled, but helped to settle themselves. The propriety of this approach notwithstanding, however, certain problems can be anticipated which will be exacerbated as the numbers crossing the border increases. In some places the scattered location of the returnees will make planning difficult, and will require the provision of services to the whole population. In others, there will be a danger that settlement will be over-concentrated. This is particularly likely in the short term. Many of those who returned between 1989 and 1990 chose to return to the border towns of Ali Gedir and Tessenei. If Habte Selassie's figures are right, in 1990, 90 per cent of the residents in the border town of Tessenei were returnees (Habte-Selassie, 1991: 8). To avoid collapse of the already devastated infastructure, the EPLF closed the town to newcomers.

This situation probably occurred because the border towns were perceived as being the safest locations. However, if my findings from investigations made in the Qala en Nahal villages can be generalized, irrespective of their ethnicity, most of the refugees want to return to the Gash and Setit valleys. Many of the refugees had been living in these valleys before their flight, and they are the most fertile and productive parts of the country. The choice of destination is therefore predictable, but can be expected to result in intense pressure on the land. Facilities have to be established to facilitate a capacity for absorption. Environmental degradation is likely to occur if a mass return occurs before this can be achieved.

Social and Economic Changes and their Implications for Reintegration

There is no doubt that provision of international assistance is the key to a successful re-integration of the Eritrean refugees. But it is also crucial that development planning for the areas that will eventually receive the returnees should take into account the economic and social transformations that the refugees have undergone in exile. Moreover, the populations in the receiving areas will also have undergone changes, and a balance needs to be struck by drawing insights from both experiences.

The Eritrean refugees in Sudan have become more involved than hitherto in national and international economic activity. They have produced for the market and have participated in wage labouring. For example, in Qala en Nahal during the mid-1980s, about 40 per cent of the arable land was allocated to production of the cash crop, sesame, and up to 35 per cent of a family's income was derived from off-farm income-generating activities (mainly wage labour) (Kibreab, 1987). Milk and ghee, which were mainly produced for subsistence in the pre-flight period, were now marketed to supplement income. Many former rural dwellers became urbanized. For some this proved a de-skilling experience, and the integration of such groups in Eritrea is likely to be an uphill task. Social networks which provided support in times of crisis have either been weakened or replaced by more commoditized relationships. The moral ties which maintained extended family life have commonly been set aside. Traditional modes of leadership have become almost meaningless. This is reflected in the amoebic multipli-cation of the sheikdoms in the six Qala en Nahal villages, which have increased over the past two decades from less than 40 to 222. At the same time, traditional resource manage-ment regimes have either broken down or have been weakened. The consequence of this is that it will be more difficult than before to manage common property resources collectively for the common good. Individual decision-making regarding production and resource allocation has replaced collective decision-making built on consensus.

The changes occuring among the Eritrean populations remaining in the war zones were different, but similarly profound. They have become much more secularized and politicized. Old communal values have sometimes been set aside, but have generally been replaced by collective solidarity and support networks based less on kin ties than on political ideology. This was due to the imperatives of the war and the influence of the EPLF and its mass organizations.

Such divergent directions of social change are likely to cause tensions, and receiving communities will have to be well prepared and supported. One important focus of dis-pute is going to be access to farm land. As a consequence of the land reform carried out under EPLF auspices, most of the returning refugees will find that their former holdings are now occupied. Whether new arable land is made available or existig holdings are re-divided to accomodate the newcomers is a crucial, and as yet largely unresolved issue.

A further fact which must be considered is that many of the refugees in Sudan had formerly been pastoralists. In exile they have become sedentarized, but because cultiva-tion in the settlements is mechanised, they have not learned the skill of ox-ploughing. Assuming that people do not return to pastoral production following repatriation, the question arises of how cultivation will occur. At present the technical, capital and organizational inputs are not available in Eritrea for mechanized agriculture. If they became available the effects may be counter-productive if the returnees are forced to replicate the dependence on services which they faced in exile. If the emphasis is going to be on small farming, based on animal traction, a mass training programme will be required, as well as effective veterinary services for the animals. It also needs to be borne

5.1 *Traditional resource management regimes have either broken down or have been weakened: evidence of heavy pressure on the environment in the immediate surroundings of the refugee villages. (Gaim Kibreab)*

5.2 *The refugee settlements have been hit hard by droughts, destroying both crops and livestock: a starved and dehydrated goat, 1990. (Gaim Kibreab)*

5.3 *Many of the refugee families in Sudan had to diversify livelihood strategies as soil fertility declined. Continuous cultivation resulted in a variety of problems, including the spread of striga (witchweed). A striga-resistant sorghum variety produced a good yield in one of the neighbouring Sudanese villages, 1991. (Gaim Kibreab)*

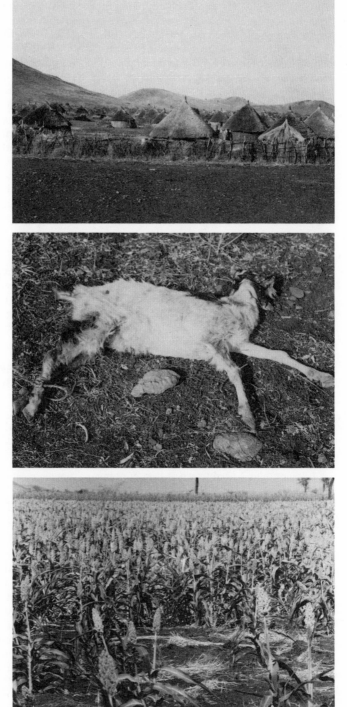

in mind that most of the kinds of plough traditionally used by Eritrean peasants are made of wood. Only the mouldboard ploughshare itself is made of metal. If such an implement were to be locally manufactured by thousands of returned refugees, excessive tree felling would accelerate the already critical problem of deforestation.

Obviously tree planting combined with clearly defined tenure and property rights should be incorporated into the reintegration schemes. But this may not be adequate. At least some of the returnees should probably be encouraged to re-establish pastoral production. During the 1980s, some refugee families in Sudan turned to pastoralism again, as soil fertility depletion from continuous cultivation in the settlements led to a diversification of livelihood strategies. Moreover, as a return to Eritrea has become a possibility, many refugees have systematically invested in moveable assets, notably livestock. Development plans for the returnees must take into account the need for pasture. At present, cattle herders from the refugee settlements migrate as far as Begemedir in Ethiopia in search of fodder in the dry season, and after repatriation it will still be necessary for herders to cross international boundaries. It would be a grave error to put an end to such activities. Concentration of livestock could be disastrous.

Overcoming the Stalemate

At the UNRISD symposium on mass voluntary return movements of refugees, held in Addis Ababa in September 1992, there were sharp exchanges between Eritrean participants and representatives of some international organizations. The Eritreans were accused of placing obstacles in the way of their people coming home. They responded by arguing that adequate funds had not yet been made available for mass repatriation. Discussion about the issue seemed to have reached a stalemate.

During the previous month, recriminating correspondence had passed between the head of the PGE (who was also the Secretary General of the EPLF) and the UNHCR, following the breakdown of negotiations in Asmara. The UN High Commissioner made little attempt to disguise her irritation:

> I must express my concern at the PGE's unwillingness to continue discussion on your project proposal as this will further delay the start of mass organised repatriation of the returnees who have made known their eagerness to return home. (UNHCR, 1992: 2)

The head of the PGE responded as follows:

> I do not think I need to repeat here our utmost disappointment in the whole approach and response of the international community, including the UNHCR, as these have been conveyed to your office several times in the past and were extensively discussed with the delegation that visited us a few days ago. I believe, however, that you will agree with me that the repatriation of the Eritrean refugees in the Sudan is not a matter that can be postponed indefinitely until the international community sees fit to address it. (PGE, 1992)

The apparent failure of communication between the parties evidenced by these letters prevailed until the intervention of the United Nations Department of Humanitarian Affairs (UNDHA). An inter-agency and donor meeting was held in Geneva in mid-April 1993, and this was followed up by a 'programme support formulation' mission to Eritrea in May, which involved the Eritrean government as well as representatives of UN agencies, NGOs and donors. Finally, on 6 June, a high-profile pledging conference for the Programme for the Reintegration and Rehabilitation of Resettlement Areas in Eritrea (PROFERI) was held in Geneva, under the chairmanship of Jan Eliasson, Undersecretary General of the UNHDA. The meeting was also attended by the President of Eritrea, Ato Issaias Afewerki.

The pledging conference was viewed as a partial success in that it brought an end to the stalemate. It bridged the dichotomy between relief assistance and development aid, which was one of the factors impeding progress in previous negotiations. A general understanding was reached that without development assistance to the areas of return, integration will not be achievable. The meeting was also very well attended. No less than 69 governments were represented, as well as 24 non–UN multilateral agencies and 37 NGOs (PROFERI, 1993).

As a first stage, it was decided to support the repatriation of 150,000 refugees and to rehabilitate areas of return at a cost of US$111 million. This figure was considerably more than UNHCR's earlier estimate of around US$31 million, but much less than the US$200 million estimate of the former CERA (which had hoped to repatriate and reintegrate 250,000 refugees over two years from early 1992). The Eritreans continued to draw attention to the fact that the new estimate was not as much as had been made available elsewhere. As has been mentioned, Cambodian returnees received cash payments, and this has also been the case for South African refugees, with each adult receiving US$1,518 as well as additional sums for children (Keats, 1992: 55). In Eritrea it was not made clear if any money at all would be made available to the returnees themselves, except in the form of food and farming tools.

Moreover, the recommendations made at the pledging conference were not matched by the provision of funds. In fact, only US$32,435,915 was actually pledged for the PROFERI programme (with a further 1.4 to 2.1 million placed under consideration by Christian Outreach and the Danish government, and several other countries only promising to look into funding possibilities). Table 5.1 gives a breakdown of the oral

Table 5.1 *Summary of oral pledges for Eritrea pertaining to PROFERI, (as of 17 August 1993)*

Donor	Amount pledged US$	Sector	Channel
Liechtenstein	6,623	Unspecified	DHA
Sweden	2,580,645	Rehabilitation	EG (Eritrean government), UN/NGO
UK	1,483,680	Rehabilitation of refugees	UNHCR
Norway	3,000,000	Unspecified	EG, UN
Switzerland	1,986,755	Rehabilitation of refugees	UNHCR, NGOs
Netherlands	1,052,632	Rehabilitation of refugees	UNHCR
UNDP	2,000,000	Program management & implementation	UNDP
WFP*	12,500,000	Food for rehabilitation & reintegration	WFP
EC	1,965,116	Agriculture, water & health	EG
Christian Aid	500,000	Relief & rehabilitation	Unspecified
Oxfam UK	800,000	Agriculture, rehabilitation water	EG
Various donors 1991-91 SEPHA appeal**	3,700,000	UNHCR repatriation programme	UNHCR
Total	32,435,915		

Source: Report on the Pledging Conference for the Programme for Refugee Reintegration, and Rehabilitation of Resettlement Areas in Eritrea (PROFERI), Geneva, 6 July 1993
* This funding provides food aid within PROFERI for up to 150,000 returnees who are currently receiving food aid in the Sudan, which would be transferred to Eritrea. WFP will seek the additional resources required within PROFERI for other returnees who are not currently receiving food aid in the Sudan.
** This amount is a carry over from the 1991–2 contributions received against previous SEPHA appeals.

Several donors are also considering further pledges. These countries include Canada, Egypt, Japan, France, Indonesia, Korea, Kuwait, Pakistan, Saudi Arabia, South Africa and the USA (Report on the Pledging Conference for the PROFERI, 6 July 1993).

pledges made at the meeting, with the sectors for which the funds should be allocated. It is revealing of donor priorities that out of the meagre US$32.4 million, only US$11.7 million was earmarked for improving the economic and social infrastructures of the refugee receiving areas.

In view of the unfavourable response from donors, the pledging conference recommended that the returnees should initially be settled in a single region, such as Gash Setit. It was also recommended that the PROFERI programme should *reduce the numbers being repatriated to a much lower level, commensurate with the funds available* (PROFERI, 1993: 35, emphasis added). Although this probably is the only option, it undermines the Eritrean government's commitment to allow returnees freedom to choose their destination and, as discussed above, it can be expected to have adverse environmental consequences.

Conclusion

It is only possible to conclude with the depressing observation that the international community has failed the Eritrean people. It seems completely ludicrous that donors should choose to allocate funds in such a way as to keep thousands of refugees in settlements rather than help them rebuild their homeland. Yet that is what has happened.

Understandably the refugees in Sudan feel let down, and the optimism of May 1991 has given way to despair. Many of those I have spoken to have described the early 1990s as the worst period they have experienced while in exile. The following testimony encapsulates a widely held perspective.

> We have been desperately waiting for our country to become free. Now it is free, yet we cannot return. For the majority, the conditions in our country make return impossible without international assistance for national reconstruction and reintegration. We have got our independence, but we are denied our freedom because we still live as refugees in spite of the elimination of the factors that prompted our flight. No refugee irrespective of his/her hosts' hospitality is free. In the past, the hope of one day returning home and the 'esprit de corps' gave us energy to endure the suffering. Now after independence out resilience is turning into vulnerability. The determination to persevere in hardship and deprivation is bit by bit vanishing into thin air. (male elder, interviewed at Qala en Nahal in November 1991)

The literature on refugees abounds with statements suggesting that the refugee experience is associated with dependency and lethargy. Perhaps there are some refugees who fit this stereotype, but they are a minority. By and large, refugees are not only skilful in coping with adverse conditions but also manage to preserve their integrity and honour, partly by a shared belief in the prospect of a better future. This was evidently the case with the Eritrean refugees in Sudan. The endurance exhibited by these people was an outcome of a strong, almost fanatical conviction that one day in the near future it would become possible to return home. Many of them actively participated in the liberation struggle. It was the dream of a free Eritrea which kept their flames of hope ablaze. In 1991, their dream of Eritrean independence became reality, but poverty has prevented mass repatriation. It is a bewildering turn of events. Resilience based on hope is being eroded. Thousands of people have been left floating in a state of limbo, and many are beginning to give up. As their will to survive breaks down, so their vulnerability increases.

The refugee problem is by its nature global in scope and it can only be tackled by co-operation on a global scale. The opening sentence of the 'Declaration and Programme of Action' of ICARA II stated that: '[T]he task of caring for refugees and finding solutions to their problems is a matter of international concern ...' (UNHCR, 1984b). Since voluntary repatriation is recognized as constituting the most durable solution to the refugee problem, the international donor community has a responsibility to help refugees re-establish themselves in their homelands. Such help should be provided to Eritreans. Failure to do so is tantamount to a denial of their human rights.

The Current Situation

Since writing this paper, the living conditions of the Eritrean refugees in Sudan has continued to deteriorate (Kibreab, 1995). However, the Eritrean government and the UNHCR have at last reached an understanding and have signed a Memorandum of Understanding. The first stage of the repatriation operation (involving 24,000 refugees) has been successfully completed. A major operation is planned for 1995/6.

References

African Charter on Human and People's Rights, 1981.

Commissioner's Office for Refugees (COR) (1993) Statistical Report, Documentation Centre, Statistics Division, Khartoum.

Habte Selassie, E. (1991) 'Eritrean refugees in the Sudan: preliminary analysis of repatriation', paper for the Workshop on the Prospects for Peace, Recovery and Development in the Horn of Africa, The Hague, 19–23 February.

IIHL (1985) 'Voluntary repatriation: a background study' prepared for the Round Table on Voluntary Repatriation, International Institute of Humanitarian Law, San Remo, 16–19 July.

International Covenant on Civil and Political Rights, 1966.

Keats, M. (1992) 'South Africa: facing reality', *Refugees*, No. 89, UNHCR, May.

Kibreab, G. (1987) *Refugees and development in Africa: the case of Eritrea*, The Red Sea Press, Trenton, NJ.

— (1991a) 'The system of asylum in African economies under pressure' in K. Ullenhag (ed.), *Hundred flowers bloom: essays in honour of Bo Gustafsson*, Almpvist & Wiksell International, Stockholm.

— (1991b) *The state of the art review of refugee studies in Africa, Uppsala papers in economic history, research report no. 26*, University of Uppsala, Department of Economic History, Uppsala.

— (1992) 'Current events in Ethiopia and Eritrea: prospects for repatriation', seminar presentation in the series 'criticsl issues in international and US refugee policy', Fletcher School of Law and Diplomacy, Tufts University, February.

— (1995) *Ready and willing ... but still waiting. Factors influencing the decision of the Eritrean refugees in Sudan to return home*, Institute of Life and Peace, Uppsala.

— (forthcoming), 'Integration of African refugees in first countries of asylum: past experiences and prospects for the 1990s', in R. Rogers and S.S. Russell (eds), *Towards a New Global Refugee System*, Fletcher School of Law and Diplomacy, Tufts University.

Lyman, P.N. (1991) 'US response to refugee and migration issues: the challenges of the 1990s', seminar presentation in the series 'Critical issues in international and US refugee law and policy', Fletcher School of Law and Diplomacy, Tufts University.

Organization of African Unity (1969), Convention Governing the Specific Aspects of Refugee Problems in Africa.

PLE (Provisional Government of Eritrea) (1992), Letter from the Secretary-General of the Eritrean People's Liberation Front and Head of the Provisional Government of Eritrea to the United Nations High Commissioner for Refugees, Asmara, 24 August.

Refugees, 1992, No. 88, UNHCR, Geneva, January.

PROFERI Report on the Pledging Conference for the Programme for Refugee Reintegration and Rehabilitation of Resettlement Areas in Eritrea (1993), prepared by M. Askwith, DHA Representative, Eritrea, 10 August 1993.

Stein, B.N. (1991), 'The actual and desireable link between programmes of ad hoc assistance to return movements and long-term development programmes for the local areas where refugees return', paper for the Symposium on Social and Economic Aspects of Mass Voluntary Return of Refugees from one African Country to Another, Harare, Zimbabwe, 12–14 March.

UNHCR (United Nations High Commissioner for Refugees) (1992), Letter from the United Nations High Commissioner for Refugees to Mr Issayas Afewerki, Secretary General of the Eritrean People's Liberation Front and Head of the Provisional Government of Eritrea, AF/D/229/92, 24 August.

— (1980), Note on Voluntary Repatriation submitted to the Sub-Committee of the Whole on International Protection, Executive Committee of the High Commissioner's Programme, EC/SCP/13.

— (1984a) Introductory Statement by the High Commissioner for Refugees, ICARA II, Geneva, 9 July.

— (1984b) Declaration and Programme of Action, ICARA II, Geneva.

United Nations (1948), Universal Declaration of Human Rights.

United Nations General Assembly (1984a), Refugee Aid and Development, A/AC.96/635, Note submitted by the High Commissioner, 1983, 21 December.

— (1984b), Declaration and Programme of Action of the Second International Conference on Assistance to Refugees in Africa, Geneva, July.

USCR (US Committee for Refugees) (1993), *East of Bosnia refugees in Serbia and Montenegro: issue paper*, September.

6 JOHNATHAN BASCOM
Reconstituting Households
& Reconstructing Home Areas

The Case of Returning Eritreans

Repatriation, after all, is not the end of a refugee migration process but 'a half-way point that must be followed by the even more difficult challenges of social, economic and political integration' (Wood, 1989: 365).

In 1984 the Executive Committee of the United Nations High Commissioner for Refugees (UNHCR) sounded a call for 'durable solutions' to refugee crises in developing countries. The ongoing search for durable solutions has been characterized by a growing interest in mass voluntary repatriation. Understandably, the focus of attention has centred on factors that can precipitate the movement of refugees back to their homeland. The repatriation process, however, is not complete when returning populations cross a political boundary. Official exile may end at the border, but after the repatriation 'event' occurs, then returning populations must face the difficult challenges of resettlement as well as social, economic and political integration.

The relative degree of success or failure in the reintegration process depends on the forms, size and timeliness of available assistance as well as conditions in the homeland. These factors – structural, exogenous and contextual in nature – are important. But refugees are the principal actors in the process of reintegration and, very significantly, they start to determine the conditions for their reintegration well before the actual repatriation event.

Much of the larger migration literature as well as recent work on repatriation focusses on factors that determine the decision to migrate (De Jong and Gardner, 1981; Koser, 1992). This study attempts to move beyond an analysis of variables that coalesce around the decision to migrate. Its main objective is to investigate ways in which repatriation decisions are linked to the subsequent process of reintegration. The study examines two key issues inspired by the research programme on refugees and returnees of the United Nations Research Institute for Social Development (UNRISD). First, how do repatriation decisions reflect a motivation to reconstitute relations between households as well as within them? Second, how do repatriation decisions reflect a mental preparation to reconstruct the local area to which refugees return? Answers to these questions can help facilitate self-organization among returning refugees as well as direct donor assistance and policy decisions linked to reintegration.

The Field Site

Sudan, since the late 1960s, has faced a large influx of displaced refugees from the neighbouring countries of Chad, Ethiopia, Uganda, and Zaire (Table 6.1). In 1967, the Eritrean diaspora to Sudan began with an influx of 30,000 refugees from the western

Table 6.1 *The number of refugees in Sudan by country of origin (in thousands)*

Year	Ethiopia	Eritrea	Zaire	Uganda	Chad	Total
1974	49.0	(included in Ethiopia)	4.5	0.0	0.0	53.5
1975	85.0	"	5.0	0.0	0.0	90.0
1976	105.0	"	4.5	0.5	0.0	110.0
1977	145.0	"	4.5	0.5	0.0	150.0
1978	270.0	"	3.5	0.5	0.0	274.0
1979	346.0	"	3.5	0.5	0.0	350.0
1980	390.0	"	5.0	69.0	16.0	480.0
1981	419.0	"	5.0	110.0	18.0	552.0
1982	440.0	"	5.0	160.0	22.0	627.0
1983	460.0	"	5.0	184.0	0.0	649.0
1984	484.0	"	5.0	200.0	1.0	690.0
1985	718.0	"	5.0	250.0	121.0	1094.0
1986	656.0	"	5.0	165.0	93.0	919.0
1987	677.0	"	5.0	90.0	45.0	817.0
1988	660.0	"	5.0	3.6	25.0	693.6
1989	663.2	"	5.0	2.0	24.1	694.3
1990	700.0	"	4.5	2.0	20.0	726.5
1991	690.0	"	4.5	2.7	20.0	717.2
1992	730.0	"	2.0	4.0-	14.5	750.5
1993	200.0	420.0	2.0	4.0	7.0	633.0
1994	160.0	380.0	2.0	4.0	4.0	550.0

Sources: Bulcha, (1988); Hamilton (ed.) (1986–95).

lowlands. By 1990, Sudan provided asylum to 700,000 Ethiopians, some 500,000 of whom were of Eritrean origin (Commission for Eritrean Refugee Affairs, 1992b). Although the Eritrean war ended on 24 May 1991 only one seventh of the refugee population in Sudan returned during the 12 months preceding the end of armed conflict as well as the first two years thereafter. The majority of Eritrean refugees remain in Sudan.

Data for this study were collected from refugees at the border location of Wad el Hileau (Map 6.1). Successive waves of Eritreans arrived in the late 1960s, mid-1970s and early 1980s as conflict moved into different regions of Eritrea. Coming to Wad el Hileau afforded safety, but refugees could still remain in a familiar habitat and in close contact to the homeland. The field site now constitutes the largest concentration of unassisted rural refugees in eastern Sudan as well as an official refugee camp for more than 10,000 refugees. Wad el Hileau has an exceptionally diverse population comprised of more than 40 different ethnic groups (Ahmad, 1986). Eighty-eight per cent of the refugees in Wad el Hileau, however, are from the Eritrean lowlands.

The author completed an intensive case study at the field site during 1987–8. The study was based on a lengthy questionnaire administered in 135 Eritrean households representing 23 per cent of the refugee households in Wad el Hileau. In early 1992 and early 1993 the author returned to the field site. Thirty-five representative households from the 1987–8 sample were interviewed again in order to assess the prospects for repatriation among unassisted or 'self-settled' refugee households. In addition, four group interviews were completed in the adjacent refugee camp. The 35 unassisted households reflect the larger 1987–8 sample in terms of ethnic distribution as well as the average year of arrival in Sudan, size of smallholdings, and size of pastoral herds.

Reconstitution of Household Relations

The broad designation of 'households relations' connotes two different levels of analysis. The relations within households (intra-household dynamics) represent one prominent

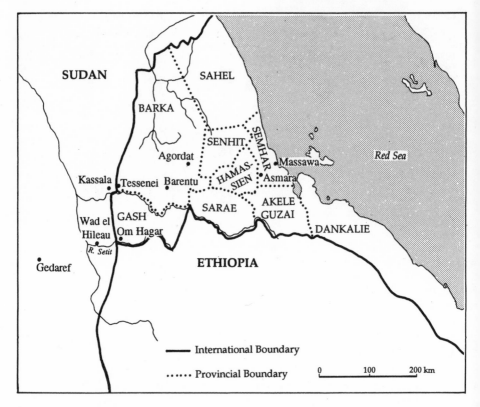

Map 6.1 *Provincial boundaries and key cities in western Eritrea.*

arena of conflict and co-operation and the relations of conflict and co-operation between households (inter-household dynamics) are another. The rules, roles and responsibilities that govern interaction at both levels are loosened by the process of social dislocation associated with flight, and then, restructured by the pressure of surviving in a new environment during exile. A basic sense of such changes during flight and resettlement is essential to understanding how they are tested yet again by, during, and after repatriation.

Inter-household dynamics
Capitalist penetration into the subsistence economies of the western lowland region was marginal at best before the exodus of Eritreans to Sudan. In spite of 62 years of Italian and British occupation (1890–52) the lowland population remained characterized by interdependent social relations and subsistent economies (Longrigg, 1974; Johnson and Johnson, 1981; Kibreab, 1987). The intertwined social obligations undergirding subsistence economies included reciprocal exchanges of food, shelter, and land as well as non-monetized exchanges of labour to plant, weed, harvest, or construct homes. Hyden (1983) argues that such culturally defined expectations create an 'economy of affection' which insulates peasants from capture by other social classes or 'the state'.

In Sudan, however, market relationships have replaced the main features of the once-prevailing social relations between households. Evidence presented in previous studies from this field site underscores the impact of transforming land, labour, livestock, and grazing rights into monetized commodities on the relations between Eritrean households during exile (Wijbrandi, 1990; Bascom 1990, 1993). Most important, the free and reciprocal exchange of labour between households has virtually disappeared:

> Although Eritreans depended on communal labor parties when they first arrived in the late 1960s, soon thereafter '*nafir* died' – to use an oft-repeated phrase of refugees. The exchange of labor for production is now a rare exception. Only nine Eritreans from my sample of 81 small-holders had participated in a *nafir* during the last 10 years. Mechanization and the agricultural wage labor market are the most important reasons for the decomposition of this center piece in the natural economy. Two forms of daily wages – a short work day (*dahawa*) between 7 and 10 o'clock and a full day of work (*yoomiiya*) – have replaced *nafirs*.
>
> Lesser kinds of redistributive arrangements are also disappearing or being replaced by monetary exchanges. Refugees reported very few instances in which relatives or friends had shared labor or beasts of burden with them since they arrived in Sudan. Other social obligations have been monetized in what amounts to fund-raising campaigns. In the event of a fire, for example, a list (*cashif*) is circulated among villagers on which they pledge cash donations. Building supplies and labor are then purchased rather than donated as they were in the past. The fact that reciprocity practices have been suspended or depleted illustrates that unassisted refugees have been unsuccessful in reconstituting their preflight economy at Wad el Hileau (Bascom, 1993: 334–5).

The very structure of refugee households reflects the severe impact of social transformation. Kibreab (1992) reports that extended families are non-existent in refugee camps like the Qala en Nahal settlement. Table 6.2 illustrates extended family relationships among unassisted refugees. It identifies the distribution of extra household members – both extended family members as well as temporary dwellers – for refugee households in Wad el Hileau. The proportion of household members who are not from the immediate family (9.2 per cent) is slightly higher than the previous estimate of 7 per cent for the village (Wijbrandi, 1990).

The scale at which decisions to repatriate are being made also reflects the effect of social transformation during exile. Only 27 per cent of the unassisted respondents in Wad el Hileau suggested that their sheik would have any influence whatsoever over their decision to repatriate (Bascom, 1994). In the succinct words of one interviewee, 'I have to decide what is best for me.' In sum, a crucial shift has occurred; community interests are now secondary and subservient to those of the household and the individual.

Table 6.2 *Distribution of added members in Eritrean refugee households at Wad el Hileau*

Household Size	No Extra Members	One Added Member	Two Added Members	Three Added Members	Four Added Members	Total Households
1-2	0	8	—	—	—	8
3-4	5	14	3	2	—	24
5-6	18	15	—	—	—	33
7-8	12	7	1	—	—	20
9-10	12	4	3	0	—	19
11-12	11	1	1	2	2	17
13-14	3	0	1	—	—	4
15-16	3	0	1	2	1	7
17+	2	1	—	—	—	3
Total	66	50	10	6	3	135

Source: Household survey conducted by author, November 1987/June 1988.

6.1 *Common property resources are apt to become 'flash points' of contention, but respondents in Wad el Hileau are confident that conflicting claims can be resolved: cattle herders sharing a 'cowad' or camp while watching over their animals.*
(Johnathan Bascom)

Meanwhile, refugee camps have experienced a marked expansion in authority figures. Kibreab (1992) reports an 'amoebic' proliferation in the number of small sheikdoms throughout the Qala en Nahal settlement. During the last 20 years the number of authority figures has grown from 40 sheiks to 220 authority figures (a 550 per cent increase). He aptly comments on the deep implications of a weakened authority structure on resource management: '... it will be more difficult than before to manage common property resources collectively for the common good of the communities concerned because individual decisions have replaced collective decision-making regarding production and resource allocation' (Kibreab, 1992: 8).

Common property resources like wood, water, grazing rights, and agricultural land are apt to become 'flash points' of contention between returnees and their compatriots who remained during the war. There are no formal systems of land measurement or registration in the western lowlands. Instead, agricultural land – once deemed 'pubic domain' during Italian colonialism – is collectively owned by respective ethnic communities (Habte-Selassie, 1992b: 7). Repatriates are apt to rely on social and cultural networks within those communities to resolve potential clashes over land ownership. Respondents in Wad el Hileau are confident that conflicting claims can be resolved in that manner. Sixty-eight per cent of the respondents in Wad el Hileau do not anticipate difficulty reclaiming their land, 21 per cent anticipate a dispute will occur, and 11 per cent are uncertain.

Intra-household dynamics

Unfortunately, dynamics within refugee households are generally envisaged in a loose, imprecise and static way. Very little attention has been devoted to the qualitative differences that exist within refugee households despite an increasing emphasis paid to refugee women and children by donors, practitioners, and researchers as well as a large body of literature that raises questions about how the household should be defined in agrarian societies (Guyer and Peters, 1987; Dwyer and Bruce, 1988; Carney and Watts, 1990). How are the rules, roles and responsibilities that govern interaction within the household restructured by the pressure of surviving in a new environment during exile?

As seen already, the process of social transformation has eroded interdependent relationships between households. Social transformation also sets in motion the breakdown of the household as a unit of production. UNHCR's planning mission for the repatriation from Sudan to Eritrea acknowledges the dissolution of the 'household' in its recommendations for developing a protocol to register refugees for repatriation:

> An issue that is likely to occur frequently at point of registration is the presentation of requests for the separate processing of individuals . . . registrars cannot be expected to engage in *social analysis* [emphasis mine] at the registration table and will need simple, readily applicable criteria with which to handle such requests routinely. Is age alone sufficient to qualify one as an

independent householder? Is marriage? What about widows, widowers and divorced persons? (Ali, 1991: 9)

Returnees from official camps will include a much higher proportion of female-headed households compared to those from self-settled concentrations where intact families are more common. One survey of 17,160 Eritreans indicated that 21.3 per cent were children under the age of five and 39.5 per cent were female-headed households (CERA, 1992a). Among self-settled populations, however, female-headed households are the exception. This is particularly true for a relatively 'stabilized population' where the short-term exigencies of flight have worn off during an extended asylum. Islamic religious structures in Sudan intensify further the expectation that women should be married, rather than single. In sum, men are making the repatriation decisions for unassisted households. Sixty-one per cent of the male respondents in Wad el Hileau indicate that they will not consult their wives at all regarding the repatriation decision. The remaining 39 per cent imply that they will tell their wives of their decision, but only one suggests that his wife will have any substantive input.

6.2 *To minimize food insecurity and other risks associated with repatriation, most refugee men prefer to return to Eritrea before their wives and children. (Johnathan Bascom)*

The dominant preference among heads of unassisted households is to go to Eritrea first, then return to Sudan and bring the rest of the family several months thereafter. Eighty-five per cent of all interviewees in my sample prefer this 'split family' tactic. They justify it on the basis of their need to register land, rebuild homes, and establish trade linkages before the whole family returns. This deployment tactic is not surprising given the protracted length of time that refugees have been away from Eritrea, the massive amount of destruction that has transpired since they left, and the risk-avoidance tactics that poor people must adopt.

Refugees in other times and at other places have chosen to do the same. Between 1985 and 1987 more than 250,000 Tigreans returned home from Sudan. Most heads of households and productive members went before the rest of the family members (Hendrie, 1992). An UNHCR consultant discovered a similar strategy among families 'stretched' between camps in southern Sudan and their origination areas in Uganda:

> ...because of the infinitely flexible shape of the families making up the refugee population...It is necessary to leave some family members in the camp/settlement to claim food rations for the whole family, etc., as well as to maintain their right to the allotted plot. Equally it is necessary to have others at the border at all times to tend the growing crops and to maintain a right to the ground and tukuls (huts). It is a perfectly reasonable and understandable system (Day-Thompson cited in Harrell-Bond, 1986).

Unfortunately, the deployment of household members on either side of the border is not consistent with UNHCR's protocol for repatriation exercises which requires that households return as a complete unit. UNHCR consultants are concerned that Eritrean households will engage in cross-border movements or split their families into locations on either side of the border in order to gain entitlements in Sudan as well as Eritrea (Ali, 1991). Advocacy for phasing out assistance to Eritreans in Sudan is growing, in large part, to mitigate against this split family approach.

In theory, UNHCR must ensure that repatriation occurs under conditions that are entirely voluntary and thereby refugees are often allowed to remain on assistance rolls indefinitely. In practice, however, repatriations range from purely voluntary to 'encouraged' or 'induced', and, even 'forced' (Stein, 1992). Increasingly, refugees are being repatriated under duress by phasing out food and other assistance and pressuring the host government to grant citizenship rights to those who do not wish to return home. These tactics, employed in the case of Somalia, are now at the centre of debate over the Eritrean repatriation as the 'politics of repatriation' are played out between UNHCR (intent on withdrawal), Sudan (dependent on refugees to obtain international assistance), and the provisional government of Eritrea (intent on securing significant assistance to facilitate reintegration).

Reconstruction of the Home Area

Too often it is taken for granted that the return of refugees to their country of origin is a 'natural' and 'problem-free' process (Rogge 1994). Reconstruction of the home area is, however, a challenging task. Significantly, that process begins as refugees collect information about conditions at home.

Like other migrants, most refugees find personal contacts to be the most effective way to begin preparing for the return home. Travellers – new arrivals, temporary visitors, and persons who have made a visit to Eritrea – are the chief source of information for potential repatriates living in Sudan. Ninety-six per cent of the respondents in this study had spoken directly with someone from their original village since the cessation of conflict. In most instances, visitors conveyed very specific and personalized information about conditions in Eritrea. Eighty-nine per cent of the respondents could identify, for example, the present condition of their former agricultural land as either overgrown, cultivated by family members, confiscated, or damaged.

Returning refugees are most apt to return to the areas from which they originally came. For that reason it is abundantly clear that the vast majority of repatriates from Sudan will resettle in the western lowlands of Eritrea. Nearly 70,000 Eritreans returned of their own accord between May 1990 and early 1993 (CERA, 1993). Table 6.3 identifies the provincial destinations chosen by 47,781 returnees who went through a formal registration process. The majority of these former refugees – more than three of every four – returned to the lowland provinces of Barka, Gash, and Sahel.

Ninety-five per cent of the sample in Wad el Hileau indicated their desire to resettle in Eritrea at the same location from which they fled, but they have serious questions as

Table 6.3 *Distribution of registered returnees to Eritrea, May 1990–April 1993*

Province	Number	Percentage
Gash	20,784	43.5
Sahel	11,421	23.9
Hamassien	4,826	10.1
Barka	4,492	9.4
Senhit	3,918	8.2
Semhar	1,575	3.3
Highlands	765	1.6
Total	47,781	100.00

Sources: CERA (1993) and CERA (1992a).

to whether the specific location from which they fled will have sufficient natural resources – grain, building materials and livestock fodder – to sustain them. Many refer to their homeland as 'empty' and to many inhabitants as 'disabled' [economically impoverished]. Respondents were asked to identify an alternative site for resettlement in Eritrea. Their shared responses suggest the likelihood of a marked population shift to the southwestern corner of Eritrea. The Setit River area offers more arable land, less proneness to drought, and close proximity to wage labour opportunities in Sudan.

Eighty-eight per cent of the respondents in Wad el Hileau believe they will be welcomed back by the current inhabitants. Returning Eritreans are, however, likely to face the same challenge as recent Namibian repatriates who found that the host community was not as willing to accommodate them as was expected (Tapscott and Mulongeni cited in Simon and Preston, 1993). Although the majority of the respondents in Wad el Hileau (63 per cent) predict that life will be easier in Eritrea, many refugees are referring to the non-material advantages afforded by return. One respondent noted that 'at home you are free to behave in all senses' while another stressed that in Sudan 'you are always a guest'. The difficulties they are most apt to face are associated with pressure on land and with new expectations held by the returning population.

Pressure on land

Rapid population increase has taken place since the turn of the century. The Eritrean population, estimated at about 1.65 million when conflict began in 1961, more than doubled in the 30 years thereafter. The impact of destroy-and-desolate-campaigns carried out by the Ethiopian military during the war coupled with rapid population growth has precipitated a severe shortage of arable land. During the war the peasantry in many regions was forced to overexploit and undermaintain its environment (Mengisteab, 1992). Peace now provides Eritreans with the 'space' to manage the fragile ecosystem in keeping with the country's zealous commitment to self-reliant development.

The prevailing precipitation pattern is a key factor in strengthening Eritrea's food security. The Sahel belt is characterized by limited rainfall. Reliable rainfall data are not available for Eritrea, but a comparison of recent rainfall data in the border region of Sudan with data from colonial records indicates that the 600 mm rainfall isohyet has shifted southward in a marked fashion (Map 6.2). The steep rainfall gradient in this region (i.e. a rate of 50 mm per 30 km) is coupled together with a shrinking rainy season. Rainfall data from an eastern-most weather station in Sudan illustrate the heavy concentration during the months of June, July and August (Figure 6.1). The constriction of the rainy season as well as its variability poses serious consequences for refugees who chose to return home. Pastoralists and small-scale cultivators are in the most precarious position.

Agriculture is the mainstay of the Eritrean economy. Four-fifths of the total Eritrean population earn their living from the land. According to a survey of two-thirds of Eritrea's 182 districts, carried out in late 1987 with the co-operation of the Eritrean Peoples Liberation Front (EPLF), 61 per cent of the rural population are settled agriculturalists, 31 per cent are agropastoralists, and the remaining 8 per cent are pastoralists (Agriculture and Rural Development Unit cited in Pateman, 1990: 179). Drought has taken its toll on each of these livelihoods. During the 1980s it is estimated that crop production declined by 40 per cent and the number of livestock fell by 50 per cent (Agricultural Commission, 1992: 92). Additional losses continued under low rainfall conditions during the first two agricultural seasons of the 1990s. The 1992 season was boosted by the best rains in 15 years. The total harvest quadrupled that of the previous season (Wise, 1993: 1). Despite record-setting harvests, imports were still needed to cover half of the country's grain needs.

The transformation of subsistence agriculture is clearly a central issue to the short-

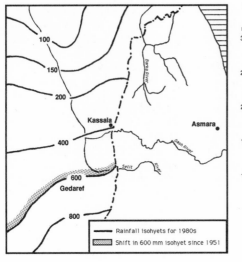

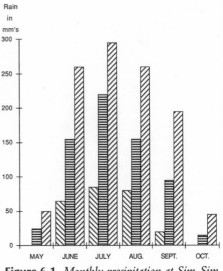

Map 6.2 *Annual rainfall in the border regions of Sudan (in mm). (Mickels and Yousif, 1987)*

Figure 6.1 *Monthly precipitation at Sim-Sim weather station, 1981–5. (Chordi, 1988)*

6.3 *The constriction of the rainy season as well as its variability places pastoralists and small-scale cultivators in a precarious position. (Johnathan Bascom)*

term and long-term success of returning
households as well as the entire country. It
is imperative that the new Eritrean state
facilitate the peasantry's access to credits,
fertilizers, improved seeds, and farm
implements as well as establish favourable
terms of trade for agricultural products.
These preconditions are needed for several
prominent reasons: a) to encourage
refugees to return to agricultural occupations; b) to generate capital locally and,
thereby, stimulate recovery and growth in
rural areas; and, c) to encourage people to
stay in agriculture and 'on the land' when
inevitable crises in climate and food
resources occur.

Eritrea's first investment code opens
the door to the privatization of large-scale
agriculture. Issaias Afewerki, chairman of
the provisional government of Eritrea, has
declared that 'Hotels, industries and
agricultural estates are on sale. Anyone can
buy them. We need money to rebuild our

6.4 *Refugee herders move small ruminants
and cattle further and further due to rising
prices for grazing rights. (Johnathan Bascom)*

economy' (cited in Misser, 1992: 47). Eligible investments in agriculture are exempt
from income tax for two years if they are under US$300,000 and for five years if they are
over US$1 million (Misser, 1992). Whether sufficient investment in mechanized
agriculture will occur to stimulate a sizeable demand for agricultural wage labourers
remains to be seen. Southwestern Eritrea is the prime location for such ventures. Ideally,
these mechanized, rainfed schemes will increase agricultural productivity and
employment opportunities in an environmentally sound manner. Eritrea can ill-afford
the kind of wholesale degradation that has characterized the spread of mechanized
agriculture in eastern Sudan.

New rural expectations

Major cultural and social transformations in exile complicate attempts to return to
traditional agrarian societies or to promote co-operative activities to work the land,
rebuild homes, and re-establish basic services (Rogge, 1991: 8). Ninety-one per cent of
respondents in Wad el Hileau believe that upon return they will go back to 'the ways of
nafir' (group work parties). Non-monetized exchanges of labour in group work parties
were the quintessential expression of the social interdependence and reciprocity that
characterized pre-flight economies in the lowland region. Although respondents readily
acknowledge that *nafir* is dying out in Sudan, they stress that it is still a 'habit' for those
who remained in Eritrea throughout the war and that new growth can be expected
because such a limited amount of money is circulating throughout rural areas.

At the same time, however, returnees have very different expectations than when
they left. Livelihoods and lifestyles have both changed. Using a sample of 380 households which returned during the first nine months of 1990, Habte-Selassie (1992a)
reports a drop from 85 per cent of the number of households being primarily engaged in
the rural economy before flight to 65 per cent engaged in agricultural activities upon
return. Virtually all exiles in Sudan have shifted to a form of agriculture that is far more
dependent upon mechanization, wage labour, and large capital inputs. The average-sized
holding before flight to Sudan was, for example, 13 feddans among interviewed

6.5 *House-raisings are a last vestige of 'nafirs' or group work parties. (Johnathan Bascom)*

households in Wad el Hileau (1 feddan = 0.44 hectares). When the same respondents were asked how many feddans they would require upon return they indicated an average of 30 feddans. The vast majority of refugee peasants have relied on tractors for cultivation in Sudan, but the mechanization of smallholder agriculture, even in the most developed agricultural zones of Eritrea, has been marginal. Over 90 per cent of subsistence farmers in Eritrea rely on draught animal power (Gebremedhin, 1992: 102). Hence, the reintegration programme will need to take into account the nature of the agrarian transformation that took place during exile, particularly among unassisted refugees in rural settings.

New urban expectations
The process of reintegration will be difficult after living in large refugee camps. Habte-Selassie (1992a) predicts an elevated desire on the part of returnees to settle in urban locations associated after their extended stay in refugee camps. He argues that long stays in large settlements of 10,000–30,000 people has inculcated a new expectation and craving for the amenities of urban life like ready access to schools, clinics, running water and flour mills. All the towns in the western lowlands – Agordat, Barentu, Haikota, Om Hager, Tessenei – will be favourite destinations. Returnees comprise 90 per cent of the residents in the border town of Tessenei already (Habte-Selassie, 1992a). To avoid collapse of the already depleted infrastructure, the provisional government of Eritrea closed the town to any more new-comers (Kibreab, 1992).

Urban employment poses another difficult challenge. Many returnees from camps will be ill-equipped – technically and socially – for farming, especially in an ecosystem that consistently receives marginal amounts of precipitation. Fifty to sixty per cent of the returnees to Namibia were unable to procure employment (Tapscott and Mulongeni cited in Simon and Preston, 1993). In Eritrea, there is already an immediate demand posed by as many as 100,000 former soldiers who require employment (Habte-Selassie, 1992b: 2).

One way in which returnees can be expected to relieve the intense demand for labour is to seek employment in Sudan. Fifty-four per cent of the respondents in Wad el Hileau already plan to travel back to Sudan after repatriation. Most obviously, Sudan offers a massive demand for agricultural labour. A traditional measure in Eritrea to cope with droughts is to work seasonally for wages in Sudan (Pateman, 1990: 180). Moreover, the principal source of income for poorer refugee households living in Sudan has been agricultural wage labour on mechanized rainfed schemes. Undoubtedly, at first many returning households will allocate their labour on both sides of the border. Male members are apt to return to Sudan during the peak of the agricultural season and entrust subsistence plots in Eritrea to the rest of the household. Informants in Wad el Hileau report that recent repatriates have already begun doing so. Substantial circular migration back and forth can be expected for other reasons as well. Eastern Sudan and western Eritrea have historically constituted a single grazing zone. Market opportunities and educational opportunities will draw former refugees back to Sudan as well. Maintaining an 'open door' policy that allows unhampered movement between regions will be vital to the success of the reintegration process in Eritrea.

6.6 *Mechanization has encouraged widespread agrarian transformation during exile in Sudan, while mechanization of smallholder agriculture in Eritrea has been marginal. The reintegration programme will need to take this into account. (Johnathan Bascom)*

Conclusion

This analysis, built on observations and data from eastern Sudan, suggests that repatriation decisions do reflect a motivation and mental preparation by refugees to participate in the process of reconstructing the area to which they return. Their contribution cannot be overlooked; repatriates' active participation is a fundamental prerequisite for the rehabilitation and development of the regions to which they return. The ongoing programme for the repatriation, reintegration and rehabilitation must provide returnees with a central role in that process for several important reasons. First,

6.7 *The refugees have had access to certain amenities, such as school, clinics, running water and flour mills. It is unlikely that they will readily give these things up following repatriation: a refugee woman grinding grain in the traditional manner. (Johnathan Bascom)*

the Eritrean people are, after all, the country's principal resource. Second, international assistance to reconstruct the damaged economy and environment has been slow to materialize. Third, rural migration can be, and often is, a positive force in agricultural development (Mollet, 1991). In the case of the Eritrean repatriation, refugees will bring a new infusion of resourcefulness, capital and skills with them to *their* homeland.

Lessons from post-war Mozambique may be useful in the Eritrean context (Myers, 1992). Rather than focus on an elaborate resettlement programme, donors and the government are being encouraged to allow people to resettle themselves and focus on the revitalization of the agricultural sector instead. This kind of approach allows the returning population more freedom in making their own choices about where to live and how to live. Shifting the focus of concern from a resettlement programme to a broader scope has advantages. Most important, it helps to: a) mitigate against tensions between 'stayees' and 'returnees'; b) encourage returnees to marshal co-operative efforts and self-help projects on their own behalf; and, c) 'dovetail' resettlement programmes together with the longer-term imperative of rural, regional, and sector development.

Recent reports describe the new country of Eritrea as 'one, grand self-help project' (Wise, 1993: 1). While Eritrea's independence is a vibrant testimony to an enduring co-operative ethic in the past, the process of post-war rehabilitation now requires new forms of co-operation. One key point of stimulus will be 'grassroot efforts' that originate among rural households. Among exiles in Sudan the commodification of social relationships has eroded the bases for productive co-operation that once existed between households. Potential returnees are confident that 'dormant' social and cultural networks can help them resolve conflicting land claims in Eritrea and that co-operative work parties are still a central component of agrarian life and society. Nonetheless, it remains to be seen how heavily returnees will actually depend on self-organization for working their land, rebuilding their homes and re-establishing basic services. If co-operative efforts do emerge among returnees will they be rooted in 'survival' imperatives, social relationships, or political associations? Undoubtedly, the answer may be all three given the formidable task of re-establishing themselves in a fragile ecosystem, the residual legacy of social relationships on which to build, and a new communal 'ethic' of collective solidarity forged by the EPLF during 25 years of conflict.

Acknowledgement

Research on which this chapter is based was funded by a generous and timely grant from the American Philosophical Society.

References

Agricultural Commission, EPLF (1992) 'Problems, prospective policies and programs for agricultural development in Eritrea', in *Emergent Eritrea: Challenges of economic development*, G. Tesfagiorgis (ed.), The Provisional Government of Eritrea and Eritreans for Peace and Democracy in North America, Washington, DC.

Ahmad, U. (1986) 'Self-settled refugees in Gedaref (Eastern Sudan)', Report for United Nations High Commissioner for Refugees, Khartoum.

Ali, T. (1991) 'Sudan planning mission for voluntary repatriation to Eritrea: registration, assistance entitlement, and population processing – 21 October–5 November 1991', Programme and technical support section mission report 91/35, United Nations High Commissioner for Refugees, Geneva.

Bascom, J. (1990) 'Food, wages and profits: mechanized schemes and the Sudanese state', *Economic Geography*, 66: 140–55.

— (1993) 'The peasant economy of refugee resettlement in eastern Sudan', *Annals of the Association of American Geographers*, 83: 320–46.

— (1994) 'The dynamics of refugee repatriation: the case of Eritreans in eastern Sudan', in *Population migration and the changing world order*, Gould, W. and Findlay, A. (eds), 225–48, John Wiley and Sons, London.

Bulcha, M. (1988) *Flight and integration: causes of mass exodus from Ethiopia and problems of integration in the Sudan*, Scandinavian Institute of African Studies, Uppsala.

Carney, J. and Watts, M. (1990) 'Manufacturing dissent: work, gender and the politics of meaning in a peasant society', *Africa*, 6: 207–41.

Chordi, V. (1988) 'South Kassala agriculture project – water component, technical support service', mission report for United Nations High Commission for Refugees, Geneva.

Commission for Eritrean Refugee Affairs. (CERA) (1992a) 'Current status of the repatriation programme and the way forward', unpublished mimeograph of conference paper, (29 April).

— (1992b) 'Appeal to donor governments', *Refugee Participation Network*, 13: 37–8.

— (1993) 'Repatriation and reintegration project', unpublished mimeograph of project proposal for 500,000 Eritrean refugees in the Sudan.

De Jong, G. and Gardner, R. (1981) 'Introduction and overview', in *Migration decision making: multidisciplinary approaches to microlevel studies in developed and developing countries*, G. De Jong and R. Gardner (eds) 1–2, Pergamon Press, New York.

Dwyer, D. and Bruce, J. (1988) *A home divided: women and income in the third world*, Stanford University Press, Stanford, CA.

Gebremedhin, T. (1992) 'Agricultural development in Eritrea: economic and policy analysis', in *Emergent Eritrea: challenges of economic development*, G. Tesfagiorgis (ed.), The Provisional Government of Eritrea and Eritreans for Peace and Democracy in North America, Washington, DC.

Guyer, J. and Peters, P. (1987) 'Conceptualizing the household', *Development and Change*, 18: 97–213.

Habte-Selassie, E. (1992a) 'Eritrean refugees in the Sudan: a preliminary analysis of voluntary repatriation', in *Beyond conflict in the Horn: prospects for peace, recovery and development in Ethiopia, Somalia and the Sudan*, eds. M. Doornbos, L. Cliffe, A. Ghaffar M. Ahmed and J. Markakis, James Currey, London.

Habte-Selassie, E. (1992b). 'Reintegration of returnees: challenges in post liberation Eritrea', unpublished mimeo for symposium for the Horn of Africa on the social and economic aspects of mass voluntary return movements of refugees, Addis Ababa, Ethiopia (14–18 September).

Hamilton, V. (ed.) (1986–95) *World refugee survey*, US Committee for Refugees, Washington, DC.

Harrell-Bond, B. (1986) *Imposing aid: emergency assistance to refugees*, Oxford University Press, Oxford.

Hendrie, B. (1992) 'The Tigrean refugee repatriation: Sudan to Ethiopia, 1985–7', *Journal of Refugee Studies*, 5.

Hyden, G. (1983) *No shortcuts to progress: African development management in perspective*, University of California Press, Berkeley, CA.

Johnson, T. and M. Johnson (1981) 'Eritrea: the national question and the logic of protracted struggle', *African Affairs*, 80: 81–95.

Kibreab, G. (1987) *Refugees and development in Africa: the case of Eritrea*, The Red Sea Press, Trenton, NJ.

— (1992) 'Prospects for re-establishment of the returning Eritrean refugees', Symposium for the Horn of Africa on the social and economic aspects of mass voluntary return movements of refugees, Addis Ababa, Ethiopia, 15–17 September, UNRISD.

Koser, K. (1993) 'Repatriation and information: a theoretical model', in *Geography and refugees: patterns and processes of change*, Black, R. and Robinson, V. (eds), 33–46, Belhaven Press, London.

Longrigg, S. (1974 [1945]) *A short history of Eritrea*, Greenwood Press, Westport, CT.

Mengisteab, K. (1992) 'Rehabilitation of degraded land in Eritrea's agricultural policy: an exploratory study', in *Emergent Eritrea: challenges of economic development*, G. Tesfagiorgis (ed.), 110–17, The Provisional Government of Eritrea and Eritreans for Peace and Democracy in North America, Washington, DC.

Mickels, G. and Yousif, H. (1987) 'The project for mechanization of agriculture in the refugee settlement areas – a study of context and beneficiaries', Report for Finnish International Development Agency.

Misser, F. (1992) 'Eritrea seeks to attract foreign investment', *African Business*, p. 47.

Mollet, J. (ed.) (1991) *Migrants in agricultural development: a study in intrarural migration*, New York University Press, Washington Square, NY.

Myers, G. (1992) 'Land tenure and resettlement in post-war Mozambique: capacity and individual choice', unpublished mimeographed paper, Land Tenure Center, University of Wisconsin, Madison.

Pateman, R. (1990) *Eritrea: even the stones are burning*, The Red Sea Press., Trenton, NJ.

Rogge, J. (1994) 'Repatriation of refugees: a not so simple "optimum" solution', in *When refugees go home: African experiences*, Allen, T. and H. Morsink (eds), 14–49, James Currey, London/Africa World Press, Trenton, NJ.

Simon, D. and Preston, R. (1993). 'Return to the promised land: the repatriation and resettlement of Namibian refugees', in *Geography and refugees: patterns and processes of change*, R. Black and V. Robinson (eds), 46–63, Belhaven Press, London.

Stein, B. (1992) 'Policy challenges regarding repatriation in the 1990s: is 1992 the year for voluntary repatriation?' paper commissioned by the Program on International and US Refugee Policy, The Fletcher School of Law and Diplomacy, Tufts University.

Wijbrandi, J. (1990) 'Organized and spontaneous settlement', in *Enduring crisis: refugee problems in eastern Sudan*, T. and Kuhlman and H. Tieleman (eds), African Studies Centre, Leiden, The Netherlands.

Wise, T. (1993) 'Hope in the Horn', *Insights, 7* (Newsletter for Grassroots International).

Wood, W. (1989) 'Long time coming: the repatriation of Afghan refugees', *Annals of the Association of American Geographers*, 79: 45–69.

7 DAVID STYAN
Eritrea 1993

The End of the Beginning

Introduction: the Provisional Government of Eritrea (PGE) May 1991–April 1993

For three months in 1993 history in the Horn of Africa appeared to accelerate; an over-whelming 'yes' for Eritrean independence in April's meticulously planned referendum opening the way for the celebration of Eritrean independence in Asmara on 24 May. Several weeks later the arrival of the 52nd state on Africa's post-colonial political stage was uncompromisingly announced by the Eritrean president's attack on the continent's political elite at the OAU's 30th anniversary summit in Cairo. Predictably, Eritrean statehood was accompanied by much misinformed media speculation about the implications of 'secession' on the Horn and Africa's post-colonial map, in which hyperbole appeared directly proportional to the dearth of factual analysis about the future political and economic prospects of the Eritrean state and its role in the region.[1]

The watershed of Eritrea's formal independence cannot be understood in either regional or chronological isolation. In many respects May 1993 merely marks the end of the beginning. For around 3 million Eritreans independence heralded the final end of 30 years of war and the conclusion of two years of provisional government by the Eritrean People's Liberation Front (EPLF).[2] It marked the beginning of a process to fashion a pluralist civilian identity from a monolithic nationalist movement against a background of extreme economic fragility. For the region's politicians the confirmation of Eritrean independence is a foundation stone of the search for a durable regional settlement, a necessary precondition for tackling the Horn's agricultural and ecological crises.

The festivities and euphoria of April and May 1993 were essentially symbolic. The referendum formally ratified the events of May 1991, legitimizing the EPLF's military victory in both domestic and international eyes. The symbolic nature of the referendum prompts two observations: first that it is the battles of 1991, not the voting of 1993, which mark the real regional shifts in power; it was the conclusion of these battles which reconfigured the region's politics with implications far beyond Eritrea and Ethiopia.[3]

---

[1] This is an amended version of an article written in 1993 and first published in *Afrique politique 1994: vue sur la démocratisation à marée basse*, edited by CEAN-Bordeaux, Karthala (Paris) 1994.

[2] Precise population figures are controversial; 1.1 million adults registered to vote in the referendum. The current domestic population is probably a little over 2 million, with around 500,000 refugees set to return from Sudan. Up to another half a million are exiled elsewhere, the majority in Ethiopia itself.

[3] Alongside the independence of Eritrea and the total reconfiguration of Ethiopia politics, the end of the war had significant consequences for conflicts in Sudan, Djibouti and Somalia. It also prompted a radical restructuring of US and Israeli policy in the region. On Sudan, Somalia and the US policies see *Politique Africaine*, No. 49, Karthala (Paris), June 1993.

7.1 *'We born today': Celebrating formal independence in Asmara, May 1991.*
(Dario Mitidieri, CAFOD)

Secondly, that however enthusiastically Eritreans embraced their referendum and independence, the focussing of public life solely on these goals during the provisional period served to obscure the economic realities facing Eritrea. Economic imperatives will condition the decisions of Eritrean politicians throughout the nineties. In the two-year period of provisional government, from May 1991 until the April 1993 referendum, crucial decisions about future policies were overshadowed by the imperatives of organizing the referendum. This reflects the EPLF leadership's caution and doubts about the limitation of their longer term economic and political options. Against this background the EPLF Central Committee declared a further four-year 'transitional' period from May 1993. Although a full EPLF congress began to debate the state's constitution early in 1994, constitutional details are to be worked out by a constitutional commission and an elected government is not scheduled to be in place before 1997.

This chapter briefly chronicles the two years of provisional rule leading up to the referendum. After discussing the background and modalities of the referendum itself, it evaluates the problems of political disentanglement from Ethiopia and the implications of the emergence of Eritrea as a significant regional force, assessing the new state's foreign policy in the Horn and the Middle East. It then examines the domestic political agenda and sketches the main economic constraints facing the nascent Eritrean state. In conclusion, the article evaluates the future through the prism of Eritrea's essential paradox, that of a cohesive political machine in charge of the continent's most impoverished economy.

The PGE's Inheritance: War and Division

This is neither the time nor the place to review the decades of political and military struggle, both within the Eritrean nationalist movement and against successive Ethiopian regimes, which culminated in the liberation of April–May 1991.[4] However, two legacies of the convoluted struggle will continue to shape the post-1991 landscape; divisions *within* the nationalist movement and the scale of human destruction wrought by three decades of war.

The effects of the prolonged internecine conflict between the EPLF and the Eritrean Liberation Front (ELF) largely accounted for the Eritreans' failure to consolidate their initial military advances against the Derg in 1977. In the civil war the EPLF politically and militarily outflanked its more parochial forerunner and in the eighties the Front consolidated its hegemony over the national movement. This ultimately brought the EPLF military victory and total dominance of the post-independence state. Yet it is the background of bitter divisions within the nationalist movement, as much as the EPLF's ideological orientations or the imperatives of war, which account for the Front's tightly centralized internal organization. Inflexible structures and ingrained political habit in large part explain the key features of the provisional period: the EPLF's legal monopoly on political power, their *dirigiste* economic stance, complete state control of the media and persistent doubts about the substance and timing of political pluralism.

Whilst the remnant factions of the ELF were largely co-opted into the state during the provisional period, two worries remain. Firstly that deep-rooted factional and individual animosities may resurface in the guise of civilian politics, particularly given the limited resources available for political patronage. The second, more immediate worry is how to reduce and reform the monolithic power of the EPLF in order to provide flexible foundations for a pluralist political system. The much delayed third EPLF

---

[4] For a full account of internal divisions see Markakis (1987: 104–45). For an initial, fragmentary account of the end of the war see Africa Watch (1991: 235-288).

congress was finally held in Nacfa, in the northern province of Sahel, in mid-February 1994. The congress renamed the organization the People's Front for Democracy and Justice (PFDJ). A 19-person executive was elected, composed largely of figures who had not been in the former EPLF politbureau.[5]

The second legacy is that of the human destruction wrought by decades of war. In evaluating the current political and economic realities there is inevitably a tendency to forget the scale and intensity of fighting in the final years of war. This will remain the dominant legacy in decades to come, not simply in terms of physical destruction of infrastructure, but also in terms of human losses and public attitudes to political authority. The battles of Afabet in March 1988, generally regarded as the turning point of the war in the north, left over 15,000 Ethiopian soldiers dead; the EPLF's capture of Massawa early in 1990 resulted in similarly heavy casualties. Whilst Eritrean losses in such battles as well as in subsequent systematic aerial bombardment were far lower than the Ethiopians', in proportion to the tiny Eritrean population they were devastating. According to the official EPLF estimate, 40,000 combatants and 60,000 civilians were killed, around 3–4 per cent of the total population. In addition 10,000 adults are permanently maimed and the state is caring for 90,000 orphans.[6] Decades of bereavement and sacrifice bind the Front to the population in an ambiguous, double-edged relationship. The EPLF commands extensive support having brought an end to the carnage, yet in return it is expected to perpetuate the memory of those sacrificed and to provide those who survived a peaceful and prosperous future. As in post-war Europe, losses in battle will remain a potent symbol of national unity. How long this can be used to legitimize the privations of the post-war state remains to be seen. Clearly there are other legacies of the war. In the wake of the defeat of the Ethiopian army in May 1991, the EPLF had 100,000 people under arms. Overnight it became the region's superpower with the largest army in the Horn. It also inherited a vast arsenal; there can be few more eloquent graveyards of the cold war than the ranks of rusted Soviet tank carcasses behind the Kagnew base in Asmara. This legacy makes demobilization of highly politicized fighters among the most pressing post-independence tasks. Lastly, the political legacy of the role played by the EPLF in the downfall of the Mengistu regime, not just by crushing the army in Eritrea, but also in assisting the Ethiopian People's Revolutionary Democratic Front's (EPRDF's) assault in central Shoa and Addis Ababa, has been to bind them more closely to the EPRDF, although the contours of this interdependence remain largely obscured.

Given the magnitude of destruction in the final years of the war the end came mercifully quickly, Assab was captured on 24 May with only minor damage and Asmara was unscathed save for scarring of the city's Italian boulevards by jubilant EPLF tank crews. One of the many ironies of the change was that its most senior actors were absent. Secretary-General Issayas Afeworki and several high-ranking EPLF officials were in London attending the hastily convened discussions under the auspices of Herman Cohen, the then US assistant secretary of state for Africa. In the event the 'negotiations' became rites of passage of the new order. With EPLF troops entering Asmara, Issayas attended the Ethiopian talks only as an observer. On 29 May, with US blessing, the secretary-general unilaterally announced de-facto Eritrean independence and the formation of a provisional government to rule Eritrea for a two-year period pending a referendum.

Ethiopia's new rulers, the EPRDF, dominated by the EPLF's Tigrayan namesakes, formally endorsed Eritrean independence during the July 1991 transitional conference in

---

[5] The second EPLF congress was held in March 1987. See 'Congress in Eritrea' L. Cliffe (1987), *Review of African Political Economy*, Winter: October 1991.
[6] P. 23, *Eritrea, birth of a nation*, Government of Eritrea.

Addis Ababa. This conference promulgated the Transitional Charter as the basis of legitimacy for the Ethiopian transitional government for up to 30 months. The conference and charter provided for the separation of Eritrea, which was approved in the presence of the EPLF leadership.[7]

Within Eritrea the three months following liberation were chaotic, euphoric and distressing. Families were reunited, casualties were confirmed as fighters regrouped and EPLF departments installed themselves in Asmara. Immediate problems of demobilization, employment and accommodation were sidestepped by the decision that fighters would continue to work voluntarily for the two-year provisional period. This decision was supplemented by a November 1991 decree on national service for all youths. Little has been published in English about what happened to the Ethiopian officers and soldiers in the chaos of May–June 1991 as Africa's largest army crumpled and upwards of 200,000 soldiers and dependants based in Eritrea fled. Officially the EPLF captured 82,000 prisoners and 44,000 dependants. Perversely, the flight of the Ethiopian army became a public relations disaster that would publicly dog the EPLF throughout the first year of the provisional period.[8] The first phase of liberation came to a close on 1 September 1991, with the celebration of the 30th anniversary of the armed struggle.[9]

Despite considerable domestic pressure to unilaterally declare immediate independence, the EPLF's decision to wait for an internationally supervised referendum two years later was based on several considerations. Firstly it gave the EPLF time both to thoroughly prepare the referendum and determine their own peacetime agenda. It also allowed the practical details of separation, ranging from the immediate repatriation of prisoners of war to the long and drawn-out process of disentangling ownership of bank accounts and fixed assets, to be negotiated with the Ethiopian authorities. The EPLF leadership has been exceedingly cautious over the timing of reform since liberation. This reflects their habitual pragmatism; about both the capabilities of their personnel and the complexities of organizing the referendum. EPLF attitudes are in stark contrast to the EPRDF who have repeatedly overestimated their organizational capacities, particularly over transitional electoral timetables. Secondly, the two-year delay stemmed from the Front's desire for international legitimacy for independence based on a popular vote rather than military victory by the EPLF. This point was made repeatedly in official statements: in the words of the Secretary-General the EPLF 'did not declare the independence of Eritrea by getting drunk on its military victory'.[10]

The April 1993 Referendum

PGE decree No. 22 of 7 April 1992 established the timing and modalities of the referendum. This defined the ballot question as 'Do you want Eritrea to be an independent

---

[7] 'Transitional Period Charter of Ethiopia', *Negarit Gazeta* (Addis Ababa, English and Amharic) 22 July 1991. Eritrean independence was legitimized under Article Two, Section C, *the right of nations, nationalities and peoples to self-determination*. Confusingly, this same article underpins the domestic Ethiopian debate about regional governments based on ethnic identity. For further discussion of the contradictions of this see *Africa Confidential* (London), 25 October 1991.

[8] 'Statement on the repatriation of Ethiopian POWs', PGE, Office of Secretary-General, (Asmara) 1 August 1991. See also the Asmara press conference of 5 September 1991, recorded in *Summary of World Broadcasts* (*SWB*) 9 September 1991.

[9] The 1 September 1991 anniversary celebrations encapsulated the historiography of the nationalist struggle more accurately than the independence celebrations of 18 months later. The country was plastered with posters of veteran nationalists and the septuagenarian Wolde-Ab Wolde Marian was guest of honour. For an idiosyncratically poignant image of both the ambiguities of nationalism and Wolde-Ab's personal position in those months, see Harding (1993: 404–8). Wolde-Ab died in May 1995. For an appreciation see *London Review of Books*, 6 July 1995.

[10] *SWB* 28 November 1992.

country, yes or no?' The organization of the referendum was entrusted to a five-man Eritrean Referendum Commission (ERC) appointed by the secretary-general. Amare Tekle, a US-based academic, became referendum commissioner on 23 April, aided by four assistants, who were appointed for their seniority rather than EPLF credentials.[11] The ERC then spent a year preparing the referendum with voting taking place on 22–24 April 1993. Of the 1.1 million people who voted, only 2,000 voted against independence or spoilt their papers, giving a final yes vote of 99.8 per cent.

However, the road to international legitimacy was not as smooth as it appeared in retrospect. Despite the EPLF's clear desire to involve the United Nations, the UN's slow response generated friction with the Eritreans. In forming the ERC the EPLF announced unilaterally that the referendum would go ahead, even without UN participation, by the target date of April 1993. It was only three months later that Herman Cohen, US assistant secretary of state for Africa, pledged US support for the referendum and in July a UN technical group finally arrived in Asmara. In the event the Eritreans got the best of both worlds in that the modalities (and therefore the result) of the referendum were settled months before the establishment of the 21-member office of the United Nations Observer Mission to Verify the Referendum in Eritrea (UNOVER) in January 1993. Their skeleton staff were joined by 100 UN observers in the second week of April, with 40 more UN staff observing polling in Ethiopia and Sudan. This token UN force was therefore both cheap (US$3 million) and too small to seriously modify the ERC's slick operation, yet it provided the required legitimacy and provided a happy ending to the UN's sorry, 40-year record in Eritrea.[12] Many governments also contributed official observers. Several hundred journalists and independent observers, many drawn from the EPLF's extensive networks of supportive Western NGO's, further supplemented the UNOVER and Eritrean monitors. Observers were unanimous in the accuracy of the result and the fairness of the poll. The head of UNOVER, Samir Sanbar, stated that 'the referendum process can be considered to have been free and fair at every stage'. Observers expressed admiration for the ERC's technical competence in running over 1,000 polling stations and issuing over a million ID cards to a population in many cases both illiterate and inaccessible.

The referendum was undoubtedly a technical success, however its political outcome was never in doubt for several reasons. Firstly the ERC had decided from April 1992 that the ballot question on independence was to be simply yes or no. Any possible alternative were excluded. Secondly, whilst in theory a 'no' campaign was permitted, indeed UNOVER was mandated to ensure 'equal access to media facilities and fairness in the allocation of both timing and length of broadcasts', in practice there was no public opposition. With political parties in Eritrea banned and the discussion of any alternative to independence excluded by the wording of the ballot, there could be no grounds for opposition to the poll. Private political publications were prohibited during the provisional period. The third reason for the certainty of the referendum result was that in order to be eligible to vote Eritreans first had to register as a citizen of the new state. Those rejecting independence were hardly likely to first opt to become a citizen of the state only to vote against its existence, particularly among exiles in Ethiopia and elsewhere who had to register in their local EPLF offices. However, such details were little commented on by foreign observers, most of whom followed only the euphoric, closing stages of the protracted referendum process. Nevertheless, it should be stressed

---

[11] The full commission was Amare Tekle (Commissioner), Taha Mohammed Nur (secretariat), Idris Galawdeos (publicity and information), Asfaha Berhe (identification board), Safi Imam Musa (election board). *Eritrea Update (EU)* April, September 1992.

[12] The decision to create UNOVER was finally agreed by the UN only on 16 December. It was headed by Samir Sanbar, a veteran Lebanese UN official. The structure and costing (just under US$3mn) of UNOVER is set out in the 13-page report of the Secretary-General *Request to the UN to observe the referendum in Eritrea,* UN General Assembly A/47/544, 19 October 1992.

that even if the modalities had been more transparent this would have made little or no difference to the eventual result.

Whereas the register of voters for the domestic population provides a fairly accurate profile of population, figures for the diaspora underestimate the size of Eritrean communities to varying degrees. Of the 340,000 who voted outside of Eritrea, 154,000 were in Sudan, 58,000 in Ethiopia and 35,000 in Saudi Arabia. The remainder were largely in the Gulf, Western Europe and North America: 15,000 Eritreans voted in the USA, with the largest concentrations in San Francisco (3,000) and Washington DC (2,500).

Table 7.1 *Referendum results*

Area	Total	Yes	No	Invalid	% Yes
Asmara	128,620	128,443	144	33	99,86
Barka	44,472	44,425	47	0	99,89
Denkalia	26,027	25,907	91	29	99,54
Gash-Setit	73,506	73,236	270	0	99.63
Hamasien	76,716	76,654	59	3	99.92
Akele Guzai	92,634	92,465	147	22	99.82
Sahel	51,187	51,015	141	31	99.66
Semhar	33,750	33,596	113	41	99.54
Seraye	124,809	124,725	72	12	99.93
Senhit	78,540	78,513	26	1	99.97
Fighters	77,579	77,512	21	46	99.91
Sudan	154,058	153,706	352	0	99.77
Ethiopia	57,706	57,466	204	36	99.58
Other countries	82,506	82,597	135	74	99.81
Total	1 102,410	1 100,260	1,822	328	99.81

(*Source*: Government of Eritrea, May 1993)

Relations with Ethiopia

Whilst bearing in mind both that only adults voted, and that demography remains heavily skewed in favour of those under 18, the figures for Eritreans voting abroad still significantly underestimates the size of the Eritrean diaspora. This is most clearly so for Ethiopia where only 58,000 Eritreans voted. Given that children of mixed marriages could also vote, well under half of those eligible to vote did so within Ethiopia. This does not necessarily imply a lack of interest in, or opposition to, the notion of Eritrean citizenship. Rather it reflects the doubt in the minds of Eritreans resident in Ethiopia of the legal implications of opting for Eritrean citizenship (a necessary preliminary step to voting in the referendum) upon their residence status in Ethiopia. The ERC's position was clear, dual nationality was acceptable. Yet the Transitional Government of Ethiopia (TGE) had no policy on citizenship or nationality. In March 1993 interim Ethiopian president Meles Zenawi said that if someone chose Eritrean nationality 'he cannot continue as an employee of government institutions, but will be allowed to live in Ethiopia as any other alien'.[13] Given the preponderance of Eritreans in the Ethiopian civil service

[13] *SWB*, 3 April 1993.

and the associated complications of creating separate tax, property and inheritance laws for several hundred thousand people, the idea of this becoming law was highly unlikely. In fact in September 1993 freedom of movement and residence were established between the two countries.

With a virulently anti-EPRDF independent press in Ethiopia, Eritrea retains consider-able political resonance within Ethiopia's unsteady transitionary political landscape. Yet much of the domestic opposition erroneously equates the independence of Eritrea with the TGE's plans for regional self-government based on ethnic identity within Ethiopia. Much of the Addis Ababa-based press portrays both as a northern, specifically Tigrinya-speaking, plot to enfeeble Ethiopia. In reality the press's stereotyping of the EPLF and TPLF/EPRDF as twins is caricatural; serious differences periodically resurface and these have been accentuated by the very different post-liberation problems facing the two organizations. Indeed there is now a curious asymmetry between the erstwhile allies, the EPRDF holding all the economic power whilst the EPLF retain the political initiative, notably in its ill-fated efforts to broker a settlement between the EPRDF and Oromo Liberation Front (OLF) in mid-1992. Undoubtedly relations are good at the highest level. This is underlined by frequent private discussions between Meles and Issayas. Yet Issayas' first official visit to Addis in July 1993 was relatively low key, and beneath the surface relations have been frequently strained by the practicalities of separation. Differences stem from two sources: the long-standing historical and ideological tensions between the two fronts, the complexity and confusion of disentangling the two states.[14]

Throughout the provisional period ad-hoc committees were formed to settle urgent bilateral issues: the use of ports, post and telecommunications, monetary issues etc. Agreements on trade, transit and port services were signed in January 1992, notably guaranteeing Assab as a free port for Ethiopia. Following the 30 July 1993 heads of state meeting, the first joint high ministerial committee (JMC) met in Asmara from 22–27 September 1993 under the joint-chairmanship of Ethiopian Prime Minister, Tamrat Layne, and the Eritrean Minister of Local Government, former EPLF Secretary-General, Ramadan Mohammed Nur. Three joint committees; political, economic and social affairs, were created and a series of protocols signed, most importantly on the 'harmonization of economic policies.[15] Issayas Afeworki was again in Addis both for the Inter-Governmental Authority on Drought and Development (IGAAD) summit in September and then in mid-October when the two leaders underlined the importance of the JMC and the need to strengthen regional co-operation, notably on Somalia, through IGADD. In terms of longer term relations between the two countries, much media attention focussed in the carefully worded statements of Issayas Afeworki immediately after the referendum. Speaking in Amharic on Ethiopian radio he stressed the need to strengthen ties between Eritrean and Ethiopian peoples, saying that economic co-operation and integration could lead to political ties, even confederation in the future.[16] However, a more immediate concern of the two governments was perceived antipathy towards Eritrean separation by Ethiopian civil servants who were blamed for many of the initial delays on bilateral issues, with both Eritrean and EPRDF officials muttering darkly about 'Amhara sabotage' of their plans. The creation of what amounts to a parallel administration around the office of the Prime Minister of the Transitional government of Ethiopia appears to have been in part a response to bureaucratic obstructionism to directives on Eritrea and other sensitive issues.

---

[14] There are historical, ideological and cultural reasons behind the differences, see Markakis (1987: 256–8).
[15] Joint communiqué, Ethio-Eritrean JMC, 27 September 1993. *Ethiopian Herald* (*EH*), 7 September 1993, 19 October 1993.
[16] Voice of Ethiopia, *SWB*, 1 May 1993.

Eritrea's Regional Relations

Given Eritrea's geographical and political isolation, the EPLF's unique status as cold war pariahs – a progressive liberation front fighting the Soviet Union's principal ally in Africa – the imperatives of securing military supplies and food aid, and the vicissitudes of exile politics, the EPLF could not have survived without an imaginative foreign policy and tenacious overseas missions. This legacy in part explains the high respect and international profile of EPLF diplomacy, which is out of all proportion to Eritrea's diminutive population and economy. The EPLF's breadth of contacts and experience within the Horn explain the lead role it has played since May 1991 in attempts to broker regional settlements, between the EPRDF and OLF in mid-1992, repeated peace initiatives in Somalia and offers in 1993 to mediate in the civil conflicts in both Djibouti and Yemen. Joint Eritrean and EPRDF negotiations in the Somalia imbroglio from early 1992 onwards were arrogantly swept aside by the US intervention, only to be revived nine months later as US and UN diplomats recoiled from their own political blunders.

Some of the salient aspects of the EPLF/EPRDF relationship have already been highlighted. For the EPLF close relations with successive Sudanese governments were of paramount importance. For three decades Sudan was the hinterland of the Eritrean struggle; a political base providing supply lines and hosting a refugee population of over half a million. The Sudanese president was the first head of state to visit Eritrea on 7–8 March 1992. Large Sudanese ministerial delegations received place of honour at ceremonial occasions and Hassan El-Turabi, *eminence grise* of the Sudanese National Islamic Front, was received with honours in Eritrea in January 1992. Political relations were buttressed by trade between the two countries and free movement of people. However, given the avowedly secular nature of the Asmara government and the large numbers of refugees in Sudan, fears of Sudanese sponsorship of militant Eritrean Islamic movements were to strain relations to breaking point by December 1994. Relations with Egypt are good and the PGE appears to have made use of rivalry between Egypt and Sudan to its advantage. Despite friction over fishing vessels and criticism of Eritrea's relations with Israel in the Egyptian press, formal relations with Egypt are cordial. In December 1991 Issayas Afeworki visited the Presidents of Yemen and Egypt as well as the Secretary-General of the Arab League and the then UN Secretary-General elect, Boutros Boutros Ghali in Cairo.

Eritrea's Dahlak Islands lie just 200 km from Saudi Arabia; with the Red Sea coastline within proximity of Jeddah and Mecca relations with the Gulf's economic giant are crucial for Eritrea. Yet past relations between the Saudi government and the EPLF have been poor. Within three months of liberation Issayas Afeworki accused Saudi Arabia (along with France) of seeking to destabilize the fledgling state. Animosity was based on both Saudi support for Eritrean factions opposed to the EPLF and a failure to provide food and material support to the Eritrean people. The former role appeared to briefly resurface with the announcement in September 1992 of the formation in Jeddah of the 'Eritrean National Pact Alliance'.[17] Although there had been low-level diplomatic contact between the PGE and Saudi during 1992, Issayas Afeworki's 1993 New Year's speech bitterly attacked the Saudi authorities.[18] Three weeks later the EPLF's Jeddah office was closed and four diplomats were expelled, jeopardizing the referendum votes

---

[17] This Eritrean National Pact Alliance was ostensibly composed of the Eritrean Liberation Front – United Organization (ELF-UO), the ELF-Revolutionary Council, ELF-Central Command and the Eritrean Democratic Liberation Movement (EDLM). By this time several key figures in these organizations had already rallied to the PGE in Asmara. Their statement of 28 September 1992 backs the referendum and full independence for Eritrea but contests the EPLF's dominance. *SWB*, 30 September 1992.

[18] New Year's Message of PGE Secretary-General, Asmara 31 December 1992. (English).

of the 35,000 Eritreans who had already registered in Jeddah. The dispute was solved by Samir Sanbar, the Lebanese head of UNOVER, just days before the April poll; subsequently the Kingdom recognized the new state, attending the May independence celebrations and sending a ship with aid. Issayas Afeworki then made a state visit to Riyad as part of his post-independence regional tour.

Eritrea's problems with Saudi coincided with the consolidation of ties with another Red Sea ally, Israel. On the surface, EPLF ties with Israel appear paradoxical; successive Ethiopian governments received significant Israeli military assistance specifically to prevent the emergence of an independent 'Arab' Eritrean state in the Red Sea. Nevertheless Eritrean leaders are open in their admiration for Israel, not simply as a source of technical and financial assistance, but as a model for development. The catalyst for these relations was unusual; an unconscious Issayas Afeworki arriving in Israel in a US air force plane on 6 January 1993 reportedly suffering from a relapse of cerebral malaria. This news was greeted with predictably outraged Arab editorials. After recovery and a return to Tel Aviv for a check-up Issayas praised the Israelis; diplomatic relations were established and Israel now plans an extensive programme of co-operation in Eritrea, notably in agriculture and health.[19]

Eritrea's ties with European states were based on aid and considerable support received from Western NGOs, notably from the UK and Scandinavia. Their aid has dropped off considerably since independence which has brought a closer relationship with the United States. The US promptly established a consulate in Asmara, in the fifties a hub of their interests in the Horn because of the Kagnew listening station. Italy is also keen to revive its bygone commercial interests. France's relations are conditioned by its patronage of the beleaguered government in neighbouring Djibouti, whose slide into civil war coincided with Eritrea's provisional period of government. In a press conference in September 1991, Issayas singled out France and Saudi Arabia for trying to destabilize Eritrea. For several months in late 1991 the PGE erroneously perceived the Afar rebellion in Djibouti as a French plot to destabilize Eritrea by 'creating a Djibouti-based Afar entity'.[20] By the time of the January 1992 visit of the French minister of foreign affairs to Asmara this curious stance had been revised. Eritreans subsequently offered to mediate between President Aptidon and the Afar rebels.

Postponing Domestic Politics

The true shape of the domestic political stage was obscured during the provisional period by the EPLF's legal monopoly on power. However, four spheres of political activity can be briefly examined: firstly the formal structures of state power, secondly the exiled opposition, composed essentially of former ELF factions, thirdly and most importantly the political process *within* the EPLF and fourthly the Front's relationship with civil society.

The formal structures of power revolve around the Central Committee (CC) of the EPLF. For the first year after liberation the Provisional Government of Eritrea announced in London was formed simply by the existing EPLF hierarchy. Even after de jure independence this remained essentially the case, although the structures and personnel have altered several times. Following the first post-independence meeting of the EPLF's full 71-member CC in May 1992, PGE proclamation 23 formalised the ad-hoc arrangements under which the country had been governed since liberation. The CC acted as a legislature for the remainder of the provisional period with the Secretary-General

---

[19] See 'Israel, Eritrea and Ethiopia: a convoluted relationship', *Middle East International* (London),No.456, 6 August 1993. For a Palestinian viewpoint see *Mideast Mirror* (London) 19 February 1993.
[20] *SWB*, 23–26 November 1991

heading a 28-member executive Advisory Council. This ruling body was composed of the heads of the 12 EPLF Departments, de-facto ministries, the 10 regional administrators and five representatives of the armed forces and navy. Immediately after the referendum the CC decreed a further mutation of government with a modified council becoming a cabinet. A National Assembly was formed comprising the whole of the CC, plus three representatives from each region and 30 additional appointed members. Ten of these seats were reserved for women, the others in principle allocated to non-EPLF figures.

Devolved, elected local authorities are frequently presented as primary evidence of the EPLF's commitment to democracy. PGE proclamation 26 of October 1992 outlined the new structures of local government. It confirmed the division of the country into 10 provinces (including the capital Asmara), plus eight urban districts, all other towns having the status of sub-districts.[21] Local elections were held for regional and town councils during the first half of 1992. These structures of central and local power were to provide the formal framework for the duration of the four-year transition period stretching to 1997. However, in May 1995 the 10 regions were reduced to six. One most notable characteristic of these arrangements is the accumulated powers of Issayas Afeworki who is simultaneously head of state, leader of executive and government, chief of the armed forces as well as secretary-general of the EPLF. This is paradoxical in that whilst Issayas has clearly eschewed any personality cult and appears ill-at-ease and uncharismatic on formal public occasions, he nevertheless remains the dominant public voice of the state. With the rare exceptions of brief comments by the GOE Foreign Minister and Eritrea's ambassador in Ethiopia, Haile Menkarios, virtually all international pronouncements during the provisional period were by Issayas himself.

The second sphere of domestic politics is that connected with the remaining factions of the ELF, the legacy of the three decades of internecine strife within the Eritrean nationalist movement mentioned earlier. The political aim of the two-year provisional period; i.e. the consolidation of the EPLF's hegemony over the nationalist project to ensure old rivalries did not scar the post-independence landscape, appears to have largely succeeded. With all non-EPLF organizations campaigning for independence they had little alternative but to support the PGE's referendum process, effectively depriving themselves of any opposition programme. Whilst an ELF representative in Rome protested to the UN against the EPLF's dominance of the referendum, all the factions opposed to the EPLF endorsed the referendum result and several Eritrean Democratic Liberation Movement (EDLM) members rallied to the GOE immediately after the referendum.[22] One by one leaders of factions returned to the fold, some taking senior positions within the provisional administration, notably the ELF-UO (United Organization) returned en masse in July 1992. Significantly, the referendum commission included non-EPLF figures. Despite the brief spectre of an opposition front composed of ELF factions, the Eritrean National Pact Alliance (ENPA), in September 1992, these forces are moribund, although some still maintain offices in Ethiopia. A more speculative opposition presence has been that of Eritrean Jihad, an Islamic grouping operating amongst lowland Eritreans within the camps in Sudan. Although Islamic political groupings exist, the significance of their presence has been exaggerated, not least by the PGE, which has repeatedly stressed that the state has enemies.

Given the marginalization of organized 'opposition' forces and the overwhelming dominance of the EPLF during both the provisional and current four-year transition it is clear that the crucial political arena is that within the EPLF itself. Internal politics, at least

[21] *SWB*, 16 October 1993.
[22] For the ELF Rome statement by Ali Musa see *Agence France Presse* (Paris) 16 December 1992. Ethiopian radio broadcast opposition groups' support for the referendum results on 21 April 1993. These included the Eritrean Liberation Front-Central Command and the Eritrean Democratic Liberation Movement (EDLM). See *SWB*, 23 April 1993. On the return of EDLM members see *SWB*, 4 May 1993.

to the outsider, were in suspended animation in the 30 months prior to the EPLF third congress, repeatedly postponed before finally being held in February 1994. Although at liberation it was assumed that a congress to decide on future policies of the Front would be held early in the provisional period, nothing happened. When pressed for explanations senior officials appear embarrassed and evasive about the delays. By the referendum the congress was said to be scheduled for July/August 1993. It was then postponed until early 1994. A preparatory committee for the third congress was appointed at the EPLF Central Committee meeting in February 1991, before liberation. However, it began work only after the fifth Central Committee meeting in May 1991. The sixth meeting in Semhar in February 1993 called for the circulation of the report by the preparatory committee. There are several explanations for the delays. Firstly there are unresolved differences over the future of the EPLF. Secondly policy divisions were compounded by the administrative overload placed on those with senior positions in the Front, leaving little time for strategic planning. Issayas stated several times that he felt the Front should have a 'non-political' role after independence. This was interpreted to mean either that the Front should dissolve itself into several competing factions, which would then form the basis of a multi-party system, or that the EPLF would assume the role of guardian of the nation, above and unsullied by the petty business of party politics. Issayas has been quizzed repeatedly on this point in press conferences. Immediately after liberation he stated that:

> The EPLF is a nationalist front embracing all sectors of society and many currents of thought. It will be a mistake to turn this broad front into political grouping which will inevitably mean a one-party state in Eritrea. Who will compete against us? We are simply serving as caretakers during the transition.[23]

He elaborated on this in November 1992:

> When we said that the EPLF will not exist, we mean to say that the EPLF will not exist as a liberation front... Our objective is to create a society where a continuous democratic system is ensured ... How this will be achieved will be up to the EPLF ... Thus while we shall not consider ourselves as a political organisation, we shall continue to participate constructively. Probably some people might think that this is because the EPLF wants to continue as a political organisation after the referendum, but we have no desire to continue as a political nucleus or as a political organisation. I would like to take this opportunity to note that there are some members of the EPLF who (hold) different views to mine.[24]

In the event the delayed third congress of February 1994 effectively maintained the structure of the EPLF intact, albeit with a rejuvenated executive committee and a new name, the People's Front for Democracy and Justice (PFDJ). Decisions concerning the modalities of the content of democracy were thus deferred to the commission charged with drafting a constitution under which elections are scheduled to be held in 1997.

Evidently tensions within the Front have to be resolved before anything definitive can be said about relations between the state and society in the new Eritrea. Undoubtedly the majority of the population have an unerringly high degree of confidence in their rulers. The EPLF having ended the war immediately restored basic services and reunited families, thus many Eritreans have unrealistic expectations of what the government will be able to provide its citizens after independence. So far government attitudes to organized civil society, be they religious, sports or commercial organizations, have tended to be interventionist; as during the armed struggle, the GOE views mass organizations as there to be organized or co-opted. This approach was strengthened by the task of mobilizing the population for the referendum. The apparatus of *kebeles*, urban neighbourhood committees, was maintained as the basic unit of urban government.

[23] Quoted in Okbazghi (1993: 23).
[24] Voice of the Broad Masses of Eritrea 27 November 1992; *SWB*, 1 December 1992.

7.2 *Children play among the remains of Ethiopia's soviet armoury, Asmara 1991. (Stephen King/CAFOD)*

These were used extensively for mobilization during the referendum.[25] Despite their entrenched secular positions, Eritrean leaders have been cautious to court both Moslem and Christian religious leaders; the population is estimated to be evenly split between Moslems and Christians. The Orthodox church in Eritrea promptly severed its links with the Orthodox church in Ethiopia and reverted back to the patriarch in Cairo.[26] Sheikh Alamin Osman was appointed as Mufti of Eritrea in mid-1992, Ethiopia having allowed no Mufti following the death of the Italian-appointed spiritual chief in 1969. However given the profound dislocations of society during the war, organized associative life outside the Front was rare at least up until 1993. The significant exception is that of traders and private capitalists. By both habit and necessity, the EPLF has adopted a heavily regulatory approach to economic activities. Price controls and state purchasing in markets for grain, sugar etc. were practised during the provisional period by the government and the quasi-official Nacfa corporation. Yet the poverty of the state places

[25] On the essential similarities between the rival policies of social mobilization of both rebel fronts and the former Ethiopia government, see Clapham (1988: 212–13).

severe limitations on such direct intervention. Numerous declarations have emphasized the government's desire to privatize state enterprises and stressed the role assigned to both domestic and foreign investment, notably from the diaspora. Yet the regulatory attitudes of the government have generated friction with private capital; retailers, taxi owners, merchants trading with Ethiopia, and exiled Eritreans looking to invest in productive activities, all complained during the provisional period about the Front's excessively bureaucratic, regulatory approach to economic development.

A Bleak Economic Outlook

The contours of post-independence politics will be determined in large measure by the acute economic constraints facing the government and people of Eritrea. The fact that these were largely masked by the euphoria of independence and the provisional period amplifies the urgency of policies to tackle the economic contradictions evident in 1993–4. Given the legacy of war and the lack of any kind of statistical base, conventional economic indicators have no meaning in Eritrea. Yet with the high dependency on food aid and other structural weaknesses, per capita incomes are very significantly below the estimated average of US$120 in Ethiopia, making Eritrea the poorest economy in Africa. With the exception of the port of Assab, Eritrea's stunted industrial and service sectors have been starved of investment for over two decades. Of the 43 state-owned enterprises inherited from the Ethiopian government, barely two-thirds were partially operating in 1993. Neither the liberal investment code issued in December 1991 nor current plans for privatization are likely to fuel industrial recovery. Brewing, food processing and textiles account for the bulk of output. Factories face persistent shortages of spare parts, raw materials, high energy costs as well as uncertain access to their former markets of northern Ethiopia. Even taking into account almost a thousand small-scale urban industries, employment prospects outside of agriculture are extremely restricted. Over 80 per cent of the population remain dependent upon an emaciated agricultural sector. Stunted and dislocated by prolonged drought and war, domestic agriculture provided only 50 per cent of the country's food needs even in a year of relatively good harvests such as 1992–3. The Food and Agriculture Organization estimated the 1993 food shortfall for Eritrea at 147,000 tons, only half the amount required in 1992. The 1993 UN Special Emergency Programme for the Horn of Africa (SEPHA II) appealed for US$80.5 million for Eritrea, US$51 million of which was for World Food Programme emergency food aid. Although pledges fell short of these targets, good rains in 1993, combined with what was still in the food pipeline from SEPHA I, meant that shortfalls were avoided. Even if the resources now being committed to agricultural rehabilitation allow recultivation and resettlement in rural areas, Eritrea will remain critically dependent on food aid for the foreseeable future. Only around 3.2 million (26 per cent) of Eritrea's 12.4 million hectares is suitable for cultivation, and of that only 10 per cent is currently being used, due to constraints of agricultural inputs and irrigation. Surveys undertaken recently indicate a sharp deterioration in rural poverty in the late eighties, two-thirds of all livestock having been lost in the last decade.[27] Eritrean agriculturalists now face the daunting tasks of simultaneously halting this deterioration whilst reintegrating a large influx of rural refugees.

---

[26] On the politics of the Orthodox church, see *Indian Ocean Newsletter* (*ION*), 18 September 1993, EH 8 September 1993. The attitudes of Orthodox Ethiopians towards Eritrea have been coloured by mounting hostility towards the Tigrayan Patriarch, Bishop Paulos, who was installed by the EPRDF shortly after taking power.

[27] *Eritrea: food, agricultural and needs assessments*, 1992 and 1988. University of Leeds/Emergency Relief Desk.

Just before the referendum the PGE launched an ambitious rehabilitation programme which required almost US$2 billion in external finance, much of it for the resettlement of refugees from Sudan and agricultural rehabilitation. Although several agricultural projects are under way, overall the new Eritrean authorities have had to radically scale down their initial, over-optimistic expectations of foreign assistance for recovery. The first US$25 million loan was signed with the World Bank in March 1993, although protocol required that it was negotiated via the Addis government, Eritrea then not being a member of the World Bank.[28] This loan was the centre of a US$145 million Relief and Rehabilitation Programme for Eritrea (RRPE) supervised by the World Bank. However, this provides less than 10 per cent of the PGE's own estimated needs. RRPE covers essential infrastructure repairs, notably for electricity generation and distribution. The GOE has had to cut the heavy subsidies on domestic services, fuel, energy and telecommunications. The other main input of foreign donors to the economy has been the Programme for Refugee Reintegration and Rehabilitation of Resettlement Areas in Eritrea (PROFERI) launched in Geneva by a UN donors conference in July 1993. The US$262 million programme aims to resettle 430,000 refugees from Sudan between February 1994 and 1997, providing supplies and facilities for the reintegration of returnees in five provinces.[29] The programme follows a long and acrimonious dispute between the Commission for Eritrean Refugee Affairs (CERA) and UNHCR about the scale and timing of refugee resettlement.[30] Since May 1991 CERA estimates that 80,000 refugees returned to Eritrea from Sudan, 65,000 of these being registered at five centres of transit and reception. The twin policies of refugee resettlement and agricultural recovery are inextricably linked to the issues of land reform and decentralization. For commercial agriculture to revive requires further reform and standardization of the country's awkward patchwork of land tenure systems. The handling of this will inevitably influence the degree to which the GOE is able to implement its desired strategies of political devolution to the 10 regions. It is anxious to reverse rapid urbanization and defuse the acute crises of accommodation and employment. In an effort to decentralize the economy new private investments were banned within a 30 km radius of Asmara. This has irked expatriate Eritreans keen to invest in urban projects. Without large-scale public investment in infrastructure, requiring significant inflows of foreign exchange, it is unlikely that ruined provincial towns such as Keren and Decamhare could quickly become regional poles of economic development.

Eritrea's monetary policy is necessarily limited and ambiguous, the new state having no independent currency. The Ethiopian birr was the sole legal tender throughout the provisional period and will remain the currency for the foreseeable future. Although many Eritreans assumed that a separate currency would be part and parcel of independence, Issayas dismissed the currency issue as 'a matter of prestige or emotional sentiment' adding 'all this has no meaning'. However, in November 1992 he said that the birr would be temporary and that a separate currency would be desirable.[31] Although the National and Commercial Banks of Eritrea set their own interest rates, exchange rate policy is determined by the authorities in Addis Ababa. The PGE was compelled to follow the devaluation of the birr, an integral part of Ethiopia's own economic reform programme, in October 1992. Yet whilst the official rate was set at EB5=US$1, the Eritrean authorities had little choice but to offer Eritreans a parallel rate of EB7.2=US$1, this being the only way for the government to secure foreign exchange. However, as Ethiopia successfully moved to an auction-determined exchange rate for the birr in 1993–4, the problem of disparity lessened. With exceedingly limited export opportunities,

[28] Eritrea became a member of both the World Bank and IMF on 8 July 1994.
[29] For a detailed breakdown of the programme see *ION*, 17 July 1993.
[30] *SWB*, 28 May 1993.
[31] *SWB*, 28 May 1993, *EU* December 1992.

remittances by exiled Eritreans remain the key source of hard currency. In the months since independence the lack of foreign exchange became acute and was in part responsible for the closure of several public services, notably the university. Economic officials spent much of the provisional period negotiating the disentanglement of Eritrean economic assets from those of Ethiopia. However, Ethiopia's use of the port and oil refinery at Assab was quickly guaranteed; in 1992, 94 per cent of cargo handled by Assab was destined for Ethiopia. Although this disentanglement was completed by mid-1993 it was only after Issayas' first state visit to Ethiopia in July 1993 and the arrival in Asmara of a delegation from the Ethiopian Prime Minister's office in September, that bilateral trade and tariff issues began to be seriously discussed. These will determine the direction and magnitude of trade and the potential for eventual economic reintegration between Ethiopia and Eritrea.[32]

Conclusion: Towards an Uncomfortable Transition 1993–7

The successful completion of the referendum and full independence brought a two-year interregnum, from military victory to de jure statehood, to a close. Independence also concluded the EPLF's extended political honeymoon; a period of hiatus in which political and economic contradictions were concealed by the imperatives of the referendum. This is not to belittle the achievements of the referendum; although the result was a foregone conclusion, the financing and smooth running of the poll were not. The meticulous organization enhanced the international legitimacy of the state. Registration and voting procedures provided census data and consolidated the government's administrative control of the territory. Yet hopes of the current Eritrean leadership being able to sustain a sense of national purpose may evaporate if the population's overblown expectations of the material benefits of liberation turn to disillusionment and competition intensifies for the meagre resources at the state's disposal. Current pledges of foreign financial assistance are woefully inadequate to ensure the orderly implementation of either refugee resettlement or the demobilization of EPLF fighters. Intense competition for jobs and housing, particularly among refugees and former fighters in urban areas, will exacerbate existing social tensions.

---

[32] A chronicle of the evolution of Ethiopian–Eritrea economic relations during the provisional period can be found in successive *Economic Intelligence Units (EIU) country reports* on Ethiopia, No.4, 1991 – No.3, 1993.

Bibliography

Africa Watch (1991) *Evil days: 30 years of war and famine in Ethiopia*, London/New York.
Clapham, C. (1988) *Transformation and continuity in revolutionary Ethiopia*, Cambridge University Press, Cambridge.
Connell, D. (1993) *Against all odds: a chronicle of the Eritrean revolution*, Red Sea Press , Trenton, NJ.
Government of Eritrea (1993), *Birth of a nation*, GOE external affairs office, Asmara, May.
Economist Intelligence Unit (EIU), *Ethiopia country reports*, various, especially No.2, 1993: 16–24.
Eritrea Update (EU) London.
Ethiopian Herald (EH) Addis Ababa.
Harding, J. (1993) *Small wars, small mercies*, Viking, London.
Markakis, J. (1987) *National and class conflict in the Horn of Africa*, Cambridge University Press, Cambridge.
Okbazghi, Yohannes (1993) 'Eritrea a country in transition', *Review of African Political Economy*, No.57: 7–28, plus 'briefings' in same edition.
Marchal, R. (1993) 'Erythrée: an 01', *Politique Africaine*, No. 49.
Pool, D. (1993) 'Eritrean independence: the legacy of the Derg and the politics of reconstruction', *African Affairs*, Vol. 92, No. 368: 389–402.
Prunier, G. (1993) 'Atouts et failles de l'Erythrée', *Le Monde Diplomatique*, April.

8

DAVID TURTON
Migrants & Refugees

A Mursi Case Study

The Mursi are a herding and cultivating people of southwestern Ethiopia amongst whom I have carried out anthropological fieldwork over the past 25 years. In this chapter I shall describe two examples of population displacement which have taken place in Mursiland since 1979 and which contrasted markedly in their implications for the 'return' of the displaced. Both were 'forced' in the sense that they were a response to adverse circumstances – drought and war respectively – but one was also 'voluntary' in the sense that (a) not all those similarly affected took the decision to move and (b) it was undertaken in the hope and expectation that the relocation would be permanent. The other was more obviously 'forced', in the sense that (a) none of the affected population saw any alternative but to move and (b) it was undertaken in the hope that it would be temporary. For one, return meant failure, for the other success.

I cannot see any justification for conducting research into situations of extreme human suffering if one does not have the alleviation of suffering as an explicit objective of one's research. For the academic, this means attempting to influence the behaviour and thinking of policy-makers and practitioners so that their interventions are more likely to improve than worsen the situation of those whom they wish to help. A broad distinction can be drawn between two ways in which we might hope to exercise such influence. One is by pointing to the lessons of past experience: this intervention succeeded in various ways and might serve as a model to be repeated elsewhere; this intervention went badly wrong and tells us what to avoid next time. But since each case is more or less different from the next, and since the local, regional and international context is likely to change in unpredictable ways, it is difficult and dangerous to identify a set of 'do's' and 'don'ts' that will apply across the board. A much more effective way in which the academic can hope to have a positive influence on policy is by examining the normally taken-for-granted assumptions upon which policies are based and which powerfully determine action, precisely because they are not made explicit. Since the first objective of any elite, whether bureaucratic, political or, for that matter, academic, must be to ensure its own survival and reproduction, it should be assumed, until proved other-wise, that the unexamined assumptions of policy-makers and planners are self-serving. Perhaps the most important contribution the anthropologist can make to improving the practice of relief and development, therefore, is to induce critical reflection on these assumptions by attempting to understand the human situation from a different cultural perspective.

The population movements I describe here differ from those described elsewhere in the book in at least four ways. Firstly, they involved relatively few people, the total Mursi population amounting to no more than 6,000. Secondly, they took place entirely within Ethiopia, so that those affected were, in a technical sense, 'internally displaced' rather than 'refugees'. Thirdly, both movements were limited in geographical extent – they covered less than 35 km, as the crow flies. Fourthly, they both took place without the involvement, or even knowledge, of outside agencies, whether governmental, non-governmental or international. I hope, however, that by examining a single case over a relatively long period some insights may be gained into our own taken-for-granted ways of conceptualizing displacement, including the much more extensive examples of it which are described in other chapters.

The very word 'displacement' implies an assumption that all human populations 'belong' in a certain place and that, in an ideal world, they would all be where they belong. This in turn implies that the identity people gain from their association with a particular place is in some way fundamental or 'natural' and that to be deprived of that identity is to lose some part of one's very humanity. My aim is to induce critical reflection upon these assumptions by examining Mursi population movements over the past 15 years and by trying to understand what these movements meant to the Mursi themselves.

Map 8.1 *Distribution of groups in the Lower Omo Valley*

Hunger and War in the 1970s

The Mursi live in the Lower Omo Valley, about 100 km north of the border between Ethiopia and Kenya. Their territory lies between the Rivers Omo and Mago and is bounded to the north by the River Mara (Map 8.1). Having no permanently occupied 'villages' they are classified by the people of the surrounding highlands and by the local administration as 'nomads' who spend their time, as one administrator put it to me, 'walking, walking, walking, holding the tails of their cattle'. In fact their seasonal movements are highly regular, limited in geographical extent and predictable. Nor are they, in an objective sense, 'pastoralists', if this term means the provision of the household's main food requirements from herding. With less than four head of cattle per head of population, they depend for over half their subsistence needs on cultivation.

There are two harvests each year, one produced by flood-retreat cultivation along the banks of the Omo and the other by rain-fed shifting cultivation in cleared woodland along the Omo's westward-flowing tributaries. Flood cultivation, although limited in extent, is relatively reliable because it depends on rain falling over the Omo catchment area, much of which lies at an elevation of over 2,000 metres (Butzer, 1971: 1). Shifting cultivation is both unreliable, because it depends on the highly erratic local rainfall, and

8.1 *A contestant psyching himself up for a bout of ceremonial duelling, Mursiland, 1970. (David Turton)*

8.2 *A woman using a pole to plant seeds during the dry season, at the edge of the river Omo. (David Turton)*

subject to falling crop yields as fallow periods are shortened in response to growing demographic pressure on available land. Cattle, the most valued material possessions of the Mursi, make an important contribution to the daily subsistence of certain categories of the population (mainly children and young men) at certain times of the year, but their prime importance to the economy as a whole is as an insurance against crop failure, when they may be exchanged for grain in highland villages.

Between 1970 and 1973 people died of starvation in Mursiland for the first time in living memory (Turton, 1977). The immediate cause of the famine was three successive years of poor rainfall but the underlying cause was a slow deterioration in the subsistence base of the Mursi economy. For most of this century they have been growing more dependent on their least reliable means of subsistence, shifting cultivation. The reasons for this include a lowering in Omo flood levels, the spread of tsetse flies from the Omo bush into the eastern grazing areas, a growth in population due partly to a net inflow of Chai (usually called Surma or Suri by outsiders) who live west of the Omo and south of Maji and with whom they intermarry and share a common language, and restrictions on dry-season grazing brought about by the setting up of the Omo and Mago National Parks (Turton, 1987, 1988).

The effects of the drought were exacerbated by an intensification of armed conflict which affected all the herding peoples of the Lower Omo during the 1970s (Fukui and Turton, 1979). The Mursi have fundamentally hostile relations with all their herding neighbours save the Chai. Enemy groups can be divided into those with whom they are periodically at war but with whom they otherwise have relations of peaceful co-operation and economic exchange, and those with whom they have no peaceful contacts of any kind. The Bodi to the north and Nyangatom to the southwest belong to the first category and the Hamar, farther away to the southeast,

belong to the second. It is with enemies of
the first category that warfare is likely to
cause most fatalities and to be most disruptive of daily life. Attacks by the Hamar,
normally in the form of cattle raids, are
expected every year and are simply another
cause of uncertainty in a highly uncertain
environment (Turton, 1989).

For the Mursi, the most serious conflict
of the early 1970s was with the Bodi, with
whom they had been peacefully co-existing
since the 1950s (Turton, 1978). During my
first period of fieldwork (1969–70), several
Mursi families were living as long-term
'guests' in Bodi territory, cultivating alongside Bodi friends and keeping their cattle in
Bodi settlements. The first signs of trouble
came in January 1970 when a large number
of Mursi cattle were taken into Bodi terri-

8.3 *A Mursi boy in the Mago settlement,
1983. (David Turton)*

tory as a temporary move to protect them from Hamar raiders. This was a strategy which
the Mursi had adopted before, with the co-operation of the Bodi, but this time their
presence was not welcomed and relations between the two groups began to deteriorate.
The first fatality came in June, when a Mursi youth was shot dead north of the River
Mara, where he and his father were living with Bodi friends.

The northern Mursi now moved their cattle either to the Omo (despite the lack of
grazing and the danger from tsetse flies) or to the far south of the country, but continued
to cultivate along the Mara and at Kuduma, the northernmost Mursi cultivation site on
the Omo. There followed four years of raid and counter-raid between the Mursi and
Bodi which disrupted not only the pastoral and (to a lesser extent) agricultural activities
of the Mursi but also (and even more important at a time of famine) their access to
nearby markets. The path to Jinka lay across the Mago valley, where they ran the risk of
being attacked by Hamar, while that to Berka took them through Bodi territory (Figure
8.1). People travelling to and from Berka accounted for the largest number of Mursi
deaths, at the hands of the Bodi, between 1971 and 1975.

The Mago Migrants: In Search of Cool Ground

In 1979 a drought-induced migration began from northern Mursiland to the Mago
Valley. An area was chosen where there was plenty of virtually untouched forest for
shifting cultivation and which was within a few hours walk of Berka, with its twice-
weekly market. But although offering the certain prospect of higher crop yields and the
advantage of close proximity to a market centre, the Mago valley was a much greater
health risk to cattle, because of tsetse flies, than the Omo lowlands. The migrants knew
that they were putting their cattle at risk but they did not see themselves as giving up
herding for an agricultural way of life. On the contrary, they hoped that, as the Mago
forest was cleared for cultivation, the tsetse problem would be reduced to manageable
proportions, allowing them to keep their cattle within a short distance of their
cultivation areas. They hoped, in other words, to re-establish the same sequence of
seasonal activities and transhumance movements as they had followed before, but now
focussed on the Mago instead of the Omo. By 1983 there were about 1,000 Mursi living
in the Mago Valley (Turton and Turton, 1984).

8.4 *A Mursi woman (centre of the picture) visiting Berka town on market day. (David Turton)*

Viewed from the outside, this move to the Mago Valley might appear as an extreme, even if voluntary (in the sense that it was open to those who took part in it to remain where they were) response to an unprecedented ecological crisis by people who should be seen as 'environmental refugees' rather than migrants. I call them migrants not only because their aim was to establish themselves permanently in the Mago valley but also because, in doing so, they saw themselves as fulfilling their 'destiny' as Mursi. If they could not make this move permanent they would have failed not only in a material and economic sense but also in an historical and cultural sense: they would have failed to replicate the kind of population movement which had made them Mursi in the first place.

The Mursi 'myth of origin' is an account of how five named clans originated at a place called Thaleb, somewhere to the southeast, and migrated in an anti-clockwise direction into their present territory, 'finding' and forming affinal alliances with other clans *en route*. Although these five clans are now seen as the historical 'core' of the population, they are not exclusive to the Mursi, for the same clan names are found amongst the Chai. The decisive event in creating a specifically *Mursi* identity was the movement of members of these clans from the west to the east bank of the Omo, around the middle of the last century. Mursi informants say that they took their present territory from its former occupants, the Bodi, who retreated north of the River Mara. But the area evacuated by the Bodi was much larger than that which the invaders initially occupied, around Kurum, in the southeastern corner of present Mursi territory (Map 8.2). It was not until the 1930s that the Mursi began to cultivate along the Mara, a move which brought them face to face with the Bodi for the first time since their initial crossing from the west to the east bank of the Omo and which made the Mara their *de facto* northern boundary.

This progressive spreading out from Kurum (now regarded as the historical centre, or 'stomach', of Mursiland) was a response to the gradual deterioration in ecological

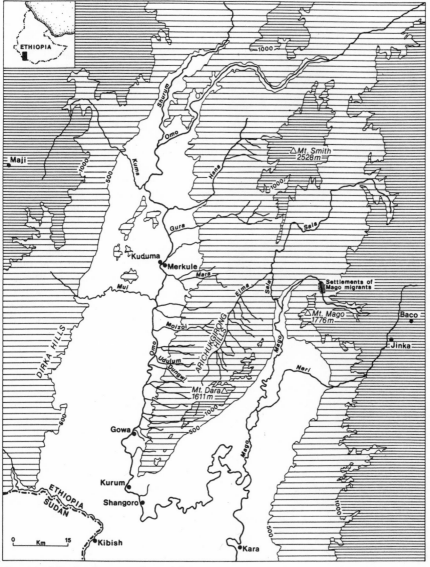

Map 8.2 *Mursiland: topography and drainage*

conditions referred to in the previous section. By 1970, with the level of Lake Turkana having fallen at least 15 metres since the 1890s (Butzer, 1971: 123), the Mara had become a dry river bed for all but a week or two during the rains. (A man in his forties told me, in 1974, that he could remember seeing crocodiles in the upper sections of the Mara when he was a child.) There was no untouched forest left along its banks and crop yields were suffering from the too continuous use of plots – for six years or more in succession.

The failure of the rains in the early 1970s, therefore, merely accentuated a problem

8.5 *A Mursi male elder at the Mago settlement, 1986. (David Turton)*

8.6 *A Mursi woman and her child at the Mago settlement, 1986. (David Turton)*

that was already present and which, with further expansion northwards blocked by the Bodi, would have led, sooner or later, to the solution adopted by the Mago migrants in 1979. Like the Mara in the 1930s, the Mago was a permanent river which offered excellent prospects for cultivation, its flanking forest having remained virtually untouched since it was last occupied (also by the Bodi) around 70 years earlier. And like the Mara, it held a major drawback for a herding people: a high concentration of tsetse flies. But even here, historical precedent could be invoked with optimism, as it frequently was, both in public meetings and private conversation. For the tsetse challenge at Mara had weakened significantly as cultivation areas were cleared along its banks. The Mago migration was not, then, a sudden or arbitrary response to an 'unprecedented' ecological crisis but part of a continuing effort to solve, by well-tried means, a recurrent problem: how to keep a satisfactory balance between available resources and population numbers.

It was also a *culturally* defined solution to this problem, by which I mean that it was facilitated by a deliberate appeal to Mursi history and traditional values. The migrants explicitly likened their move to the occupation, by people of their parents' generation, of the Mara valley. They saw themselves, like those earlier pioneers (and as the latter doubtless saw themselves in relation to yet earlier ones), as domesticating the wilderness, clearing the forest and making the grassland fit for cattle herding. This tradition of a restless search for a land 'flowing with milk and honey' is summed up by the Mursi in the phrase *kalamo ba lalini*: we are [a people who are] looking for (*kalamo*) cool (*lalini*) ground (*ba*). Seen as a search for 'cool ground', then, the Mago migration was not only consistent with traditional Mursi values: it was a validation of them. In the eyes of the migrants, it was they who were the 'true' Mursi, not the 'stayees' whose concern for their cattle had made them unwilling to risk making the first move to the Mago.

There is a contradiction, or at least tension, here between the identity which derives from an historical association with a particular territory and the identity which derives from a tradition of movement into, and appropriation of, *new* territory. As we shall see in the next section, the Mursi see their 'Mursiness' as essentially based on their *actual* occupation of what Anthony Smith calls, in his discussion of the territorial aspect of ethnic identity, an 'actual terrain'(1986: 28) : to leave that 'terrain' is to lose one's Mursi identity. And yet, as a political group, the Mursi are a product of the continuous occupation of new territory, not only historically but also structurally. That is, their internal territorial divisions have been formed by a process of 'replication' (Dyson-Hudson, 1966: 259) which is a consequence of expansion, such that each division is a miniature replica, and potential equivalent, of the whole. It is this tension between an identity based on continued occupation of an actual terrain and an identity based on a continuous 'search for cool ground' which allows new political divisions to be formed and to become, in time, culturally and linguistically (i.e. 'ethnically') distinct.

The Mago migration, however, was a failure. By the late 1980s the migrants had admitted defeat in their efforts to keep their cattle in the Mago valley and the majority had returned to their former cultivation areas along the Omo and in the Omo bush belt. All that was left of the 1,000-strong settlement of the mid-eighties was a group of about 150 cattleless Mursi for whom the nearby market had become not just an occasional resource in times of hardship but a constant factor in their subsistence calculations. Another factor which may have contributed to their decision to stay was the arrival, in 1987, of an American missionary organization, the Society of International Missionaries (SIM). A clinic was opened and a missionary couple took up permanent residence in 1988. Although much reduced in numbers, the agricultural and increasingly 'peasantized' Mursi of the Mago valley had become a useful additional resource for the remainder of the population, giving them convenient access both to the market in Berka and, for the first time, Western medical assistance.

The Ariholi and Gongulobibi Refugees

The mid-1980s saw a huge qualitative 'progression' in the technology of warfare in the Lower Omo Valley. At the time of my first visit to the Mursi (1969–70), the principal weapons of local warfare were 8mm Mannlicher long rifles and carbines which had been carried by Italian troops during their occupation of Ethiopia between 1935 and 1940. They were obtainable with relative ease from traders operating from the highlands on both sides of the Omo Valley, in exchange for cattle, ivory and leopard skins. Some indication of their easy availability is provided by the fact that a long rifle or carbine, standing for four head of cattle, was part of most bridewealth payments I recorded amongst the Mursi between 1969 and 1974. At that time there appeared to be a relatively equal balance of military power amongst the Mursi and their neighbours but this balance was drastically upset when automatic rifles began to find their way into the Lower Omo from the southern Sudan in the mid-1980s.

The Nyangatom were the first to acquire these weapons – mainly AK-47s but also M-16s (Abbink, 1993: 220) – in any numbers. Their main suppliers were their allies the Toposa, living in Equatoria Province of the Sudan, who had in turn been supplied by the Sudan Government as part of its policy of arming local 'militias' to fight the Sudan People's Liberation Army (SPLA). With the help of these weapons, the Nyangatom were able to expand northwards, driving the Chai out of their traditional grazing areas around Mt Naita on the Sudan/Ethiopia border. By 1986–7 the majority of the Chai had resettled in the Maji foothills (Abbink, 1993: 221) and it was then that the Nyangatom turned their attention to the Mursi.

In February 1987 a large force of Nyangatom killed several hundred Mursi, mainly women and children, in a single attack near the Omo Mago junction (Turton, 1989; Alvarsson, 1989). Immediately after the attack the entire population of the two southern Mursi territorial sections, Ariholi and Gongulobibi, sought refuge with their northern neighbours of the Dola section, mainly along the River Moizoi, thus becoming refugees in their own country. They had recently harvested their flood-retreat cultivation areas and were in the process of storing the crop. Their next agricultural task would have been the preparation of plots for the rain-fed crop, which is planted following the first heavy rain in March or April. They therefore not only had to abandon the harvest they had already taken in, but also seek new areas for rain-fed cultivation from the northern Mursi who were already under considerable pressure from the returning Mago migrants.

When I visited northern Mursiland 10 months after the Nyangatom attack, I was told that it would be five years before the Ariholi and Gongulobibi people could hope permanently to re-occupy the land they had evacuated and then only if the Mursi as a whole were able to acquire automatic weapons with which to make an equivalent attack on the Nyangatom. They saw no immediate prospect of this, since the highland traders who were their only source of firearms were unwilling or unable to supply them with automatics and repeated requests to the Government for help had fallen on deaf ears. They were confidently expecting a second Nyangatom attack in the next few months and the way they spoke about the potential consequences of such an attack gave some indication of how they thought about their Mursi identity. They would have to evacuate their territory altogether, they said, and attach themselves, in family groups, to neighbouring peoples. Their clan and family names would survive but there would be no more Mursi. What they seemed to be contemplating, therefore, was not the disappearance of the Mursi as a physical population, but the loss of their Mursi identity. Because they saw this as linked to the occupation of a particular territory it was, in their eyes, more problematic and fragile than their clan identities which they saw as linked to a 'land of dreams' (Smith, 1986: 28).

The expected second attack did not, however, materialize and, in the 1989–90 dry season, under pressure of extreme hunger, the refugees returned to their Omo cultivation sites. But they stayed only long enough to take in the harvest, a pattern that was repeated the next year. During a visit to Kurum in January 1991, I was shown the site of settlements, goat compounds and grain stores which the Nyangatom had burned after they had been hurriedly evacuated by the Mursi immediately before the 1987 attack. Whereas, before the attack, Kurum would have been occupied throughout the year, it was now used only for flood cultivation and the people there were planning to return to the Moizoi as soon as possible after the harvest. This was because of the overwhelming military superiority of the Nyangatom, who were finding it increasingly easy to obtain automatic weapons from Sudan (Tornay, 1993). During this visit I saw no Mursi carrying automatic rifles, but they were much in evidence among the Nyangatom.

An event which occurred at Kurum during January 1991 (and which was the reason for my visit) indicated that, for the refugees, their re-occupation of this area was not just a matter of regaining access to economic resources but also of maintaining their political identity, not so much as Mursi, but as members of a territorial section, or political subdivision, of Mursi. This was the long-overdue creation, by means of a three-day ritual, called *nitha*, of a new male age set, the first to have been created since 1961. Each of the three main territorial sections into which the Mursi are divided, Ariholi, Gongulobibi and Dola, holds its own *nitha*, in that order, Ariholi taking the lead because its territorial base is Kurum, the 'stomach' of the country. It was the Ariholi *nitha*, then, which took place at Kurum in January 1991. The other two sections held theirs about six months later.

The main events of the *nitha* take place in and around a specially constructed enclosure of branches, with a tree at its centre (Woodhead, 1991). The enclosure at Kurum was built around a highly unimpressive tree, about six feet tall. This tree was chosen because, having a long life ahead of it, it would grow and flourish together with the members of the new age set who were thus identified both with the tree and with the place where it was rooted. By holding the *nitha* at Kurum, under the eyes of the Nyangatom as they sported their Kalashnikovs on the opposite bank of the Omo, the Ariholi Mursi were, among other things, making a symbolic defence of this place, which they still considered unsafe for permanent reoccupation but upon the continued occupation of which their Ariholi identity depended. They knew that their *de jure* claim to Kurum was at risk because their *de facto* occupation of it had become relatively tenuous. One way in which they would be able to bolster this claim in future would be by pointing to the fact, concretely symbolized by the tree around which the main events of the *nitha* had taken place, that the most recent age set had been created there. What had happened to the Ariholi Mursi then was analogous to what was predicted to happen to the whole Mursi population in the event of a second Nyangatom attack – dispersal as refugees, dependence on surrounding populations for the means of survival and the potential loss of their political identity.

Conclusion

It is evident that the displacement of supposedly 'pastoral' populations will have different causes and consequences depending on the relative contributions made by pastoral and non-pastoral activities to subsistence. For those, like the pastoral Somali, who inhabit areas where agriculture is impossible, displacement will occur through the loss of animals due to drought or disease and/or the loss of pastureland due to warfare or appropriation by the government (Merryman, 1982). For those, like the Mursi, who depend heavily on cultivation, displacement is more likely to be the result of falling crop yields than loss of purely pastoral resources. Agriculture was so important to the survival of the Mago migrants that they were prepared to risk, and indeed accept, increased stock losses due to trypanosomiasis in order to achieve higher crop yields, while the Ariholi and Gongu-lobibi refugees were displaced, by warfare, not from pastureland but from agricultural land. This simply reminds us that survival in the arid and semi-arid areas of East Africa and the Horn requires movement, fluidity and adaptablity, not a tradition-bound commitment either to one particular place or one particular mode of subsistence.

The two cases of displacement I have described were objectively different in their causes and consequences but what interests me here is the subjective meaning these differences held for the displaced. Both the migrants and the refugees were forced, by circumstances beyond their control, to leave their home areas, pushed in the one case by famine and drought and in the other by war. But because they were taking over new, unoccupied territory, the Mago migrants were able to see themselves, not as victims of circumstances beyond their control, but as pioneers, treading almost literally in the footsteps of their heroic ancestors. The Ariholi and Gongulobibi refugees saw themselves as losing territory and with it their identity as members of autonomous political subdivisions within the Mursi population. They were refugees both in the sense that they had been given hospitality and assistance by their neighbours and in the sense that they would, in due course, assume the political identity of these neighbours – they would become members of the Dola territorial section. They were in the process of losing one locally based identity and gaining another, while remaining Mursi.

The irony here is that is was the Mago migrants who were set on a path which would have led them, had they been successful, to a separate cultural as well as political identity. A transition from pastoralism to settled agriculture, as a consequence of herders moving into highland areas unsuitable for cattle herding, seems to have been a feature of the Omo Valley and its surrounding highlands for hundreds of years. The traditions of several highland cultivators, including the Teshenna (Abbink, 1991), and the Majangir (Stauder, 1971: 1) suggest a general movement of peoples from lower-lying areas, northwards into the Ethiopian highlands. We can see this process taking place today with the surviving 'rump' of 150 or so migrants in the Mago valley and with the Chai who have moved into the Maji foothills under pressure from the Nyangatom. The opportunity to look closely at one case – that of the Mago migrants – allows us to see that the transition can only begin because those who are making it are able to hide its revolutionary implications behind a mask of traditional values, through an appeal to oral history.

An indigenous account of Mursi origins can take one of two forms. It can either focus on a journey of five 'original' clans from Thaleb, a 'land of dreams' which cannot be identified with any known place, or it can focus on the relatively recent occupation of an 'actual terrain' – Kurum and the area between Kurum and the River Mara. Thaleb, however, is not the territorial base of *Mursi* identity, since it is not only Mursi clans who claim this origin and members of the half a dozen or so Mursi clans who do not claim it are nevertheless fully Mursi. Mursi identity is linked essentially to the relatively recent occupation of their present territory and it is clear that the Mursi themselves think of it, as compared to their clan identities, as impermanent and problematic. Clan identities are not only older, as a matter of empirical fact, than the politico-territorial divisions they cut across but they are seen as 'given' by the people themselves: they are the 'stuff' of social life out of which relatively fragile politico-territorial units are constructed (cf. Schlee, 1985 and 1989; Turton, 1994).

The phrase 'population displacement' contains the implicit assumption that a given population has its own proper 'place', 'territory', or 'homeland'. Liisa Malkki, in an article based on her research among Hutu refugees in Tanzania (1992), has pointed out that the 'naturalised identity between people and place' (p. 26) to be found in the literature on nations and nationalism is the result of 'a powerful sedentarism in our thinking' (p. 30). This 'sedentarist' cast to our thought is reflected in the way anthropologists have constructed an ethnographic map of the world out of territorially based and therefore physically demarcated 'societies', 'peoples' or 'ethnic groups'. In 'sedentarist' thinking these are seen as given in nature and the identity people derive from association with a particular territory is therefore seen as equally 'natural'.

The assumption that it is 'natural' for human beings to berooted in a particular place has given us 'a vision of territorial displacement as pathological' (Malkki, 1992: 31). Both refugees and migrants have thus become a 'problem', not only for administrators and politicians but also for researchers and scholars. If history 'is always written from a sedentary point of view' (Deleuze and Guattari, 1987: 23, cited by Malkki, loc. cit.), so also is anthropology. Anthropologists have, for example, given much attention to the causes and consequences of the 'nomadic' movements of hunters and herders, discovering that these cannot by any means be attributed solely to environmental pressures, but have largely ignored the causes and consequences of 'sedentism' (Salzman, 1980: 10–11). And if history and anthropology are always written from a 'sedentary point of view', they are also always written about territorially based 'tribes', 'societies', 'nations' or 'ethnic groups' as though these were given in nature and as though they could, in principle, be unambiguously labelled as one thing – pastoral, agricultural, nomadic, etc. – or another.

The case I have described should allow us to gain some distance from these normally unexamined assumptions about identity and territory and to realize that political identity (by which I mean identity based upon the occupation of an 'actual terrain') can be conceived of as inclusive as well as exclusive. The unity of the Mursi is not conceived of by them in terms of ethnic exclusivity, if we mean by 'ethnic' a unity which is based on the assumption of a common origin in space and time. It is conceived of as an amalgamation of ethnically distinct (clan) groups on a territorial basis. The important point here is that the resultant unity is thought of as recent, temporary and fragile, not as the triumphant end product of an historical process of 'nation-building'. This is in contrast to the exclusivity of the nation-state which, at least in theory, 'brooks no communal attachments at levels between the nation and the individual' (Sharp and McAllister, 1993: 20).

The idea that voluntary repatriation is the 'natural' solution to the 'refugee problem' in Africa and Asia may be one result of the assumption that it is 'natural' for any human group to be rooted in a particular place. The case described here suggests that 'going home' may not necessarily be the desired outcome of population displacement for the displaced. Voluntarily making a new home for themselves in a new area may be perfectly consistent with their history and with their view of themselves as a distinct group.

Postscript: Development Refugees?

While most population displacement in Africa in recent years has undoubtedly been due to famine and war, growing numbers of people, in Africa and elsewhere, are also being forced off their land in the name of development. According to the World Bank, for example, 1.2 to 2.1 million people are forcibly relocated each year because of hydro-electric dam projects (World Bank, 1994, cited by McDowell, 1995, p. 179). Since this chapter was written, it has become clear that the threat of such 'development induced displacement' also hangs over the Mursi, not because of dam construction but because of a wildlife conservation project to be financed by the European Development Fund and focussing on three national parks, two of which, the Omo and Mago National Parks, enclose the best agricultural and pastoral resources of the Mursi (Turton, 1987, p. 170, 1995).

In a report submitted to the Ethiopian Wildlife Conservation Organization (EWCO) in 1978, the Mursi were seen as a major threat to the viability of both parks. It was recommended that they be removed, not only from the parks themselves but from the area between them, on the grounds that 'the Omo and Mago will lose their value as national parks if vested human interests are permitted to exist between them' (Stephenson and Mizuno, 1978, p. 41, cited in Turton, 1987, p. 179). There did not seem much likelihood, at the time, that these recommendations would be taken seriously by the hard-pressed administrative authorities upon whom, the report states, 'the onus of resettlement of the people falls fairly and squarely' (op. cit., p. 49). During the 1980s there was a growing reaction against the dominance of European ideas in determining conservation policies for Africa (e.g., Anderson and Grove, 1987) and it seemed reasonable to expect that this reaction would influence the EWCO to adopt a more positive approach to the involvement of local people in national park development.

This expectation is not borne out, however, by the final report of the feasibility study, carried out in 1993, for the 'Southern Ethiopia Wildlife Conservation Project' (Agriconsulting, 1993) and related documents. True to the European image of 'wild Africa', the report describes the Omo and Mago Parks as 'impressive wildernesses' (pp. 125 and 137), even though every square inch of the lower Omo valley has been formed by thousands of years of human use and occupation (Turton, 1977). The political usefulness of describing an area as a 'wilderness' is, of course, that it implies (a) that there are very few people living in and/or using it and (b) that those who *are* living in and/or using it are a threat to its 'wilderness' character. Thus the local people, already made into 'squatters' in their own territory by the drawing of (as yet ungazetted) boundaries on a map, are automatically defined as obstacles to conservation and sustainable resource management. The report also accepts without discussion the increasingly outdated definition of a national park as an area where human settlement is prohibited. Whenever it speaks of the need to gain the 'goodwill and cooperation' of local people, it always describes them as 'neighbouring rural residents' and as 'living in areas adjoining the

8.7 *A hotel in Jinka, where tourists travelling mainly by road from Addis Ababa stay on their way to and from the Mago and Omo national parks. One of the major attractions of the trip is the opportunity to see and photograph Mursi – especially women wearing their lip plates. It is expected that the volume of tourist traffic will greatly increase once a planned all-weather road linking Jinka and Maji with a bridge across the Omo has been completed. (David Turton)*

National Parks' (e.g., p. 5). The implicit logic is clear: the current occupants of the parks should be, and ideally would be, resettled.

The logic is made explicit in another document, setting out the aims and objectives of a two-year 'preliminary phase' of the project (*Project Proposal for a Wildlife Conservation* (sic) *in Southern Ethiopia*, April 1994). Based on what it describes (p. 13) as the 'very serious environmental degradation currently taking place' (but for which there is no evidence in the Agriconsulting report), this document sets out a number of urgent objectives for the preliminary phase, among which is the resettling from the Omo area of 1,200 'families' (p. 10) amounting, therefore, to at least 6,000 people or the equivalent of the entire Mursi population. This will be achieved 'with the collaboration of the local administration ... The project will assist with the timely supply of materials (for building new houses) hand tools and where necessary food aid for six months ...' (p. 10). Those who are not resettled (presumably because they live in areas adjoining the two parks) will be 'sensibilised ... in order to minimise conflictual or unsustainable resource use' (p. 9). The terms of reference for consultants providing 'technical assistance' to the project include the requirement for a 'sociologist or socio-economist' whose task will be to undertake a 'socio-economic survey ... concerning families to be resettled'.

If acted upon, these proposals would almost certainly lead to the kind of impoverishment for the Mursi which has been experienced by the victims of development-induced displacement generally: 'unemployment, landlessness, marginalisation, food insecurity, loss of access to common property, erosion of health status, social disarticulation and cultural stress' (McDowell, 1995, p. 179). Indeed, the measures it is proposed to take to facilitate the resettlement of 'squatters' are so minimal that one can only conclude that those who have designed the project will be happy to see local people bear the main burden of its costs, even to the extent of being forced off their land and provided with six months' food aid 'where necessary'.

There are not just humanitarian grounds for concern here. The accumulated evidence of wildlife conservation practice in Africa suggests that failure to put the interests and wellbeing of the local *human* population at the centre of a project, by including them in its formulation and implementation, is likely to ensure that it does not achieve its long-term objectives. As Charles Schaefer comments in a review of Adams and McShane (1992),

> ... almost every conservation scheme conceived in the West, financed by Western aid and implemented by European or American naturalists has ignored the single most important factor in conservation – humans ... Africa's wildlife must live in an environment of increasing human population and if species are to survive, a happy medium between the two must be reached. To accomplish this....Africans who have lived on land with wild animals as neighbours for hundreds of years, must be the primary concern of conservation efforts. (1994, p. 51)

There are already a number of examples from African countries of imaginative attempts to come to terms with this (one would have thought) obvious truth by involving local people, to varying degrees and with varying success, in the design and management of conservation projects. It is to be hoped that it is not too late for the EWCO to rise to the same challenge with its Southern Ethiopia Wildlife Conservation Project. Given the substantial funding involved (over 16 million ECU) and the size and significance of the area to be developed, there is an opportunity here for Ethiopia to establish one of the most exciting and influential wildlife conservation projects in Africa – or to add one more case to the catalogue of humanitarian outrages that have been perpetrated in the name of development.

References

Abbink, J. (1991) 'The deconstruction of "tribe": ethnicity and politics in southwestern Ethiopia', *Journal of Ethiopian Studies*, XXIV (November): 1–21.

— (1993) 'Famine, gold and guns: the Suri of southwestern Ethiopia, 1985–91', *Disasters*, Vol. 17, No. 3: 218–25.

Adams, J.S. and T.D. McShane (1992) *The myth of wild Africa: conservation without illusion*. W.W. Norton & Co, New York.

Agriconsulting (1993) *Feasibility study for a wildlife conservation project in southern Ethiopia: final report*. Agriconsulting, mimeo, Rome.

Alvarsson, J-A. (1989) *Starvation and peace or food and war? Aspects of armed conflict in the Lower Omo Valley*. Uppsala Research Reports in Cultural Anthropology, University of Uppsala.

Anderson, D. and R. Grove (1987), 'The scramble for Eden: past, present and future in African conservation', in D. Anderson and R. Grove (eds) *Conservation in Africa: people, policies and practice*, Cambridge University Press, Cambridge.

Butzer, K. W. (1971) *Recent history of an Ethiopian Delta: the Omo River and the level of Lake Rudolf*, Research Paper No. 136, Department of Geography, University of Chicago, Chicago, IL.

Deleuze, G. and F. Guattari (1987) *A thousand plateaus: capitalism and schizophrenia*. University of Minnesota Press, Minneapolis.

Dyson-Hudson, N. (1966) *Karimojong politics*. Clarendon Press, Oxford.

Malkki, L. (1992) 'National geographic: the rooting of peoples and the territorialization of national identity among scholars and refugees', *Cultural Anthropology*, Vol. 7, No. 1: 24–43.

McDowell, C. (1995) Conference Report: Conference on Development Induced Displacement, Refugee Studies Programme, University of Oxford, 11–14 January 1995, *Disasters*, Vol: 19, No. 2: 178–9.

Merryman, J.L. (1982) 'Pastoral nomad settlement in response to drought: the case of the Kenya Somali', in A. Hansen and A. Oliver-Smith (eds) *Involuntary migration and resettlement: the problems and responses of dislocated peoples*, Westview Press, Boulder, CO.

Salzman, P. C. (1980) *When nomads settle: processes of sedentarisation as adaptation and response*. Praeger, New York.

Schaefer, C. (1994) Book Review: *The Myth of Wild Africa: conservation without illusion* by J.S. Adams and T.D.

McShane, W.W. Norton, 1992, *Walia: Journal of the Ethiopian Wildlife and Natural History Society* 15: 51–2.

Schlee, G. (1985) 'Interethnic clan identities among Cushitic speaking pastoralists of northern Kenya', *Africa*, 55: 17–38.

— (1989) *Identities on the move*. Manchester University Press for the International African Institute, Manchester.

Sharp, J. and P. McAllister (1993) 'Ethnicity, identity and nationalism: international insights and the South African Debate', *Anthropology Today*, Vol. 9, No. 5: 18–20.

Smith, A. D. (1986) *The ethnic origins of nations*. Basil Blackwell, Oxford.

Stauder, J. *The Majangir: ecology and society of a southwest Ethiopian people*. Cambridge University Press, Cambridge.

Stephenson, J. and A. Mizuno (1978) *Recommendations on the conservation of wildlife in the Omo-Tama-Mago Rift Valley of Ethiopia*. Report submitted to the Wildlife Conservation Department of the Provisional Military Government, Ethiopia, Addis Ababa.

Tornay, S. (1993) 'More chance on the fringe of the state? The growing power of the Nyangatom, a border people of the Lower Omo Valley, Ethiopia (1970–1992)', in T. Tvedt (ed.) *Conflict in the Horn of Africa: human and ecological consequences of warfare*. Research Programme on Environmental Policy and Society, Department of Social and Economic Geography, Uppsala University, Uppsala.

Turton, D. (1977) 'Response to drought: the Mursi of south west Ethiopia', in J. P. Garlick and R.W.J. Keay (eds) *Human ecology in the tropics*, Taylor and Francis, London.

— (1978) 'War, peace and Mursi identity', in K. Fukui and D. Turton (eds) *Warfare among East African herders*, Senri Ethnological Studies, No. 3, National Museum of Ethnology, Osaka.

— (1987) 'The Mursi and national park development in the Lower Omo Valley', in D. Anderson and R. Grove (eds) *Conservation in Africa: peoples, policies and practice*, Cambridge University Press, Cambridge.

— (1988) 'Looking for a cool place: the Mursi, 1890s–1980s', in D. Johnson and D. Anderson (eds) *The ecology of survival: case studies from Northeast African history*, Lester Crook Academic Publishing/Westview Press, London/Boulder.

— (1989) 'Warfare, vulnerability and survival: a case from southwestern Ethiopia', *Cambridge Anthropology*, Vol: 13, No.2: 67–85. (Reprinted in *Disasters*, 15: 254–64).

— (1994) 'Mursi political identity and warfare: the survival of an idea', in K. Fukui and J. Markakis (eds) *Ethnicity and conflict in the Horn of Africa*, James Currey, London.

— (1995) *Pastoral livelihoods in danger: cattle disease, drought and wildlife conservation in Mursiland, Southwestern Ethiopia*. Oxfam Research Paper No. 12, Oxfam (UK and Ireland), Oxford.

Turton, D. and P. Turton (1984) 'Spontaneous resettlement after drought: an Ethiopian example', *Disasters*, 8: 178–89.

Woodhead, L. (1991) *Nitha* (52 mins, colour) 'Disappearing World' Series, Granada TV, Manchester (Anthropologist: David Turton)

World Bank (1994) *Resettlement and development: the bankwide review of projects involving involuntary resettlement, 1986–1993*. Environmental department, mimeo, Washington, DC.

9

K. N. GETACHEW
The Displacement & Return of Pastoralists in Southern Ethiopia

A Case Study of the Garri

Introduction

Displacement is not a new phenomenom for the peoples of the Horn. This is particularly so for the pastoral groups of the lands divided by the Ethiopian, Kenyan and Somalian national borders. Here is one of the most ethnically dynamic and politically volatile areas of Africa, where population groups have long traditions of almost continuous local warfare and frequent enforced migrations. It is important to recognize that people draw on their notions about these past upheavals in trying to cope with those of the present. Nevertheless, the robust and adaptable customs of the past have been placed under increasing strain by the unprecedented scale of social trauma. The violence of the modern era is something new.

For as far back as anyone can remember, warfare has defined the boundaries of social units, or divided units into sections to form separate collective identities, or established who had grazing rights in specific locations. Not surprisingly, the fighting was most intense during periods of drought. But these confrontations had limits. Armed engagements generally followed predictable patterns, and were soon followed by pressures for a truce or reconcilliation. Killing was relatively limited, partly because of the weapons used, and partly because payment of compensation to aggrieved relatives could be expensive in terms of livestock.

Even groups which lost decisively were not wiped out. They took refuge with friends and relatives elsewhere, becoming incorporated as clan siblings, vassals or, if they remained organized and strong, as allies. All the groups of the area speak Cushitic languages (Oromo and/or Somali dialects), and share many customs, attitudes and beliefs. So it was relatively easy for families to shift from one ethnicity to another, often taking on new cultural traits or passing on their own. Marriages and networks of live-stock alliances between families of different, even opposed, ethnic groups were a crucial insurance against disasters (there is a large published and unpublished literature relating to intra-ethnic relationships in the area, eg. Donaldson-Smith, 1896: 221–9, 1904: 680–9; Neuman, 1902: 376–8; Maud, 1904: 552–79; F.0. 401/10&11, 1907; Gwynn, 1911: 113–39; Hodson, 1927; I.M. Lewis, 1955, 1960; H.S. Lewis, 1966: 27–46; Turton, 1975; Schlee, 1989; Baxter, 1991).

A well-known oral tradition among several groups illustrates the point. The Garri, Garrimarro, Ajuran, Sakuye, Rendille and Boran all know the story of *keed-guurai*, the long trek to the southeast (see Haberland, 1963; Getachew Kassa, 1983, 1988; Schlee,

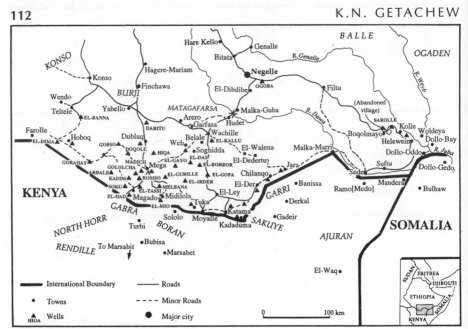

Map 9.1 *Southern Ethiopia*

1984, 1989). This migration was caused by a ferocious Boran assault on all their neighbours. Many people fled into Somali areas, where some became clients (*sheegat*) and
others were accepted as allies. Those who remained became clients (*tirisso*[1]) of the Boran.
Yet, some years later the Boran and other non-Somali groups, including the Garri, had
sufficiently set aside their differences to form an alliance to stop Somali expansion.

These flexible inter and intra-ethnic relationships proved to be remarkably resilient
during the terrible epidemics and great famine of the nineteenth century. The livestock
of many groups was wiped out by disease, known as *tiite cinaaca guuraca* ('the time when
the rib cages were black with flies'). Afflicted pastoralists were forced to take refuge in all
directions, and seem to have been accepted and accomodated. Boran groups welcomed
refugees from Garri, Gabra, Garrimarro, Sakuye, and Arssi. Relatively unaffected Garri
and Garrimarro clans acted in a similar way, and so did Somali clans, who hosted
displaced Boran. In some cases entire clans were adopted by their former enemies, and
consequently it is possible to find clans with the same name distributed among different
ethnic identities (a point noted by, among others: Turton 1975; Haberland, 1963;
Schlee, 1984, 1989; Getachew Kassa, 1983, 1985, 1988, 1989, 1990; Baxter, 1991).

However, towards the end of the century, different kinds of pressures began to be
felt, making such collaboration more difficult. The establishing of Italian Somaliland and
the Kenya Colony, and the expansion of the Ethiopian Empire divided grazing lands
between three states. The arbitrary nature of the boundary lines, and the efforts of
colonial administrators to restrict movement, led to tensions. For example, British
colonial administrators in Kenya created so called 'tribal areas' and the Galla-Somali line
in 1910, with fixed boundaries and police patrols, in an effort to control nomadic
movement. The location of these demarcations quickly provoked antagonisms with
various groups, including several from southern Ethiopia who found themselves denied
access to their pastures. The situation was also excacerbated by the introduction of
firearms. Colonial administrators armed their allies and encouraged them to raid other
groups. Thus the Garri were armed against the Ogaden and the Degodia in 1915.

---

[1] The term *tirisso* in the Boran language denotes not only 'client' but also 'quasi-adopted'.

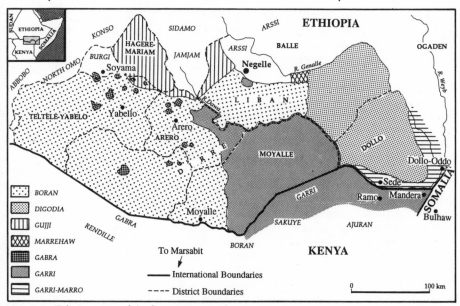

Map 9.2 *Ethnic groups of the former 'Boran administration'*

Moreover, the location of the pastoralists in the border zones, and their persistence in wandering over frontiers, made them scapegoats when conflicts arose between governments (Hamilton, 1977). Occasional border incidents between government troops occurred as early as 1900, and continued throughout the 1920s and 1930s (Zaphiro, 1907; Hodson, 1927; I.M. Lewis, 1955, 1980; Tsehai, 1969). Inevitably, those ethnic groups whose territory stretched across the national boundaries became involved in these conflicts, and as a consequence, the Garri, Boran and Gabra were driven out of some of their pastures in northern Kenya losing their territory to Somali clans. Following a policy of divide and rule, colonial administrations fostered antipathy between neighbours, and emphasized cultural differences.

On the Ethiopian side of the border, the government tended to support settled, non-Moslem Boran clans against other groups, particularly Moslem Oromo and Somali pastoralists. However, this policy was reversed under Italian rule between 1936 and 1941 (Trimingham, 1952; Perham, 1974). During this period, Boran allies of the overthrown Ethiopian government suffered considerable loss of livestock and land, as well as numerous mortalities. After liberation in 1941, the government rewarded them and took revenge on the Oromo and Somali pastoralists. Since the Italians had armed their pastoralist allies with guns, there was some resistance (an uprising known by the name *Jig-heer*). The rebels were crushed and the underlying causes of the rebellion remained unresolved. During the following decades, the tension between the Boran and other groups of the region, and particularly betwen the Boran-dominated local administration and the non–Boran pastoralists, continued without resolution. The government's strategy was to create tribal areas, and to restrict migration. Any group whose member crossed another group's territory risked being punished. The policy aggravated competition over resources, and raids using guns became ever more prevalent.[2]

---

[2] This information is from interviews with *Aw* Yisahaqow Racha, *Haj* Mohammed Haj Hassan and *Aw* Eiya Qalla at Negelle, Moyalle and Hudet in 1983 and 1990. Sophisticated guns and ammunition have gradually become important to pastoralists of Ethiopia and other parts of the Horn. The are now essential for groups to be able to remain in the pastoral sector and to defend their communities, because the governments have not been able (or willing) to provide security.

The situation deteriorated further from the 1960s. Following independence, the government of Somalia claimed the territories of neighbouring Kenya and Ethiopia, and thereby dragged the border clans into the middle of an intra-state conflict. Oppressive administrative strategies attempted to prevent pastoralists crossing national boundaries and to enforce permanent settlement in locations where government controls could be imposed. Large numbers of soldiers were garrisoned in the main towns, and the local populations suffered the full impact of the smouldering antagonisms which eventually led to the Ogaden War of 1977–8. Large numbers of destitute people were forced to flee, and were made to live in official refugee camps where conditions were often awful. Others took up arms against the military forces and local allies of their own repressive regimes. Rather than trying to resolve long-standing ethnic conflicts, governments provided modern weapons to one group to fight against another, and fomented ethnic strife in the neighbouring states by supplying, hosting and training dissidents. Somalia armed Ethiopian insurgents and Kenya and Ethiopia armed the Somalis who were fighting the Barre regime. Since the late 1970s, the region has been awash with modern automatic rifles and ammunition, thousands of people have been almost continuously displaced and separated from their means of livelihood, and humanitarian aid has been a constant requirement. This remains the case in the mid-1990s.

Up until 1991, one of the most adversely affected pastoral groups in southern Ethiopia was the Garri. In the following sections I describe their experiences since the 1960s. Most of them fled to Somalia in the 1970s, where they spent more than a decade in UNHCR refugee camps. They returned to Ethiopia towards the end of the 1980s, with assistance from a UNHCR repatriation and rehabilitation programme. An assessment is made below of the UNHCR operation. The chapter also notes some of the innovations the returnees brought back from Somalia, and comments on the changes years of social upheaval have made in the Garri way of life.

The Garri and Their Ethnic Setting

The traditional Garri grazing grounds extend from southern Ethiopia into Mandera, Wajir and Marsabit districts of northeast Kenya. A few Garri clans also live in southern Somalia in Af Goi and Af Maddo. The Garri population of Ethiopia is about 81,000. They speak their own dialects, Afan-Kofar and Darawa. In addition, the Boran Oromo dialect and standard Somali are widely spoken, and some Garri businessmen have learned Amharic, Ki-Swahili, English and Arabic. The two Garri dialects are closely related to the Garrimarro Rahanwein dialect (*Af-Maymai*). The Garri share many values, including spiritual values, with Gabra, Sakuye, Ajuran and arguably also with the Garrimarro. They are strong adherents of the Islamic faith, many being followers of Sufi sects such as Salihiyya and Qadiriyya. In addition, neighbourhood ties have resulted in the adoption of some Boran customs.

Traditionally, economic activity among the Garri is dominated by pastoralism. Camels and goats are particulaly important, but sheep and cattle are also reared. In addition to herding, trade in animal products has played a crucial role in livelihood strategies, and the Garri are also known for their basketry and wood carving. In the past, farming and crafts like smithing and pottery were generally despised. However, there have been settled Garri living along the Dawa river and other fertile areas for a long time, growing maize, millet and other crops. Nowadays, the loss of livestock has forced many more Garri to turn to agricultural production, or urban-based economic activity, such as running small hotels and shops, or market trading in towns like Negelle, Moyale, Wachille and Arero. Garri women, as well as men, have become involved in these new activities.

Although Garri commonly recognize affinal and other kinds of social networks which cut across ethnic divisions, as a group they have frequently been hostile to their neighbours. They have tended to be in intermittent competition over water sources and pasturage with the camel-keeping Degodia and Marrehan Somali clans, and with the agro-pastoral Garrimarro, and Gujji. However, the most tense relationship has been with the Boran. The Boran form part of the Oromo 'nationality', which has played a significant role in Ethiopian national politics.[3] They value cattle more than camels, and therefore have different pastoral management strategies to those of the Garri and Somali clans. They are also non-Moslems. Most of them are followers of their own religious beliefs (associated with *Waq*, the Sky-god). As noted above, in the past the Boran and the Garri were occasionally able to set aside their differences, and sometimes even formed alliances against other groups. But, with the formation of colonial states, the antipathy which often prevailed between them became an aspect of government policies. The support given to the Boran by the Ethiopian administration greatly exacerbated divisions. The government's hostility was particularly galling to the Garri in that, unlike several Moslem groups, they had supported the Emperor against the Italians. By the 1960s, the Garri were ready to take up arms to protect their livelihood and, together with many other Moslems living in Boran region, were prepared to to support incursions from Somalia.[4]

Resistance and Flight

In 1963, following a series of raids and counter-raids by Garri and Boran warriors in Dirre, the government intervened militarily, assisting the Boran against all Moslem pastoralists. Massacres ensued, in which scores of Garri were killed, including the chief, Robow Hassan Gababa, and six prominent clan elders. The response was a guerrilla campaign against the Ethiopian army, led by Alyow Hassan Gabbaba. Meanwhile, across the border in Kenya, Hasaan Goro, a Garri, was also leading an armed struggle against oppression by Moslem pastoralists. Together these conflicts have become known as the *Shifta* wars.

The consequence of the rebellion for Moslem pastoralists in southern Ethiopia was immense. The administration armed the Boran who guided the Ethiopian army in assaults on the Garri and their allies. Villages were burnt, livestock and property was taken, and Moslem families were killed indiscriminately. People escaped in every direction. Many went to Somalia or to relatives in urban centres like Negelle and Moyalle, others submitted to Ethiopian army protection. Once the resistance movement had been suppressed, the government stationed troops all over Garri territory, taking particular care to police places where livestock could be watered (e.g. Wachille, Udet, Wallena, Dedertu, Lei, El Der, Dedertu, Jara, Malaka-Mari and Qadadduma). Somalia's claim to the Ogaden meant that the loyalties of all Moslem groups continued to be suspect, and increased government backing enhanced the local dominance of the non-Moslem Boran.

However, unrelenting oppression (which reached a new peak during the 1974–5 drought) inevitably encouraged the Garri and the Somali clans to look towards Somalia. The Somalian government was most willing to exploit the situation. It had in fact already been encouraging dissident groups in Ethiopia. In the political turmoil which followed the fall of Haile Selassie's regime, Somalia stepped up these activities, supporting a Somali liberation front in the Ogaden which helped spread insurrection through much of

---

[3] According to many informants from both groups, educated elites and politicians have been responsible for the ongoing conflict between the Boran and Garri. They have frustrated efforts by elders to mediate because they have derived personal benefits from the fighting.
[4] Since 1991 this situation has been reversed, with the Boran's enemies being supported by the Transitional Government.

Borana region. The Garri refer to events at that time as 'when people were caught by force' (gāāf-nāām-ya-ban).[5]

In early 1977, the Somalian army entered Ethiopian territory in an attempt to annex the whole Ogaden. It met no resistance until the troops reached Ogoba, near to Negelle town. For a short time it looked as if the Somalian forces were going to be victorious but, having secured Soviet and Cuban support, Mengistu's government was able to launch a counter-offensive. By mid-1978, the Somalian regular army had been forced to withdraw. Guerrilla fighting contined until the early 1980s, provoking vicious responses, including several large-scale massacres of civilians. Much of the Moslem population, including many Garri, fled into Somalia, where most of them spent years in refugee camps. Those who remained faced destitution, hunger and forcible relocatlon to protected villages. Men were in danger of conscription into the Ethiopian armed forces, and of being sent to fight in the war in Eritrea.

UNHCR and the Return to Ethiopia

There are no accurate figures for how many Ethiopians became refugees in Somalia, nor for how many have returned to Ethiopia. There are several reasons for this, including the following: (1) the social upheavals in southern Ethiopia, western Somalia and Northern Kenya since the 1960s have pushed populations in both directions, sometimes at the same time; (2) there are ambiguities about nationality among the nomadic groups of the border region, because they have customarily ignored state boundaries in their migrations to water sources and pasturage, and because there has been a great deal of mixing between people of different ethnic identities; (3) during the 1970s and 1980s, the Somalian government persistently exaggerated refugee numbers in order to secure foreign aid. Nevertheless, it seems likely that the total population that was forcibly displaced over the Ethiopian/Somalian border between 1960 and 1990 was well in excess of 200,000. Apart from Garri families, it included Gabbra, Gujji, Marrehan, Arssi, Garrimarro, Gurra, Degodi, Watta, Sidama, Gere and some islamicized Boran. Many individuals fled back and forth more than once.

Most of the Garri refugees in Somalia had a terrible time. Life in the camps was grim. Much of the humanitarian aid intended to help them appears to have been used for other purposes by corrupt government officials, and little protection was provided from the frequent raids on the settlements by local Somali clans. Moreover, men were placed under pressure to join the national army and to fight in the civil war going on in the north (Africa Watch, 1991: 96; interviews with returnees in Hudet, 1989).

By the early 1980s, some of the refugees seem to have wanted to go back to Ethiopia although, as an Africa Watch report put it: 'Civilian refugees were caught between two evils, and their return to Ethiopia often indicated merely that conditions in Somalia had deteriorated not that those in Ethiopia had improved' (Africa Watch, 1991: 96–7).

For its part, the Somalian government was heavily dependent on finance and commodities brought into the country by the aid agencies working with refugees, and strongly resisted any efforts by UNHCR to facilitate repatriation. Meanwhile, the Ethiopian administration attempted to counter Somalian government assertions, proclaiming that the refugees were in no danger and should return through Ethiopian government-controlled reception centres. They were after their own share of any available international aid.

UNHCR and other humanitarian agencies were placed in an extremely difficult

[5] Information from interviews with Aw Mude, Maalim Ibrahim Genemo, Hassan Guracha, Yisahaqow Racha, Aw Alyow Qaliti, Ali Jillo and Haj Mohammed Haj Hassan in Gababa, Qadaduma, El-D'er, Moyalle, Hudet and Arero (1983, 1989 and 1990).

situation. They had no choice other than
to try to work with the Mengistu and
Barre regimes, two of the most oppressive
and despotic governments in Africa.
Unfortunately some international staff
appear to have been easily fooled. The first
attempt at supported repatriation occurred
in May 1980, when fighting was still continuing in Borana region. A team of UN
officials visited Ethiopia at the invitation of
the Mengistu adminstration. The following observations were made in their
report:

9.1 *The Ethiopian administration successfully
used aid as a means of extending state control:
children participating in a literacy campaign
launched by the government among the Garri
living in Liban, 1985. (K.N. Getachew)*

The UNHCR representative broadly agrees
with the [Ethiopian] government peception
of the situation, and feels that on both
humanitarian and pragmatic grounds a
comprehensive approach is needed; this would include assistance for both displaced and [other]
affected populations in Ethiopia thus reducing the incentive to swell the number of refugees in
neighbouring countries.... [The Ethiopian government] feels that the UN system is taking a
one-sided view of the situation by launching a large-scale assistance programme in Somalia and
doing almost nothing in Ethiopia. They feel that this will only aggravate the situation in
attracting a large number of people to cross the border. (Zaki Hassan, UNICEF Executive
Board, 'Report on a visit to Ethiopia, 13–17 May 1980', Addis Ababa, quoted in *Africa Watch*,
1991: 97).

The implication was that the refugees in Somalia were economic migrants. It was a
remarkably ill-informed view, given what was known about atrocities in Ethiopia and
the appalling circumstances of many families in the refugee camps. Nonetheless, UNHCR
decided to promote repatriation, without having a capacity to monitor the consequences.

In the event, neither UNHCR not the Somali and Ethiopian governments proved
capable of co-ordinating the population movements of the 1980s. Having experienced
atrocities in the camps, many refugees decided to go back to Ethiopia, but they were
aware of the dangers involved. Mengistu's regime had given assurances of amnesty but
some influential Garri, as well as some leaders of other groups, were known to have been
detained and even formally sentenced to prison terms. The Ethiopian government had in
fact passed legislation for this purpose. Article 12 of the Revised Penal Code of 1981
stated that attempting to leave the country without official permission was a 'counter
revolutionary act', equivalent to treason. It was punishable by between five and 25 years
imprisonment.

The effectiveness of the humanitarian interventions aimed at helping the returnees
was further hampered by the ongoing lack of co-operation between UNHCR and the
two governments involved. The Ethiopian administration refused to recognize returned
refugees as a specific category, and insisted that international aid should be extended to
former guerrilla fighters and prisoners of war released by the rebel fronts. It successfully
used aid as a means of extending state control. In Somalia, the government continued to
maintain that Ethiopia was unsafe, and that the return of refugees should be discouraged.
For years, it would not contemplate a tripartite agreement for repatriation. International
pressure eventually forced the acceptance of such agreement in 1986. However, few
displaced people were prepared to place much faith in the offers of support made by
government officials and aid agency staff, and a glance at the activities of the UNHCR
office at Negelle reveals that this was an accurate assessment.

The UNHCR field office at Negelle was one part of the repatriation programme set

9.2 *The Garri returnee settlements at El-D'er, 1991. (K.N. Getachew)*

under way in 1986. Full-time staff comprised a manager, a medical doctor, drivers for 15 vehicles, and several repatriation 'co-ordinators'. The Red Cross was also involved in the operation, providing some medical care, and Ethiopian government employees were engaged in projects to improve wells, build roads and clear fields for farming, mostly using local labour on a food-for-work basis. Among the people involved in running these schemes were highly motivated and altruistic individuals. But there were also other staff who were ignorant of local circumstances and unsympathetic to the returnees. Furthermore, few decisions could be made without reference to Ethiopian officials whose primary concerns were to do with party policy, security and the imposition of state authority.

Those refugees who chose repatriation under official auspices had to follow a carefully regulated procedure. Returnees were brought from the Somali camps to Dollo-Gedo, a Somalian border town. They were then accompanied by a UNHCR official to the Ethiopian border town of Dollo-Oddo. After being photographed and registered, they were transferred to Boqolmayo, a temporary UNHCR receiving centre. After staying one night they were transported to the central UNHCR receiving and dispatching centre at Negelle. They remained at Negelle for a week or more, receiving medical check-ups, treatment and vaccination. They were then re-registered, photographed again, and asked about their ethnic identity, clan, religion, language, former residence, number of dependants, and choice of destination for settlement. Goverment security officers were involved in these interviews, and records were kept for each individual.

Finally, the returnees were supposed to be provided with food rations for two months, a small amount of money (1,050 birr), farming tools and cooking utensils. They were then taken to the sites selected as their homes, where they were meant to receive donated food in monthly distributions. But, in practice, many families who arrived after 1986 received very little food, let alone money or donated items. Moreover, the decision of where to settle returnees was sometimes made by UNHCR or government officials without reference to stated preferences, and several families found themselves located far from their former areas. For example, Garri Marrehan and Gujji returnee settlements were established in Boran territories (near Arero and El-Gofa, and in Liban) while Gabra, Arssi and Gurra families were located in Gujji areas. Given the past conflicts over grazing and water rights, this kind of insensitive mixing up of population groups against their will was unlikely to result in the emergence of harmonious neighbourhoods.[6]

Not surprisingly, as the situation in Somalia deteriorated, the vast majority of refugees did all they could to avoid regulated 'voluntary' repatriation and settlement. They escaped from their camps without assistance, many of them travelling back to Ethiopia via Kenya. Between 1986 and 1990, as few as 7,200 people were registered by UNHCR as having returned under the agency's auspices.[7]

However, irrespective of whether the refugees returned through formal channels or

---

[6] Since 1992 it has been a direct cause of bitter disputes. Hundreds of people have been killed.
[7] Information from various unpublished UNHCR reports and interviews carried out in Negelle during the late 1980s.

managed to avoid them, the life they faced back in Ethiopia was, at best, only a marginal improvement on that in war-torn Somalia. The early 1980s had been a period of severe drought, and the Ethiopian army had made every effort to destroy the local pastoral economy, restricting access to water points and pasture, confiscating livestock and imposing restrictions on movement. The government had also adopted a strategy of exploiting and encouraging hostilities between groups, particularly between the Garri and the Degodia, and between the Boran and the Garri, the Degodia, the Gujji, the Arssi and the Marrehan. The Boran were provided with modern small arms. The consequence was a spiral of violence, which remains a serious problem in the 1990s. In spite of the the continued provision of humanitarian assistance, much of the population remains destitute.

An Assessment of the UNHCR Repatriation and Rehabilitation Programme

Having outlined the difficult context in which UNHCR was operating, I now make some more specific comments about the running of the Negelle field office. I have already made clear that the office's attempts to co-ordinate repatriation and to provide aid were ineffective. The purpose of this section is to highlight some of the inappropriate methods used which ought to be avoided in the future.

(a) UNHCR staff lacked knowledge and understanding of the local situation:
The UNHCR local employees, who carried out much of the day-to-day running of the office were almost all new to the region, and did not speak the Boran and Somali languages. Like the international staff, they needed continuous help with communication, and tended to depend upon interpreters provided by the security services. As a consequence, misunderstandings between returnees and UNHCR officials were common, with the statements of returnees often being deliberately misinterpreted. This was a problem which continued right up to the end of the programme (I observed it occuring myself in 1990 while working among returnees in Udet, Negelle, El-Ley, Malka-Mari and Arero). There were even cases in which a breakdown in communication led to people being unjustly imprisoned for alleged trouble-making.

(b) There was no serious consultation with the returnees:
Doubtless partly because so little was done to overcome the problem of communication, there were no serious efforts made at consultation with the returnees. From the perspective of the Garri, Gabra and Gujji families who I spoke to, decisions were made by government officials, the party, the security and UNHCR officials. All of these powerful groups were viewed as having a contemptuous attitude, and some individuals were known to be actively hostile, regarding displaced people as allies of the Somali enemy.

(c) The inadequate resources made available for the programme did not reach afflicted populations because of incompetence and theft:
The resources allocated by UNHCR to support the returnee families it repatriated, let alone the displaced population as a whole, were inadequate. Moreover, a large part of what was donated never reached those targetted, but seem to have been used to enrich senior officials working in the operation.
    The first manager appointed to Negelle refused to give the returnees cash. Instead he bought and distributed cheap highland goats and cattle. Virtually all the animals quickly died, either because of local diseases against which they had no resistance, or because of

9.3 *The small-stock market in Negelle town, August, 1994. (K. N. Getachew)*

the arid lowland environment. His decision had been made without consulting the returnees, and it was rumoured that the money he had made by purchasing highland animals was enough to establish his family in a fine house in Addis Ababa. He was eventually replaced, but embezzlement and incompetence continued.

Partly because of the endless complaints made by returnees, UNHCR decided to start providing cash to each family. However, many families were given only a fraction of the money allocated to them, and some were given nothing, being informed that they had already received it. As for the food ration, many did not receive anything for four or five months at a time, and when food finally was distributed a considerable proportion was usually missing. Much of it ended up in the urban markets, having been embezzled by returnee camp officials and the lorry drivers.

At the returnee villages where I spent a short period in 1990, the Garri households attempted to deal with the situation by dividing up. Some family members would be sent to towns like Moyalle, Arero, Mega or Negelle in search of work, others would go to look for food among relatives who had not been displaced, and a few would hang around in the village or at the UNHCR office in Negelle, complaining that no food had arrived. This situation had dragged on for years, but no-one seemed at all interested in their plight. No schools had been built in the returnee settlements nor teachers allocated to hold classes, and the only formal health care was a rare visit by a Red Cross medical team. Sanitation was poor and there were many deaths from diseases which could have been easily treated. Mortality rates appeared to be especially high among Garri families located in remote areas (e.g. Hudet-Bima, El-D'er, Malka-Marri, Jara and Walena).

(d) Monitoring was completely inadequate:
As will be apparent from the above remarks, monitoring of the UNHCR operation was inadequate. There seems to have been no inspection of the way the Negelle office was run, and perhaps more disturbing, UNHCR was unable to protect the people it had

encouraged to repatriate. When the fighting in the war in the north intensified at
the end of the 1980s, the returnees were
effectively abandoned. Numerous Garri
men were captured, sent to Negelle for
military training and then transported to
the war zones. This prompted others to
flee the returnee camps, leaving women
and children to their own devices.

(e) Decisions were frequently taken without preliminary or ongoing research:
It has already been mentioned that there
was virtually no consultation with returnees. In addition, there were no steps taken
to gain an adequate understanding of local
issues. Although the UNHCR programme
was run over several years, no significant
social research was attempted before
making decisions. Often it would take
some time before a decision was made, but
this was due to bureaucratic bottlenecks.

9.4 *The returnees are more interested in
Islamic learning than 'non-returnees': teaching
the Koran at El-D'er returnee settlement,
1991. (K.N. Getachew)*

When it actually became possible to decide about something, haste was usually
considered to be essential, and there was no effort made to assess the consequences or
debate alternative strategies.

As a result, the cultural, historical and environmental implications of UNHCR's
activities were largely ignored. People were sometimes settled among their clan enemies,
and often in places where there were no water sources, nor materials for building or for
firewood. Furthermore, it was assumed that all returnees would take up a life of
subsistence farming, irrespective of their previous pastoral economy or their experiences
in exile. Even if this had been a reasonable expectation, most settlement sites were totally
unsuited for agriculture. For example, the Garri settlements at Hudet, Walena, Gof and
Lei are in areas where it is not even possible to graze cattle. These are places where camel
and small-stock pastoralism is the only locally sustainable economy, but such a prospect
seems to have been anathema to the authorities. It is difficult to avoid the conclusion
that the UNHCR programme was in effect co-opted by the Ethiopian state, and was
aimed not at reintegrating the returnees, but at keeping them separated so that they
could be watched and persecuted.

A Note on the Longer Term Social Effects of Exile

In the early 1990s, the Garri continue a struggle for survival in difficult circumstances.
Old customs remain a powerful influence, and have helped shape approaches to re-
establishing communities. Partly because international humanitarian interventions have
had such a very limited impact in terms of the distribution of resources, many of the most
impoverished have turned to better-off clan members. They have received *hiirb*, a dona-
tion of livestock, food or money collected from the clan as whole, or they have begged
dabarre, a loan of livestock for up to three generations, or they have resorted to a socially
acceptable form of 'theft' from close relatives with whom they have a special 'joking'
relationship. In this manner families have begun rebuilding lost herds, and the networks
of debt and reciprocity which bind people together are slowly being reconstituted.

9.5 *Garri returnees engaged in cultivation of maize and millet in April 1991. Before the displacement, farming was on a much smaller scale. (K.N. Getachew)*

However, it is also clear that divisions have emerged within and between Garri communities, often associated with experiences of displacement. Those who have returned from Somalian refugee camps tend to have different attitudes and a different world view to those who remained in Ethiopia. If political stability can be established, and the economy and security situation improve, these differences may be resolved as neighbourhood ties develop, and a new consensus evolves about reasonable and moral modes of behaviour. But such a process is likely to be slow, will be linked with profound changes in the Garri way of life, and can be expected to be a significant cause of local tension during the years to come.

Drawing on my own observations, I conclude this chapter with a few remarks about some of the most noticeable differences between those who went to Somalia and those who did not.

Repatriated Garri have taken on a form of ethnic identity which sets them apart. They are known as *qohati* (returnee). This identity is used in conversations with 'non-returnee' Garri, and has proved useful as a means of avoiding some forms of taxation, membership of certain government-run organizations, and military conscription (until 1989). Also the returnees are more interested in Islamic learning than 'non-returnees', have tended to look towards the staff of international organizations for administration rather than government officials, and are somewhat more dismissive than 'non-returnees' of political revolutionary or party rhetoric. Their relative independent-mindedness has led to tensions with officials and with some traditional Garri elders.

In addition, the returnees have introduced new ways of doing things, some of which directly challenge convention. They build different sorts of houses, using different building techniques. They embroider their clothes and are more concerned about decoration of the home. They consider it important to have household utensils and furniture, and they tend to keep poultry for eggs and meat. Furthermore, returnee men do not despise farming. If they are located in arable areas and have some camels or cattle, they will use animal traction for ploughing – shocking behaviour to conservative pastoralists.

Perhaps most striking of all, returnee women are much less inhibited than 'non-returnee' women (Getachew, 1991). Many of them do not hesitate when it comes to participation in public debates. They tend to insist on marrying men of their own choice and to challenge the custom of widow inheritance. Several have gone so far as to run households without the protection of any adult males, choosing to fend for themselves and their children without recourse to traditional modes of support. Much to the amazement of 'non-returnees', such female household heads are accorded equal status to male household heads by the staff of UNHCR. Their autonomy has become a possibility because returnee women have turned to commercial activity in locally unprecedented ways. Some of them have opened small shops or tea rooms. Others have become involved in the sale of firewood, milk and eggs, or in long-distance trading in smuggled goods and *chat* (a stimulant drug). In a society where many people still expect women to be totally dependent on men, these radical introductions can be viewed as a shameful affront.

References

Africa Watch (1991) *Evil days: 30 years of war and famine in Ethiopia*, London, New York.

Asmarom Legesse (1973) *Gadar: three approaches to the study of African society*. New York, Free Press.

Baxter, P.T.W. (1991) 'Introduction' in P.T.W. Baxter (ed.) *When the grass is gone: development intervention in African arid lands*, Scandinavian Institute of African Studies, Uppsala.

Donaldson Smith, A. (1896) 'Expedition through Somaliland to Lake Rudolf', *Geographical Journal*, Vol. VIII: 221–39.

— (1904) 'Africa between the River Juba and the Nile', *Geographical Journal*: 680–89.

F.O. (1907) British Foreign Office papers, copies held by the Institute of Ethiopian Studies Library, Addis Ababa.

Getachew, K.N. (1983) 'A history of the Garri upto 1941', BA thesis, Addis Ababa University, Addis Ababa.

— (1984) 'Some notes on the Garri traditional crafts'. Eighth International Conference of Ethiopian Studies, Institute of Ethiopian Studies, Addis Ababa.

— (1985) 'Research Report on Garri–Boran relations', unpublished ms, Institute of Ethiopian Studies, Addis Ababa.

— (1988) 'Die Garri Sud-Äthiopiens – wer sind Sie und was macht Sie zu einer ethnie?' MA thesis, University of Bayreuth, Bayreuth.

— (1989) 'The expansion of Boran into Boran Region of Southern Ethiopia', unpublished ms, Institute of Ethiopian Studies, Addis Ababa.

— (1990) 'A descriptive account of coffee slaughter (*Bun-Qalle*) ceremony of the Garri of southern Ethiopia', Proceedings of the First National Conference of Ethiopian Studies. Institute of Ethiopian Studies, Addis Ababa: 13–29.

— (1991) 'Change of role and status among pastoral Garri women, southern Ethiopia', in Tsehai Berhane Selassie (ed.), *Gender issues in Ethiopia*, University Press, Addis Ababa: 7–15.

Gwynn, C. (1911) 'A journey in southern Abyssinia', *Geographical Journal*, Vol. 38, No. 2: 113–39.

Haberland, E. (1963) *Galla Sud-Aethiopien*. Kohlhammer, Stuttgart.

Hamilton, D. (1977) 'Schedule of international agreements relating to the boundaries of Ethiopia', *Ethiopian Observer*, Vol. 16, No. 2: Addis Ababa.

Hodson, A.L.W. (1927) *Seven years in Southern Abysinia*, London.

Lewis, H.S. (1966) 'The origins of the Galla and Somali', *Journal of African History*, Vol 7, No. 1: 27–46.

Lewis, I.M. (1955) *Peoples of the Horn of Africa, Somali, Afar and Saho – ethnographic survey of Africa, North East Africa, Part I*, Institute of African Studies, London.

— (1960) 'The Somali conquest of the Horn of Africa', *Journal of African History*, Vol 1, No. 2: 213.

— (1979) 'Pre- and post-colonial political units in Africa', in Hussein M. Adam (ed.), *Proceedings of the International Symposium*, Vol. 2, Mogadishu: 352–69.

— (1980) 'The Western Somali Liberation Front (WSLF) and the legacy of Sheikh Hussein of Bale,' in J. Tubiana (ed.), *Modern Ethiopia*, Balkama publications du CNRS, Sophia-Antipolis: 402–512.

Maud, P. (1904) 'Exploration in the southern borderland of Abysinia', *Geographical Journal*, Vol. 23: 552–79.

Neumann, O. (1902) 'From Somali coast through southern Ethiopia to the Sudan', *Geographical Journal*, Vol. 20: 376–8.

Perham, M. (1974) *The Government of Ethiopia*. Faber and Faber, London.

Schlee, G. (1984) 'The Oromo expansion and its impact on ethnogenesis in Northern Kenya', Eighth International Conference of Ethiopian Studies, Addis Ababa, unpublished proceedings.

— (1989) *Identities on the move*. Manchester University Press, Manchester.

Trimingham, J.S. (1952) *Islam in Ethiopia*. Frank Cass, London.

Tsehai B. S. (1969) 'Menelik II conquests and consolidation of the southern provinces', BA (history) Addis Ababa University.

Turton, E.A.R. (1975) 'Bantu, Galla and Somali migrations in the Horn of Africa – a reassessment of the Jubar/Tana area', *Journal of African History*, Vol 16, No.4: 519–37.

10 AHMED YUSUF FARAH
The Plight & the Prospects
of Ethiopia's Lowland Pastoral Groups

This chapter draws on a series of short fieldwork visits to lowland locations in Ethiopia, carried out between August and October 1992. It also derives insights from some of the detailed studies made of Ethiopian pastoralists by myself (Farah, 1989) and other social anthropologists (eg. I.M. Lewis, 1961; Baxter, 1965, 1978). Most of the material was originally presented in a series of consultancy reports (Farah, 1992a, 1992b, 1992c, 1992d), prepared for the ERCS/IFRC (the Ethiopian Red Cross and Red Crescent Society and the International Federation of Red Cross and Red Crescent Societies). The primary purpose was to come up with policy suggestions, which might be of help to the Red Cross Movement in its relief operations among some of Ethiopia's most impoverished populations.

In 1992 it was estimated that there were about 300,000 Ethiopians who urgently needed humanitarian assistance. The majority of these people were Somali, Afar or Oromo groups, living in marginal, lowland locations. The most vulnerable had lost the bulk of their livestock, were unable to cultivate their fields and were facing near-famine conditions. Particularly in the areas near Jijiga in Afarland, and near Negelle in the south, their main source of aid was the ERCS/IFRC (see Table 10.1). Staff working for the Red Cross organizations therefore needed to gain an understanding of the kinds of constraints facing such pastoralists and former pastoralists on a day-to-day basis.

In the following sections I introduce the traditional Somali, Afar and Oromo ways of life, and then go on to examine the breakdown of security in lowland areas, the inadequacies of the aid operations, and some of the characteristics of particularly distressed population categories (which I found to be the locally displaced, returnees, Somali refugees and demobilized soldiers). In the last part of the chapter I briefly comment on some of the possibilities for future humanitarian intervention.

Somali, Afar and Oromo Livelihoods

Ethiopia's Oromos, Afars and Somalis manifest important common characteristics. They all speak Cushitic languages, and a remarkably extensive interaction and cultural assimilation has taken place over the centuries, even between groups which express hostility towards one another. This has notably been the case in the vicinity of Jijiga and Negelle. On the one hand, there are some Oromo groups who have become 'Somali-ized', while on the other hand, there are Somali groups who have become 'Oromo-ized'. The Jarso who are antagonistic to the Geri in Jijiga provide a quintessential example of the former, while the latter is exemplified by Garri and the Gabra in Boran. Marriage relations,

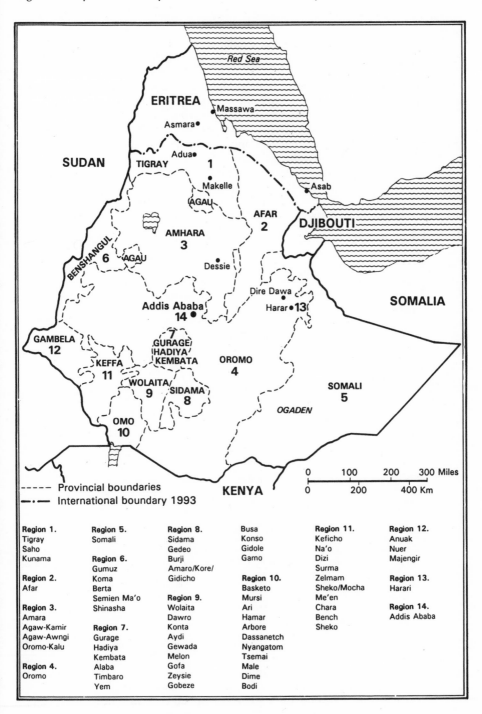

Map 10.1 *Regions of Ethiopia, 1991*

neighbourliness and pastoral economies provide foundations for common interest and co-operation.

There is also a widely held view among these lowlanders that they have been neglected or exploited by the previous governments of Ethiopia. The regimes of Haile Selassie and Mengistu are perceived as having been dominated by an Orthodox Christian, highlander elite, who were distrustful or actively hostile to the Moslem Afar and Somalis, and who despised the 'animist' Oromo.

Nevertheless, social organization does not generally lend itself to integration into large, organized population units. For instance, there are 14 Ethiopian Somali political organizations (which basically replicate the major Somali clans), and there are four political groups representing the Ethiopian Oromo nationality. The Afar are the exception, currently having just two main political organizations, the Afar Liberation Front and the Afar People's Democratic Organization.

Table 10.1 *Location and religious belief of the major ethnic groups assisted by the ERCS/IFRC*

Name of the group	Religion	Ethnic category	Location
Gadabursi	Muslim	Somali	Jijiga
Geri	"	"	"
Jarso	"	Oromo	"
Afar	"	Afar	Northeast
Garri	"	Somali	Negelle/Boran
Gabra	"	"	"
Marehan	"	"	"
Digodi	"	"	"
Arssi	"	Oromo	"
Boran	Mixed	"	"
Guji	"	"	"

Notes
1. *Name of the group* refers to the most common local-level classifications.
2. *Religion* refers to the dominant religion of the group. 'Mixed' indicates that some members of the group are Christian, others are Muslim and others adhere to traditional beliefs.
3. *Ethnic category* refers to broader ethnic classifications, related to linguistic divisions.
4. *Location* does not refer to areas corresponding with the post-1991 boundaries of regions and districts. 'Jijiga' is a town (and also the common name for its vicinity) located in the north of the present Somali Region (of Ethiopia). 'Northeast' is now mainly made up of Afar Region. 'Negelle' is a town located in the South of Ethiopia. Its vicinity was until recently called the 'Boran Administration', taking its name from what has been in the past the dominant local ethnic group. 'Boran Administration' is now divided between Oromo Region and Somali Region (see Map 9.2 on page 113).

The Somali

The livelihood of the predominantly nomadic Somali has been analysed in detail by I.M. Lewis (1961), and more recently in my own work (Farah, 1989). A kinship-based, patrilineal descent system, which is supplemented by a customary contract (*xeer*), is the basis of social organization. Each Somali has a place within a relatively small social unit, and also recognizes relationships with wider spheres of kinsmen. Social life is characterized by a remarkable degree of egalitarianism between men, a fact which goes some way to explain the tumultuous nature of Somali political activity.

The highest organizational unit has been designated by Lewis as the 'clan family'. Usually this is a symbolic social entity whose widespread members, in many cases extending across the borders into neighbouring countries, are tied together by the sense of being the descendants of a common ancestor. Dir, Isaq, Darod, Hawiya, Digil and Rahanweyn, constitute the total Somali nation. The last two 'clan families' are primarily agricultural groups found in southern Somalia, while the other four are mainly pastoral groups, inhabiting territory in Ethiopia, Kenya and Djibouti, as well as Somalia.

Below this highest level of grouping is the 'clan', which Lewis described as having considerable local political significance in particular circumstances. Clans are associated with specific locations frequented by its nomadic members. Visits to wells and trading centres provide a degree of regulation to otherwise rather erratic migrations associated with the requirements of the livestock. Clans are divided into what Lewis called 'primary lineages', units which commonly practise exogamy (i.e. marriage occurs between lineages and not within a lineage). These are in turn made up of corporate clusters, known as *dia*-paying groups, which count four to six generations to a common male ancestor.

A *dia*-paying group may comprise a few hundred to a few thousand souls. It is the most important social segment in daily life. A strong sense of solidarity based on agnation is reinforced by a binding customary contract *xeer*, which most importantly sanctions the collective payment and receipt of blood compensation (*dia*). The *dia*-paying group is neither a residential unit, since its members move among wider kinsmen, nor an endogamous unit. Indeed a Somali man regards females belonging to his *dia*-paying group as sisters and traditionally never married them (although such rules are now sometimes being undermined, particularly in urban and sedentary contexts). Among the Somali, only very close kinsmen (a man and his sons or brothers) reside and migrate together.

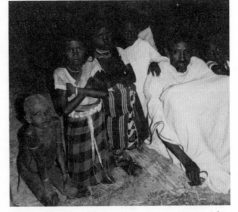

10.1 *An Afar elder enjoying an evening with his children, August 1994. The style of clothing seen in the photograph is typical of the Afar, and clearly sets them apart from neighbouring groups. (K.N. Getachew)*

10.2 *Among the Afar, the* finaa *is the institution that defends clan territory and enforces decisions of the clan chief and council elders. It is made up of young men selected from all the lineages of the clan. The photograph shows* finaa *men guarding their clan chief, August 1994 – note the automatic rifle. (K.N. Getachew)*

The Afar

The literature on the Afar is patchy, largely unpublished and often difficult to obtain. Aid agency reports suggest that the Afar are organized on the principle of clanship and, by implication, that they have a social organization comparable to that of the Somali. However, currently ongoing fieldwork by K.N. Getachew indicates that superficial similarities disguise important differences (personal communication). The total Afar nation (made up of populations living in Ethiopia and in contiguous territories of Djibouti and Eritrea) are divided into two major groupings: Adohi-Murra ('the white-people') and Asahimara ('the red people'). These widely scattered and unwieldy entities are known to be divided into different segments, which have been described as clans. However, the morphology and actual function of Afar social units is unclear.

From the material available, it would seem that the most important social unit may be designated as the 'minimal lineage'. This unit appears to correspond with the Somali *dia*-paying groups. Both are founded upon descent and customary contract. But the Afar minimal lineage is further strengthened by a tendency among its members to reside together, and relations are further cemented by an inward-looking endogamy rule that encourages patrilateral cross-cousin marriage.

Most probably, the Afar clan leaders have more authority than their Somali counterparts (who in practice hold only nominal powers and depend upon persuasion to enforce decisions). The external recognition of an Afar Sultanate, the political effectiveness of particular Afar sultans, and long-term local warfare with the Issa in the Awash Valley, may have had the effect of reinforcing social hierarchies, and may explain the Afar's relative social cohesion.

The Oromo

The Oromo make up one of the largest language clusters in Africa (there are an estimated 20 million Oromo-speakers). Most of them live in Ethiopia, where they are the biggest 'nationality'. They consist of numerous groups which have often been mutually hostile. The best known of these are the Arssi, Boran, Guji, Karaiyu, Lega, Macha, Afran Kallo, Raya, Tulama and Wollo. Some have been the focus of fine anthropological and historical studies, and there are also useful overviews which relate to all Oromos (literature relating to Ethiopian Oromo-speaking groups includes: Bartels, 1983; Baxter, 1965, 1978, 1983, 1986, 1991, 1994a, 1994b; Hassen, 1990; Hutlin, 1987; H.S. Lewis, 1965; Gidada, 1984; Van de Loo, 1991).

There is a great deal of cultural variation between Oromo-speaking groups, and between Oromo individuals and families. Many more Oromos have been integrated into the Ethiopian state system and the national economy than Afars and Somalis. Baxter has described modern Oromoland in the following way.

> Oromoland varies from parched desert to forested mountains. The different groups have different histories and now demonstrate diversities in culture, ways of life and religion. Many men and some women are now urbanized professionals, craft workers and labourers, and many others are merchants and traders, but most Oromo maintain themselves as cultivators and/or stock keepers, ranging from densely settled plough farmers to transhumant and nomadic pastoralists.... Most would describe themselves as Muslims, Orthodox Christians, Roman Catholics, Lutherans or Pentecostals, but the daily religious behaviour of most continues to be rooted in traditional responses ... Indeed, whatever variations there may be by group, religious affiliation or education, all Oromo seem to share basic and crucial sets of understandings as to what the proper relations between people, and between people and God, should be. Moreover, any Oromo-speaker, whatever his or her dialect, can be readily understood by any other throughout Oromoland. (Baxter, 1994b: 167)

The social organization of the Oromo is more complex than that of the Somali and the Afar. Clan membership constitutes only one aspect of social organization. For example, among the Boran (the largest Oromo group of Southern Ethiopia, and one which has been very badly affected by recent upheavals), social life is regulated in a variety of ways. The group is divided into two great exogamous moieties, Sabho and Gona, each being associated with one of the two main, hereditary spiritual leaders, known as *Kaalu*. These moieties are subdivided into clans, but these are diffuse units, having no head, nor a senior lineage, nor any territorial loyalties (Baxter, 1965: 67). Boran men also belong to generation sets (*Luuba*), which perform a series of ceremonies (*Gadamoji*) every eight years. A man's set is determined by that of his father and grandfather, and in many ways a member is seen as replacing his grandfather. All Boran men become members of a set and set activities are synchronized, although the set as a whole never meets. Superficially the sets appear to have a similar role to generation-set systems among other African groups (including other Oromo), but the Boran system has much less direct association with political administration. Its purpose is essentially ritual and moral.

Traditionally, some Boran could be viewed as in a 'better' ritual condition than others, as some were older, healthier, or stronger than others, but none were politically superior to others. According to Baxter, the moral solidarity of the Boran was maintained largely by the repetition of commonly held sentiments in ceremonies, combined with the ever present fear of hostilities with non-Boran (Baxter, 1965: 76). However, state support for government chiefs, and periodic alliances with government forces has fostered greater social stratification than hitherto, and in some places, a hierarchy has emerged connected with territorial control. It is sometimes accepted that senior figures should administer resources, including such crucial needs as pasturage and water.

Pastoral economies

The vast majority of the communities which the Red Cross Movement is assisting in lowland Ethiopia are pastoralists, whose primary stock is either cattle or camels. Cattle herders found in disaster-stricken areas are predominantly Oromo-speakers (although Oromo groups of Southern Ethiopia, notably the Arssi and Guji, also practise crop production). The Somali groups and the Afar pastoralists mainly keep camels (although a considerable number of the Afar also raise cattle and small stock).

Each nomadic family possesses unalienable rights over its primary stock, either camels or cattle, and supplementary herds of small ruminants (sheep and goats). The small ruminants are raised for their economic value. In addition to the milk and ghee derived from them, they are slaughtered to satisfy the domestic meat requirement and to entertain important guests. They may also be sold to earn cash, for purchase of household goods such as grains, salt, sugar, tea, soap, razor blades, clothes, shoes, etc.

The traditional staple diet of the nomads, which consists mainly of animal products – milk, meat and occasionally purified ghee, is still very significant. However, it is important to emphasize that traditional foods are increasingly being supplemented with grains exchanged with the proceeds from livestock sales and animal products. Dependence upon grains increases at the height of the dry season – November to April, and at times of drought, when livestock yields are drastically reduced. In contrast to the 'consumer' and 'market commodity' significance of the small ruminants, the cherished primary stocks tend to be regarded as 'pastoral capital', and social solidarity revolves around them. Thus Somali camels are collectively herded, collectively defended against aspiring rival social units and also collectively raided from hostile groups. Many feuds are caused by conflicts over particular camels or cattle, or over securing sufficient pasturage and water. Primary stocks are hoarded and kept from the market except at times of extreme need. As a rule, they are only slaughtered on ceremonial occasions.

Ideally, coveted camels or cattle change hands only in very significant traditional exchange arrangements. Most importantly, they are exchanged with women, who beget children as wives of lineage members, and maintain valuable affinal relations which

10.3 *Most of Ethiopia's pastoral communities can be viewed as in a difficult period of transition: Afar household, 1994. (K.N. Getachew)*

become valuable at times of food scarcity or political upheaval. Animals are also exchanged in cases of blood compensation. Only camels or cattle can console the aggrieved for the loss of a kinsman. In effect, the primary stocks act as a repository of values and an indicator of status.

A possible danger of stock hoarding is overgrazing and consequent environmental damage. However, there is a too ready tendency among researchers and government officials to simply assume that this must be occurring. It has been an explanation given for oppressive strategies aimed at discouraging livestock production, notably the introduction of sedentarization and villiagization programmes, and the levying of a pastoral 'head tax'. This policy was a major cause of the famine in 1962, and was responsible for impoverishing the people of the Ogaden in the late 1980s (Dolal, 1992: 186).

In fact, pastoral groups are generally very aware of the dangers of overgrazing and try to take steps to avert it. They know about the effects on the environment, and are also wary of concentrating herds because of the possibility that diseases will be spread (veterinary services have always been inadequate). A widespread husbandry practice is the seasonal splitting up of family stock units, so as to make maximum use of the scarce and seasonally varying pastoral resources. Among both cattle and camel keepers, men will take dry animals, which require less water and can move quickly, to distant grazing lands. Lactating cattle or camels as well as small ruminants are kept in the less mobile nomadic hamlets, where wives and small children attend to them. In most instances where overgrazing occurs, it is due to the concentration of animals in particular places. This is usually a result of misguided development schemes or because of the need for protection at times of war.

Nevertheless, force of circumstances mean that most of Ethiopia's predominantly pastoral communities can be viewed as in a difficult period of transition – from nomadism towards settled village agriculture. The Geri and Jarso in Jijiga were traditionally nomadic groups who eventually adopted settlement and cultivation. Similar examples occur across the border in northwestern Somalia, where segments of the Gadabursi and Habar Awal Somali clans, living in Borama and Gabiley districts, adopted settlement and cultivation at the turn of this century (See I.M. Lewis, 1961: 109–10). Moreover, in Negelle, one can see small-scale rain-fed agriculture being initiated by some pastoral families aspiring to produce supplementary crops. The upheavals and forced population displacements of recent years have tended to accelerate such processes. For some groups a largely pastoral economy is still a viable option, but this may not be so for much longer.

The Breakdown in Security

The point has been made above that the pastoral groups of the Ethiopian lowlands traditionally shared certain characteristics. Raiding, feuds and local warfare were common, but it was in everyone's interest not to allow the violence to escalate. In recent decades, however, ethnic conflict has been a major problem in many areas, and continues to hinder relief and development work. In some places it is the main cause of impoverishment. How has this situation emerged?

Basically it has been caused by three interrelated factors. Firstly, as former pastureland has been seized by the state for agricultural purposes, competition between pastoralists over scarce resources has become intense. Secondly, local rivalries have been absorbed into larger confrontations, and can no longer be resolved or contained by means of traditional ritual, such as the payment of blood compensation. Thirdly, the various full-scale wars being fought in the Horn have made many effective, modern small arms cheaply available (notably automatic rifles). This means that relatively petty squabbles can rapidly result in numerous mortalities, and escalate into intractable and widespread feuding. Access to such weapons can also enable a less well off group to attack local elites, undermine established procedures, and create political anarchy.

Ethiopia's Moslem pastoralists have been adversely affected by these developments since Haile Selassie's return to power after the Second World War. The regime was generally unsympathetic to the needs of pastoralists, and the state's requirements for cash and commodities for its growing bureaucracy resulted in it limiting land rights in nomadic areas using legal instruments (Gamaledin, 1992: 178). Land was allocated by the state for agricultural production. These strategies affected all pastoralists, but the Afar and Oromo were hit hardest. Moreover, the Christian-dominated government viewed Islamicized Oromos and Somali clans as having been collaborators during the Italian occupation. It exacted revenge by restricting their access to pastures, and generally supporting non-Moslem Oromos in local arguments. By and large, Mengistu's regime later adopted a similar policy.

In some areas wars had periodically been fought between Moslem and non-Moslem pastoralists for generations. Indeed this could be a means of asserting an ethnic identity. For example, among the Boran, the peace and gentleness which were expected to prevail within Boran homes was highlighted and supported by the attitude towards a non-Boran. At the time of their transition to married adult status, Boran men were supposed to kill a male adversary and submit his male organ as a trophy. The adversary had to come from a hostile group, often a Somali clan. A man who would hesitate before slapping his own naughty child would have no qualms about castrating a foreign baby, leave it to bleed to death and dance with his trophy (Baxter, 1965: 65). Such customs perpetuated local hostilities. Nevertheless, the violence was relatively limited and, as has

Traditional peace-making ceremonies are still performed among pastoral groups, although it has become very difficult for elders to contain the violence.

10.4 is a photograph of Yisaqow Racha, one of the Garri elders of Liban, praying for peace in 1985 while performing a customary coffee 'sacrifice' ceremony, known as bunqalle.

10.5 is a photograph of a dispute settlement held in accordance with Afar custom in February 1995. The dispute was over the abduction of a young woman by a man and his relatives before she could be given in marriage to her father's choice of groom. It was resolved after three days of negotiations, and was followed by a wedding ceremony between the woman and the man who captured her.

(Both photographs by K.N. Getachew)

been mentioned, interaction and even cultural assimilation was possible. Divisions became much more impervious as anti-Islamic state policies took effect. Increasingly they lent local resonance to national and international disputes.

State-supported persecution of Afar, Somali and Islamicized Oromo pastoralists intensified in the 1960s. Among the Afar this was linked to the promotion of large-scale mechanized commercial enterprises (particularly after 1971 in the middle Awasha Valley), most of which were managed by foreign agro-businesses in joint ventures with the state. This produced a few wealthy Afars, but discouraged smallholder agricultural production among the nomads, who found themselves denied access to grazing land, including riverine locations and valuable highland territory (which was adversely affected by the bungled diversion of the Awash river). Eventually the Mengistu regime's programme of nationalizing rural land in the Awash Valley provoked the defiance of the Afar Sultan, and the formation of the Afar Liberation Front in 1975 (Gamaledin, 1992: 179). Guerrilla warfare and population displacement followed.

Meanwhile, Ethiopia's Somalis had become caught up in an international conflict. Many Somali clans straddled the Somali–Ethiopian border, and had long migrated back and forth with their herds. Consequently, Ethiopian Somalis had no choice but to be drawn into the wars between Ethiopia and Somalia over the Ogaden, tending to support their Somali Moslem brethren. In contrast, other pastoral groups, particularly non-Moslem Oromos such as the Boran, offered allegiance to the Ethiopian government. After the Ethiopian victories in 1964 and 1977, the position of many Somalis in Ethiopia became completely untenable, and more than a million took refuge in Somalia, Kenya and Djibouti (some estimates put the figure at almost 2 million). Some idea of the Ethiopian government's hostility towards Somali pastoralists is indicated by the fact that in 1977, 75 per cent of the land area of the Ogaden was being used for crops, even though rainfall is generally insufficient to support regular cultivation and extensive farming could only have ecologically damaging effects. Formerly 90 per cent of the Ogaden had been pasture (Report and Assessment of Jijiga Development Project, cited in Dolal, 1992: 186).

The majority of Ethiopian Somalis and Afars have now returned to Ethiopia, in recent years being accompanied by thousands of Somali refugees from Somalia. Rangeland is now at a premium, at a time when population pressures have greatly intensified. Not surprisingly, division between Moslems and non-Moslems remains an issue, continuing to influence patterns of social strife in much of the peripheral lowlands. In some locations, as herds have become more concentrated, a broad division between cattle people and mainly Moslem camel people has compounded matters. A heated discourse takes place between the groups from the two pastoral economies. Cattle people tend to find fault in camels, arguing that their flat feet crush the grass grazed by cattle. Camel people claim that the grazing cattle eat the surface grass to the roots, and thus cause depletion of pastures.

Moslem Oromos find themselves in a particularly difficult situation. The cattle-herding Arssi Oromo, for example, are Moslems who have absorbed segments of various Somali groups (Geri, Karanle and Ajuran). On the one hand, they sympathize with the Moslem Somali in their fights against non-Moslem, Christian/'animist' Oromos. On the other hand, they are drawn into supporting Oromo causes. In particular they tend to entertain the Oromo Liberation Front's (OLF) concerns about being dominated by the Ethiopian People's Revolutionary Democratic Front (EPRDF).

A similar point might be made about Ethiopian Somalis who have ended up in alliance with non-Moslem Oromos. The most prominent example is the case of the Digodi of Liban district. Here again external issues are crucially important. The Digodi have supported their Boran neighbours against virtually every other Somali clan in Liban, among whom a powerful group is the Marrehan. The Boran have had long-standing feuds with the Marrehan, and have, in the past, come off better because of Ethiopian government support. One section of the Marrehan, the Bon-Marrehan, claim that the Boran have occupied parts of their traditional territory along the Dawa river. This land is said to have been plundered from those Bon-Marrehan families currently living at relief centres in Negelle town. The Digodi have a long-standing feud with the Marrehan, and antagonisms have been compounded by political developments in Somalia. The Marrehan belong to the Darod clan-family, which dominated Somalia's politics after independence. The Digodi belong to the Hawiya clan-family which is on an opposed side in Somalia's present civil war. Thus, the recent conflict in Negelle, which has had an appalling impact on the population, can partly be interpreted as a spreading of the Somalian upheaval into Ethiopia. Without Ethiopian government support, many Boran have found themselves very exposed. Some have lost everything.

The above cases indicate that, while the religious divide remains significant, it is nowadays only one cause of externally exacerbated conflict. In the political turmoil of Ethiopia, localized conflicts are increasingly being taken up by a range of political factions, all of which seek an ethnically based, rural constituency in order to struggle for influence at regional centres of power. In the turbulent transitional period, the EPRDF is reluctant to impose order, lest it be accused of partisan interference. The change of government removed, however corrupt, the existing law and order enforcing machinery, and the interim government has not yet been able to adequately replace them, particularly in isolated rural areas. Some factions have tried to capitalize on the situation and seize the initiative in disputes, hoping to be able to bargain from a position of strength when national stability is attained. In the current circumstances, antagonisms are deliberately aggravated by ambitious individuals, even among closely related populations.

The ongoing conflict between the Guji and Boran in Dirre district clearly illustrates the trend. In the past, the Boran dominated the politics of this area since they persistently supported the previous governments in Ethiopia. Now they appear to be at odds with the new administration, and the Guji have seized their opportunity. The Guji occupy land which stretches up into the fertile highlands. Since 1991, the opening up of the economy and the change of government has provided a range of new opportunities, a fact which has been underlined by the successes some Guji have met with in illicit gold mining. Their political leaders want to gain a regional influence commensurate with what they assert to be their people's numerical and economic strength. Leaders of both Guji and Boran factions directly and indirectly encourage their followers to resort to violence. A somewhat similar competition for power within a district has emerged in Jijiga. Interestingly in this case external involvement extended to mediation. The conflict is between the 'Somali-ized' Jarso and the Somali clan, the Geri (who, like the Marehan, belong to the Darod clan-family). Ostensibly the problem is over rights to territory, but the Jarso appear to have been mainly concerned with gaining equal status with the Geri clan. The Jarso claim that the Geri, who were the traditional local aristocracy, regard them as lowly and do not even marry their daughters. Fighting was fierce, and many people were killed because of the use of automatic weapons. Several villages were destroyed and a considerable number of people fled to the relative safety of neighbouring areas.

The process of reconciliation was undertaken jointly by elders of the neutral Gadabursi clan, sultans of the protagonists, and EPRDF representatives. Its success has led to the return home of most of the displaced Jarso (for example to the villages of Tulli Gulaid and Eil Ahmar). The Geri, however, have been more cautious. Many have been sceptical about the reconciliation and wary of return. They appear to have come off worse in the fighting, losing much of their livestock, and have had concerns about access to food and land in their former home areas. They are doubtless sensitive to the fact that things will not be the same as they once were.

These conflicts cause tremendous hardship, and they will have to be resolved or at least contained before the general well-being of the populations concerned will improve. Insecurity also hinders the relief efforts. Humanitarian relief workers are usually viewed as neutral, and of benefit to everyone. Violence is rarely directed at them by protagonists. However, the breakdown in law and order, social tensions, the ease of access to automatic weapons, and the concentration of scarce commodities in the hands of aid personnel makes them a target for bands of robbers. Theft of vehicles, food and other goods, sometimes involving armed ambushes, have became a serious threat. Relatively affluent local people are also at risk.

The response of communities dislodged by all this civil strife has followed a predictable pattern. People flee to the nearest secure location; either among a neutral social unit or a town. They attempt to take with them what they can carry, and to salvage at least some of their livestock. This makes them vulnerable to attack, and most displaced groups lose their remaining animals in the course of their flight. Once sanctuary has been reached, the next concern is to find a source of food. This commonly involves a further trek to a place where relief is offered.

In the past, locally displaced groups could seek help from a more powerful neighbour. There is even a Somali word for the kind of protection offered to people whose lives are in danger, *magan*. But this customary philanthropic altruism, which extended to both sheltering and feeding victims of war, cannot deal with the current crisis. The host communities may themselves be widely affected by drought and civil strife, and the scale of local displacement is unprecedented. Some attempts to provide assistance are still made. For example, the Moslem, Oromo-speaking Arssi managed to afford protection to a few displaced Marehan Somalis in Negelle. However, the vast majority of displaced pastoralists, including the majority of the displaced Marehan, have found themselves destitute, and have become dependant on the Red Cross Movement's food distributions.

Inadequacies of the Relief Programme

Chronic insecurity has disrupted the local economy, and reduced the capacity of the traditional moral obligations to meet the needs of suffering kinspeople. It has severely exacerbated the impact of the long-term drought which has affected most lowland areas. Government services, which have always been very limited and sometimes even counter-productive, are now almost non-existent. This has made relief aid the most important local resource that is currently available to the displaced and impoverished, and there is no doubt that the ongoing programme is saving lives.

However, relief efforts are inadequate to sustain good health. Food distribution is irregular, and is only of wheat grain, occasionally supplemented with pulses and oil. It falls far short of the current demand. For example, in the Awash Valley, the Red Cross Movement is pledged to feed 80,000 Afar nomads. This is known to be only a small proportion of those in need, but even such a limited objective has not been consistently attained.

Many areas also do not have a supply of safe drinking water, and medical facilities are insufficient. Water is often only provided from temporary systems. These consist of taps linked to water bladders made of soft synthetic material, which have to be regularly refilled. Where they are available, relief medical services mostly consist of a few over-worked staff trying to do the best that they can in a makeshift tent. Such arrangements are essential in the initial emergency stage, but there is little sign of them being improved or replaced by more permanent facilities.

The scarcity of relief aid has fostered intense competition for access to donated items. Each ethnic group or clan strives to obtain a large share of whatever is available, just as in the past they competed for pasturage and water. At the same time there is competition among the relatively better off within each group to secure resources with which to dispense patronage, and thereby maintain their local dominance.

This latter form of competition is particularly fierce among Somalis. The social upheaval in Somalia displaced a considerable population there, and many of them have joined their kinspeople living in Ethiopia. These Somalian Somalis include people from urban centres as well as farmers and nomads. Thus, politicians, educated professionals, and former wealthy traders now compete against traditional clan leaders for the control of relief aid and its attendant benefits.

The tendency for elite groups to secure aid at the expense of the most disadvantaged appears to be less pronounced among Afar and Oromo populations. Here it is usually possible to collaborate with the acknowledged leaders to distribute food and to identify the most needy. Indeed, the Afar appear to have a capacity to live in relative harmony among themselves, even in very adverse circumstances. But among the Somalis, lack of co-operation between traditional leaders and influential urban groups, and competition among these powerful men for the support of their kinspeople, undermines the employment of the clan system for distribution of food. The situation is compounded by the fact that the aid organizations have no alternative method, but continue to collaborate closely with the very individuals who are embezzling supplies for their own ends.

These problems with the aid operation are partly a matter of insufficient funding and resources. There is, for example, a serious shortage of trucks, which is exacerbated by a lack of spare parts. Often it is simply impossible to reach relief centres in remote locations. However, another factor is an unwillingness among able and qualified personnel to leave their relatively comfortable (and safe) positions in the major towns. This applies as much to the NGO community as it does to government employees.

There is a real danger that the current recipients of aid will be left with nothing when the relief effort eventually winds down. It might be observed that these marginal areas did not have any resources in the past, and the populations seemed to have managed. But it needs to be recognized that many families have now spent prolonged periods in relief centres or in towns. A significant proportion will be unwilling or unable to return to the rigours of the traditional pastoral way of life. They have become less self-sufficient than they used to be and, like other Ethiopians, they look to the state to provide essential services. If the new government does not provide them, and they continue to feel overlooked and ignored, there is already ample precedent for armed resistance.

Categories of the Most Distressed

In this section I comment on the categories of people who currently seem to be most in need of assistance.

The locally displaced
The locally displaced groups currently receiving relief aid are victims of drought or local warfare. Drought is fairly common in Ethiopia's lowlands, and can be particularly severe in Negelle district and in the Afar region. Fortunately in 1992 the rains were reasonably good. However, numerous families have been unable to take advantage of this, because of insecurity. Fighting was intense in many areas following the change of government in May 1991. There are signs that hostilities are abating in some places, but large popula- tions remain concentrated at relief centres, and will probably require seeds and assistance

with restocking before they are able to leave. There has been less violence within the Afar population than among Somali and Oromo groups. However, some Afars have been displaced by the almost continuous low-level warfare with their arch-enemies, the Issa. In addition, the Afars in Ethiopia receive and quietly accommodate kinsmen dislodged by the civil strife in neighbouring Djibouti, where the Afars dominate the armed opposition to one of the Horn's remaining despotic regimes.

Among the locally displaced nomadic groups in Boran province, the displaced Marehan appear to be the most disadvantaged. They have lost virtually all their animals following attacks by Boran and Guji Oromos and Digodi Somalis.

In Jijiga, the Geri and Jarso generally produced a grain surplus before the social upheaval which severely destroyed settlements and property. The reconciliation initiative undertaken in June 1992, under the auspices of EPRDF, led to the relocation of the displaced to nine homeland villages. This seems to have been a remarkable achievement, but many families have chosen to remain in transit camps, rather than actually go back to their former areas. They still have fears about security and they have no livestock to look after. Significantly, it is only those families who managed to retain some of their animals who have re-occupied their former homes and pasture.

The returnees

Until the civil war disrupted supplies, the Ethiopian refugees in Somalia had mostly lived in camps which had been provided with enough donated food. Moreover, many of the camps had schools, hospitals and an effective water-supply system. As a consequence, children born in Somalia have had little experience of their parents' former way of life. They, and their parents, now have new expectations. These are not going to be met if they go back to remote rural areas, and many families will resist taking up nomadic pastoralism as a means of survival.

For these reasons, the Somali returnees are most conscious of their needs, and assertive about what they hold to be their rights. Since they were used to a system based on individual refugee entitlement, they are hostile to the current community-oriented, cross-mandate approach. They are particularly aggrieved by the fact that they have not received the repatriation and integration package which they assert was promised to them by UNHCR. The recent refusal of the returnees in Negelle to be counted in the early 1990s illustrates their frustration with the relief programme as a whole.

Although support for the repatriation of Ethiopian refugees from Somalia has been the stated policy of UNHCR since January 1990, it took many months for mass repatriation to actually occur. Delays have been partly to do with the upheavals in Ethiopian and Somalian national politics, and the return of the Ethiopian population has been complicated by the flight of thousands of Somalian refugees. However, things moved more swiftly from early 1991.

Teferiber, which lies north of Jijiga town, was a desolate village in early 1991. In February it suddenly become a bustling reception centre, and is now a camp sheltering a mixed population of Somali refugees and returnees. This has also happened at Dherwenaje, the other camp in Jijiga district where a considerable number of Ethiopian returnees are settled. Both these camps have lively markets, where food aid and other donated commodities are traded. The returnees and refugees are able to exchange wheat grain for the livestock and animal products of nomadic groups that have retained their herds (including those based in northern Somalia). Also, pulses and oil are much in demand in Jijiga town, and merchants will come to the camps whenever there is a distribution. As elsewhere, food relief is used by recipients in a variety of ways in order to maximise the benefits, and the camp markets have become an important aspect of the district economy.

Arssi, Digodi, Geri, Garri and Gabra constitute the dominant returnee groups in the former Boran Administration. Many Arssi returnees and some Geri originated from Bale province and have expressed a desire to return. They are aware that there are limited economic opportunities in their home area, but they have no wish to remain in Negelle as the relief assistance they presently receive is inadequate. Their decision to return ought to be honoured, and arrangements for transport should be made as early as possible.

Other returnees currently residing in Negelle town are likely to want to remain there. Many of them had been living in refugee camps located close to important regional towns in Somalia (Beletwein, Qoryoley, Bur Dhubo and Luq), and want to continue residing in an urban environment. The most enterprising among them have introduced valuable innovations. Some women returnees have started long-distance milk trading. They go to the rural villages, buy milk and transport it for sale in Negelle town to make a profit. Others participate in street trading, while some male refugees increased the vigour of the trade between Moyalle and Negelle town.

The remaining returnees living near Negelle town, are from local groups: Garri, Gabra, Guji and Boran, and many of them live outside territory covered by the ERCS/IFRC operation. The majority of these returnees are already integrated into their former home areas. They are difficult to separate from kinsmen who did not flee abroad in that they are not concentrated in a particular place. Nevertheless, some of them (especially those living in Gabra and Garri communities) are badly in need of help.

Although the cross-mandate approach of the aid organizations is still in an embryonic stage, it is supposed to target populations which are most in need, irrespective of their returnee or refugee status. But, when a potentially vulnerable population is dispersed, it takes a considerable amount of local research to locate them and to establish whether or not aid is required. This is not happening, and at present it is sometimes hard to avoid the conclusion that the new approach is simply diffusing the responsibilities of national and international agencies. It leaves many distressed people to their own devices.

It also needs to be stressed that, although many of the returnees to Negelle are from nomadic groups, a considerable proportion have spent over a decade in refugee camps. This prolonged dislocation has induced a sedentary inclination among them. Possibly there is a case for setting up agricultural projects along the unexploited perennial Genale and Dawa rivers.

Refugees from Somalia

Contrary to the advice of international organizations, the EPRDF has adopted a policy of encouraging Somali refugees to settle in official camps. This already appears to be creating something of a dependency syndrome. There are also serious public health hazards because sanitation and hygiene are not adequate. Moreover, the concentrations of population in marginal and thinly forested locations can be expected to have severe environmental consequences.

In Hararge province, the refugees are located in relatively well-established camps, which keep mutually hostile clans apart. At Teferiber and Dherwenaje virtually all the residents are from non-Isaq groups which were associated with the Barre regime. Many of them are Gadabursi. They fled Somalia because of fears of reprisal by the Isaq-dominated Somali National Movement (SNM), following its successes against Somali government troops in February 1991, and the declaration of a northern Somaliland Republic (in May). As mentioned above, there are also Ethiopian Somalis living in these camps as returnees, these are mainly from border clans. Isaq refugees, who were displaced from Somalia by government atrocities before the SNM's victories, are situated at Harta Sheikh and neighbouring camps.

In Negelle, probably the most significant Somali refugee group consists of families connected with the former Barre regime's military establishment. Reportedly, they fled the military operations carried out by a faction of the United Somali Front in Somalia's Gedo region in March 1992. Some battered military trucks and a fleet of civilian vehicles brought by this group indicate government connections and a well-off background. The vehicles have been impounded by EPRDF, since their legal status is uncertain at the moment (however, private vehicles whose owners produce appropriate documents are said to be released). Although they are accompanied by some members of other Darod clans, the majority of this relatively small but distinctive Somali refugee group belong to the Marehan clan. On crossing the border into Ethiopia they were ambushed and robbed of some of their vehicles, ammunition and other wealth by the Ogaden Darod. After this incident, the EPRDF escorted them to the present site for their protection.

In Negelle, there are also clusters of Gadabursi and Isaq families. They want to proceed to Hararge region, so as to join their displaced kinspeople in the existing camps where they believe they will receive some assistance. Many of them are currently stranded in Negelle town because of lack of funds with which to pay travel costs.

Demobilized soldiers

Most of the demobilized soldiers receiving relief aid are located in the vicinity of Negelle town. Placed in an isolated pastoral region, which is distant from Ethiopia's centres of administration and business, and not close enough to Somalia and Kenya to allow informal, cross-border trade to thrive, Negelle has the hallmark of a strategic military town. It has acted as a bastion against possible invasion from Somalia, and it is therefore not surprising that a significant number of its current population consist of demobilized soldiers and their families. In fact these comprise the largest group of ERCS/IFRC beneficiaries in the district.

The demobbed soldiers come from a wide range of backgrounds. A significant few are managing to earn a regular income and are quite well-off. Others are living in penury, many of them disoriented young men, who were taken out of primary schools and recruited into the army by force. There are also several older, experienced veterans, some of whom had retired and were receiving their pensions, but were called up for service in the last years of Mengistu's rule as the government's situation became desperate. They too now find themselves dependent on handouts. In addition, the ex-soldiers are from different ethnic groups. They include, for example, Arssi, Borana, Amhara, Gurage and Tigrai. Those belonging to ethnic groups from other parts of Ethiopia have little prospect of social or economic reintegration in the location from which they originally came, and most have no choice other than to remain in Negelle.

Ex-soldiers have been allocated plots and some families have managed to construct houses. Several have applied for agricultural land, but many say that they cannot afford the registration fees and other charges. In addition to the insufficient relief food, some ex-soldiers have received a small sum of money (50 birr per month) from the special Commission for Reintegration of Demobilized Soldiers. However, this financial assistance was terminated in September 1992.

Like returnees from refugee camps in Somalia, the demobbed soldiers are eager to wrench as much as possible from the humanitarian organizations, and they tend to express their needs in vehement terms. This is partly to do with the expectations that come with education and with experience gained by working in different parts of the country. It is important that any rehabilitation initiative designed to benefit them should take their particular characteristics into account. To regard this category, or indeed any other needy groups, as a homogenous unit is erroneous. Some would swiftly achieve self-sufficiency given the necessary inputs. Others will require longer term help, including some kind of training in marketable skills.

10.6 *Up until now development efforts in Ethiopia have prioritized permanently settled communities at the expense of pastoralists: the livestock market of Warar, northeast Ethiopia, July 1994. (K.N. Getachew)*

Notes Towards a Constructive Policy for Ethiopia's Pastoralists

Up until now development efforts in Ethiopia have prioritized permanently settled communities. Even during periods of relative political stability, basic services in pastoral lowland areas have been minimal, and public facilities have been concentrated in the more densely populated central highland farming regions. Moreover, whatever has been available in the lowlands has been largely limited to the permanent residents of the towns and larger villages. This has continued in spite of the obvious needs of particular pastoralist groups, and the evidence that promoting sedentarization is counter-productive.

This neglect of pastoralists has extended to the UN agencies and the NGO sector. It still remains a problem, as evidenced by the fact that the number of organizations prepared to work with pastoralists remains depressingly low. With the exception of Jijiga, where many NGOs work among the displaced Somalis, most pastoral areas are ignored. For example, in the Afar region, the Red Cross Movement is usually the only operational NGO (although recently SCF has been working on a small scale).

The predjudice has also applied to humanitarian relief at times of famine and drought. Interventions have been modelled on programmes implemented (often unsuccessfully) in the ox-plough, highland peasant economies. Policy has been largely based on individual rights entitlement, and rarely upon a community-orientated approach – notwithstanding the occasional showpiece rehabilitation or development scheme of dubious utility. The assumption has tended to be made that families required food until they could harvest their crops in the following season. In effect, if they were not farmers they were encouraged to become so.

However, there are signs that things are changing. The interim government of Ethiopia, the UN agencies and the NGO community appear to have finally recognized the inappropriateness of previous approaches. The current alternative strategies, which discourage free distribution of food and focus upon community rehabilitation and development, certainly represent a step in the right direction, and might prove constructive in the long term if they are adequately resourced.

It is important to demolish established but eclectic categories that unhelpfully differentiate needy victims of disaster, and to try to find ways of dealing with distressed populations as disadvantaged communities. In this respect, the cross-mandate and parallel operations approach, which is currently advocated by the government, UNHCR and major NGOs, has considerable potential – provided issues of accountability and responsibility between the various agencies can be sorted out.

If better organized and more effectively managed, there is no doubt that food-for-work and cash-for-work programmes can act as useful alternatives to free distribution of food. They can help organize the labour that is necessary to construct, maintain or improve essential community services in nomadic areas. However, it is important that these initiatives should not undermine traditional corporate activities, rather they should supplement customary forms of solidarity and co-operation. Probably some means of distributing cash rather than food would be the optimal strategy, because it would encourage the development of trade networks into these economically marginal zones.

An obvious point, which nevertheless needs to be made since it is persistently overlooked, is that food-for-work or cash-for-work programmes, to have any meaningful effect in the nomadic areas, should be designed to improve the production of livestock. For example, protection of existing water holes or construction of new ones in places where scarcity of water is acute; construction of dip tanks for veterinary purposes and health posts.

The introduction of basic services in pastoral areas must also take the existing local modes of life into account. In the short to medium term it is likely that the way to provide inexpensive veterinary and public health facilities will be to train locals and supply them with drugs. Some nomads have had experience of rudimentary veterinary and medical services provided by government outreach systems. These could be reactivated quite easily.

Integrated regional programmes, which facilitate pastoral movements ranging across contiguous areas in neighbouring countries, would help improve the quality of livestock, and thereby raise well-being of nomad families and the economic importance of the livestock sector. This policy is currently supported by the interim government of Ethiopia and it is to be hoped agreements can eventually be reached with governments in Eritrea, Kenya and the currently war-torn Sudan and Somalia.

However, it would be mere romanticism to imagine that the currently displaced and impoverished populations of the Ethiopian lowlands will one day all return to traditional nomadic livelihoods. Many former pastoralists have become sedentarized, and no doubt the trend will continue. In Jijiga, a significant number of Gadabursi, Geri and Jarso have started cultivating. In Negelle, demobilized farmers and enterprising former nomads show a keen interest in small-scale, family based agriculture. In Afar region, commercial farms are being handed back to the Afar people, but are unlikely to be made available for grazing. Without accelerating a process which can only place more pressure on the fragile soils, it is essential that steps are taken to make lowland agricultural production sustainably viable.

Bibliography

Bartels, L. (1983) *Oromo religion: myths and rites of the western Oromo of Ethiopia – an attempt to understand*. Dietrich Reiner, Berlin.

Baxter, P.T.W. (1965) 'Repetition in certain Boran ceremonies', in M. Fortes and G. Dieterlen (eds) *African systems of thought*. Oxford University Press, London.

— (1978) 'Boran age-sets and generation-sets: Gada, a puzzle or a maze?' in P.T.W. Baxter and U. Almogar (eds), *Age, generation and time*. Hurst, London.

— (1983) 'The problem of the Oromo, or the problem for the Oromo?' in I.M. Lewis (ed), *Nationalism and Self-Determination in the Horn of Africa*. Ithaca Press, London.

— (1986) 'The present state of Oromo studies', in *Bulletins des études africaines de l'Inalco*, Vol. 6, No. 2: 53–82.

— (1991) ' "Big Men" and cattle licks in Oromoland', in P.T.W. Baxter (ed.) *When the grass is gone: development intervention in African arid lands*. Nordiska Afrikainstitutet, Uppsala.

— (1994a) 'Ethnic boundaries and development: speculations on the Oromo case'. in *Inventions and boundaries: historical and anthropological approaches to the study of ethnicity and nationalism*, Roskilde University, Occasional Paper no.11, IDS, Roskilde.

— (1994b) 'The creation and constitution of Oromo nationality', in K. Fukui and J. Markakis (eds), *Ethnicity and conflict in the Horn of Africa*, London: James Currey.

Dolal, M. (1992) 'Pastoral resources, human displacement and state policy: the Ogaden case', in M. Doornbos, L. Cliffe, Abdel Ghaffar M. Ahmed and J. Markakis (eds), *Beyond conflict in the Horn*. London: James Currey.

Farah, A.Y. (1989) *The milk of the Boswellia forests: production of frankincense among the pastoral Somali*, PhD thesis, London School of Economics and Political Science.

— (1992a) *Some poor peasant communities in rural Tigrai of Ethiopia: relevant propositions regarding grassroots rehabilitation, disaster prevention and development activities*, a consultancy report prepared for the ERCS/IFRC. Addis Ababa, Ethiopia.

— (1992b) *Priority rehabilitation needs of the neglected marginal Afar region of Ethiopia: preliminary examination*, a consultancy report prepared for ERCS/IFRC, Addis Ababa.

— (1992c) *Essential rehabilitation needs of the displaced and distressed groups in Negelle: preliminary investigation*, a consultancy report prepared for ERCS/IFRC, Addis Ababa.

— (1992d) *Reconciled and resettled Geri and Jarso clans in Jijiga: examination of an agricultural rehabilitation programme*, a consultancy report prepared for ERCS/IFRC, Addis Ababa.

Gamaledin, M. (1992) 'Pastoralism: existing limitations, possibilities for the future', in M. Doornbos, L. Cliffe, Abdel Ghaffar M. Ahmed and J. Markakis (eds), *Beyond conflict in the Horn*. James Currey, London.

Gidada, N. (1984) *History of the Sayyo Oromo of the south western Wollega, Ethiopia from about 1730–1886*. PhD thesis, Johan Wolfgang Goethe University, Frankfurt-am-Main.

Hassen, M. (1990) *The Oromo of Ethiopia: a history 1570–1860*. Cambridge University Press, Cambridge.

Hutlin, J. (1987) *The long journey; essays on history, descent and land among the Macha Oromo*, PhD thesis, Uppsala University, Uppsala.

Lewis, H.S. (1965) *A Galla monarchy: Jimma Abba Jifar, Ethiopia 1830–1932*, University of Wisconsin Press, Madison.

Lewis, I. M. (1961) *A pastoral democracy. A study of pastoralism and politics among the northern Somali of the Horn of Africa*, Oxford University Press, London.

Van de Loo, J. (1991) *Guji Oromo culture in southern Ethiopia*, Dietrich Reiner: Berlin.

11 JULIUS HOLT
Looking Beyond the Towns

Facts & Conjectures
about Rural Returnees
in the Ogaden & 'Somaliland'

It seems scarcely possible to discuss the circumstances of any Somali without immediate reference to his or her clan affiliation. This remains true of people involved in mass movements across international boundaries which allow their formal identification as 'refugees' or 'returnees'.[1] The hundreds of thousands of people who fled from Ethiopia into Somalia during the Ogaden war in the late 1970s are most readily identified as members of the Ogaden clans. And people who from late 1990 fled into the Ogaden at the downfall of the Siad Barre regime did so because they were Ogadenis in particular, or members of the Darod clan-family in general, or Isaaqs trying to get 'home' to north-west Somalia. By the same token, the recent war of secession in that region was most readily identifiable as an Isaaq-clan affair, producing a multitude of Isaaq refugees in Ethiopia. In post-war 'Somaliland',[2] tensions are interpreted either as a power struggle involving Isaaq sub-clans, or as the result of ambiguities in the allegiances of non-Isaaq people: the Gadabursi in the northwest, or the Warsengeli and Dolbahante (Darod) in the east.

But if clan relations constitute the essential, shorthand explanation of conflict and refugees, they are neither a sufficient nor often even a particularly interesting element in the consideration of returnees. To those commentators – Somalis and non-Somalis alike – who might find this a heresy, the response would be that an apparent obsession with categorization by clan and sub-clan alone has led to a remarkable paucity of any other recorded information about the identity of refugees and returnees. Which area did they flee from, or return to? How many are of town origin, how many of rural origin? How many were purely livestock herders, how many also farmers? Is it the intention of refugees to return to their original environments? Have returnees resumed their original occupations?

Such matters are not merely of academic or 'human' interest. They should be at the heart of debate about induced repatriation or assistance to voluntary returnees. But that debate has mostly continued with little effort to obtain substantial information beyond the enumeration of the refugee camp populations. Perhaps the notorious difficulty of

---

[1] The term 'returnee' as used in this chapter includes people returning to the Ogaden who were refugees in Somalia; people returning to north-west Somalia/'Somaliland' from refuge in Ethiopia; people who had migrated voluntarily to southern Somalia (including children born there to migrant families) and were forced to flee 'home' to the Ogaden or to north-west Somalia/'Somaliland'.

[2] 'Somaliland', which retains the borders of the former British Somaliland and of the subsequent northwest region of independent Somalia, is not internationally recognized as a sovereign state. But at the time of writing, the former Republic of Somalia was in no sense a functioning polity. In this paper the term 'Somaliland' is used merely for convenience, and does not imply any opinion about the legal status of the territory.

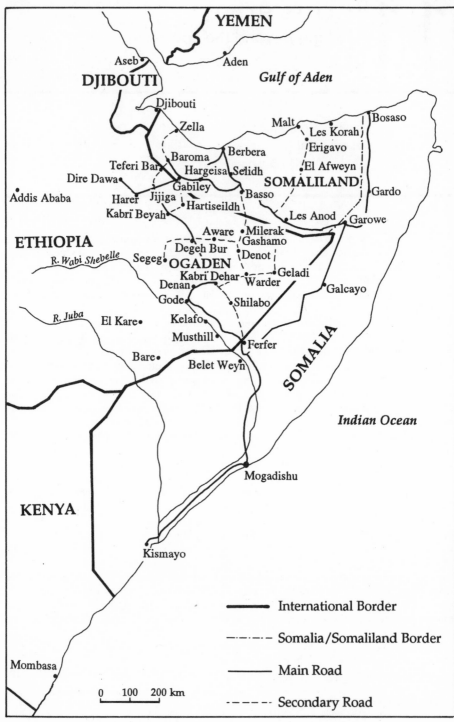

Map 11.1 *Somalia, Somaliland and the Ogaden*

counting Somali refugees in camps has diminished what appetite there might have been for undertaking other enquiries. At all events, in mid-1991 there was little available information about the returnees who were visible to the authorities and agencies in camps, and none about those who were not immediately visible because they had merged with town populations or had melted into the countryside.

Two Surveys

The two rapid rural surveys which form the basis of this paper were designed to provide broad statements about human nutrition and economic conditions, and the position of returnees in this context.[3] They were not designed as specific, sociological inquiries to answer the above questions, but some observations were recorded which seem worth discussing here.

The Ogaden needs-assessment study (Holt and Lawrence, 1991), carried out in August/September 1991, set out to answer two basic questions:

- what was the status of food availability in the Ogaden in a roughly six-month perspective?
- what was the capacity of the Ogaden to support the economic reintegration of the returnee populations?

A perennial concern about conditions in the Ogaden was sharpened by the combined effects of drought and the return of an uncounted population who, from previous information on Somalia, might be calculated to number more than 300,000. The similarly designed survey of rural Somaliland (Holt and Lawrence, 1992) in November/December 1991 had a similar inspiration. The territory had emerged from three years of war and two of drought. The large-scale return of refugees to the main towns was a relatively easily observed phenomenon, if largely unquantified. The return of refugees to the countryside was all but unseen, although the number could be deduced to be over 100,000.

At the time of survey, the chief focus of official concern in the Ogaden was not the returnee population already in the countryside but rather some 40,000 people in camps at Gode and Kelafo towns on the Wabi Shebelle river. The question was, could they be reinstalled into their previous localities and, by implication, into viable economic activity? There was no recorded information about their economic status before they had fled into Somalia.

Similarly, the prominent question concerning Somaliland was not about the returnees already at 'home' but rather about the potential, officially induced return of upwards of 200,000 people who remained in camps in the Eastern Harerghe region of Ethiopia. Some judgement of the economic conditions of rural Somaliland, especially in view of a recent history of drought, would help to determine whether the potential rural returnee contingent could be absorbed. In his account of the Hartishek camps in December 1991, in which he also laments the lack of accurate demographic information, Ryle (1992) suggests that those who had already left for Somaliland were largely the better-off former town-dwellers, while former farmers were more reluctant to return because of the uncertain prospects for agriculture.

The majority of the population in the two biggest towns, Hargeisa and Bur'o, had returned either from Ethiopia or from other countries of refuge. Despite their uncertainty about the numbers of people in the countryside and the proportion of returnees amongst them, there was a general feeling amongst officials that if people had

[3] The surveys upon which this paper is based were carried out by Save the Children Fund with generous funding support from the British Overseas Development Administration, the United States Office for Foreign Disaster Assistance, and Comic Relief.

11.1 *Returnees from Somalia to Ethiopia at Kebri Bayeh camp, Hararghe region, July 1991. (UNHCR/21027/A. Hollmann)*

chosen to return to the countryside, then they must have had something to go back to. This was not an unreasonable assumption, although, as in the Ogaden, there was a tendency to accompany it with an attitude of 'out of sight, out of mind'.

Quite soon after the beginning of the first (Ogaden) survey the question arose of the circumstances of rural returnees. This was not due to the astuteness of the survey team but because of the insistence of our hosts that we should understand an important problem.

Who is rural?

The term 'rural returnees' in the title is meant to indicate returnees living in rural areas as opposed to those living in towns. Does this also mean that they are of rural origin, and/or that they are pursuing a productive rural life? It is first necessary to consider what 'rural' means in context.

In areas where the majority of the population are settled smallholders, a village is virtually always smaller than a town, but is more accurately distinguished by the fact that its members are essentially primary producers, and not administrators or traders. The same distinction holds between the encampments and the towns of the rangelands inhabited by Somali pastoralists, and is not affected by the fact that these groups are usually very small and mobile, and subject to frequent changes in membership.

However, what English-speaking Somalis tend to call a 'village' is something different. It can be quite small, with fewer than 30 houses; but a large proportion of these houses will be fixed, of wattle-and-daub or stone construction. Typically, the village is sited at a substantial water-point of some kind, and a main track or seasonally motorable road runs through it. The village is home to clan elders and other people of local influence, traders, tea-shop owners and a few resident pastoralists. Every day people will arrive with livestock for watering, but men from encampments within a few hours walk will also come to the town to socialize over tea and, with luck, *kat* (the leaf of the shrub *Catha edulis*, transported from the Ethiopian highlands and chewed for its stimulant properties). There may be a weekly livestock market.

These settlements are towns in embryo, but usually without administrative status. They are particularly numerous in the Haud area, which straddles the eastern Ogaden and southern Somaliland. This extensive plain is very short of available ground water, and in the absence of wells and springs much use is made of small, cement-lined reservoirs or tanks (*berkas*) placed in depressions to collect rainwater run-off. These become settlement sites, and now account for perhaps 5 per cent of the rural population.

The surveys were limited to the encampments in which the majority of Somalis live. Nevertheless, it soon became clear that returnees were to be found at every level: in the main towns, in the special camps near certain of these, in the 'village' settlements, and in the pastoral and agro-pastoral encampments.[3] There is undoubtedly a strong tendency for refugees who have fled from rural areas to return to rural life if they can. If not, then they will be found in towns or in the associated camps.

The largest group of such returnees in the Ogaden are the people who fled from rural life there into central and southern Somalia between 1977 and 1979, and had spent up to 14 years based at refugee camps alongside refugees of town origin. Food aid and to a limited extent land or other means of income generation were made available to them, and many more children received at least an elementary school education than would have been the case at home in the Ogaden.

Most had few livestock in Somalia and returned with none. We now know that this was not so great a barrier to their acceptance back 'home' as might be supposed, even though the majority could not become more than marginally economically active with the number of livestock which their relatives could put together for them (or to which they had retained some entitlement).

Fourteen years defines a generation of children who have grown up in the peculiar circumstances of large refugee camps where they have had little or no opportunity to develop the special skills of pastoral husbandry, but every opportunity to identify themselves with urban, or at least sedentary, life. It is likely that many of these older adolescents and young adults will drift back to towns at the first opportunity, and that in the absence of a major upswing in economic activity in the Ogaden or Somalia they will substantially increase the numbers of urban unemployed and perhaps contribute to civil instability. For the present, they may be considered as temporarily rural returnees.

Who is Urban?

Where people have fled from towns and returned to them, there is no problem of definition. But there are populations such as those at Gode in the Ogaden, or at Boroma in Somaliland, who originally lived in or very near the town and were more or less settled into agricultural life before they fled. These could reasonably be classed either as urban or as rural returnees, but perhaps the latter classification would improve their call upon the authorities to help them resume agricultural activity.

[3] During the symposium, it was suggested that care should be taken in labelling populations as 'pastoralist' and 'agro-pastoralist', since the combinations of both activities amongst different peoples were so varied as to render the terms unclear, if not redundant. Without entering into this debate, we should note here that in this paper the terms are used to distinguish between people who, *in the relevant rainy season before the surveys*, had purely engaged in livestock production and those who had also cultivated some amount of land. According to our enquiries, there was a high tendency for the distinction to hold good for the same people over several previous years.

Enquiries amongst 100 randomly chosen families at the returnee camp at Gode in August 1991 revealed that 34 had originally lived in or around Gode, and almost all of these had been engaged in irrigated agriculture before they fled. Including those from the Kebri Dehar and Shilabo areas, fully 46 per cent of the sample had been settled[4] farming families, as opposed to 41 per cent who had been pastoralists and agro-pastoralists. Given that they represent a very small proportion of the original rural population, the relative concentration of previously settled Ogadeni farmers in the relief camp points to their particular difficulty in resuming their former occupation.

Almost every rural Somali family has at least one member – usually male – who spends greater or lesser periods of his life in town, or, often enough, labouring or trading in other countries. It is a phenomenon which has grown throughout this century, and which has offered a contribution to family economic security through trade and remittances. On balance this must be assumed to more than compensate for the loss of labour for herding, although it is common to hear older people complaining bitterly of the loss of the young to the attractions of town life. Most of those who have no salaried position or major capital investment in town may be expected to return to rural life sooner or later. If political accident makes this sooner, it seems reasonable to class these people as rural returnees.

Another kind of rural–urban migration is more permanent. As with any rural community, education beyond the elementary stage has a high propensity to remove the individual from rural life for good. A first-generation town settler is likely to become the arbiter of a new, permanent rural–urban link which rural kin can use to send children to school in town, obtain credit and improve trading opportunities. In return, they may bring animal products to the urban family, or keep livestock for them as a major form of saving and investment. But the balance of advantage appears often to be in favour of the rural kin. This remains the case when the town in question is a big centre, however distant: Dire Dawa, Djibouti, Aden, Jeddah, Addis Ababa, Nairobi, but above all Mogadishu and Hargeisa until the recent catastrophes.

Here political accident has wrought a dramatic reversal. People remaining in towns where they were government administrators, teachers or technicians have lost their salaried employment. People returning to their own towns from Mogadishu and elsewhere in Somalia have equally lost their salaries, or their trade, and anything but the cash they could bring if they were not robbed on the way.

But such people have not only gone back to the main towns. They are to be found in some numbers at the smaller towns and the settlements. At settlements where the water comes from *berkas*, a frequent complaint was of the diarrhoeas amongst children from towns as far away as Mogadishu who were not used to the polluted water. They were also said to be more vulnerable than local children to the year-round malaria caused by mosquitoes breeding without control in the *berkas*.

Finally, returnees from towns as far away as Mogadishu were present, albeit in small numbers, at the pastoral encampments. As with the far greater number of formerly rural returnees, they could be found as whole families or as parts of families. A man might stay in the local town whilst his family lived with relatives in the countryside; or a woman whose husband had been killed, or had deserted the family, might stay in town to try to collect charity or official rations whilst her children lived with pastoral relatives to benefit from a better environment and available milk.

---

[4] This refers to members of the Ogaden clans as opposed to the far greater number of settled, flood-retreat cultivators in large villages on the banks of the Wabi Shebelle at Imi, Kelafo and Mustahil who are ethnically distinct from the Ogadenis, although mainly Somali-speaking. They are of varied origins, but are together referred to as 'Reer Bare'. The settlements are of long standing, and proportionately few of the population became refugees in the 1977–8 Ogaden war compared with the Ogadeni clans.

Who Bears the Burden?

Both surveys were assisted by helicopters, which allowed a representative sample of the population to be studied over an extensive area. At each of the encampments visited, a record was taken of the number of returnees present. In the Ogaden, returnees were widely found amongst pastoralists and agro-pastoralists alike, but there was considerable variation between the 78 survey sites. Whilst 27 per cent had no returnees, in 10 per cent more than half the families were returnees, and in one case the whole group were returnees. It was calculated that overall, the proportion of returnees amongst the rural population was 28.5 per cent (with a confidence interval of 21.5–35.5). With a rough estimate of the Ogaden pastoral and agro-pastoral population at 920,000 (that is, excluding the settled farmers on the banks of the Wabi Shebelle river), this suggested that amongst them were more than 260,000 returnees.

In Somaliland there were great regional variations in the concentration of refugees, with some 40 per cent in the western, largely agro-pastoral sites, 10 per cent in the central, largely pastoral sites, and only 3 per cent in the east, including the Haud and the northeast mountain areas. The great majority of returnees were from the Ethiopian camps, and the small number of returnees from southern Somalia were almost all found in the east. It was estimated that about 20 per cent of the total pastoral and agro-pastoral population of Somaliland were returnees, numbering some 130,000 or as much as 180,000 depending on the generosity of the estimate of the whole population. In contrast to the Ogaden, the number of returnees in towns is almost certainly greater than in the countryside.

In sum, the resident rural population all over the Ogaden has borne a far heavier burden of returnees than the townspeople, whilst it is in the western part of Somaliland that the rural burden has been particularly heavy. In addition, it was a widespread claim amongst families at the survey locations that they were called upon for help, in the form of animal products and cash from the sale of livestock, by relatives who were returnees in the nearby towns and settlements.

Comments on the Nutritional Evidence

Some of the nutritional observations made in the latter half of 1991 may still be of interest, especially since in neither territory had direct food aid been distributed to the greater part of the rural population. If there is no recent evidence of epidemic disease or major mortality amongst children, nutritional anthropometry can offer an objective indication of the adequacy of energy intake, although a one-off survey cannot refer beyond the recent past.

The first observation was that there was not a famine. The weight and length of children up to approximately 10 years of age were measured to determine the incidence of acute malnutrition. It was found that children up to the age of about five years (110 centimetres in length), that is, those usually considered most vulnerable to the effects of food deprivation, showed a mean weight-for-length per cent of somewhat above 90 per cent.[5] The equivalent figure for the older children was under 90 per cent but above 85 per cent. In the classification now generally adopted in Ethiopia, this would mean that the younger children were on average in a 'satisfactory' condition, whilst the older ones

---

[5] That is, the mean value of the results expressed as a percentage of the 50th percentile according to the NCHS international reference standards, and calculated for groups of children falling within various length categories.

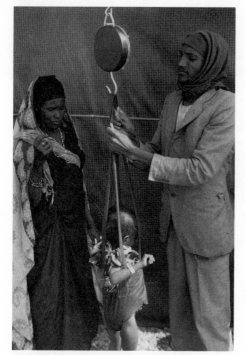

11.2 *The nutritional situation was by no means ideal, but there was not a crisis: nutritional status of children being observed, Teferi Bev Camp, Ethiopia, 1991. (UNHCR/21045/A. Hollmann)*

showed a 'poor' condition. The picture presented was by no means ideal, and there seemed to be little room for any deterioration in access to food. But there was not a crisis of the kind observed at the time of writing in southern Somalia or in surveys carried out in the Ogaden drought of 1974–5 (Mehari *et al.*, 1977) when the overall mean weight-for-length percentage fell below 82, as opposed to a level of around 88 in 1991.

Another significant finding was that in both the Ogaden and Somaliland there was impressive evidence that available food had been shared out equally amongst resident families and the returnees who had joined the group. There was no significant difference in the anthropometric results as between resident children and returnee children. In the Ogaden the major, significant difference was that the children of agro-pastoralists were of lower nutritional status than those of pastoralists.

In western Somaliland, where returnees from the Ethiopian camps are concentrated, it was found that the greater the proportion of returnee children in the group, the better was the nutritional status of the group as a whole. It is not possible to give definite reasons for this, but it was noted that in the west in general, nutritional status was significantly higher than in the rest of the territory. In other words, the difference showed itself geographically rather than by the mode of subsistence.

The local sorghum and maize harvest some two months before the survey could have made little overall difference, since a lack of seed and to some extent a lack of rain, but above all the late return of farming people from the camps, had resulted in minimal production. Two conjectures appear reasonable, especially if taken together. One is that by their proximity to major markets such as Hargeisa and Boroma, and also to the relief camps just across the border in Ethiopia, the western groups have relatively more regular and cheaper access to grain of food aid origin. It is tempting to speculate further (although there is no information to help us here) that the greater is the number of returnees in the communities, the greater also is the tendency to retain direct links to the camps and the wheat grain. This may be through relatives still there, or through residual, direct claims on rations due the manipulation of family ration cards.

The second conjecture is simpler. It is that the children of the west had more milk than those elsewhere. There was no significant difference in the observed and reported family livestock holdings between the west and elsewhere, taking into account the two modes of subsistence. But the livestock in the west were observably in better condition than those in the east, and livestock traders at the central markets of Hargeisa and Bur'o were commonly making a substantial distinction in the price they would pay for animals of the same age and type coming from the two general areas.

The Redistribution of Food Aid

In his chapter of this book, Richard Hogg highlights the 'constant two-way flow of goods, services and people between the two areas' of Hartishek and Somaliland. The surveys described here offer striking evidence of the geographical extent of the flow of the single most important good, namely the wheat grain distributed in the camps both at Hartishek and in the Aware district.

In the Ogaden, the maize and sorghum which were being eaten came mostly from the recent, mediocre harvests of the agro-pastoralists rather than from trade with the agricultural highlands. But amongst pastoralists in the survey, almost half said that wheat was the only grain which they were eating, whilst a further fifth said they were eating wheat as well as other cereals. The consumption of wheat, all of it of food aid origin, spread far into the eastern Haud area and to the south-west across the Wabi Shebelle river (where some amount also came from the airlifted grain distributed at Gode and Kelafo relief camps).

In Somaliland, the spread of wheat grain from Hartishek and Aware was even more remarkable. It was the principal or only grain eaten not only in the west, but also in the centre, and far into the southeast beyond Las 'Anod, and around the northeast town of 'Erigavo. Only in the far western coastal plain near Djibouti, and in the far east and northeast towards the port of Bosaso, was rice reported to be the principal grain eaten. Since rice and wheat flour are commercially imported, and are generally sold at about twice the price of wheat grain, all but the wealthiest people were eating these commodities only because their markets were beyond the reach of the wheat trade. During 1992, wheat grain from Djibouti, also of food aid origin, began appearing on the market in Hargeisa, presumably at competitive prices (personal communication with J. Pearce, SCF, Hargeisa).

An Inescapable Equation

There was much that could not be known about the rural economy of the Ogaden and Somaliland from rapid surveys. It was clear that, as is the case with pastoralists elsewhere in Africa and beyond, grain accounts for at least half of the food calories consumed over the year by most rural people in the territories surveyed, and this phenomenon predates the recent drought and warfare. Given the recent history of severely limited trade in livestock and commodities between the Ogaden and Somalia, it was difficult to understand how all the cash was obtained month after month to keep the wheat grain flowing through the markets. The lapse in the most lucrative livestock trade for Somaliland, that with Saudi Arabia, posed a similar question, if not as extreme as in the Ogaden. Remittances from relatives elsewhere were undoubtedly part of the equation, but their overall contribution must have been seriously reduced by the reversal in the fortunes of urban people and possibly by the residual effects of the Gulf War on the employment of Somalis, *inter alia*, in that region.

However, the essential equation for pastoralists must be in the exchange of livestock for grain, and this is also true of most agro-pastoralists in most years. The information obtained in the surveys on livestock holdings and market prices over a wide area allowed a calculation of the terms of trade and their implications. The conclusion was that despite livestock losses to drought, under the prevailing exchange conditions the Ogaden pastoralists would in general just about 'break even' in the following 12 months, but only if the market did not deteriorate for them. That is, with reasonable rains, they would be able to maintain a viable holding of livestock whilst buying sufficient grain for survival. In the case of Somaliland, in the west much would depend on the resumption of successful agriculture. Amongst pastoralists, the prospects for the year were far worse in the east than elsewhere unless either the price of animals rose steeply or grain became much cheaper.

Some of the recommendations arising from the surveys are no doubt now dated, whatever their value at the time. But the basic equation appears to hold. Grain has got to come into the region from somewhere at prices which allow the maintenance of a viable livestock economy. The closing of relief camps, and the phasing out of aid grain as an essential source of food, are things devoutly to be wished. But towards the end of 1991 it seemed clear that in the short term more food aid, whether in the form of free distributions or under a subsidized marketing arrangement, would be needed if some measure of economic stability, let alone regeneration, was to be achieved. It also seemed clear that if the official repatriation of hundreds of thousands of people to Somaliland were to be politically feasible, it should come with a high price tag in continued aid to ensure that the first result was not increased hunger. Insofar as circumstances may be considered to have changed in the ensuing period, they must still be judged in the same light.

References

Holt, J. and M. Lawrence (1991) *An end to isolation – the report of the Ogaden needs assessment study 1991*, The Save the Children Fund, London and Addis Ababa, October.
— (1992) *The prize of peace – a survey of rural Somaliland*, The Save the Children Fund, January.
Mehari, G-M., R. Hay, L. Yacob and M. Maffi (1977) 'The initial experience of a consolidated food and nutrition information system, analysis of data from the Ogaden area', *Environmental Child Health*, Vol. 23, 29–36.
Ryle, J. (1992) *Where there is no border*, Save the Children Fund, London, January.

12 RICHARD HOGG
Changing Mandates
in the Ethiopian Ogaden

The Impact of Somali
'Refugees & Returnees'
on the UNHCR

Introduction

The Greater Ogaden,[1] covering the former autonomous administrative region of Ogaden and lowland areas of Eastern Hararghe, is a politically and ecologically marginal part of Ethiopia – existing on the periphery of the Ethiopian highlands, inhabited largely by Somali pastoralists and economically, culturally and geographically tied to Somalia.[2] Civil war in Somalia has resulted in a flow of Isaak refugees from the north of the country into camps in Eastern Hararghe and more recently to a massive influx of Isaak, Ogadeni and other Somali refugees and returnees escaping the war in the south of the country, in particular the destruction of the capital, Mogadishu. This human tragedy has been compounded by drought and famine in the Ogaden, fighting between local Somali clans in the Jijiga and Kelafo areas, and intermittent insecurity both within the Ogaden and along the main Dire Dawa–Jijiga road. In April 1992 the UN temporarily suspended its relief operation in the south of the area following the murder of the UNHCR co-ordinator for Gode.[3]

The Ogaden today is a tangled skein of different actors, political, relief and humanitarian organizations. The following case study concerns the response of one agency, UNHCR, to the refugee/returnee crisis in the Ogaden. The central argument of the paper is that a) it is meaningless to talk of returnees or local people in the context of the Ogaden – the distinction between the two is at best blurred and at worst misleading, (while this has finally – since June 1992 – been recognized by the UNHCR in its new cross-mandate approach it has been a long time coming, and still requires considerable fine-tuning); b) the policy of UNHCR should be to target economic assistance to the whole of the Ogaden and to neighbouring areas of Somalia, rather than to only one side of the border; and c) it is the UNHCR mandate itself which, because it focusses on the discontinuities between different actors and regions, obscures the nature and strength of the interdependencies and linkages which exist between different groups in the society and different neighbouring territories. It is these interdependencies/linkages which need

[1] In the rest of the paper, unless otherwise specifically indicated, I use the term Ogaden to refer to the Greater Ogaden as a whole.
[2] Under the new largely ethnically based administrative arrangements of the Ethiopian Peoples' Revolutionary Democratic Front (EPRDF) transitional government in Ethiopia, the Greater Ogaden including the Issa-dominated Dire Dawa and Gurgura districts to the north of the area, is set to become part of the Somali administered 5th Region of Ethiopia.
[3] Since then the UNHCR has not returned to the south of the Ogaden, but provides funds to the Emergency Preparedness Group of the UNDP in Addis Ababa to operate as the 'lead' UN agency in the area – part of the new cross-mandate approach of the UNHCR.

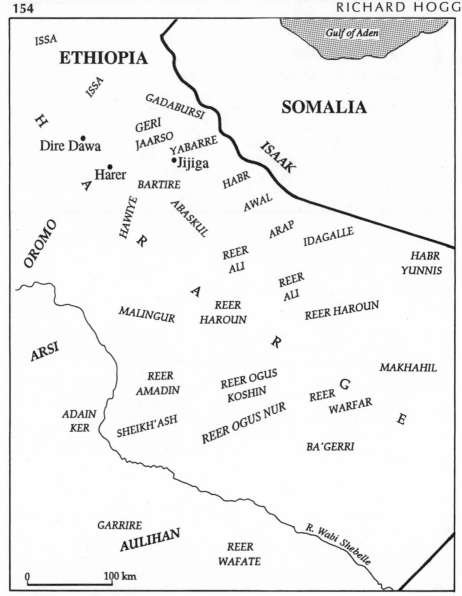

Map 12.1 *Somali clans of Hararge Province*

to be developed and strengthened in any rehabilitation–cum–development programme in the region.

The Land and People

The Greater Ogaden covers approximately 240,000 sq km in the southeast corner of Ethiopia. Most of the area lies between about 1,500m in the northwest to 300m in the south. The land, with its low and variable rainfall and often poor soils, is best suited to nomadic pastoralism. Agriculture is practised in better watered areas and along the banks of the Shebelle river. The majority of the population are Somali-speaking pastoralists, who are divided into different but interrelated clan groups each with their own traditional clan territories (see Map 12.1 for major clan areas). Fighting over grazing and water is common between distantly related clans; even closely related groups will sometimes fight over access to grazing and water.

Many of the clan territories in the Ogaden stretch across the international border with Somalia, and visiting between relatives and friends on both sides of the border is common. Many pastoralists in the Ogaden use clan watering points and grazing areas in Somalia, and it is common for wealthy merchants to own shops and houses in both countries. Historically, the Ogaden combined with the neighbouring parts of Somalia, have formed a single economic zone where goods, people and services have flowed freely if not always officially.

Because of the constant traffic in people across the border estimating the population of the Ogaden has always been fraught with difficulties. In a recent series of over-flights of the area carried out by Save the Children Fund, UK, in 1991 it was estimated that the total rural population of Greater Ogaden, excluding the refugee/returnee camps, was about a million (Holt and Lawrence, 1991: 24).[4]

The Genesis of a Crisis

The crisis of the Ogaden is a crisis of politics compounded by economics and geography. Wars between Ethiopia and Somalia in 1963–4 and 1977–8 for control of the Ogaden resulted in large outflows of Somali from the area.[5] Most fled to Somalia where they became absorbed into the local economy and society , while others became permanent refugees in refugee camps, absorbing large amounts of UNHCR and international donor money over the years.

Links between the refugees in Somalia and their home areas in the Ogaden were carefully maintained, and throughout the eighties the Ogaden benefited from substantial inflows of grain from the refugee camps just across the border in Somalia. This cross-border trade in grain, livestock and other commodities largely supported the Ogaden economy during these years, and the Somali shilling was (and still is) the main currency of the area.

With the gradual break-up and disintegration of Somalia, first in the north of the country in the late eighties as attacks on government-held towns by the Somali National Movement (SNM) increased, and later in the capital and centre and south of the country by United Somali Congress (USC) forces, the flow of refugees and returnees was reversed. By 1989 there were well over 300,000 refugees registered in camps in the northern part of the Ogaden: Rabasso, Daror, Kamaboka, Harshin and Hartishek. This flow greatly increased after the fall of Mogadishu in early 1991. According to UNHCR planning figures for June 1992 there were a total of over 594,000 refugees and 117,000 returnees in the northern part of the Ogaden (administratively, Eastern Hararghe).[6]

The figure for registered returnees does not include the vast majority of those returning from Somalia who were simply re-absorbed by the local population.

---

[4] According to official government figures from the Central Statistical Agency, 1988, the total rural population of the Greater Ogaden is estimated at 1,359,000.

[5] Some small towns in the area, such as Teferi Ber in the north-east of the region and Durwale in the Jerer Valley (this latter town has never been rebuilt) have been destroyed twice in the last 30 years as a result of the conflict.

[6] UNHCR recognizes, however, that these figures are based on card rather than head counts. As many people have more than one card the actual numbers of people living in the camps is likely to be far less than the card count suggests.

According to the Report of the Ogaden Needs Assessment Study (Holt and Lawrence, 1991) over 260,000 returnees or nearly one-third of the rural population of the Ogaden were living with relatives or friends, i.e. had been re-absorbed back into the local community. The cost of this sudden influx of people and mouths to feed on the local economy, which was already under considerable pressure as a result of drought, was shattering.

The Problem

The problem of the Ogaden today is multi-faceted:

1 There is the long-term problem of a marginalised economy, largely oriented to Somalia and the Middle East. The civil war in Somalia and the collapse of the Somali economy has had unintended consequences on an already fragile local economy.
2 There is the immediate human tragedy of people being forced to flee Somalia and find succour in the Ogaden. Many of these are returning to their original homes, but for some others it is a new country, with which they have few connections. For many, they have known of nothing else but refugee camps for the past 14 to 15 years.
3 There is the problem of drought-affected pastoralists in the Ogaden, whose difficulties have been compounded by the influx of returnees from across the border and the loss of grain supplies from the refugee camps in Hiraan region in Somalia.
4 There is the problem of internally displaced people, who because of inter-clan fighting have lost their homes and means of livelihood. It is estimated that upwards of 150,000 people have been displaced as a result of fighting between Geri and Jaarso northeast of Jijiga and Reer Barre and Ogadeni around Kelafo on the Shebelle river.
5 Finally, there are the difficulties created for all aid agencies working in the Ogaden as a result of the new political dispensation in Ethiopia, with its accent on regional autonomy and ethnically based political parties. In the Ogaden there are a variety of largely clan-based political parties, each with their own agenda and interests.

The Dilemma for UNHCR

UNHCR's dilemma is as follows: while it is willing to offer assistance to help the refugees and registered returnees in the short term it does not want to get sucked into a situation of supporting permanent refugee/returnee camps. So far, since the organization first became involved in 1987 in establishing refugee camps in the Harshin area for Isaak refugees, the situation has if anything deteriorated. For a time, after the assumption of the SNM to power in northern Somalia and the proclamation of the Somaliland Republic the prospects looked good for a repatriation of at least a large number of Isaak refugees from the camps. However, these hopes have been dashed by the resurgence of inter-clan fighting in Somaliland this year, and in the meantime, fighting elsewhere in Somalia has seen a continuing flow of people into the Ogaden. In addition, the organization has found itself increasingly involved in providing assistance to internally displaced Somalis – on the grounds a) that it is the lead agency in the area and therefore in the best position to help them; and b) that it is largely arbitrary in any case who gets assistance as an internally displaced Somali or returnee. As a result the UNHCR commitment to the area has steadily expanded rather than contracted over the last four years.

It was probably inevitable that in the complex situation it found itself in in the Ogaden the role of the UNHCR was likely to expand. The refugees/returnees crossing the border were merely the symptoms of a much larger regional tragedy being played out in the Horn, viz., the collapse of Somalia as a political and economic entity. Any agency that became involved in the area simply to help refugees/returnees was likely to be drawn into this wider conflict, especially as the disintegration of Somalia coincided with a period of marked political instability in Ethiopia following the fall of the Mengistu regime in May 1991, which unleashed a series of localized inter-clan conflicts in the Ogaden. These conflicts had resulted by early 1992 in upwards of 150,000 internally displaced Somali dependent on international assistance.

Without the large inflows of relief grain from Somalia to depend on, following the economic dislocations in that country from the late 1980s onwards, food had become increasingly scarce in the Ogaden by 1990. By 1991 much of the south of the area was gripped by famine. At the same time local people had to support a growing number of returnees crossing the border from 1987–8 onwards. Without UNHCR grain to the refugee/returnee camps, much of which inevitably found its way onto local markets, many more Somali throughout the Ogaden would have died. By 1991 food relief intended exclusively to support refugees/returnees was propping up a whole regional economy. Given this situation the price of a sudden UNHCR withdrawal would have been catastophic.[7]

It is hardly surprising therefore that local people are opposed to any downgrading of the UNHCR role in the area.[8] They have too much to lose. In a sense the UNHCR, just because it did come to the rescue in 1987 of what it then largely perceived as a discrete category of *refugees*, has steadily got itself trapped by the aid-dependent nature of the local economy in the Ogaden into playing, at least indirectly, a longer term 'developmental type' role. Extracting itself from this position is going to prove very difficult given the volatile political and economic situation in the area, where, not only is there a chronic structural food deficit, but also a host of different and competing political groups.

Until there is improved security in Somalia/Somaliland the problem of the refugees in Ethiopia is unlikely to go away. To this extent the UNHCR has to play a waiting game. However, there is already a strong indication, from many of the returnees at least, that even if peace is restored in Somalia they would rather try and make a life for themselves in the Ogaden – in other words they have genuinely returned home, and, as they perceive it, it is largely up to the UNHCR working with government and other agencies to make sure that the economy of the area is strong enough to absorb them. In so far as the refugees are concerned, however, the majority of whom are Isaaks, who are already living in their own clan territory, most are reluctant to go home to Somaliland while there is no apparent solution to the interlinked problems of lack of security and the poor economic prospects in the country.

The problems of Somaliland have been compounded by the failure of the international community to come to its assistance. Without this international assistance, which appears largely conditional on international recognition of Somaliland, it is difficult to see how Somaliland will escape the inevitable slide into anarchy so many Somali predict.[9] In this context, the camps in Ethiopia are subsidising the Somaliland economy in two important ways i) by providing free rations to Isaak, and to a lesser extent Gadabursi, refugees; and ii) by the illegal flows of grain from the refugee camps which find there way across the border into Somaliland.

[7] This position changed in the south of the Ogaden from 1993. Some of the large in-flows of grain going into Somalia inevitably found it way up north.
[8] This has been brought home recently by the vociferous demands of many returnees to continue to be allowed to stay in the relief camps in Eastern Hararghe in spite of UNHCR attempts to get them back to their home communities.
[9] Since October 1992 with the signing of a peace agreement between the main warring factions in the Somaliland conflict, the security situation in the country has much improved.

Given the poor state of the Somaliland economy as well as the close relationship that exists throughout the region between insecurity and targeted food relief, the obvious strategy for UNHCR to adopt in the circumstances is to try to spearhead a revival of the Somaliland economy (see Ryle, 1992). At least such a revival would immediately relieve the pressure on the refugee camps in Ethiopia. Such a strategy, however, inevitably runs foul not only of arguments over the limitations of the UNHCR mandate – these arguments are invariably put by UNHCR personnel when they *do not* want to become involved in a particular area – but also the implicit recognition such a package might contain of the independent status of the Somaliland Republic. For a UN agency this is particularly delicate ground. During the early 1990s in Eritrea it was only possible because of the already implicit recognition by the international community of the de facto independent status of the territory and the promise of the Eritrean provisional government to hold a referendum in 1993. However, UN involvement in Eritrea remained very limited until after 1993, and in the case of Somaliland not even token recognition has been granted. As a result Somaliland is left largely to the sphere of non-governmental agencies, while the UN directs its attention to explicitly humanitarian rather than longer term development assistance.

The major problem of the UNHCR approach – which is largely forced on it by its own restricted mandate, is that by dividing the population of a particular area into different categories – refugees/returnees/local – it is distorting and effectively hiding the structural continuities which exist between all three categories, and between the Ogaden and Somalia itself. By looking at the problem differently, and accepting the underlying economic and structural continuities, UNHCR may be able either by itself or in partnership with other agencies, to come up with a more practicable, and possibly expeditious, solution to the immediate problem of what to do with the refugees/returnees in the Ogaden.

An Approach from Socio-economics rather than Political-Economy

The international border with Somalia is largely an artificial creation of nation states. So far as the people living in the Ogaden and neighbouring areas of Somalia are concerned the border is meaningless – they cross it at will and many have friends, relatives and property on both sides. Pastoralists have always crossed the border in search of grazing and water – although in some areas this has recently been curtailed because of land mines on the Somaliland side of the border. The main distinction of the border at the present time is that it is safer on one side than the other, and the Ethiopian side has refugee camps.

Many of those who have fled across the border to escape the fighting in Somalia are either originally from the Ogaden or have close relatives and clansmen in the area. These may be returnees or refugees according to the UNHCR, but the point is that it is almost impossible to tell in many cases – because the distinction is artificial, a product of the world of bureaucracy rather than the world of Somali clan and family relationships. Certainly there are genuine refugees who have no close or clan connections with the Ogaden, but it is hard to credit that the large numbers claiming refugee status have no connections with the area.[10]

Talk of repatriating Isaak refugees in Hartishek camps to Somaliland, when there is a

---

[10] It is clear for instance that many of those registered as refugees by UNHCR at Teferi Ber camp are in fact Gadabursi returning to their home area after many years of absence. Many have farms just outside the camp to which they move every day during the planting and harvest seasons.

12.1 *Food distribution to returnees from Somalia at UNHCR's Teferi Ber camp.*
(UNHCR/21030/07.1991/A. Hollmann)

12.2 *To be effective in the Ogaden either the UNHCR has to be more than just a refugee*
organization and openly take on some of the baggage of a development organization or it has to
more strictly interpret its own traditional mandate while striving to build institutional links with
other UN agencies: new arrivals at Hartishek, 1991. (UNHCR/21023/A. Hollmann)

constant two-way flow of goods, services and people between the two areas, is difficult to understand. There is a cultural and economic continuum. The discontinuities are created by massive flows of aid into the camps on the Ethiopian side, and increased insecurity on the Somaliland side. So long as these discontinuities exist so will the problem of 'refugees'. The only sensible approach for the UNHCR to take is to treat both sides of the border as one economic and relief zone, and given improvements in security, to even out the flows of relief and development aid to both.

Inevitably, however, such an approach would involve, firstly, the political will to work in Somaliland on longer term rehabilitation and development activities *whatever* the official UN position on the political status of Somaliland, and, secondly, the development of an effective *modus operandi* for UNHCR to either work through other bilateral/multilateral agencies or extend its own mandate to include an explicit recognition of a) the importance of cross-border or regional operations which transcend the normal national operations of the agency; and b) the inevitable continuity which exists between humanitarian and development assistance. To treat the symptoms of a problem without addressing the underlying causes is merely to compound the problem in the future.

Unlike the majority of the refugees in the camps in the Ogaden, who have some notion of ultimate return to their 'homes' across the border, many of the returnees to the Ogaden appear to want to stay. For them at least the Ogaden is 'home'. The extent to which they will manage to stay, however, will depend critically on the balance of economic opportunities on either side of the border. Many of the better-educated returnees if they cannot find suitable paid jobs in the Ogaden will simply return to Somalia/Somaliland once the situation improves across the border. The fate of the returnees therefore is closely linked to the longer term development of the Ogaden economy and its capacity to provide them with useful employment.

Returnees, however, are not an isolated category nor can assistance be offered to them in isolation from the rest of the community. While registered returnees live in camps, because they are unwilling or cannot return to their home areas, most returnees, few of whom have ever been registered, have been re-absorbed into the local population. While they tend to be better educated than the majority of the local population who stayed on in the Ogaden during the 1970s, and have different kinds of expectations, *all* have a need for longer term development assistance. At the very minimum therefore, apart from short-term emergency relief, there is a pressing need to build up the capacity of the local economy, through longer term programmes, to feed its growing population.

New Approach

After much soul searching UNHCR has finally, since June 1992 recognized the limitations of its traditional humanitarian approach to the problem of refugees/returnees in the Ogaden as summarized below:

a) define the categories of people eligible for assistance in terms of their status as *refugees and returnees* (according to the operational definitions used by UNHCR);
b) register them;
c) put them into camps and feed and clothe them;
d) after the emergency phase is over repatriate the refugees as soon as possible and provide reintegration packages for the returnees;
e) end of problem.

The trouble in the Ogaden has been that i) the conventional definitions of what is a refugee/returnee/local do not hold; ii) it is extremely difficult to register people, for just about everyone can claim to be a refugee/returnee in need; iii) local people are also in need but are largely left out of the relief process altogether (and feel aggrieved as a result);[11] and iv) the conventional distinctions between emergency, rehabilitation and development phases are difficult to make in the context of an economy in permanent crisis. After nearly four years in the Ogaden UNHCR has realized that its conventional approach is unlikely to lead to an early withdrawal from the area. As a result the agency has been forced to re-examine its mandate.

However, it is one thing to recognize the need for a change of direction but it is quite another to establish a workable institutional framework to allow it to happen. Since June, 1992 when UNHCR in Addis Ababa first outlined the broad principles of its new cross-mandate approach,[12] the implementation of the new approach has been constantly delayed, as the other agencies working in the Ogaden with UNHCR, such as Oxfam, Save the Children Fund,UK, and UNHCR's own counterpart organization, the Administration of Refugee Affairs (ARA), while welcoming the UNHCR change of tack have complained vociferously about the pace of the change. The core of the complaint is that there has been insufficient consultation between the agencies concerning the programming and implementation of joint activities.[13]

Far from representing the radical change of direction it might at first appear the rationale for the new approach is that it actually allows UNHCR to return to its roots as a 'refugee' organization while handing over responsibility for its accumulated non-traditional responsibilities in the Ogaden, particularly longer term support to returnees, to other interested agencies. The new approach is therefore as much a recognition of the limitations of the UNHCR mandate as an expansion of it. By getting the returnees out of the camps and back to their home communities, for example, UNHCR can justifiably argue that they are now the responsibility of the community as a whole, while, by supporting collaborating agencies with development funds the organization can argue that it is supporting long-term development activities in the area while remaining true to its original mandate.

While in theory such an approach at least recognizes UNHCR's wider responsibilities to support other agencies in the field – a belated recognition of the inter-connectedness of all interventions in the Ogaden, in practice what has happened is that a) there is no defined institutional machinery to allow for such collaboration; and b) it is the UNHCR which sets the terms and timetable for the cooperation. The other parties to the agreement are merely expected to fall into line. So for example, in August–November 1992, when the returnees were expected to leave the camps, it was UNHCR which set the agenda. The 'returnees', 'local communities', and 'co-operating agencies' were merely expected to rubber stamp the arrangements.[14] Until, however, greater attention is paid to sorting out the institutional arrangements between the co-operating agencies – on an equal footing – it is difficult to see how the cross-mandate can hope to work. The

[11] There have been numerous instances over the last year of local pastoralists holding up UNHCR trucks in order to steal the food they are carrying to the camps.

[12] While there has been little attempt to clearly enunciate the principles of the cross-mandate, the approach signifies an inter-disciplinary approach between different agencies working towards a common goal.

[13] An example of this at the end of July 1992 was the announcement by UNHCR that it intended to allow only two weeks for all returnees to leave the camps. In future, reduced rations were to be channelled to the returnees' home communities on the basis of need for a period of six months. Only after protests from other agencies working in Jijiga was the timetable for returnees to leave the camps extended.

[14] This was most visibly brought home to me when UNHCR started to carry out, in September 1992, pre-liminary surveys of returnees in the camps prior to sending them back to their communities. When it was suggested to the UNHCR representative in Jijiga that insufficient time had been allotted to carry out the surveys it was pointed out a) that no more time was available and b) that UNHCR was not a research or development agency so could not be expected to carry out detailed survey work.

simple principle at stake is that no agency should accept increased responsibility without proper representation in the decision-making process. It is how to achieve this level of consultation and joint decision-making that UNHCR needs to work on urgently.

Role of Returnees

Many returnees, because of their educational background and experience in working in Somalia and elsewhere – many have travelled widely and worked in the Middle East – represent potentially a dynamic force in the local economy. For years the Ogaden has been a relative backwater, lagging behind the rest of Ethiopia and Somalia as well. After the exodus of Somali from the area after the 1977 war with Somalia, there were few educated people left in the region. The majority of what few jobs there were went to Ethiopians from the highlands. Since the fall of Siad Barre in Somalia, and the return home to the Ogaden of large numbers of people, the situation has radically changed. Educated and qualified Somalis are clamouring for jobs, and others are setting up small businesses and farming co-operatives. Even in the remotest of Ogadeni towns educated returnees are to be found. One of the main problems they face is adjusting to the relative lack of opportunities in the Ogaden. Jobs are few and far between.

Nevertheless, the returnees act as a catalyst for development. In the rural areas it is the returnees who are spearheading ideas for change, and making demands on development and relief agencies working in the area for longer term development assistance and training. This new willingness and confidence to change is not confined to the men. Returnee women have been in the forefront of opening new businesses, and play a leading role in the long-distance lorry trade in goods from Somaliland and Djibouti.

The present influx into the Ogaden of large numbers of qualified local people offers a challenge as well as a danger. The challenge is that their energies can be harnessed to develop the Ogaden economy, the danger is that they will grow disaffected because the opportunities for employment will not materialize. At present the only large-scale development project in the area is the African Development Bank financed South East Rangelands Project (SERP) with its headquarters in Jijiga. The project however has few resources to develop an area covering almost one-third of Ethiopia. The challenge for the UNHCR is to work together with SERP and other agencies to rebuild the local economy. Already there is talk of UNHCR providing additional funds for rehabilitation to be channelled through SERP. However, while this may seem an obvious direction for the organization to move it is circumscribed by bureaucratic problems and, in spite of the cross-mandate approach, continued UNHCR coyness about involving itself too closely in development.

Comment

Refugees and returnees are products of an official bureaucracy. The procedures to deal with them are products of the same bureaucracy. To the people themselves, however, they only become refugees and returnees by entering the world of UNHCR. Otherwise, in the Ogaden, they are Ogadenis, Isaaks, Gadabursi, Abaskuls etc. In other words they have a cultural and clan identity. It is this identity which gives them leave to expect help from their fellow clansmen and near relatives.

It is this world of the Somali 'refugee/returnee' that UNHCR must enter to understand the economic and cultural continuities which lie beneath the surface. The Ogaden is economically and ecologically part of Somalia. Historically, the border is the creation of a relatively recent political process. Effectively, Somali on either side of the border trade in a single economic zone. People and livestock have always moved across the border. The recent influx of people is probably unprecedented in scale but the underlying processes at work are culturally and historically determined – exposed to insecurity Somali have always retreated to their own clan territories. By and large they come not as strangers but as kinsmen.

The very scale of the influx has overwhelmed the local economy and society. However, it is not through targeting aid at official categories of people that the problem will be alleviated, but through an understanding of the economic and cultural interdependencies which exist in the region as a whole. This requires a re-direction of assistance away from 'refugees/returnees' to the revitalization of the regional economy as a whole and the larger community of which it is a part.

The Institutional Challenge

The Ogaden case directly challenges traditional UNHCR orthodoxies about a) what is or is not a refugee or returnee; b) agency emphasis on national state identity rather than local ethnic identity as a basis for registration; c) the arbitrary nature of political lines drawn on a map, when they can clearly be seen on the ground to divide ethnically homogeneous communities and economically interdependent regions; d) the essential continuum which exists between short-term relief and longer term rehabilitation and development assistance; e) the severe limitations in the field imposed by the traditional and rather arbitrary institutional divisions between and mandates of the different UN agencies, which effectively block inter-agency cooperation; and, finally, f) the lack of any clear-cut institutional mechanism to allow for the effective implementation of cross-mandate operations.

To be effective in the Ogaden either the UNHCR has to be more than just a refugee organization and openly take on some of the baggage of a development organization or it has to more strictly interpret its own traditional mandate while striving to build institutional links with other UN agencies, such as the UNDP, which can take on responsibility for the more overtly developmental needs of the area. At present the main problem is that the UNHCR is being pushed and pulled in different and often contradictory directions. The organization rests on a set of formal political assumptions about nation states, which cannot do justice to the diffuseness of such concepts as nationalism/statehood/ethnic identity in Africa today and, in particular, the inter-penetration of economic and political factors in triggering mass movements of population. In the disintegrating fabric of post-colonial Africa, when such population movements represent as much an economic as political expression of the retreat to the primordial loyalties of clan and tribe, UNHCR has to establish a new set of guiding principles and necessary institutional arrangements to allow for a more effective interdisciplinary approach to the problem of population displacement. Only such a step can turn present UNHCR rhetoric about the new cross-mandate approach in the Ogaden into a meaningful reality.

References

Central Statistical Agency (1988) *Statistical abstract*, Ethiopian Government, Addis Ababa.
Holt J. and Lawrence M. (1991) *An end to isolation – the report of the Ogaden needs assessment study*, Save the Children Fund UK, London and Addis Ababa.
Ryle, J. (1992) 'Notes on the repatriation of Somali refugees from Ethiopia', *Disasters*, Vol. 16, No.2.

13

M.A. MOHAMED SALIH
Responding to Situations of Mass Voluntary Return

Past Experience in Sudan

The Addis Ababa Agreement

In this chapter I present some observations about the Sudanese experience in the years following the Addis Ababa Agreement – the peace settlement which marked the end of the first civil war between the South and the North (1955–72).

I do not intend to discuss the immediate political context of the negotiations in 1972, which had placed considerable pressure on both sides to find some means of resolving their differences, nor to dwell on the details of the repatriation exercise. These issues have been examined elsewhere (see, for example, Allen, 1989; Akol, 1994). Suffice it to say that the agreement was based on the following key considerations: (1) regional autonomy, with the setting up of a Southern Assembly and the appointment of a president of the Southern Region, (2) an amnesty for all exiled Southerners, (3) the incorporation of Southern guerrillas into the national armed forces, (4) economic, social and cultural development programmes, (5) the training of Southerners to assume public responsibilities.

The terms of the agreement have been heavily criticized by various interest groups and, with the benefit of hindsight, scholars have tended to argue that it was doomed from the start. In 1983 war broke out again, and continues to be waged at the time of writing. It is, however, too easy to dismiss the Addis Ababa Agreement as a failure. It led to one of the first and largest assisted mass voluntary return operations, and was a foundation of peace in Sudan for almost a decade.

Both because of what was initally achieved and because the experiment with the politics of compromise ulimately did not work, the Sudanese experience in the 1970s offers useful lessons for planning and implementation of programmes in comparable post-war situations. The lesson that I emphasize most strongly here is to do with the linking of relief to development, and particularly to the establishing of viable national institutions. In this context, it is worth drawing attention to the terms negotiated in Addis Ababa.

For obvious reasons, the Sudan Government tended to take the view that under-development, rather than religious intolerance or the oppression of ethnic minorities was the primary cause of the war. A connection was therefore made between the return of the population and longer term reconstruction. 'Rehabilitation' and 'resettlement' were the expressions used, and the needs of repatriated refugees were not placed above other displaced people. It was also recognized that assistance in the post-war situation could not be separated from setting up the administration of the new Southern Region, and

13.1 *There was widespread destruction during the first civil war in Sudan, but facilities and services had always been minimal: Juba port in 1972. (UNHCR/1805/W. van de Linde)*

that efforts needed to be co-ordinated in negotiation with Sudanese officials, rather than implemented by international agencies on an ad hoc basis.

These points are illustrated by Chapter IV, Section 2, Article 2 of the Addis Ababa Agreement, which stipulated that:

> ... although resettlement and rehabilitation of refugees and displaced persons is administratively the responsibility of the Regional Government, the present conditions in the Southern Region dictate that the efforts of the whole nation of the Sudan and international organizations should be pooled to help and rehabilitate persons affected by the conflict. The Relief and Resettlement Commission shall coordinate activities and resources of the organizations within the Country.

Assisting return in the 1970s

The extent of devastation in Southern Sudan during the first civil war was never adequately assessed. Certainly there was widespread destruction of schools, health centres, bridges and government offices, and the complete suspension of most public services. However, facilities and services had always been minimal, so it was more the opportunity cost of the fighting which was damaging. There were also the costs associated with the destruction of communal life, the most obvious indication of which was the scale of population displacement. About a million people had fled their home areas, 200,000 of whom were refugees, mostly in neighbouring countries. In these circumstances 'rehabilitation' was a daunting prospect. It required not only the rebuilding or replacing of what had once existed, but in many respects actually initiating the development process for the first time.

However, even before engaging with the problem, there was a prior issue to be dealt with, that of ensuring consensus over the state's monopoly on the use of force. Sensibly,

Map 13.1 *The repatriation to Southern Sudan following the Addis Ababa Agreement of 1972*

the Addis Ababa Agreement gave priority to the absorption of ex-military personnel. An 18-month transitional period was devoted to regrouping, selecting and training 6,000 officers from the 'Anyanya' guerrilla forces, and their incorporation into the national army. The second step was to train and establish the remaining guerrillas in their villages or in the public sector. Many were employed in road construction or as forest and game wardens. This took about two years (1972–4).

13.2 *Infrastructure was in a better condition than it had ever been: the new Nile bridge near Juba, capital of the Southern Region, photographed in 1974, soon after completion. (UNHCR/4047/W. van de Linde)*

During the same period, ex-government employees began to be reinstated. Consideration was given to the skills they had gained abroad and some were sent on short courses. This was considered important so as to have a functioning administration as soon as possible in order to cope with the return of the mass of displaced people. Most of these people had received little or no formal education and, while they looked to the state to provide some basic services, they had a potential capacity to sustain themselves relatively quickly through established modes of agricultural and pastoral production. However, thousands had lost their herds and found their farms overgrown, and there were also disputes over access to pasture and land to sort out. Moreover, there were high expectations that life would rapidly improve, and it was recognized that it was essential for people to see the benefits of peace almost immediately in order to sustain it.

The enthusiasm of international agencies for relief programmes was not as pronounced in the mid-1970s as it was to become. In those years several were prepared to support integrated schemes, and this enabled the Sudanese authorities to take a developmental approach. For various reasons, the funding provided under central government auspices was meagre (much less than anticipated by the negotiators in Addis Ababa), but the regional government was able to raise its own revenue. The UN granted about US$20 million for the rehabilitation efforts, the World Bank lent US$10.7 million for agricultural and livestock projects, Kuwait and Abu Dhabi built the Southern Region's health and education networks, and Yugoslavia funded the building of the adminstration and parliament buildings. Emphasis was placed on the training of teachers and medical personnel, the installation of new, rural public health and water supply facilities. 423 primary schools and three teacher training institutes were rapidly constructed or repaired. The Federal Republic of Germany, the United Kingdom, the Dutch government and UNHCR all supported the construction of roads and bridges. Over 1,300 miles of gravel roads were graded between 1972 and 1974.

Importantly, the assistance efforts targeting at returnees were absorbed into the national and regional agricultural development plan. The rehabilitation policy aimed to create an enabling environment, and to encourage self-reliance. Between 1972 and 1975 a total of 119,260 hand tools and 40 tons of various seeds were distributed free of charge to the returned families. The World Bank loan was used to purchase and introduce some 2,000 ox-ploughs and to set up a central seed-bulking station in Yei with 11 sub-stations in various parts of the Southern Region.

In 1975, by which time most of the displaced people had arrived back in their home areas, the South was still very poor. Communications remained impossible in many places during the wet season, there were virtually no local savings for investment, almost no manufacturing, an acute shortage of skilled staff in the public sector combined with a lack of employment opportunites for uneducated people, and the informal economy benefited very few. Nevertheless, infrastructure was in a better condition than it had ever been. Even more significantly, according to observers from the International Labour Organization, for nearly all foodcrops, the area under cultivation was higher in the 1973/4 season than before the start of hostilities. Independent commentators at the time agreed that things looked promising.

Linking Relief and Development

Five main factors contributed to the success at linking relief and development in Sudan during the mid-1970s.

1 The Addis Ababa Agreement had been preceded in 1971 by an attempted communist coup. This undoubtedly made the major aid donor countries more willing to help Sudan than would otherwise have been the case, and adequate funds were made available at an early stage.
2 It was in the political interest of Nimeri's government in Khartoum to end the war and encourage foreign investment. This was partly because Nimeri had originally come to power in alliance with the communists, and was not in a situation in which he could gain the co-operation of the old political parties or the main Moslem factions.
3 The programme in Sudan was an early instance of assisted mass return (which built on some of the precedents set in Algeria in 1962). There was as yet comparatively little pressure to run short-term emergency relief schemes. Donors were prepared to support institution building and aid workers were prepared to work under national supervision. Moreover, most funds were not earmarked in restrictive ways. For example they were not generally made available only for particular groups of repatriated refugees.
4 Many of those involved in the programme, both Sudanese nationals and staff of international agencies, had a highly altruistic attitude. They revealed remarkable determination, tact and patience. Potentially explosive situations were defused, and the provision of aid was well co-ordinated and effectively monitored.
5 Although economically very impoverished, large parts of the South are fertile and reasonably well watered. Other areas can provide good seasonal pasture for cattle. The large-scale distribution of agricultural inputs could therefore have rapid effects. Food self-sufficiency was achieved much faster than would have been the case in much of northeast Africa.

Unfortunately, the gains made did not last. The threat of communism in Sudan waned, and so did donor interest. Nimeri began to cultivate friendships and alliances with Islamic leaders who were opposed to the settlement in the South, and were eager to introduce Islamic law in the whole country. Divisions opened up in the Southern Regional Assembly, notably over the issue of dividing the South up into three smaller regions. International aid agencies started operating ever more independently, both of the Sudanese authorities and of one another. The central government pushed through large-scale projects in the South, such as the Jonglei canal scheme, which seemed of benefit only to the North. As resouces became scarcer, corruption became a problem, and adminstration in the South became incapacitated.

By 1980 it was clear that the expectations of many southerners were not going to be met. Civilian employment opportunites had dried up for ex-guerrillas, and those incorporated in the Sudanese armed forces resented being overlooked for promotion. Tensions were further increased by more influxes of returnees from Uganda following the fall of Amin. They were acompaned by a quarter of a million Ugandan refugees. Unlike the returnees in the mid-1970s, many of these later migrants had attended schools, and they

13.3 *Sudanese children from a variety of ethnic backgrounds playing together near a small trading centre, north of Malakal, Southern Region, 1980. (Tim Allen)*

became increasingly influential in Juba and in the most fertile southern parts of the Southern Region (around Yambio and Yei). There had been a series of army mutinees by Southern soldiers during the later 1970s. In the early 1980s, conflict over 'redivision' and the threat of Islamicization eventually culminated in the Bor mutiny and the drift back to full-scale civil war in 1983.

Prospects for Bridging the Gap Again

The current war in Sudan is having appalling consequences, and it is hard to see an end to it. However, assuming that some kind of settlement is again negotiated, will it be possible to learn from the 1970s? Could the gap between relief and development be bridged again (and hopefully the development process be sustained for longer)?

It is difficult to respond to these questions optimistically. It seems that the scale of suffering in Southern Sudan has probably been even greater since 1983 than during the previous war. Infastructure built during the 1970s has been destroyed. According to Sudanese government reports, in 1990, 97 per cent of primary schools, 95 per cent of junior secondary schools and all senior secondary schools in the South were closed. In the same year, 80 per cent of all health centres (including hospitals) had been shut down. Displacement is on a huge scale. Over 400,000 people have become refugees in Ethiopia, Uganda and Kenya, some of them crossing into war zones in those countries. Something like 2 million others have been internally displaced, and the ethnic composition of much of the country has probably been permanently changed. Reconstruction will present awesome difficulties, and a commitment from the international community which may not be forthcoming.

Furthermore, even if national and international political pressures are brought to bear, a compromise is reached, and resources are made available, the approach of the international community to post-war reconstruction has changed for the worse.

The current approach is to channel funds through international NGOs rather than local NGOs and other national institutions. Most international NGOs are not interested in working together with government officials. They generally establish parallel structures

13.4 *Before the return to war: a wedding celebration near Nasir, May 1981. (Tim Allen)*

through which to channel resources, often by-passing or co-opting the state sector almost entirely. In addition, international NGOs not only reject co-ordination by local authorities, but also refuse to be co-ordinated by international bodies (such as UN agencies). They are also in competition with each other over funding and areas of operation. They unite only when there are efforts to regulate them.

Moreover, partly because international NGOs insist on operating independently and partly because all aid has become more prone to the political influence of the media, relief operations have become a much more attractive proposition for funders than a commitment to long-term development. Experiments with integrated rural development in the 1970s are set aside as impractical, especially in Africa where governmental administration is perceived as weak and ineffective. Quick, spectacular, well publicized, emergency-orientated relief is something that can be presented as caring and charitable, even though large amounts of money are used up in overheads and in salaries for international staff. Continuous food handouts have become a norm and, in spite of what is claimed in aid agency propaganda material, no real effort is make to empower the poor so that they can struggle for their own interests.

These tendencies had already become apparent in Southern Sudan during the early 1980s, particularly in areas where there were large numbers of refugees, often with very damaging results. A situation is created in which local tensions are exacerbated, as international NGOs play one faction off against another in order to operate without constraint, and planning becomes almost impossible. The present situation is that international NGOs are engaged in a continuous fight to secure their own interests. They have become expert in diverting attention from development to unsustainable piecemeal responses.

Similar points can be made about UNHCR. Like the international NGOs (which it commonly funds), UNHCR has become much less willing to respond to the longer-term needs of displaced people. It, too, solicits support from the big donors by emphasizing its role in emergency relief, and it has been placed under pressure not to become involved in any development programmes. Supposedly, such programmes are taken on by other UN organizations once the initial crisis has passed, but this does not occur in practice because of donor priorities and the overall lack of co-ordination between agencies.

I can readily imagine that if the time comes when it is again possible to consider resettlement and rehabilitiation in the South, international NGO representatives will maintain that there is no indigenous expertise in handling such situations. Some use may be made of the experience of Sudanese humanitarian Christian and Moslem organizations, and of other local agencies which have been working among displaced groups and in the war zone. International NGOs may choose to absorb them as 'local staff' or 'implementing partners'. But it will be clear from whom policy is dictated. It is probable that no serious attempt will be made to establish Sudanese institutions, and government ministries will have only nominal control over funds. The achievements of 1972–5 will be ignored.

DOUGLAS H. JOHNSON
Increasing the Trauma of Return

An Assessment of the UN's Emergency Response
to the Evacuation of the Sudanese Refugee Camps
in Ethiopia, 1991

This paper is based on my experiences working as a consultant for the World Food Programme (WFP) in Operation Lifeline Sudan, Southern Sector, at various times in 1990-91, and particularly during the emergency operation at Nasir following the return of the Sudanese refugees from Ethiopia in June 1991. There I was in charge of the WFP field operation and was involved in monitoring and reporting from June to August. What follows is inevitably a worm's eye view. I cannot comment authoritatively on the major relief decisions taken during that emergency: who made them, when, and why. I can describe the consequences of some of those decisions, and by asking questions about the international response to the plight of the Sudanese returnees, I hope that we can ultimately arrive at answers that will explain the UN's specific failure to implement effectively a programme of emergency aid and assisted resettlement.[1]

Itang Refugee Camp in the Southern Sudanese Relief Strategy

The civil war in the Sudan has been marked by the absence of relief to the rural areas of the Southern Sudan affected by the war. International politics were the main obstacle to such relief. In 1983–7 the United States supplied the government of Sudan with considerable amounts of military equipment, and the State Department, the National Security Council in the White House, and various US development and relief bodies spoke with different voices concerning relief issues in the Sudan. While the USAID office in Khartoum was extremely critical of the government of Sudan's handling of relief, by 1987 the National Security Council in Washington was willing to accept Khartoum's assertion that only 3 per cent of the population of the Southern Sudan lay outside government control. NGOs already operating inside the Sudan were reluctant to jeopardize their existing projects by becoming involved in relief operations outside government areas. Though the international community had evidence of massive internal displacement by 1986, no concerted relief activity was begun inside the rural Southern Sudan until late 1988 and early 1989, with the UN Operation Lifeline Sudan (OLS) and the International Committee of the Red Cross (ICRC) programmes.[2]

The Sudan People's Liberation Movement/Sudan People's Liberation Army

---

[1] Citations which follow are from widely circulated reports and memos, or from open meetings.
[2] The Norwegian People's Aid (NPA) provided food to displaced people at Narus, on the Sudan–Kenyan border, from 1986–8, but this aid was restricted to that camp.

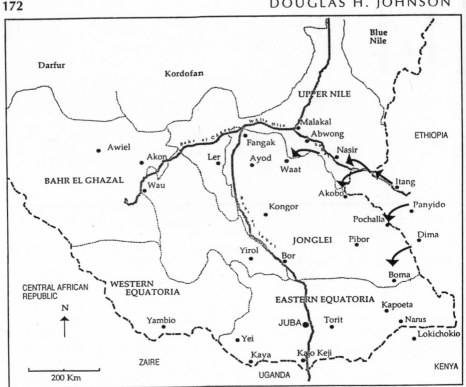

Map 14.1 *Southern Sudan: Influx of Sudanese returnees from camps in Ethiopia, May/June 1991. (UNICEF/OLS)*

(SPLM/SPLA) thus had few options available for securing relief for the civilian population. International relief was available, however, to refugees, and with Ethiopia offering a safe haven the refugee camp at Itang, supplied by UNHCR and other agencies, became the main channel of relief to the Southern Sudanese civilians, and to certain adjacent parts of the Southern Sudan. The Ethiopian government ensured that the SPLM/SPLA was able to run the Itang camp (and later other camps) without much oversight from the UNHCR. The SPLM camp administrators thus enjoyed far more autonomy and far less international scrutiny or accountability than the SPLM's Sudan Relief and Rehabilitation Association (SRRA) later did under OLS. There were some disadvantages to this. Health and sanitation facilities were not always up to standard, and early in 1990 there was a serious outbreak of cholera and other diseases in Itang. The Ethiopian government also discouraged the establishment of 'self-help' schemes, so that refugees were prevented from growing most of their own food.

Numbers of refugees were not carefully monitored, because of double registration and the failure to deduct figures of returnees. But surrounding Itang were settlements of persons (mainly Nuer with their cattle) who, though displaced by the war, were not officially registered as refugees. Thus, even though some food supplies were diverted to the SPLA (which had nearby bases), there was a large number of civilians who benefited from the presence of Itang without being registered as refugees.

Itang camp became a centre for commercial activity. During the dry season the people of the Sobat and Pibor rivers came to Itang with their cattle and canoes, sold their cattle for Ethiopian currency, bought food in large quantities (larger than could be carried overland), and brought it back by canoe to their homes in the Sudan. Small markets grew up inside the Sudan, especially at Jokau and Nasir, where goods from Ethiopia and Itang were sold for Ethiopian and Sudanese currency. Relief supplies from Itang were dispersed over a wide geographical area through kinship networks which straddled the international border. Many Nuer living inside the Sudan, some as far as a week's walk from Itang, regularly received relief items from the camp which they were unable to get through the OLS network. By the dry season of 1991 refugees originally from the border area began planning for an eventual return to the Sudan by sending part of their maize ration (locally grown maize from Nekemte rather than hybrids) to members of their families living along the Pibor and upper Sobat. This successful crop (though planted in limited amounts) helped to alleviate food shortages for some returnees when they evacuated Itang in May 1991, before they were really ready to leave.[3]

Operation Lifeline Sudan and Displaced Persons

By contrast, between April 1989 and May 1991, OLS was unable to provide significant quantities of relief of any sort, either through UN agencies or allied NGOs, to the areas along the Ethiopian border or most inland districts. Because there were no agreements for official cross-border operations, and the Sudanese government refused to sanction barge or overland relief convoys during the appropriate seasons, insufficient quantities of food, seeds and tools were delivered to the Sobat, Nasir, Waat and Pibor districts, all of which had suffered from failed harvests in 1988–90. Late in 1990 there was an additional burden of new refugees fleeing government militia activity in Bahr al-Ghazal, southern Kordofan and parts of Upper Nile. People entering the Sobat on their way to Ethiopia late in the rainy season were forced by local flooding to settle in and around villages near Nasir. Even though local people had been unable to accumulate a sufficient reserve for their own needs through cultivation, they shared what they had with the displaced persons; thus local stocks of food were degraded by the flight of refugees, even before the much greater strain of the influx of returnees.

Very little food could be got to Nasir by UN Twin-Otter relief flights. OLS was aware, however, that the passage of the refugees would have its effect on the local community in the dry season of 1990–91. A proposal was therefore made at the OLS Project Meeting in Kenya in October 1990 to supply Waat district and the Sobat valley by overland convoys in 1991. This proposal was accepted by all present, including UN representatives from Khartoum. A similar recommendation was made in principle by the Multi-Donor Technical Mission (MDTM) on Refugees and Returnees in Ethiopia only a few months later. Noting that many persons still continued to come to Ethiopia because of the insufficient supply of food and the inadequate services inside the southern Sudan, the MDTM suggested that relief programmes inside Sudan be increased.[4]

There was thus a general agreement among donors, NGOs and UN agencies working in both the Sudan and Ethiopia that an essential strategy in coping with the refugee problem inside Ethiopia was to concentrate more on programmes to alleviate distress inside the Southern Sudan. There was also a clear awareness among those working inside the Sudan that the time to begin was the dry season of 1991.

There were three essential elements to the proposed OLS strategy for the 1991 dry

---

[3] For an account of the economic importance of Itang to people living inside the Sudan, see UNICEF Operation Lifeline Sudan, *The return to Southern Sudan of the Sudanese refugees from Itang camp, Gambela, Ethiopia. A report on their current situation, numbers, areas of origin and present location along the Baro, Pibor and Sobat rivers of Southern Sudan*, UN, Nasir, Southern Sudan, 31 August 1991, 5–7.

[4] Multi-donor Technical Mission on Refugees and Returnees, *Report on mission to western region Sudanese refugee camps*, February 1991.

season: the improvement of flood control along the 60+ km Jalle to Kongor road, the stockpiling of food at chosen locations from Bor to Waat, and the distribution of seeds, tools, and fishing equipment to increase food production. The first part meant that the flood-protection embankment which ran parallel to the Jalle-Kongor road had to be repaired and strengthened, either through the use of earth-moving machinery, or through food-for-work labour programmes. This would not only have ensured that the main north–south supply route to the interior was kept open longer in the year, it would also have helped local people reclaim their fields and villages from the river flooding which had caused continuous dislocation since 1988. Reclaiming the land was a necessary part of the stabilization of the local population and the revival of agriculture. The second part involved the pre-positioning of food at strategic points so that food for-work projects could be supplied and other food stocks conserved during the dry season. The third part was aimed at reversing the recent contraction of agricultural activity due to loss of tools and seed stocks during the war. If all three parts of this proposal had been implemented the area available for resettlement and cultivation would have been increased, and food production would have expanded (at least in some places).

WFP was the largest transporter of food in this area and had brought convoys from Kampala to Bor and Kongor late in 1990. The WFP office in Khartoum, however, refused permission for the movement of convoys into the Southern Sudan in the dry season of 1991, and also embargoed the distribution of that food which was already stored in the area. Thus the flood-embankment improvement scheme, which was essential to increasing food security, was never implemented. UNICEF did deliver seeds, tools, and fishing equipment, but as this was not coupled with the distribution of food during 'the hungry period' early in the cultivating season, it had a far more limited effect than intended.

The WFP office in Khartoum offered no justification for its effective suspension of relief activity in the southern sector of OLS, other than the disapproval of the government of Sudan. WFP projects in government-held areas were not affected.

The general weakness of OLS was described in a USAID assessment report in 1991. Contrasting the SPLM's blanket approval for truck, air and barge movements of relief supplies with the government of Sudan's selective and limited approval (which never sanctioned barge movements and disallowed truck convoys for almost the entire 1990–91 dry season), the report concluded:

> The GOS policy in respect to OLS operations in southern Sudan has been clearly capricious, if not blatantly obstructionist. The net effect of the GOS ban on barge movements and limitations on truck convoys has been to prevent WFP making any food deliveries to the four neediest areas (Ler, Yirol, Waat and Nasir) visited by our team, as well as to other needy areas such as Akobo, Boma, and Pibor.[5]

The report concluded that the OLS umbrella was inadequate to meet 'all critical needs in southern Sudan' and recommended that the US government should be prepared to support other means of supplying relief, even if that meant going outside the authority of OLS.

The International Response to the Evacuation of Itang

OLS was thus unprepared in 1991 to receive any substantial number of returnees, either from Ethiopia or from the Northern Sudan. Not only were there insufficient relief items inside the rural areas, there was almost no operational relief network in those districts from which refugees had left, and to which they would return. In 1989 and 1990 small

---

[5] USAID, 'Southern Sudan assessment final report, April 21, 1991–May 31, 1991' (Contract No. FDA-1006-0-00-0017-00): 1–2.

groups of refugees did leave Ethiopia and return to their home areas to monitor the progress of relief activities there. Relief workers on the ground were aware that any substantial improvement in local conditions could attract returnees from both Ethiopia and the Northern Sudan and felt that this should be taken into account in planning.

The need for such forward planning was clear in early 1991 as the disintegration of the Mengistu government accelerated. The SPLA certainly recognized some need to plan for a return to the Sudan, and discussions concerning the return of at least some refugees were held in Itang (and perhaps the other camps) as early as January 1991. The speed of the collapse of the Mengistu government took more than just the SPLA by surprise, and the evacuation of the camps had to take place earlier and more quickly than anticipated, but it is significant that even though the SPLA had some contingency plans, neither the UN and other agencies nor the major donors had made similar plans.

Itang came under stress some months before the evacuation, when its supply routes were cut and no further food was coming in. The Ethiopian People's Revolutionary Democratic Front (EPRDF) agreed in principle to allow relief supplies to continue to the camps, but as this depended on the repair of strategic bridges, this pledge could be redeemed only some months later. All personnel of international agencies in Itang were withdrawn in March and April. After the fall of Gambela and the general disintegration of security throughout Gambela district, the vast majority of the Itang refugees evacuated the camp and began their trek along the Baro back to the Sudan on 26 May 1991. The fact of the evacuation was reported to Nairobi on the OLS radio network soon after it began, and before the returnees arrived in the Sudan. Evidence of harassment of the returnees was clear for several weeks. Not only was testimony forthcoming from the returnees themselves, but a UN team on the Baro witnessed the Sudanese air force bombing Jokau (where the first group of returnees were assembled), and bodies of returnees shot by bandits along the Baro (and even the Sobat) were seen floating in the river past Nasir throughout early June. But even this evidence was later disputed.

Given the controversy that later developed over the returnee centres in the Sudan, it is important to recall just what the SRRA asked for at the beginning of the emergency. At a public meeting with UN, NGO, donor and press representatives in the SRRA office in Nairobi on 29 May, the newly appointed Executive Secretary for Relief specifically asked for immediate, *short-term* relief for up to 300,000 returnees, saying that it was *not* the SRRA's intention to establish refugee camps in eastern Upper Nile. Rather, they hoped that those returnees originally from eastern Upper Nile would be rapidly re-absorbed into their home communities, and that the rest would be provided with food to see them through their journey to their more distant homes. There was a need for the international community to persuade the new government in Ethiopia to allow relief to be brought to the refugees, and also a need for a short-term air drop. After this there would be a need for development in the returnees' home districts. The regional Food For Peace (FFP) officer (representing USAID) commented that, *even if people had left Ethiopia*, USAID was using its contacts to settle the situation in Ethiopia itself. When he then suggested that the supply route along the river via Itang was probably the best way to move large quantities of food to the Sudan, the Executive Secretary agreed that it was necessary to bring pressure to bear on the new authorities in Ethiopia to respect the rights of refugees, and he repeated that an air drop was only a temporary solution.

Thus, from the start both the SRRA and the UN agencies involved approached the problem of the Sudanese returnees in two stages: 1) immediate, temporary assistance (primarily in food) to see the returnees through the initial period of their arrival, and 2) the dispersal of returnees to their home areas as soon as possible, where their needs would be incorporated into the main activities of OLS.

The immediate task was to find out how many persons would need temporary

14.1 *The UN Operation Lifeline Sudan was unprepared in 1991 to receive any substantial number of returnees: new arrivals, near Nasir, May 1991. (UNHCR/21051/B. Press)*

assistance, and for how long. A UNICEF/ WFP presence was established in Nasir by 2 June 1991 and sent daily radio messages back to Nairobi monitoring the arrival of returnees and their food and health needs. It was on the basis of these reports that immediate planning was to be made. In the end some 132,000 persons were recorded as moving up to or through Nasir. This was not the total number of returnees, because some did not stop to be recorded but went directly on to settle along the Sobat, or directly to Waat, Ayod and Kongor districts. There were other groups who went directly to the Pibor river and settled near Akobo (perhaps as many as 20,000). There were also the needs of local people to be considered; having low reserves of their own, they were now expected to share what they had with people with no other resources, for an undetermined period.

By 11 June it was reported that nearly 100,000 returnees had been registered in and around Nasir, of which about 40 per cent were children, 40 per cent women, and 20 per cent men.[6] These figures were available to the senior WFP team who negotiated a schedule of relief with Khartoum.

The agreement which was announced on 16 June allowed for only 1,000 MT of grain (no other foods and no non-food items such as shelter material or blankets), to be divided equally by barge and airdrop. Any further deliveries would have to be re-negotiated. Both the amounts and types of food allowed were inadequate to known needs; pulses, salt and oil which were needed to provide a balanced diet were excluded from the food basket. There were limitations imposed on the number of days an airdrop could fly, so there were long gaps built into the agreement between the termination of the airdrop and the arrival of the barge from Kosti. Later in the year supplementary airdrops were negotiated, but never enough to meet existing needs, and at no time was an unbroken delivery of supplies by either airdrop or barge agreed or guaranteed. There were numerous interruptions to deliveries when food stocks ran low and rations had to be cut. This had an adverse effect on the health of the returnees.

Khartoum did not allow food to be delivered to other places, such as Akobo, Waat or Ayod, where the returnees were headed. Nor did it agree to the spacing of barge deliveries along the Sobat. The concentration of the relief effort at Nasir meant that the dispersal of returnees to other areas was inevitably delayed.

In addition to this, the provision of seeds and tools was also inadequate, largely because of the restrictions placed on the mode of delivery. It was clear by mid-July that the majority of returnees (some 90,000) would have to stay in the Nasir and Sobat area

---

[6] The proportions altered somewhat by the time all registers had been analysed. Of 132,000 returnees recorded, about 17 per cent were adult males, 22 per cent adult females, and 61 per cent children under 14 (most of whom were living in family groups).

during the remainder of the rains before they could hope to move to other settlement areas. In order to improve their own food security, and thus reduce their dependency on relief food, it was necessary to provide them with seeds and tools in time for the second planting in late August. This deadline was not met. This had a particularly adverse effect on some 20,000–30,000 ex-Assosa refugees from the Blue Nile, who were not native to the Southern Sudan, could not go back to their old homes due to insecurity, and had no local kinship networks on which to draw for support.

The situation was far worse for between 10,000 and 20,000 ex-Dimma refugees who went to Pakok, near Boma and came under UN care. There, despite the presence of a landing-strip which could receive a C-130 transport plane, relief food was sent in insufficient quantities.

The government of Sudan's objection to a comprehensive emergency relief programme and schedule was at least consistent with its attitude towards relief in the SPLA-held areas since late 1989. The UN's unwillingness to push the issue was also consistent with its proven reluctance to take a stand with Khartoum on relief issues in the Southern Sudan. In addition to this, the hesitations of one major donor government appeared to hinder both the planning and implementation of a comprehensive relief and resettlement programme.

There was a marked ambivalence towards the returnees on the part of the US from the start. A USAID representative expressed scepticism about the news of the evacuation of Itang as early as the 29 May Nairobi meeting. Ultimately US officials based in Nairobi were willing to help once the scale of the problem became clear, but original offers of aid were soon cut back, particularly in the provision of boat transport which could have expanded the radius of food deliveries from Nasir; thus dispersing to some degree the returnee settlement over a wider area. There were a number of other voices offering conflicting opinions.

For some weeks after the evacuation of Itang US government sources claimed that the refugees were still in Itang: the WFP office in Khartoum was told this (and therefore was initially unwilling to credit UN reports from the field), and several agencies preparing to go to Nasir were also told that no refugees had left Itang. This caused some delay in persuading donors of the urgent need for relief; it also helped Khartoum to justify its resistance to relief proposals. When it was no longer credible to dispute the fact of the evacuation, US sources then claimed that there had been no need for it. Certainly the behaviour of some units of the SPLA in their hasty retreat from Ethiopia (such as the looting and destruction of the GTZ logistics base at Mizan Teferi) raised doubts about SPLA motivation for the evacuation of all three refugee camps. The most frequently voiced criticism of the SPLA was that they had moved all refugees out of Ethiopia to preserve their 'meal ticket'. There was concern among all agencies early in the emergency that this may have been the case, and the forced diversion of the ex-Assosa refugees from Maiwut to Nasir by the Nasir command of the SPLA was certainly one clear attempt to manipulate the distribution of returnees, and therefore influence the response of the relief community.[7] This example aside, however, there was little in subsequent SPLA and SRRA behaviour during the emergency to justify the accusation. There may, in fact, have been conflicting opinions within the SPLM/SPLA about what to do with the returnees, which was reflected in the contradictory statements made about just what happened at Itang. Even though Itang camp itself was not directly attacked by the advancing forces of the anti-Mengistu coalition, the SPLA and the refugees themselves had the destruction of Tsore camp in Assosa in 1990 as an example of what to expect. Given the subsequent behaviour of the Anuak in southwestern

---

[7] Alastair and Patta Scott-Villiers, and Cole Dodge, 'Repatriation of 150,000 refugees from Ethiopia. A case study in manipulation of civilians in a situation of civil conflict', unpublished mimeographed paper, October 1992.

Ethiopia, and the very late establishment of EPRDF authority in Gambela, the SPLA seems now to have been justified in their fears for the safety of the Sudanese refugees. The same voices critical of the SPLA for 'cynically' using the refugees as a 'meal ticket' would have been equally critical if the SPLA had 'cynically' abandoned them to the sort of harassment which did take place when groups of Sudanese passed through Anuak country in 1991 and re-entered Ethiopia in 1992.

The prevailing insecurity in Gambela and other parts of the southwest in mid-1991 was soon beyond dispute, yet no direct dialogue was established between US agencies in Ethiopia and the relief personnel in the field in the Sudan to examine outstanding questions. The continuation of surreptitious denials (whose ultimate source remained difficult to trace) only added to the uncertainty surrounding the emergency and whether, or how, the US was going to support the UN in responding to it. Throughout the summer US sources continued to dispute the UN figures of returnees, without giving evidence for revising downward these estimates. This had the effect of supporting Khartoum's objections to the relief effort by suggesting that the scale of relief requested by the UN was exaggerated. This seems to have been a further factor in the unnecessary delay in the WFP airdrop.

The denial that the Sudanese refugees had been in any personal danger in Ethiopia was linked to another proposal which was made early in the emergency, and which was related to the US's relief and development programme for Ethiopia, rather than the Sudan. The same USAID report which had been critical of OLS had this to say about the Sudanese returnees in early June:

> Neither Nasir, Akobo, nor Pibor are currently accessible by road, and none has an airfield capable of accommodating more than a Twin Otter aircraft. The only conceivable way large quantities of food could be delivered to those areas, therefore, is by an expensive and cumbersome air-drop procedure. The assessment team believes that a more workable solution would be to effect immediate resumption of food deliveries to refugee camps in Ethiopia in order to signal continued international involvement in the camps and, hopefully, to entice those who have abandoned the camps to return to them. While pursuing a policy of rationalization of food deliveries to the camps based on actual populations, it may also be worthwhile to undertake a regulated, and necessarily limited, cross-border feeding operation from Gambella [sic] to Nasir, Akobo, and Pibor using the SPLA barge. Such a program could assist the present populations in those areas, provide 'bridging' assistance to allow fleeing refugee populations to return to their Ethiopian camps, and demonstrate that international assistance can reach needy persons in Sudan even in the absence of inflated population figures in refugee camps.[8]

The same author later elaborated on this proposal in a widely circulated memo:

> ... although we recognize the right of returnees to settle where they please within the Sudan, we would recommend against providing international support for any local settlement project which may (and probably will) be proposed by the SRRA. Within the context of present-day southern Sudan, a local settlement scheme would undoubtedly be fraught with administrative and security problems, and would likely entail expenditures on infrastructure and agriculture that would at least have the appearance of involving the USG [US Government] in a development program.
> ... security in Ethiopia is likely to improve during the next several months while security in southern Sudan may well deteriorate, particularly in Nasir. When faced with worsening security and a cessation of food assistance where they are, a lack of improvement in the security situation in their home areas, and both improved security and food availability in Ethiopia, returnees who have nowhere else to go may well decide to take refuge once again in Dimma, Fugnido [sic] and Itang. To the extent the international community can encourage this movement to take place in an orderly and regulated manner, refugee hardship can be minimized, refugee numbers can be verified, and more effective camp administration can be imposed. REDSO/ESA/FFP recommends that this course be followed both to preserve lives and conserve scarce resources.[9]

---

[8] USAID, 'Southern Sudan assessment': 5.
[9] Thomas O. Brennan, 'Southern Sudan emergency field visit of July 12–20, 1991: update and recommendations on returnees from Ethiopia', paras 36 and 37.

This was accompanied by a timetable for the cessation of the distribution of relief items in the returnee centres, so as to require the return of remaining displaced persons to Ethiopia. This proposal was repeated in August.[10] Neither the UN nor the ICRC endorsed the plan, and in fact it was not even supported by the US embassy in Addis Ababa. Despite this, the idea was kept alive until it was clear that the Provisional Government of Ethiopia also would not support it.

Two comments are necessary: 1) This proposal failed to address the *immediate* problem, as any supply through Gambela and Itang would have to await the re-opening of the road (which was at best some months distant). 2) There never had been any real question of resettlement *schemes* (along the Ethiopian model), or even long-term returnee/refugee *camps* requiring sustained administration and infrastructure.[11] The question was how to reintegrate returnees into secure rural districts. This had been the original SRRA proposal, and it was the goal that OLS was trying to achieve. The US proposal deflected the relief discussion from the main issues at hand. It also appeared to rescind the earlier recommendation that the US should be prepared to support a number of different ways of meeting 'all the critical needs in southern Sudan'.

The ICRC Operation at Pochalla: A Comparison

The ICRC concentrated its attention on returnees from Itang and Funyido who showed up at Pochalla, directly on the Sudan–Ethiopian border. Though beginning their operation later than the UN, and having fewer people to look after (variously estimated, at different times, at between 75,000 and 90,000), they obtained a far more comprehensive agreement from Khartoum than did the UN. The number of relief flights was not restricted (as the number of days for the WFP airdrop was), and the ICRC used three planes in a daily combination of airdrops and airlifts, bringing in a full food basket of grain, pulses, oil and salt (and even sugar and tea), supplementary feeding, shelter material, medicines, blankets, cooking utensils, and eventually seeds and tools. The ICRC took the attitude that it should bring in as much as it could while it could, knowing that permission could be rescinded at any time. When, by the end of the year, it became clear that most returnees could not go home, the ICRC even entered into negotiations with the local Anuak on setting aside unused land where returnees could self-settle, outside of any 'camp' structure.

The scale of the ICRC operation highlights the inadequacies of the UN's overall performance, and raises the question of why the UN, too, did not obtain a more satisfactory blanket agreement for the returnees under its care.

Strategies of the Returnees

The Sudanese returnees found that they were required to remain mobile inside the Sudan during the height of what turned out to be a very heavy rainy season. Many of the first arrivals who originally came from homes along the Sobat, the Pibor, and Waat went directly home. Others from more distant districts travelled as far as they could, and spent the remainder of the rainy season in places like Waat, Ayod, and the lower Sobat. Many others followed reports of incoming relief and travelled between the main centres: some from Pochalla left before the ICRC airlift began and went to Akobo (where a small-scale

---

[10] 'Southern Sudan emergency – refugees returning from Ethiopia: the view from both sides now', 8 December 1991, unclassified, Nairobi 021090.

[11] The SPLA authorities at Nasir (who later split off from the mainstream SPLA) did float the idea of a reconstituted Itang at Nasir, but this was firmly resisted by the UN and appears not to have been supported by the SRRA. See Scott-Villiers and Dodge, 'Repatriation of 150,000 Refugees from Ethiopia'.

14.2 *Why did those senior UN officials responsible for making the final decision in UN/OLS not act on field reports concerning the importance of pre-positioning food during the dry season of 1991? Cooking wild grasses, Pochalla, Sudan, May 1991. (UNHCR/21050/B. Press)*

operation was supervised by Medair); people along the Pibor travelled between Akobo and Nasir. But a large number were unable to move far beyond the distribution centres circling Nasir because of the prevailing insecurity in their homes, or uncertainty along the way. Thus, many persons from the White Nile and southern Blue Nile had no choice but to stay in the Nasir area during the rains. Those from Bahr al-Ghazal also could not easily leave Pochalla.

Even some Nuer and Dinka who attempted to return to their old homes along the Sobat found that they had been displaced. The internal war in the Sudan up to 1988 meant that new groups moved into areas vacated by the refugees. Thus, the Nuer who returned to Jikmir found their old villages occupied by families of the formerly pro-government militia who had previously chased them into Ethiopia. The Dinka of Baliet found a number of Lou Nuer from Waat in their area. Given the low level of food stocks along the Sobat, and the fact that there was no direct provision for local food needs throughout the emergency, there was frequently tension between locals and returnees. Many of the returnees thus constructed small communities of ex-refugees along the middle and lower Sobat, drawing on friendships and links forged in Itang, rather than on the links which existed before the war.

Returnees who could not rely on language affinity or kinship networks in their host areas still had to find some way to draw on local resources. Having no other entitlements, they used many non-food items obtained in exile to barter for food. Thus returnees progressively had to shed their clothes, blankets, mosquito nets, cooking pots, and other similarly scarce items in order to obtain food when relief supplies were cut back or were not forthcoming. This further impoverishment of returnees was of great concern to relief workers in the UN-supervised operation as they were unable to provide similar useful and necessary items on the same scale as the ICRC.

Seeds and tools, along with some additional food, were distributed to returnees around Nasir late in the dry season of 1992, enabling most of them to disperse to other areas where they could try to self-settle and cultivate. Delays in this dispersal and the general lateness of the rains meant that many of these cultivations were not successful. Sources of wild food to the east of Nasir were rapidly depleted, and there were numerous confrontations, over fishing and collecting rights, between returnee communities and local Nuer – who were also adversely affected by the lateness of the rains and were congregating around the river banks as a result. Soldiers of the Nasir faction of the SPLA sided with the local Nuer in their harassment of the remaining returnees. Some 13,000 people from southern Blue Nile subsequently left the Sudan for Ethiopia, soon to be followed by another few thousand Nuer, Dinka and Shilluk refugees. The failure of the international relief effort in the Sobat thus contributed directly to the re-introduction of Sudanese refugees to Ethiopia in 1992.[12]

Unanswered Questions

The lack of a well co-ordinated, comprehensive and sustained relief effort in the areas of UN responsibility had the cumulative effect of increasing the trauma of return for the Sudanese coming out of Ethiopia who, though they had begun planning their own return, were forced by the political situation to move before they were ready. The time of year in which the evacuation was made and the remoteness of the regions to which the returnees went would have made any relief programme difficult to implement. Yet the ICRC were faced with many of the same problems as the UN and appear to have handled them better. The two main factors contributing to the overall failure of the UN effort were the lack of UN preparedness, despite two years of OLS, and the apparent unwillingness of a major donor to support systematic reintegration of returnees inside the Southern Sudan. In outlining the reasons for this failure, I feel I must end by posing some questions, for which I still have no satisfactory answers:

1 Why did those senior UN officials responsible for making the final decisions in UN/OLS not act on field reports concerning the importance of pre-positioning food during the dry season of 1991?
2 To what extent can 'development' be divorced from 'relief' in any resettlement programme, voluntary or otherwise; and are donors justified in insisting on such a divorce?
3 Is it ever justified to focus on the needs of returnees to the exclusion of the needs of their host communities, who often bear the brunt of the burden of assisting returnees prior to (and sometimes even during) a major relief operation?
4 To what extent were the humanitarian needs of the Sudanese returnees in the Sudan ultimately subordinated to political considerations of US policy in Ethiopia?

Postscript

Since this paper was written (1992) evidence has come to light following the disintegration of the SPLA-Nasir faction (aka SPLA-United, aka SSIM/A), indicating that the relief restrictions imposed by Khartoum and advocated by at least some US personnel were employed by the former to encourage a split within the SPLA, and by the latter to bring about a change in SPLA leadership.

[12] See Wendy James, this volume, and 'Uduk asylum seekers in Gambela, 1992. Community report and options for resettlement', report for UNHCR, Addis Ababa, 31 October 1992.

15 WENDY JAMES
Uduk Resettlement

Dreams & Realities

The abstract humanitarian motives and neutral professional standards of relief, development, and in particular resettlement operations are increasingly bedevilled by politics. The context is plainly one of competing interests at every level, rather than a benign framework of governmental or international justice and reason holding the arena while good is done for the suffering people by disinterested third parties. Sometimes no particular expertise or vast expenditure is needed to evaluate a community's needs on the ground; common sense and a general knowledge of the region can help one tap into the people's own requirements as they see them and put forward some modest proposals. However, their reception, and ultimate fate, are at the mercy of political and strategic factors at regional, national and international levels. These factors may seem to relief personnel quite beyond their control, and arbitrarily outside their professional concern in formulating and implementing proposals. But it is becoming very clear that agencies, especially those dealing with resettlement, are constrained by and drawn into politics. This is partly because resettlement, the making of a new home, whether on one side or another of a civil war front line, or in a neighbouring country, entails very political questions of new patterns of access to land and other regional goods. It also entails new lines for the seeking and redistribution of resources from outside, and the construction of new local links of indebtedness, dependency, and their converse, patronage, out of which local power may be built.

At different times and places, I have had the opportunity to visit a substantial displaced population, mainly Uduk speakers from the Blue Nile Province of the Sudan, and to help formulate proposals for relief and resettlement under very different conditions. Since 1987 they have been on the road, trekking from one place to another and sometimes back again as the tides of war have come and gone in the Sudan and in Ethiopia, and as relief and aid projects have waxed and waned. More or less as a cohesive group, the survivors have now travelled over 1,000 km and crossed the international border five times (see map).

Originally displaced from the northern Sudan, well over 20,000 Uduk have been temporary beneficiaries in a succession of relief schemes: a UNHCR camp near Assosa during the Mengistu period in Ethiopia; a further UNHCR camp at Itang near Gambela, after a period back in the Sudan without any relief; a UN Operation Lifeline Sudan distribution centre for returnees at Nasir, and a succession of failed resettlements there; a temporary UNHCR camp for asylum seekers at Karmi back in Ethiopia, and thence finally a semi-permanent resettlement scheme at Khor Bonga, further upstream on the Baro River. Neither the UNHCR nor the Ethiopian authorities wish to re-establish the old-style refugee camps which existed up to 1991 in the Gambela region. The UNHCR in Addis Ababa is approaching the renewed influx of Sudanese asylum

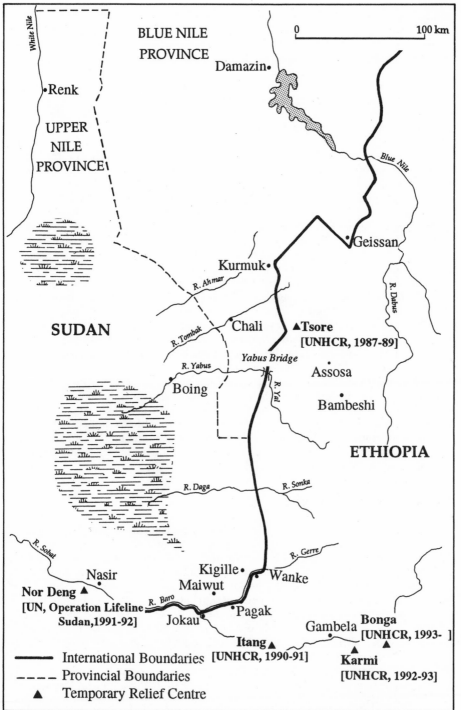

Map 15.1 *The central Sudan–Ethiopian borderlands, showing where international relief assistance received by the Uduk, with approximate dates.*

seekers from mid-1992 rather through a series of smaller settlement schemes and the encouragement of partial self-sufficiency from the start, in the context of the proposed 'cross-mandate' approach to the meeting of regional relief/development requirements of all needy groups in border areas. As an element in this overall strategy, after an agreement in late 1992 between the UNHCR and the Ethiopian government, 13,000–14,000 Uduk (with a few others from the Blue Nile region) are being resettled on a semi-permanent basis at Khor Bonga in the Gambela region.

The resettlement needs of this community, as they see them, have always been relatively modest. Nevertheless, because of the security situation and political struggles at local and international level, until late 1992 it proved extremely difficult for aid agencies and relevant political authorities on either side of the border to reach an agreement on and to implement any effective or lasting relief schemes. Many interests and organiza-tions were delaying and obstructing what could have been done for this and other small displaced groups on the basis of both humanitarian obligation and modest local develop-ment advantage, because they were caught up in overt politics in one way or another and angling for bigger fish and greater influence. From the time the Uduk found them-selves on the front line of the Sudan civil war, various powerful interests have sought to use them to advantage; I have heard them described as pawns or bait in the aid game, even as being 'farmed' by the Sudan People's Liberation Army (SPLA). The story of the Uduk, from 'below', surely illuminates the way in which relief and development aid to civilians has been caught up in higher policy-making and strategic considerations throughout northeast Africa.

This chapter examines specifically some contrasts between the way in which very similar, common-sense resettlement proposals which I helped formulate for the Uduk were received by agencies and political authorities in two different places/times: first in Nasir in 1991–2, and then in the Gambela region of Ethiopia, 1992–3. The major irony is that survival for this community has turned out to be more problematic in their own country, whether north or south, than it has been in Ethiopia. Though Sudanese, on three separate occasions they have found it impossible to live in the Sudan and left it more or less voluntarily for Ethiopia; a country which, for different political and strategic reasons at different times, has held out the possibility of a little protection, a little food, and maybe – though this is still something of a dream – a new 'home', where people can once again grow food for their own children.

Background story of displacement

Most of the Blue Nile refugees now displaced to the Gambela region, though not all, speak the Uduk language as their mother tongue. They used to live in small villages, cultivating and even selling sorghum, maize and sesame, raising a few animals, hunting and collecting wild foods. Their hilly and wooded region just south of Kurmuk was similar to that of the Nuba peoples in the southern part of Kordofan Province. They shared a way of life with a whole series of agricultural minority communities in the foothills and valleys of western Ethiopia and the fringes of the Sudanese plains, speaking languages such as Kunama, Berta, Meban, Hill Burun, Gumuz, Komo, Kwama, Shyita, and Mao.[1] Many of these communities have become relatively invisible as distinct ethnic groups in the course of current disturbances. The majority of their individuals, with little education and depending on a traditional subsistence economy, have melted into the general population of the rural areas, often adapting to locally dominant languages and cultural practices.

1 General ethnography and history of the Uduk, these related groups and the border region may be found in James (1979, 1988a) and Donham and James (1986).

In spite of the massive displacements which must have taken place, these people have, we must hope, survived as well as they can in the less accessible foothills, valleys and plains (only a future historian will be able to say whether being unknown to the international and national NGOs and the media will be to their disadvantage in the long run). The Uduk belong historically to this border zone of linguistically varied, but culturally related and intermarrying peoples which straddles the frontier from the Blue Nile to the Baro-Sobat valleys. On the Ethiopian side it is now constituted as the Ethiopian administrative region of Bela Shangul.

It is because, in a sense, of a series of historical accidents that the core of the Uduk-speaking people have become unusually 'visible' as a distinct ethnic group in tbe course of recent generations. This is partly because their home area was transferred and retransferred several times between the northern and southern Sudan for reasons of administrative convenience; and partly because their home area was made the focus of evangelical Christian mission activity at a relatively recent date. The Sudan Interior Mission (SIM, now Society of International Missionaries) began work at Chali, the central market village of their country, in 1938. At this time, the area was administered as part of the (southern) Upper Nile Province; but in 1953, just before independence, when the Christian mission work was going well, the area was transferred to the (northern) Blue Nile Province. At the time of independence, in 1956, when the first Sudanese civil war had already begun, the Uduk thus found themselves already on a conceptual front line. They were now a community administered as part of the northern Sudan, but associated by religion and geography with the South and seen by increasing numbers of northerners as potential sympathizers with the Southern disaffection. This no doubt encouraged many of them to convert to Christianity from the mid-sixties onwards as the war worsened – this was after the missionaries had to leave, and the leadership of the church network was left in the hands of the local people.[2]

The circumstance of being located in the 'fault line' between North and South has since left peoples like the Uduk exposed on the civil war front. The SPLA surged northwards in the mid-1980s to overwhelm first the northern Upper Nile and then the Kurmuk district of the Blue Nile. Their first flight in 1987 followed widespread reprisals against local civilian populations by Sudanese forces. The southern Blue Nile people, perceived as dark-coloured, African-language-speaking and partially Christian, were assumed *en masse* sympathetic to the SPLA by the Sudanese government as well as by some of the liberation movements then active in Ethiopia. Their strengthening leadership and growing commitment to open Christian activity made them better known, as a group, than they had ever been before; and there was indeed a good deal of support among them for the Southern cause in general. They became conspicuous in a new way in Nasir in 1991–2, as a large non-Nilotic community under the SPLA umbrella, far from home, in poor condition and without local kin networks to draw on for help. There was much discussion over targeting relief aid to them at that time, the international agencies recognizing their particular distress but the Sudan Relief and Rehabilitation Association (SRRA, relief wing of the SPLA) reluctant to allow any special treatment which might arouse the jealousy of other returnees and locals in the Nasir region. The Blue Nile community there in fact included several ethnic and language groups among its total population, which was on best judgement well over 20,000 and possibly as many as 24,000. But they were increasingly spoken of simply as 'the Uduk' as they became something of a pawn in the arguments over food aid. They tended to be taken for a more uniform, distinctive and bounded ethnic group than was the case, and increasingly as 'a people with a problem'. But it must be remembered that

---

[2] Detailed information on the impact of tbe mission may be be found in James (1988a, Chapter 4; and 1988b).

it has been the events themselves of the civil war in the Sudan and contemporary struggles in Ethiopia, as well as the intermittent and uneven effects of relief policies from one side or the other, which have first thrown together and then dispersed the people of this refugee community – several times. The ethnic community identifiable today as being in particular distress has been shaped by the very specific difficulties of surviving in this doubly marginal zone, where the North/South boundary in the Sudan meets the international frontier with Ethiopia, and where a substantial displaced population has to seek protection and patronage of some kind. Ironically and conversely, in the aid context, needy populations have become in themselves a resource for politicians – whether guerrilla commanders or local and even national organizations and their leaders. Far from being a people with a problem of displacement, the Uduk are in their modern form a people *created by* this problem. In the course of the trek from their homeland the Blue Nile group have naturally done what they could to seek secure patronage and relief, from whatever source; and have been obliged to move so many times not only because of the changing military situation but also because of the competition over scarce relief aid, and the fact that this competition has been drawn into the political struggles of the region as a whole.

The Trek: and the Discontinuities of Relief

The following outline summarizes the story of the repeated displacements of the Uduk since 1987, indicating the main reasons at different times for the suffering and mortality of the people.[3] Although evidence is incomplete, it is beyond doubt that more people have died over this period as a result of malnutrition and illness, than from direct attacks arising from military hostilities. Some of the avoidable deaths have taken place out in the bush far from any relief centre, but a good proportion have occurred in or near one of the centres where relief was supposedly to be provided, in particular Itang and Nasir. At no point in the period from 1987, up to 1993 and the Bonga resettlement scheme, have the people been given permission to cultivate on a scale really sufficient to help them feed themselves, although this is precisely what they have begged to be allowed to do. The difficulty arises of course partly from national and local political argument, especially about rights in land for or on behalf of the displaced, whether in a foreign country or in their own, but a contributing difficulty has also been the sharp line maintained internationally between emergency relief and development aid.

1. Early 1980s in the Kurmuk District
The early 1980s was a period of recurring drought all over northeast Africa and the Kurmuk district was one of those regions in the Sudan where rural people were threatened by destitution. One of the means of survival open to young men without much education was to seek wage labour on new mechanized agricultural schemes to the north, or to join the army, and a number of Uduk did so, though the trend did not last long.

2. 1985–6, the relief effort and the rise of the SPLA
Following the end of the Nimeri regime in 1985, a large international relief effort took place in the Sudan. Some agencies dealing with the Blue Nile Province targeted the particular needs of the southern part of the Kurmuk District, and entrusted the church leadership in Chali with the distribution of aid sent down from Khartoum by trucks.

---

[3] Information was obtained from agencies and from a series of interviews with displaced people from the Blue Nile since 1988; in Khartoum, Nairobi, Nasir and the Gambela area. Further detail for the period up to 1990 can be found in James (1994).

The harvest of 1986 proved a good one, but ironically this led to further suspicion being focused on the Uduk around Chali, because as the most 'visible' of the southern communities of the province, they were thought to be sending supplies on to the SPLA. There had been northward advances by the SPLA from 1984, until by 1986 they were passing through the Kurmuk District. The local civilian population were subject to increased interrogation and harassment by the security forces, and in 1986 many people were arrested and tortured. A number of young men were by this time willing to be recruited into the SPLA; the best judgement is that the numbers involved were comparable to those who had gone into the national army. Again, the flow of recruitment has not been kept up, and there have been deaths in action among those who joined the SPLA, as well as retirements back into civilian life.

3. 1987, the spread of the civil war and displacement to Assosa

In the early months of this year, engagements having taken place locally between the SPLA on the one hand, and government soldiers and the Rufaa Arab militia on the other, the security forces mounted major reprisals against the rural population of the southern Blue Nile (the Uduk having become identified as a particular 'ethnic' target). The villages were systematically burned and the fleeing population shot at. A number of people lost their lives in these actions, and some were later discovered to have died of thirst after fleeing into the bush. In addition a number of Uduk were among labourers killed as SPLA suspects on several cultivation schemes in the north of the region. At the end of March, under SPLA encouragement, the population of the outlying Uduk villages fled *en masse* to Ethiopia, and a new UNHCR camp was established for them and others of the district at Tsore, near Assosa. These were joined in May by the people from the main church village at Chali, but only after they had been under direct military threat from the local Sudanese government garrison. The SPLA took the town of Kurmuk near the end of 1987, held it for a month, and then it was retaken by Sudanese forces. These events caused further refugee influxes to Tsore.

4. 1988 and the success story of Assosa

The refugee relief programme at Tsore operated well. Uduk now remember this time as a relative paradise compared with what happened later. They say that the children thrived; the land was cool and pleasant, and it was on the whole only the old people who became ill and died there. The UNHCR was very pleased with the co-operation of the people in the relief programme; the Uduk in particular acquired the reputation of being 'model refugees', as they had maintained their family groups and their patterns of leadership, had brought tools and equipment with them, and had known how to grow a few vegetables and put the forest and bush to productive use. They joined committee structures and built up their Christian activities (with some modest help also from the SIM). Although there was a wide range of language and ethnic groups represented in Tsore, the Uduk were in the majority (26,000 out of 35,000 by October 1989, according to the UNHCR).

5. 1989, and the rise of civil strife

This year saw heightened tension on both sides of the international border. A refugee camp mainly for Oromo on the Sudan side in the Yabus valley was overrun by the SPLA in the middle of the year. The SPLA advanced and towards the end of the year took Kurmuk for the second time. They also took all the smaller garrisons in the district, including Chali, where a few of the local people, including some Uduk, were still sheltering with the soldiers. But as before, Kurmuk was retaken very quickly by the end of the year, followed by the outlying garrisons. Further waves of new arrivals were reported at Tsore, which now contained a very varied population representing all shades of political sympathy, eventually totalling 42,000 of which it is understood that 28,000 were registered as Uduk.

6. December 1989 – January 1990, the sacking of the Assosa camp

Following the recovery of Kurmuk, military activity gathered pace on both the Sudanese and the Ethiopian sides. As the Sudanese army pursued the SPLA southwards from the Kurmuk area, forces opposed to the then Government of Ethiopia overran Assosa, and in their approach from the northwest destroyed the UNHCR camp at Tsore. The majority of the Uduk fled southeastwards, away from Kurmuk, then back down through the hills and west towards the Yabus Valley. On the way they were ambushed in a ravine by local elements supporting the Oromo Liberation Front (OLF), and numbers were shot or fell to their deaths, including women and children. The survivors emerged into the Sudan at Yabus Bridge (where some retreating SPLA soldiers were also gathered). Here they faced bombing by the Sudanese air force, and tried to shelter in the hilly country to the south (still a part of their old homeland), but heavy weapons were brought to the river and fired into the hills. They were weak by this time, and many died of illness and were buried there. The main body of the people moved further west into Meban country to seek help from the SPLA, but they were unable to provide much help and strongly advised the people to move right down south to Itang, back in Ethiopia.

7. February–July 1990, adrift in the front line of the Sudanese war

This was an extremely difficult time for the refugees as they were not in receipt of any relief aid at all; it was the dry season and they had to move a great distance through very sparsely populated country. The UNHCR in Addis Ababa had lost contact with them, and no UN or other agency operating on the Sudan side took up their plight. This is just one clear example of the seeming inability of the international agencies to initiate aid projects; they come forward mainly when requested to do so, a situation in which local patronage of the needy flourishes. According to their own accounts, many of the Uduk became very thin and ill, and some died, on this journey. Some discussions were initiated, I believe by the SPLA, in April–May over the possibility of an extension relief centre being established at Pagak, in the Sudan but right on the international border, a place which was accessible from Itang and could theoretically receive assistance. The advance party of the Uduk were encouraged by the SPLA to build huts here, and a substantial number did so. But this plan was soon aborted. It is not clear whether the main reasons for the failure of the 1990 Pagak proposal included a shortage of UNHCR funds, or lack of endorsement by the Ethiopian government, or a concern about security (the Sudanese bombers left their card here too). But the outcome was that the people had no further option but to accept SPLA instruction to return across the border and go right down to Itang – trucks were even sent out to meet some weak stragglers. By July, apart from a few groups who settled independently in hills near the border, all survivors had shown up in Itang, constituting the 'ex-Assosa' community which was as a whole in what is officially termed 'poor condition'. They were directed to settle in Village No. 6, though it is very likely that a number of ex-Assosa survivors of various other ethnic groups were among the groups of 'new arrivals' registered later, in Village No. 4, or perhaps never registered at all. Some Uduk, for example, were living at Tarpam near Itang, it seems without the knowledge of the UNHCR. The registered number for Village No. 6 in early 1990 was 22,779.

8. Mid-1990 to mid-1991, sojourn in Itang

The 'ex-Assosa' people did not immediately improve as much as the UNHCR and agencies had expected.[4] Mortality remained high, and the people themselves remember Itang as a place of death – they say that people of all ages were dying, and not only the old. Four or five were being buried in the same hole. Being newcomers and socially marginal within the administrative structure of Itang, itself largely controlled by the

---

[4] See the UNHCR multi-donor mission report on the western camps (1991: 3, 14, 29).

SPLA, it is possible that this community was not in receipt of its proper share of incoming relief. Nor did they have the kin links with neighbouring regions of the Southern Sudan which many of the other Itang refugees did have. Their sojourn, however, came to an early end: with all the others they evacuated the camp in late May/early June 1991. A few made their own way off in the direction of the Daja Valley; but most, after a couple of weeks camping in the bush, came under strong pressure from the former Itang camp administration and the SPLA to come downstream with everyone else to Nasir for their own safety. The returnee relief programme run by Operation Lifeline Sudan (OLS) (Southern Sector) out of Nairobi had just begun there. At Jokau, on the way, many of the Uduk witnessed another bombing attack by Sudanese planes – the second time they had been welcomed back to their own country in this way.

15.1 *Nor Deng on the Sobat river, near Nasir, a month after the Uduk returnees arrived from Itang in the early rainy season, 1991. (Wendy James)*

9. Mid-1991 to mid-1992, sojourn in Nasir

The 'ex-Assosa' or Blue Nile refugees were allocated a site on the south side of the Sobat, already that of an existing Nuer village (Nor Deng), and shipped across the river in small boats. This became one of seven centres for relief distribution around Nasir. Nature and politics combined to hamper the effective delivery of relief. No road transport was possible to this flat and waterlogged region; because of the war there had not even been a barge up to Nasir since 1986. Flood levels were high in 1991, and within a few weeks most of the relief distribution centres were partially washed out. There had been argument from the start about the scale of necessary relief operations. Not only were there suspicions that the SRRA/SPLA claims for returnees around Nasir and else-where were exaggerated, but in June/July/August there was a serious failure in co-ordination between those international agencies based in Addis Ababa, which had been responsible for the refugees in the Ethiopian camps, and those based in

15.2 *Unloading a dinghy at Nor Deng, October, 1991; part of a rare barge delivery. (Wendy James)*

15.3 *A local Nuer boy with a model aeroplane carrying a cargo of maize. (Wendy James)*

Nairobi which attempted to meet some of their needs as returnees in the Sudan. The former even refused for some weeks to accept the fact that Itang and the other camps had been evacuated; and maintained for some time as an option the proposal that those who had left should be encouraged to return. There was continuing disagreement about the level of need, which contributed to the inadequacy of the UN relief programme as a whole. The main responsibility for this however, beyond the UN's lack of political muscle, must lie with the Khartoum regime: UN 'development' aid was completely banned in the SPLA areas, and emergency relief was restricted in kind. It was also subject to delays, cancellation and interference.[5] Relief arrived at first in Nasir by an irregular series of air drops of grain, with supplementary food and medicines airlifted by small Twin Otter plane. Negotiations eventually made it possible for occasional barges to reach Nasir from the North via Malakal, but each proposed journey had to be bargained over separately and no regular schedule was ever established. Khartoum permitted nothing but grain to be delivered as food relief, and flight permission to specified places and for specified amounts had to be renewed each month by the Sudan Government. Even when 'full' daily rations were being delivered to Nor Deng, they fell seriously short in amount and kind from what is regarded as a minimally adequate calorific value, let alone a proper food basket.[6] As stocks from each air drop or barge supply ran low deliveries were cut to alternate days. Wild resources were very limited, and began to run out. In September, after such a period of half rations, there was a two-week gap when absolutely nothing was delivered, and by late September into October, rates of illness and mortality shot up in Nor Deng. It was recognized clearly by the agencies as the largest of the most vulnerable returnee communities around Nasir, along with two or three others – the vulnerable category also included, for example, the centre Pananyang for unaccompanied minors. It was from about this time, late September/October, that the first split in the SPLA, made known at the end of August in the bid for leadership of the movement by Riek Mashar and other Nasir-based commanders, began to complicate further the politics of aid in the region.

Resettlement Proposals, 1991

The World Food Programme (WFP), a partner in OLS, had invited me in July 1991 to visit Nasir and prepare a report on the refugees from the Blue Nile. In mid-August I put

---

[5] See the chapter by Douglas H. Johnson in this volume for an analysis of the 1991 returnee crisis as a whole.
[6] Detail may be found in James (1991a, 1991b, 1992b).

forward a modest and low-profile set of suggestions for the relief and resettlement needs of the community, the tenor of which is clear in these short passages:

It is agreed generally, by agencies and by returnees, that the creation of permanent large camps in the Sudan for returnees, on the Itang model, would be wrong... Two main principles are widely seen to govern the question of the vast majority of the returnees now in the Sudan. First, they must be supported by relief inputs in the places where they are at present settled, for the duration of the current rainy season. Second, from December or so onwards, when dry conditions have returned, a policy should be generally followed of encouraging the dispersal and resettlement of the returnees, preferably to their home areas ...

These general principles apply to the population of Nor Deng as to others in the Nasir region and elsewhere. However, this particular centre poses problems common to all in an acute form. This is because it is a large and overcrowded settlement; and because the majority of its population cannot go home in the dry season, unless there is a national peace agreement ...

In the short term, this population is almost entirely dependent on direct relief inputs into Nasir. These people cannot seek supportive networks of friends and relatives in the vicinity. Rather to the contrary, there is evidence that, at least during periods of reduced or suspended food inputs, they are being impoverished through unequal bartering of their valuables for food from the local villages ...

[There is] evidence of the potential capacity of the present returnee community in Nor to re-establish a productive economy, given security and a suitable environment. Not only could they become largely self-sufficient under these conditions, but they could contribute significantly to regional trade networks, perhaps especially through the cultivation of oil-bearing plants, such as sesame and groundnuts. There is likely also to be spare labour capacity, and a willingness to engage in seasonal wage labour on a modest scale.

A further important point is that the traditional patterns of reciprocal working in the fields and sharing of the product could prove a good base for the formation of small-scale co-operatives. In the pre-war villages, the unit accustomed to working on a broadly co operative basis was fairly small, but in the succession of refugee camps the people have lived in since 1987 they have had considerable experience in the organization of productive work and the handling of common resources on a larger scale. They have also had experience in the operation of committee structures and the keeping of records ...

The most satisfactory way forward is for the formulation of a resettlement scheme, or better, a series of mini-schemes, within the SPLA-controlled areas of Sudan. The border regions from the Jokau River northwards to the Daga Valley would be environmentally and socially very acceptable to the people, and it is possible that some will wish to make their own way there in the dry season independently. These could be assisted with appropriate returnee kits. If it is thought that the security of this region is adequate, a phased plan could be constructed to encourage people to go there, with assistance and local inputs from SRRA, agencies and NGOs. By the later part of 1992, given basic security, returnees who settle here should be largely self-sufficient and making a contribution to the regional economy.[7]

These proposals were sympathetically received, within the general strategy of the SRRA and international agencies to help all the returnees disperse from Nasir and move back home, or at least to some temporary place of settlement. In late September, I made a follow-up visit. The long-distance options had been ruled out for logistical or security reasons. But the idea of a local move on the lines indicated seemed acceptable, indeed it had gained a lot of momentum from constructive discussions among the SRRA/ SPLA, the UN, and the people. Pagak, on the upper Jokau, had emerged as the particularly favoured locality. The suffering in Nor Deng was visibly increasing, and some kind of

---

[7] James (1991a: 6–9, 23–5, 27–9.)

15.4 *A present of coffee from the author, who had known Tumge's family in happier times; the coffee-pot had been on the road for several years, as had the dog. (Wendy James)*

resettlement plan had become very urgent. It was clear to me that once the floods receded and the river could be crossed, the people were likely to leave the Nasir region on their own if there were no plan; and the general expectation of a Sudanese offensive in the dry season made this even more probable. Nor Deng was a frighteningly vulnerable potential target if there were to be fighting in the Nasir area. In an update report of mid-October, I wrote:

In the August Report on Nor Deng, the importance of maintaining regular food inputs to the Nasir area, especially to Nor Deng, was emphasized. Not only has this not happened, but the amounts have consistently been well below any recognized adequate minimum. The average per head of sorghum per person per delivery is 355 g, and for extended periods of time this delivery has occurred only on alternate days. Moreover, apart from two days in August when beans were delivered by air drop, the only food supplied has been grain. The results of this systematic under-nourishment of the returnees have now become evident. Death rates and the spread of serious illness have been reported by the medical teams as reaching alarming levels (see IRC reports and sitreps; as many people died in the last week of September as in the whole of July). Nor Deng is one of the three centres in the Nasir region to show very serious deterioration, and of these it is by far the largest. It is imperative that arrangements for improving supplies, and for widening the range of food input, are made.

There are three further important reasons why the medical-nutritional situation in Nor is deteriorating, and why it is difficult to foresee any improvement:

a   There has been depletion of the wild foods seen to be available in the bush in July. Moreover, the bushland has been repeatedly flooded and many plants are no longer growing. The floods have themselves restricted access to many areas and slowed down the work of seeking wild foods. Women have to ask men to wade through water chest-deep to get access to one of the few plants still found – a type of wild okra.

b   People have tried to relieve the overcrowding in the centre of Nor by moving out. Some have done so successfully, but others have found their new grass huts flooded out, and have had to move a second time, sometimes back closer to the centre. The overcrowding problem remains with its obvious implications for the spread of disease. Initial progress was at last made in early October with a latrine scheme.

c   Sorghum was planted in a large field behind the settlement, but has been completely wiped out by a combination of two factors: floods/waterlogging, and the browsing over the whole site by locally owned Nuer cattle. Fishing equipment has still not been made available in any visible way to this community.

For all these reasons, in addition to the problems of political-military security in their present situation, the ex-Assosa population must be regarded as a highly vulnerable group for whom resettlement is a matter of urgency.

The options for resettlement in the upper Sobat basin were spelled out in detail, after the Nasir SRRA (a little later redesignated RASS – the Relief Association of Southern Sudan) had specifically pointed to Pagak as a plan they would recommend at a public meeting with the Blue Nile chiefs on 2 October 1991. Both formally in the meeting and informally afterwards, there was general enthusiasm and agreement with this idea. So the updated report backed it strongly:

The main advantages of a scheme in the Pagak area from the point of view of the Uduk and their associated groups are as follows:

a   There is woodland and sandy soil of the type they are used to cultivate. They are very anxious to move to a place where they can grow crops with their own hands and not be dependent on intermittent and inadequate help from outside. The woodland has roots and leaves of the kinds they normally collect as part of their diet. There is small game. The river is of a more manageable kind than the Sobat for them to fish in, and they can make fishing baskets and dams to catch fish there. There will be cultivable strips of land along the river bank as it recedes and a few crops could be sown in October–November. Maize can be sown and harvested between April and July next year. There will be plenty of building materials to hand in the woodland, and space to construct a series of dispersed settlements. Firewood will also be obtainable.

b   There are related communities in the vicinity, on both sides of the border – especially Koma groups. The Uduk expect a welcome, and expect to be able to buy seeds and other necessities from the Koma. They also expect that small merchants would be able to reach the area and bring salt, soap and other goods to sell. They expect to gain resources through growing sesame and groundnuts, in particular, and to acquire a few animals again. They feel that Pagak is a place they could rebuild their homes.

c   Pagak is already known to the Uduk, as the advance guard who came down from Assosa in 1990 were instructed to build houses there.... The houses are still there, and although they may need repair, they represent a definite link with the place and make the idea of resettlement very realistic.

The advantages of a resettlement scheme on these lines to the UN and relief agencies would include the following:

a   The scheme is logistically feasible. River transport is possible at least as far as Jokau before the river level falls at the end of the year. This means could be used for an initial assessment, and later for the transport of sick people and other vulnerable categories. Most adults and youngsters could walk the whole way.

b   If there is a possibility of peaceful cross-border movement, this site is one where supplies could be brought from Gambela. A truck road goes to Pagak. At the same time, supplies from the Nasir side would be possible, assuming they can be brought to Nasir in the first place.

c   The main argument for backing such a scheme is that if it were successful, the ex-Assosa group would no longer be a burden and a problem to the agencies. Their dependence at the moment is total, and the international community is not even able to meet the minimum standards to support life and health adequately. There is a desperate short-term need for assistance, but by comparison with the case of the minors, for example, the ex-Assosa group does not demand long-term planning. Relief inputs will be necessary until mid-1992, but thereafter only general development assistance such as is needed across the southern Sudan should be needed. Given regional security and good growing conditions in the next season, the community could not only be largely self-supporting but could be making a contribution to the regional economy, by producing valuable crops such as groundnuts and sesame for exchange and trade....

The principle should be clearly accepted and understood from the start that the move to the Pagak region is for the assisted self-settlement of a community still well able to build, cultivate and support itself to a good extent. The resettlement can be implemented as a relatively low-profile exercise within the context of the general relief programmes for the Sobat basin. The new settlement should not need long-term agency support, or permanent monitoring. It will not be appropriate to lay down the infrastructure of an agency administered 'camp' or resettlement centre. The settlement zone should be physically dispersed over as wide an area as possible, even reaching over a distance of some miles, to allow for some bushland and the planting of well-spaced fields of different types between the individual clusters of homes. These conditions will make for a healthier environment than a dense 'camp'-style settlement.

The Relief Stalemate in Nasir, 1992

At first the 1991 Pagak proposal for the Uduk was welcomed on all sides. But as the rainy season came to an end and the 1992 dry season followed, obstacles arose; and as even the next rains began, there was no real action to settle the people there or anywhere else, and the arguments had got lost in stalemate. The population had partly got lost too – some had died of illness and malnutrition, some had struck out on their own and made a dash for the government-controlled area north of the Yabus River, or disappeared from view by settling anonymously in the hills and valleys along the border. A number had been beaten and threatened, and at least two killed, by SPLA soldiers and local Nuer.

How is it that the plan ran into difficulty? With hindsight one can see that the dramatic bid for leadership of the SPLA by the Nasir commanders, which failed and led to a real split and internecine fighting as early as October, changed their local priorities and heightened the stakes in all negotiations with the international agencies. The earlier SRRA policy had been to disperse all returnees back in their home areas or temporary settlements across the Southern Sudan, with the help of the agencies. But following the inter-SPLA hostilities from October onwards, many returnees found their routes home were cut off and realized they would not be able to leave in the dry season. The SPLA-Nasir and reconstituted RASS began to use the presence of returnees as an argument for continuing emergency relief aid to Nasir, and perhaps this was one of the strongest cards they could play in pressing for external assistance from whatever source. The visible presence of needy groups unfortunately became, in this situation, something of a resource in itself, as the Nasir leadership struggled to build up its economic and political position.

The stakes were also raised as discussions proceeded within the UN agencies over the resettlement of the Uduk. One idea under formulation by the UNHCR, which would have built considerably on the Pagak scheme, envisaged a full-scale and expensive settlement project, complete with infrastructure, radio, airstrip, and resident international monitor. Although this plan was understandably not endorsed, discussion of it as a possibility apparently gave encouragement to the Nasir leadership in seeking to maximize the potential investment input of the agencies to the Nasir-controlled region in general. They certainly demanded that any move of the Blue Nile returnees to the Jokau Valley should be preceded by the placing of adequate supplies and facilities there. Not in itself unreasonable, this demand added to a growing weight of suspicion among the agencies that the SPLA-Nasir and RASS had their own priorities and that without adequate monitoring the returnees would not get their due anyway. Discussions over what should be done about the Uduk in Nasir went through several stages through the first four to five months of 1992. One counter-proposal made by the Nasir authorities was that they should be transferred *downstream*, to Pulang (or Ulang), and a site visit was made; but the Uduk spokesmen refused to accept this plan, pleading for permission to move upstream to the drier hilly country near the border to such a place as Maiwut where they could cultivate in peace and (it was hoped) well away from banditry. The UN also favoured this plan (on the lines of the 1991 recommendations), but the Nasir authorities continued to insist on advance supplies being placed in Maiwut, and in various other proposed sites as well, for other needy communities. The UN was unable to meet the funding, logistical and monitoring needs this assistance would have entailed.

The outbreak of inter-SPLA fighting in various parts of the South added to the logistical as well as political problems of relief delivery in 1992. It also clearly diminished the confidence of donors, whose attitude to the region seemed to follow the realignment of Western policy after the change of government in Ethiopia. International support for the new regime in Addis Ababa seemed to entail very gentle handling of the Khartoum government, with which it had good relations. One consequence was a reluctance by the US to put pressure on Khartoum over its war in the south and the suffering of the civilians there. In March 1992 the expected offensive of the Sudanese forces southwards began. What was not expected was that they would pass through Ethiopian territory in the Gambela region, by-passing Nasir as they struck at the far south (thus causing renewed flight from various other returnee centres, such as Pochalla for example, where there were also a few Uduk, later stranded in the Atepi camp near the Ugandan border). There seemed to be a lack of international political will, not only to contain this new aggression of what was widely agreed to be an abhorrent Sudanese regime, but even to give effective help to civilians caught up in the turmoil.

By the beginning of 1992, the water levels had gone down, and the Blue Nile people were assisted in crossing the Sobat. But they were not encouraged to think they could move upstream, or anywhere far away from Nasir, where they were told it would be more difficult for them to receive relief. They were directed to occupy a more spacious site on the north bank of the river, some 2 km north of Nasir town. It was hopefully named 'New Chali' (by an emerging factor from among the people themselves). OLS staff were surprised that the people did not build there; but the people themselves regarded the site as even worse than Nor Deng, being absolutely flat and liable to flooding in their opinion, and in any case they were hoping and planning to move away from Nasir before the rainy season. They claim that they received no relief grain after January (when the last barge was unloaded at Baliet further downriver, even this effort being attended by hostilities). Other relief which did reach Nasir, such as supplementary food for children, was on occasion being diverted from them, even taken in front of their eyes from the feeding clinic by RASS officials who warned them not to report it to the UN. They were obliged to spend a lot of time seeking wild foods, farther and farther out in the grassy plains and bush. Violence and banditry increased. It may be that the women's widening search on two to three day expeditions led them near some military encampment in the bush; but this was unwitting, and the search for wild food was desperate. Many women described being surprised, even at night, and threatened by armed men. Men too reported being attacked on expeditions into the deep bush looking for honey.

The most serious incident of this type occurred in connection with fishing. The SPLA had developed the practice in the Itang refugee camp earlier of following refugees on fishing excursions and demanding a share of the fish. Armed soldiers continued this in Nasir. A share was normally handed over but on one occasion a man was shot dead for refusing. What the Uduk felt to be a lack of official concern over this incident, after they made a formal complaint direct to what they called 'the government' [*hakuma*], i.e. Commander Riek Mashar, greatly increased the community's feeling of insecurity in Nasir.

At least one small party (specifically of Meban) had decided to leave the Nasir area as early as August 1991, and they made it 'home' to the Sudan government-controlled southern Blue Nile. From early 1992 there was a steady leakage as people moved away in small groups for the more hilly and wooded valleys to the north. A substantial party originally from Chali itself, led by senior members of the church community, decided to leave Nasir in April. This party was ambushed in the hills south of the Yabus, by what were assumed to be and reported as elements of the SPLA-Nasir. The story later gleaned by those who ventured northwards in May–June to investigate is that some of the men were killed, and some of the women and children taken away, partly as labour to assist 'the Nuer' in taking grain from the fields planted by Meban who had fled to Sudan government territory. A few Uduk did manage to follow them north across the Yabus River and get 'home', though the home areas had been almost completely evacuated years before. Without this problem of hostilities on the road, many more people might have attempted to go back home in early or mid-1992, who in fact decided to remain self-settled in the Daja area or join the move back to Ethiopia.

The Eventual Move to Maiwut

As the rains approached and there was no sign of increased relief coming in to Nasir, the request of the Uduk to be allowed to seek a place to cultivate became desperate. At one point it was put to the Uduk spokesmen that perhaps the men could go ahead and prepare a site near Maiwut leaving the families to follow later; this was rejected by the Uduk who felt that their community security depended to a large extent on sticking together. The arguments continued, and contributed to a delay in the final decision, which itself meant that the ideal time for clearing and planting (April–early May) was missed. Eventually, a written request was made to Commander Riek Mashar by the representatives of the people, and permission was given. Some of the Blue Nile people, the Berta-speaking 'Funj' in particular, decided to stay in Nasir in the hope of getting transport downstream later. The residual Uduk/Meban population, estimated by a UN headcount at 11,500, left by 10 May 1992 in a series of four parties to settle in Maiwut and Kigille. They were given some medicines, seeds and tools, but rations for only eight days, and there was to be virtually no back-up. Very weak people were assisted with boat and truck transport.

Although the SPLA provided a minimal escort (there seem to have been just two guards for each party of several thousand) on the journey from Nasir, there were incidents. One attack near Jokau resulted in the death of a guard, and that of the attacker (who turned out to be a Lou Nuer). On a separate occasion, at Maker near Jikmir, attackers shot dead one Uduk man and wounded two others.

The groups who tried to settle in Maiwut and further on at Kigille and Katang in May included the most vulnerable categories (some more confident individuals and small groups went straight on northwards, in the steps of others who had already settled independently). They started to plant. But there was a shortage of rain in June when the crops were still very young, and the prospects looked poor. A feeding scheme was set up in Maiwut but operated on a very limited scale. The wild resources were finished up very quickly; the remaining seeds were eaten, and the UN and agencies had great difficulty in getting more than token relief through.[8] Visitors to Maiwut in June reported very serious hunger, and emaciation of children. They also reported that the local Nuer were demanding shared facilities with the Uduk newcomers.[9]

The local population of the Maiwut/Kigille area includes some Koma (in fact representatives of two or three different Koma language communities), and it is acknowledged by all that this is historically a part of the Koma homeland; on this basis

---

[8] It is understood that on 18 May, 4 MT (metric tonnes) food and additional seeds were sent, and on 18 June 3 MT of food and 1.5 of Unimix; no more food was sent, but some seeds and 1.3 MT of Unimix were sent on 23 June together with some medicines for the establishment of a health and feeding centre.

[9] See for example the report of Sharon Hutchinson to SCF (1992).

the Uduk might have been recognized as related people having a general claim to be accepted and welcomed as temporary settlers. The majority of inhabitants seem now, however, to be mobile pastoralist Nuer, who have been expanding into the zone of the Ethiopian foothills. When these returned from their cattle camps on the Baro in June, tension between the returnee settlers and the local pastoralists increased. In addition, although the leadership of the SPLA-Nasir and RASS authorities was well disposed in principle towards the Uduk, lack of discipline and hunger among the ordinary soldiers led to looting, and banditry. There were two particularly serious incidents: the first was the beating up of one of the most senior of the Uduk men who had assisted the UN food distribution (not only in Nor Deng/Nasir, but previously in Itang and Assosa). He was attacked as he went to meet the truck which brought one of the few loads of relief from Jokau ever to reach Maiwut. It is understood that the culprit was held for a few days and then released without the case being properly settled. The other serious incident was the spearing to death of an Uduk man, Chila Ita, in the Nuer maize fields. There was hunger and mutual distrust: people with early crops (such as okra, and pumpkins) found soldiers in their fields, helping themselves. It should be made quite clear that the SPLA-Nasir as such never mounted a campaign against the Uduk or other Blue Nile refugees; what violence they suffered was the result either of general insecurity in the region or of indiscipline among the troops, or it stemmed from growing opportunism by the local civilian population. Complaints were made by the Uduk spokesmen to the local Commander in Maiwut, but while sympathy was expressed, no effective action was taken. It became clear to the Uduk, partly from their conversations with the local Koma, that the soldiers would certainly expect to take a share of their harvests if and when they matured. Some Koma expressed it thus: 'We eat together with the Nuer, and so they will expect to eat from you too.' At the same time, there is evidence that discussion of possibly resuming a movement back to Ethiopia was current among the population of the Nasir region as a whole; even the SPLA-Nasir leadership had publicly made it clear they regarded it as a final option for survival.

Itang Again

The prospects both for immediate survival and for the longer term safety of the community in the Maiwut-Kigille area looked extremely slim by late June; meetings were held and the people decided to leave. They did so quite openly, starting out by day. The move was spearheaded by the Gindi group, who left Kigille and proceeded through Wanke towards Itang; and they were followed by the majority of the rest; those in Maiwut proceeded via Pagak. The remainder stayed to work on the fields, but some of these decided to leave later, in mid-August, with the blessing in fact of the SPLA leadership in Maiwut. They were joined by a party of other refugee/returnees, who had formerly been in Itang but originally came from widely scattered places in the Southern Sudan, and included Nuer, Dinka and Shilluk. The residue of the Uduk, at least several hundred, remained behind in the Kigille/Maiwut area, their presence unknown to the relevant representatives of OLS. The agencies no longer had the people or resources even to monitor the situation outside immediate relief centres like Nasir; in October 1992, when I passed on the information that there were still Uduk in the Sudan, the reaction was disbelief.

It seems that the Uduk decision to move out of the Sudan and seek help in Ethiopia, where so many in real distress had been helped before, was looked on with sympathy by the SPLA-Nasir leadership. The community's willingness to see what help could be found in Ethiopia might even have been seen as a testing of the waters, a paving of the way for others. On the journey the Uduk were looted of most of their remaining possessions not only by the Gaajak, known to be a border threat, but also by some SPLA-Nasir soldiers even before they left the Sudan. Some died of exhaustion on the way, but while there were armed threats and detentions, this was for the sake of property, and no-one actually shot at them. By this time there is no doubt that everyone was desperately poor and hungry in the whole region, and it is likely that that several parties might have thought there to be some general advantage in allowing the Uduk to arrive back at Itang in a state of really severe destitution and starvation. Perhaps it was thought that these supposed 'favourites' of the relief agencies, now really on the edge of survival, would kick-start the relief operations again on the Ethiopian side.

It was not known to the Uduk that Itang had been finally closed as a refugee camp in February 1992. However there was a very substantial population of Ethiopian highland settlers there, displaced by the droughts of previous years. A UNHCR Programme Assistant from Addis Ababa arranging for the final clearance of various items happened to be there when the first Uduk arrived about 24 June; he reported them as around 200. A second report gave about 500 on 1 July, and a UNHCR mission estimated them at 3,000 by 6 July. Immediate emergency food and help was made available through collaboration between local government and various charities. A fuller survey of the problem had to be postponed because of security incidents which broke out in the Gambela region in mid-July. Meanwhile enquiries were made of OLS in Nairobi as to relief provision on the Sudan side of the border; the first replies received from Nairobi (where the scale of the Uduk evacuation was then not known) were interpreted as relatively reassuring, and so recommendations were being developed in Addis Ababa for the Uduk to be persuaded to return whence they had come.

Violence and the Flight to Gambela, Mid to Late July

During the first week or so of July, a large number of Nuer, including many women and children, converged on the locality of Itang. It is clear that many, if not the majority, were from the Sudan side. They had come in search of food, they said, under the leadership of the prophetic religious figure Wurnyang. He held a peace-making ceremony, witnessed by Uduk and others then at Itang, between representatives of the Nuer and the Anuak. On 11 July, a series of violent incidents began in the Gambela region. Demands were made upon Ato Agwa Alemo, Representative of the Transitional Government, by soldiers of the Gambela People's Liberation Movement (the GPLM, of which he was the head). These demands were reportedly in part to do with the provision of food relief. Their outcome was, however, the assassination of Ato Agwa in his own home. A later incident is said to have included the killing of some Ethiopians at a post near Akada on the road to Itang, by armed Anuak. Two days after this (clear evidence is not available but it seems to have been 17–18 July) the Nuer in Itang, who had already looted food stores and shops, according to an eye-witness attacked an incoming truck loaded with food, threw out the driver and unloaded the sacks. As they came in to the Itang market area singing loudly and carrying the food, they were shot at by government soldiers. The market was full of children, who had received their ration at the feeding centre and were now congregating in the market area to search for scraps of food on the ground. A large number of armed Nuer then responded by firing indiscriminately upon the Ethiopians, soldiers and civilians alike, in the market area.

Many were killed, women and children included, and probably some Uduk, it is thought, who were in the way. Uduk and Anuak however were not the target. Ethiopian women and children scattered as did the Uduk; and most managed to make their way, sometimes together, up to Gambela, either by road or along the river. A substantial number of people died on this trek, even more, the oral evidence suggests, than had died on the first leg of the journey to Itang. A number of Uduk children and a few adults were lost at the time of the violence; some were looked after in Anuak homes and the UNHCR has since been engaged in tracing them and trying to reunite them with their families.[10]

The majority of the Uduk arrived in Gambela quite quickly, though in very poor shape. Many townspeople took pity on them, bringing out food from their own kitchens. Initially squatting in the vicinity of the UNHCR compound, they were removed to open ground south of the main bridge, until the local authorities and agencies agreed that they could be transferred to Karmi, a former famine resettlement site from the 1970s, as a temporary measure. This move took place on 28 July, and a headcount produced a figure of 9,000–10,000. A six months' emergency budget was secured.

Karmi Transit Site for Asylum Seekers: 'New' Resettlement Proposals

In September–October I was able to visit Karmi and to prepare a report for the UNHCR in Addis Ababa. The first task was to encourage the completion of population lists, already under way. The total number (all individual names) turned out to be over 13,000. The UNHCR recognized the *bona fide* claims to asylum of the Uduk and some other Sudanese groups who had arrived back in Ethiopia with them, although reluctant to re-establish refugee camps in the region. Proposals were being sought and canvassed on possible resettlement schemes, and I was able to draw together ideas already in the air, and frame some recommendations. These were very close in essence to what had been recommended on the Sudan side, but had never been properly implemented. Second time around, in a foreign country rather than their own homeland, these proposals received a serious hearing and helped lead toward a resettlement scheme. I quote a few passages from the report:

> The morale of the present community in Karmi is remarkably high, considering the suffering they have been through over the last few years.... The administrative institutions of the 16 groups and their leadership remain in working order, as does their active church organization and community life based on several church groups. Leadership positions have in some cases changed, mainly because some former community leaders are still in the Sudan, but in all cases others have taken their place. The community is anxious to seek a safe place in which to live and re-establish subsistence farming.... They wish to be located as far as possible from the Sudanese border ...

> ... It should first be stated quite plainly that repatriation of this community en masse to their original homes in the Kurmuk District of the Sudan is out of the question at the moment, and for the foreseeable future. At present, the Sudan government does not even control the whole of what was the Kurmuk District, and if there should be renewed offensives by either the government or the SPLA, this very zone would be the front line. Eventual repatriation is what the people would like when there is a stable peace in the Sudan, but it must await that time.

> A return move to the neighbouring region of the southern Sudan is also out of the question at present. The UN relief operation, conducted with a number of NGOs under Operation Lifeline Sudan, is seriously handicapped in its efforts to support the lives and livelihood of the local population of the Sobat basin, let alone the still-stranded core of last year's returnees from

---

[10] Some of the families involved, and the children, are depicted in the documentary *Orphans of Passage*, directed by Bruce MacDonald for the Granada TV series 'Disappearing World: War'. Filming was done in Karmi transit site near Gambela in January 1993 (transmitted on ITV, 18 May 1993).

15.5 *Uduk children gathered to listen to makeshift music. (Wendy James)*

Ethiopia. The handicaps are partly logistical, but primarily political, in that the Sudan government places severe constraints upon the kind and quantity of UN aid. In particular, a UN request to re-open an airstrip at Maiwut, or at Daja, for emergency relief, has been repeatedly and consistently refused, and political factors have halted relief by barge since early 1992. The NGOs are scarcely able to operate in the Nasir region at present. Security conditions have become more perilous over recent months: and it is public knowledge that when the SPLA leadership left Nasir at the beginning of October, the general population was exhorted to leave for Ethiopia should there be any trouble.[11]

On the table to date there had been three main proposals; all of them were relatively long-distance ones, and this in itself weighed against them. One was to return the people to Nasir, which had already been recognized as unreasonable, and possibly against the UN mandate. The second was for them to go Dimma, one of the old camps far to the south where there was land allocated for refugees; but this was a very long distance and in the opposite direction from their homes; it was also fairly limited in size and already occupied by a considerable number of Nuer refugees. The third was for them to go back to Assosa, also very far but at least in the direction of home. The Ethiopian (rather than the Sudanese) side of that region, around Bambeshi, was and remains a long-term possible solution for their resettlement on the Ethiopian side; but the cost and security problems of the move, in addition to a range of varied opinions as to its suitability, ruled it out as an early option. So a local solution was proposed, at least for the medium term, and this is the scheme now being implemented.

> Consultations with the authorities in Gambela, experienced long-term residents and with the Uduk community revealed that it would be realistic and feasible to implement a very early transfer from the transit site at Karmi to a zone further eastwards, up the Baro river and some 30–40 km along the road from Gambela.... The area of Bonga has been a historical place of refuge for the Koma people (linguistically related to the Uduk) for some generations; although there are only a few individuals there at present, it is well known that from the late nineteenth century, this has been a place where Koma lived. There have been other settlers who have come and gone in the past, including gold-seekers. In recent times, an SPLA camp was located here, but has since been evacuated. All those consulted confirmed that a settlement scheme here would not infringe existing rights to the area, and the small community present in the village near the bridge welcomed the idea in principle.
>
> The Bonga area, enclosed in a basin formation within a ring of surrounding hills, appears at first sight very suitable for cultivation by traditional hand tool methods. The land is undulating and rocky, and would not be suitable for tractors. The traditional Uduk farming system includes two main types of fields, one on heavy soil near a river, where maize is the main crop, and the second on lighter sandy soil often near low hills, where sorghum and sesame are the main crops. They are experienced in growing a wide range of crops, including groundnuts, beans, fruits, vegetables and tobacco, and in raising modest numbers of animals (cattle, goats, pigs, and chickens). The two Uduk leaders who participated in the site visit expressed enthusiasm over the possibilities of raising crops and eventually being able to feed themselves in the Bonga area,

---

[11] James for UNHCR (1992a: 9).

even at an early date producing some surplus for local trade. The locals stated that two crops of maize could be raised per year....

One of the very positive factors in the consideration of a scheme in the Gambela area is the opportunity for seasonal employment at the state cotton farm at Abobo. Both the Abobo *awraja* authorities and the farm manager expressed keen interest in recruiting labour on a seasonal, rota basis, and the Uduk community themselves are keen on this proposal.... The cash earned from the cotton farm would help integrate the Uduk into the local economy and society.

Other sites for possible settlement in the Gambela area were suggested and discussed, but several were ruled out on the grounds of insecurity....

For the above reasons, it is therefore proposed that a formal request to the UNHCR and Ethiopian authorities be made as soon as possible to approve the establishment of a semi-permanent settlement focused at Bonga for the Uduk asylum seekers at Karmi and those of their kith and kin who may join them.... At best, the first main harvest (November–December 1993) could be a watershed; relief could then be scaled down. The total period over which UNHCR should bear responsibility for relief needs might be up to two years, or a maximum of three years. This is a provisional suggestion and is subject to detailed planning by relevant experts....[12]

Khor Bonga: a New Home for the Uduk?

The Bambeshi/Assosa option was favoured by some authorities in Ethiopia, but eventually, by the end of 1992, the UNHCR and Ethiopian government had agreed, with the strong support of the local authorities in Gambela, to back the Bonga option. Planning and arrangements for the infrastructure began immediately; and the move from Karmi began in late January 1993. There are signs that the resettlement scheme could become a success.[13]

The actual content of the recommendations made for the settlement of the Blue Nile refugees in the Nasir region in 1991, and those made for their settlement in Ethiopia in 1992, is very similar. In each case, longer distance resettlement possibilities were considered but set aside, for reasons both of cost and of security. A return to the other side of the border, whence the people had come, was initially looked at as an option in each case by one UN agency or another, though later rejected. Both reports draw attention to the need for relieving overcrowding on a temporary site; at least temporary access to land to cultivate on a small-scale but dispersed pattern, and also access to woodland, stony or hilly ground. In these circumstances it is argued that the people had the ability to work together and not only help themselves but also make a contribution to the local economy through trade and wage labour. While in both cases other refugee/returnee or displaced communities had also to be considered, the claims of the ex-Assosa group to particular targeting were recognized by the UN and international agencies in both cases. These points were at first listened to sympathetically by the authorities [SPLA-Nasir] on the Sudan side, but very little came of the plan for settlement. In Ethiopia similar resettlement suggestions were made; and by contrast, the recommendations, being acceptable to both regional and central government in Gambela and Addis Ababa, were taken up.

The question remains as to why there was this very different outcome; and the answer has to be a purely political one, on different levels. On the Sudan side, although this was arguably their home country and the SPLA owed them something, relations with that body deteriorated, especially after the split, and tensions mounted with the local population as a result of the war situation and the relief difficulties. On the Ethiopian side, although it was a foreign country, relations with the local population were good from the start, Uduk voluntarily seeking work on Anuak farms and getting paid for it in food, taking firewood for sale in Gambela town and so on. The Gambela region as a whole was attempting to recover from war and rebuild its economy. The presence of international asylum seekers meant an increase in incoming resources, and

---

[12] Ibid: 11–13.
[13] See James (1995) for a progress report on this scheme.

the new local authorities in Gambela were very willing to take on the role of protector towards groups leaving the patronage of the SPLA. On the international level, it must be admitted that the attitude of donors and governments in the region also made it easier for the funding of schemes to assist groups leaving SPLA-controlled territory, even as international refugees, than it had been for assisting civilians within any part of it. The change of approach within the thinking of agencies in the region, especially perhaps the UNHCR, with regard to the old line dividing relief from development and with regard to the 'cross-mandate' principle, no doubt helped provide the wider context in which the resettlement could be put into effect. These are just some of the many ironies in this case of the Uduk 'returning' to Ethiopia, a foreign country, to make a new home.

Relief, development and resettlement cannot operate in a neutral vacuum. Even the UN is drawn into politically structured situations locally and internationally which constrain the form its actual activities can take. In practice, whatever the noble neutrality of UN rhetoric (and I passionately endorse the vital importance of the principle which can, should and must, as far as humanly possible, protect those in danger), it operates on the ground under political constraint. The humblest people themselves know this to some extent. Let me close with a song from Karmi transit site, composed for the lyre and here translated from the Udak, which plays upon a memory of the sufferings in the Sudan and the prevarications of the UN in Nasir:

So what can we eat?
With all the children too?
I'll go and dig wild roots
Why's the UN denying us our grain?
My feet are bruised
We're from the long, bitter road
With the children too
Oh, UN, oh!
I've been strung along by the white people
Riek Mashar's behind it somewhere
He calls himself the Captain

But my feet are hurting me
Oh, UN, oh!
Oh, Nairobi!
What can we eat at home?
The children are struck by hunger up to death
The Nuer ask 'What's this, what's that?'
While I'm scratching for roots
He calls himself the Captain
Riek Mashar, so there he is!
Oh, UN! Why don't you take us to Nairobi! [14]

[14] Sung by Weila Ragab; recorded by Granada TV's 'Disappearing World: War' programme during the making of *Orphans of Passage*, January 1993.

References

Donham, D. and W. James (eds) (1986) *The southern marches of Imperial Ethiopia: essays in social anthropology and history*, Cambridge University Press, Cambridge.

Hutchinson, S. (1992) 'Potential development projects for the Sobat valley region: a set of proposals prepared for Save the Children Fund (UK)', SCF/UK, London.

James, Wendy (1979) '*Kwanim Pa: the making of the Uduk people. An ethnographic study of survival in the Sudan–Ethiopian borderlands*, Clarendon Press, Oxford.

— (1988a) *The listening ebony: moral knowledge, religion and .power among the Uduk of Sudan*, Clarendon Press, Oxford.

— (1988b) 'Uduk faith in a five-note scale: mission music and the spread of the Gospel', in W. James and D.H. Johnson (eds) *Vernacular Christianity: essays in the social anthropology of religion presented to Godfrey Lienhardt*, JASO/Lilian Barber, Oxford/New York.

— (1991a) 'Background report and guidelines for future planning: Nor Deng centre for Sudanese returnees', WFP/Operation Lifeline Sudan, Southern Sector, Nairobi.

— (1991b) 'Vulnerable groups in the Nasir region: update on the Blue Nile returnees (Nor Deng) and resettlement proposal', WFP/Operation Lifeline Sudan, Southern Sector, Nairobi.

— (1992a) 'Uduk asylum seekers in Gambela, 1992: community report and options for resettlement', UNHCR, Addis Ababa.

— (1992b) 'Managing food aid: returnees' strategies for allocating relief', *Refugee Participation Network*, Vol. 13, June 1992: 3–6.

— (1994) 'War and "ethnic visibility": the Uduk on the Sudan-Ethiopian border', in K. Fukui and J. Markakis (eds) *Ethnicity and conflict in the Horn of Africa*, James Currey, London.

— (1995) 'The Bonga scheme: progress to 1994 and outlook for 1995', UNHCR, Addis Ababa.

UNHCR (1991) 'Report of the muiti-donor technical mission on refugees and returnees to Ethiopia: report on mission to Western Region Sudanese refugee camps', Addis Ababa.

16

E.A. BRETT
Rebuilding War-Damaged Communities in Uganda

The Institutional Dimension

Institutional Failure and Political Crisis in Northeastern Africa

As a student in the late fifties I shared the post-colonial dream for Africa. Independence was to set free local initiatives long suppressed to serve foreign interests and protect backward 'traditional' elites. Economic liberation and Pan African Unity was to follow, while ethnic conflict would disappear when the colonists no longer needed to divide and rule. The new discipline of Development Economics promised a rapid take-off into sustained growth as soon as new governments established a rational planning process, imposed their will on dominant foreign interests, and took control over the commanding heights of the economy. New parties emerged to compete for positions in new parliaments where it was assumed that Africans would emulate the successful transitions to democratic rule already completed in Asia. Only racists or reactionaries predicted a collapse into war and bankruptcy.

Forty years of experience has turned these dreams into nightmares. Economic failure has reduced most countries to foreign dependence, while civil war has reduced the worst to anarchy. Here external agencies – the UN, major donors and international NGOs – have almost become surrogate governments, and there is talk of a need for direct intervention to defend helpless populations from the devastating effects of almost terminal social breakdown.

This situation creates critical short- and long-term problems. In many places the domestic capacity to respond to immediate crises – of famine, violence, displacement, or disease – has disappeared. The authority of the state is contested by rebels or has withered away, so services can only be provided by external agencies which are demanding the right to defend themselves if they are to continue to operate. These immediate crises, however, are the result of fundamental institutional failures – responding to the symptoms does not solve the problem, so donors who come to deal with short-term emergencies find themselves wrestling with long-term problems. If they leave without restoring political and administrative order and productive capacity, conditions soon degenerate to the level which forced their earlier intervention.

Thus the solution to even the most immediate problems requires the initiation of a long-term process of institutional reform and economic reconstruction. The political and economic failures which produced the descent into economic crisis and war were a function of irrational policies and inappropriate institutions. Political centralization, command planning and authoritarian bureaucracies in the post-colonial state placed

203

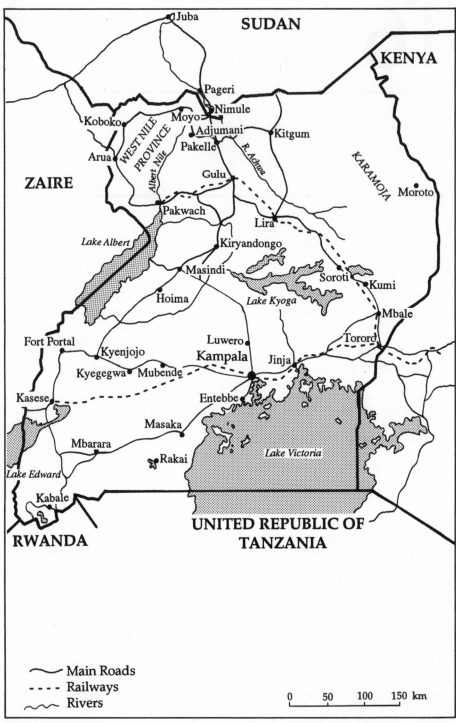

Map 16.1 *Uganda*

immense power in the hands of governments. Most regimes operated a 'winner takes all' strategy, abusing their authority to allocate economic resources to benefit themselves and their clients rather than society as a whole. Underdeveloped information systems and limited skills, combined with the systematic destruction of autonomous political, economic and social structures in civil society, marginalized all of the groups excluded from the inner circle, leading to economic decay and political conflict. With the elimination of all legitimate avenues for political competition and compromise, excluded groups, usually organized on regional/ethnic lines, had no alternative but to rebel, setting in motion the processes which are still precluding sustained development all over Africa.

The problem confronting local leaders and their foreign advisors in many African countries thus involves nothing less than a radical reform of the whole institutional framework created during the transition from colonial rule at the end of the fifties. And this process must be carried through in the most adverse circumstances – in countries dominated by the legacy of civil war and economic collapse. The process will take many years and have different modalities in different places. If it is to be prosecuted with intelligence and sensitivity, however, we must understand the underlying reasons for the original failures, and identify successful alternatives which have been shown to work under the adverse conditions which now prevail in the least stable countries in Africa.

Civil wars are best ended through a process of reconciliation and reconstruction designed to restore faith in the representativeness and equity of the political and economic systems. Several countries are now attempting to do this in Africa, but there is little doubt that Uganda has now produced the most successful record of sustained progress. Here committed political leadership and positive co-operation with donors has virtually ended chronic civil conflict and produced per-capita economic growth of about 5 per cent for seven years. This has involved a willingness to bring former enemies into the political system, build new representative structures and allow private firms and voluntary agencies the freedom to operate without external controls.

This experience is of the greatest importance to other countries which are now seeking for solutions to similar problems. The rest of this chapter will therefore review the processes which led to the breakdown of legitimacy and economic management in the seventies and early eighties, and then examine the institutional reforms which have enabled it to deal with the crucial problems of political and econonomic reconstruction which confronted the NRM regime in January 1986, and which are still having to be dealt with now.

The Politics of Conflict and Exclusion

Ugandans, like many of their neighbours, have suffered grievously from past failures to settle conflicts through a legitimate and effective system of rule and thus without recourse to violence. One foreign invasion, two military coups, and extended periods of civil war have inflicted terrible damage – hundreds of thousands dead or injured, massive losses of physical assets, the constant diversion of resources from civil to military uses, the loss of a large proportion of the educated elite, the capacity to co-operate in whole communities undermined by a legacy of suspicion and mistrust.

The roots of this conflict lie deep in a history dominated by regional, ethnic and sectarian exclusion and conflict. During the colonial period governance was dominated by Europeans, commerce by Asians and administration was based on a local authority system which reinforced ethnic rather than national loyalties and identity. Economic development, and with it access to education and promotion in the modern system, was heavily concentrated in the cash-crop producing areas in the south which were dominated by long-standing monarchical traditions. Recruitment to positions of authority among the African community favoured Protestants rather than Catholics. Most of the north, excluded by poor transport links, was relatively deprived, served as a labour reserve and provided the army with most of its recruits.

At independence a complex semi-federal constitutional settlement was arranged to accomodate the conflicting demands stemming from the complex of regional, ethnic and religious rivalries generated by these differences. These gave rise to multi-party competition between the Uganda People's Congress (UPC), the Democratic Party (DP) and Kabaka Yekka (KY). The UPC, led by Milton Obote, was dominated by anti-monarchical, Protestant and relatively deprived northern groups. It encountered strong resistance from the DP dominated by Catholics (including many Catholic northerners) and by southerners, and from KY representing traditionalists from Buganda, the dominant ethnic group in Uganda under British rule. Threatened by an internal take-over in the mid-sixties, Obote used the army to arrest his opponents, remove the traditional rulers and establish a centralized republican constitution. This initiated a period of prolonged political instability and conflict which has yet to be finally resolved.

In 1966 Obote used the army to destroy his enemies, in 1971 it displaced him and handed power to Idi Amin. Part of the army remained loyal to Obote, so Amin spent his first years organizing a violent purge of potential military opponents and a reign of terror to suppress civilian dissent. More than 50,000 Asians – much of the business and professional class – were expelled and many of the African elite were executed or fled. This eliminated all autonomous voices in civil society, and destroyed the capacity of the economy, the state and the army to function effectively. In 1979 he paid the price for this when he invaded Tanzania and was decisively defeated by the Tanzanian army and Ugandan irregulars. At the end of 1980, after a period of unstable interim governments, new elections were held and the UPC led by Obote returned to power and initiated a stabilization programme with World Bank and IMF support which initially had some success.

However the election results were thought to be fraudulent, southerners felt that they were excluded from a corrupt regime, and civil war broke out on two fronts in 1981–2. To the north and west of Kampala (the 'Luwero Triangle') the National Resistance Movement (NRM) led by Yoweri Museveni fought a guerilla war against Obote's national army and against Okello's forces after Obote was replaced in a coup during 1985. During these years Obote's and Okello's soldiers used systematic violence to terrorize the civilian population. Many thousands died, were injured, tortured, or raped so most people fled from the worst-affected zones, taking refuge with friends and relatives in neighbouring areas. In West Nile, Amin's home area, many politicians and soldiers had gone into exile in Sudan, but they took the civil war into Arua and Moyo districts when Obote returned. The government's punitive response provoked wide-spread displacement, with whole communities decamping to the Sudan where they lived as refugees. In both West Nile and Luwero people found ruined homesteads and overgrown farms when they were actually able to return in the second half of the 1980s.

Following Museveni's victory in 1986 the war did not end but shifted to different parts of the country. Defeated soldiers returned home to the north and north-east, and the ousted political leadership organized itself into movements opposed to the new regime. In Teso in the north-east the problem was less political hostility to the NRM than the exclusion of the local elite from positions of authority, and the decision by the NRA to disarm local militias and thus subject the community to cattle raiding from their neighbours, the Karimojong. Among the Acholi in the north, a group which had been dominant in the army of the Okello regime, resistance was not only organized on secular lines but also in the millenarian Holy Spirit Movement led originally by Alice Lakwena, then by Joseph Kony.

16.1 *People of Luwero returning to ruined homesteads and overgrown farms following the NRA takeover in 1986. (Claudia Moreno/Oxfam/CGM/2)*

From late 1986 to the end of 1991 these areas north and east of the Nile were devastated by a civil war which reached its peak in 1987–8 when the Lakwena movement mobilized thousands of soldiers, defeated the NRA in key engagements, and advanced to within 150 km of Kampala before being turned back. Thereafter military conflict continued in seven districts (Gulu, Kitgum, Soroti, Kumi, Lira, Apac and Palissa) where small-scale bands of rebels, loosely associated together, roamed the countryside living off the local populations and attempting to disrupt the activities of the security forces. Here dislocation was compounded by cattle-raiding from the Karimojong, their eastern pastoral neighbours, who were able to exchange cattle for guns through Somali traders and roamed freely across the region stripping it of hundreds of thousands of animals.

The rebels originally had considerable support, but this declined after 1988 as their resources ran out and their demands on the civilian population became increasingly destructive. By 1990 the main political groups had come to terms with the NRM and resistance was confined to a few hundred members of the Holy Spirit Movement and roving bands with no political programme. Once a reasonable degree of security had been established attention could be shifted from pacification to development, and planning could begin on an ambitious Nothern Uganda Reconstruction Programme (NURP), mainly funded by the World Bank. During the war none of the UN agencies, apart from the World Food Programme, entered the area – their personnel were prohibited from doing so by security guidelines until 1991 – so external assistance was provided almost exclusively through NGOs. The various projects, mainly designed to restore infrastructure, which now make up the NURP were formulated during 1991 and the programme officially opened in the middle of 1992.

Death and disruption were not as extensive in these areas as they had been in Luwero and the northwest, but they have nevertheless left deep scars. Whereas Obote's military

16.2 *Distribution of relief items in Gulu district under the auspices of ACORD (an international NGO), as part of a programme of rehabilitation in the war zone, 1989. (Tim Allen)*

campaign attempted to terrorize the civilian population into submission, Museveni's combined a military response to aggression with appeasement and political negotiation. Major errors were made in the early years – there were serious cases of abuse against the civilian populations by some units, the army failed to protect the region against the Karimojong and, indeed, local people believe that many of the soldiers were also involved in cattle rustling themselves. In Kumi District in 1990 a third of the population was rounded up at short notice and moved into camps where many died.

However it was quickly realized that this strategy was counter-productive, reinforcing opposition and confirming the allegations about the regime made by the rebels. The regime never gave up its commitment to defeating the rebellion and establishing a monopoly of force, and it was to spend more than half its budget on the army during these years. However it also introduced a general amnesty for all rebels willing to give themselves up.

Museveni himself made regular visits into the area where he personally investigated allegations of abuse; serious cases were drastically punished, often by public execution. A Minister for the North took up permanent residence in Gulu, a Presidential Commission was set up to negotiate for peace and initiate development projects in Teso. Elected local councils were allowed to operate throughout the region, many of them led by former rebels. Several members of these councils were killed by rebels. Nevertheless, they became actively involved in attempting to get development started, in negotiating with rebel groups, and in assisting external agencies in relief activities. Rebels willing to leave the bush were granted amnesty and an attempt was made to reintegrate them into society by allowing them to join the NRA or local defence units. The exiled political leadership was encouraged to return and the local leadership was given positions in government when they agreed to bring their forces out of the bush. By 1992 it seemed probable that the civil war had ended. Large-scale demobilization took place in 1993, with support from the donors for generous redundancy payments.

The Institutional Logic of Reconciliation and Reconstruction

National integration depends on the existence of an institutional system which protects the civil rights of all of the major social groups and ensures that their claims on resources will not be excluded through the arbitrary exercise of monopoly power. This need not involve full equality of opportunity – significant levels of inter-generational inequality which is transferred through the inheritance of assets, skills and contacts through kinship and social networks, exist in even the most successful modern societies. However success does require some capacity to meet two requirements – that upward mobility is not forcibly closed to those with the appropriate skills and, more important still, that rewards to those in positions of authority depend on their contribution to social welfare. The latter presupposes an institutional framework with enforceable accountability mechanisms – one which ties control over political or economic power directly to the effective performance of the services which organizations are established to provide.

Where this is so the privileges derived from the exercise of power must be earned by providing public services, and this, in turn, will allow people to acknowledge the justice of the legal and social constraints which they must accept if the system is to function. This sense of justice will ensure that they obey the law, perform the duties implicit in their economic function, accept their own incomes as just and refrain from attempting to expropriate the assets of others. The most successful versions of this system involve a combination of representative democracy – to impose effective limits on the power of those who control the state – and competitive markets – to impose efficiency on those who control the economic system.

These requirements have been systematically ignored in post-colonial Africa. Authoritarian rule and economic monopoly have confined power to an arbitrarily chosen elite which has been sheltered from the need to base their claims on effective performance. Gross inequalities, predation and economic decline have delegitimated the state and produced an endemic disregard for law and economic regulation. Particular groups – notably ethnic groups excluded from political power from regions marginalized by the collapse of economic and social provision – have lost all faith in the integrity of the national system and taken up arms to demand regional political autonomy.

This process, as we have seen, had reduced Uganda to ruin by the mid-eighties. Reconstruction has involved a systematic attempt to overcome the jealousy and mistrust engendered in three ways. Opponents have been incorporated into a 'broad-based' political management system, a programme of constitutional review and administrative reform has begun, as has a programme of economic liberalization and reconstruction which has tried to take account of the needs of marginalized as well as central regions of the country. National political integration, the reform of the state and the liberalization of the economy have all had to proceed in tandem – together they have overcome the belief that the regime would serve the interests of one group to the exclusion of all others, provided a basis for a continuous improvement in public provision, and thus allowed people to hope that life would be better in the future than it had been in the recent past.

This has imposed serious limits on the freedom of action of the dominant elite, and required heavy support from foreign donors. The process is stll far from complete – the state has yet to establish its capacity to deliver effective services; sectarian or ethnic conflict could break out again if key groups were to reject the constitutional settlement; economic collapse would quickly follow any withdrawal of foreign support. For Ugandans at this point the main task should not be to celebrate their recent achievements but to investigate and address the many failures and weaknesses. Their neighbours, however, still suffering the costs of continuing conflict, should ask themselves what it is that has allowed this much progress to occur in so short a period.

Political Reconciliation and Integration

In 1986 military victory allowed the NRM to take power and appoint its own cabinet. It set up a 'broad-based' regime, recruited from all of the major political parties. This included Moses Ali, a former supporter of Idi Amin, who had been a leading figure in the main guerrilla operation in West Nile during the early 1980s. This helped to ensure that the anti NRM revolt in the north did not cross onto the west bank of the Nile. However Moses Ali was subsequently arrested on suspicion of treason and held without trial

16.3 *School children celebrating Independence Day, Moyo district, 1988.*
(Tim Allen)

for a considerable period. When brought to trial, the case was dismissed. Subsequently leaders of rebel groups in Gulu who came to terms with the regime were also drawn into the government, while a policy of 'ethnic balancing' was thereafter applied to promotions in the civil service.

The National Resistance Council, the central policy-making body for the NRM in the bush, became the legislative body for the country as a whole. Its 'historic' members remained, and their numbers were supplemented by new Ministers and their Deputies. In 1989 country-wide indirect elections were used to elect 158 representatives to it from the old constituencies, together with 34 women, one from each district (subsequently increased to 39). It has to approve new legislation and can (and does) criticise the performance of the government.

Power at the centre was complemented by a local government system of Resistance Councils (RCs) operating at five levels – Village, Parish, Sub-County, County and District. These use direct elections at the village and indirect elections at higher levels. Their powers were very limited, but the system has nevertheless drawn hundreds of thousands of people into the decision-making process and allowed them to organize community initiatives and criticise the activities of central and local officials. The system was set up in 1986, and all councils were re-elected in 1989 and 1992. These were actively contested and many incumbents excluded. In 1992 the government agreed a decentralization policy which will increase their power over local officials hitherto responsible to the Ministry of Local Government or the other line ministries. This process should involve fundamental changes in the location of political and financial power.

The RC system has been crucial for the process of political reconciliation and integration – many former rebels now occupy prominent positions at all levels and are devoting their energies to the search for resources for their districts rather than war. Their existence has reduced competition for resources at the centre and enabled a system of ethnic pluralism to operate. This reduces the scope for centralized control and manipulation (and further decentralization has many opponents as a result), and reduces ethnic competition and jealousy by giving all groups control over their own resources. It has also been crucial for the international NGOs, involved in relief and development work across the country. RCs serve as the initial point of contact with communities, and as the forum in which agreements are negotiated on procedures for the distribution of resources and the identification of beneficiaries. They have been used to organize pump maintenance, registrations for food distributions, primary health care committees and income-generating projects. Without them the agencies would have to operate through remote central ministries out of touch with local realities, or set up their own administrative structures.

RCs were set up in rebel as well as peaceful areas. This was only possible because many people continued to recognize the legitimacy of the state – in the most disturbed areas few people were prepared to stand in the first elections. Thereafter they were seen by rebels as instruments of government and many of their members were killed.

However, the fact that elections were open and ex-rebels allowed to participate made it possible for opponents of government to take part, especially after 1989. They saw RCs promote local projects and demands, where necessary against the opposition or neglect of the central ministries. Although the NURP was ultimately to be based on projects brought forward from the ministries, all the district councils were active in promoting their own interests and policies while it was being set up.

If decentralization is successfully implemented, it should, in fact, increase national integration by persuading local interests that they have the dominant role in determining the allocation of resources in their own areas. Enormous improvements are required before this becomes a reality – local administrative capacity is negligible because of a lack of skills, financial resources and supervisory capacity. Redistributive fiscal mechanisms must be put in place to ensure that resources are transferred from central funds to allow the poorest districts to provide services comparable to the richest. Central ministries must be persuaded to give up some of their authority without attempting to sabotage the system as a whole. Most important, local people must make effective use of democratic accountability to control corruption and incompetence in politicians and officials. The willingness of government to delegate authority to elected local officials has certainly been critical to the success of post-war reconciliation and reconstruction. Now a long-term process designed to consolidate and improve capacity at all levels is essential if these gains are not to be lost. This will raise new problems and challenges.

The process of political reconciliation and integration has taken place thus far in a context which has excluded direct competition between the established political parties. The President has not as yet had to compete in an election and this has allowed him to behave as a benevolent despot (some might see him as Africa's leading philosopher king), drawing in as many groups as possible and not having to serve the interets of a single party and exclude those of all others. This is possible because the NRM acts as an 'umbrella organization' rather than a party and because parties are allowed to exist, but not to campaign openly for candidates at elections. This has made it difficult for government to form a consistent approach to policy based on a coherent ideological position, and excludes the development of unified opposition movements which can present alternative strategies to the electorate and thus provide them with viable options. What it has done is to allow political notables to be elected on an individual basis (often in the knowledge that they represent one or other of the main parties) thus enabling them to criticize, but not to form a unified alternative government.

This situation has been subjected to considerable criticism from the political elite, though it appears to have widespread support in the population as a whole which fears that multi-party competition will lead to the politics of ethnic and sectarian conflict of the past. The recent history of Angola – where the defeat of UNITA in the 1992 election brought back civil war – strongly supports this view. The Constitutional Commission has now recommended that the existing system limiting overt party competition be retained for at least five years. This, of course, runs against modern democratic theory which many Ugandans fear will be imposed on the country by donors. No doubt free party competition will be the best way of organizing political democracy in the long run, but recent history suggests that great care needs to be taken before introducing it into situations still dominated by antagonistic conflict along ethnic or sectarian lines.

The Role of External Agencies

In 1986 the new regime inherited a bankrupt treasury, hyper-inflation, a large foreign debt, an unsustainable external deficit, a paralysed civil service and ruined infrastructure.

The state sector supposedly controlled the 'commanding heights' of the economy, but hardly functioned; most resources were allocated through illegal deals in the black economy so they could not be subjected to rational regulation. These problems were most acute in the war zones, but affected the whole economy. They were intensified by civil war, but were mainly the result of an institutional system which gave the political leadership access to unaccountable authority and created perverse incentives which rewarded corruption and inertia rather than performance and initiative.

The new regime could not have generated the resources and enforced the institutional changes required to rebuild economic capacity and repair past damage. The need for broad-based government made it difficult to eliminate corrupt elements and adopt policies which would reduce the arbitrary power of influential groups and individuals. Yet some form of 'structural adjustment' was inescapable. Leaving the existing structure as unchanged would have precipitated further decline and impoverished everyone not in a position to exploit the existing allocation of political or economic power. Thus growth and reconstruction depended on access to foreign aid and on the ability to ensure that resources would be used to improve services rather than be appropriated by the elite. This meant that political and economic structures – local governments, business ventures, NGOs, voluntary groups – had to be operated in such a way that they oculd be made accountable to citizens, customers and beneficiaries.

Thus reconstruction has been heavily aid dependent. Donors provide more than half of the resources required to sustain imports and finance the budget, and to deliver services in many parts of the country. Economic policy is directly subjected to external contol by the World Bank and IMF, and new initiatives in every sector depend directly on agreement from donors willing to carry the costs. Increasing debt (almost US$3 billion by mid-1993) and reduced revenues resulting from the collapse of coffee prices now means that the government cannot even find counterpart funds to back official loans or to maintain existing low levels of government spending. These weaknesses are most pronounced in the peripheral areas directly affected by civil war where local administration is almost at a standstill with pitiful salaries only paid months in arrears and no resources at all to sustain services. Thus the management of the reconstruction programme has come to depend on external agencies – multilateral and bilateral donors and NGOs – as much as that of the national government. Traditional notions of sovereignty have little relevance here, and any evaluation of outcomes must recognize that they depend as much on the judgements and performance of external as opposed to that of local political structures.

This inevitably creates serious tensions since adjustment involves fundamental changes which have direct and often negative consequences for social groups but are introduced at the behest of donors accountable only to external authorities. The latter have their own agendas, their own advisors who are often given very generous terms of service and salaries. Their local knowledge can be limited and partial, and their judgements are based on their own economic and organizational theories. They come into disrupted situations like Uganda with a strong belief in the need for change, and very limited faith in the capacity of local elites which they blame for past failures. They are not beholden to local interests and can thus demand changes which might threaten the support base of the regime. At the same time the problem of how they themselves are made to account for the adequacy of their performance has not been seriously addressed, so many believe that their position in these countries gives them power without responsibility.

Local people recognize their dependence and are grateful for the assistance they receive, but this is tempered by resentment arising from their lack of control over decisions, what appear to be the excessive rewards offered to expatriates, and the ignorance of local conditions which the latter often demonstrate. Adjustment always implies some reduction in immediate consumption to reduce fiscal and balance of payments deficits, so it always creates some resentment. While reduced consumption actually stems from the country's need to stop living beyond its means, it is attributed to the policies like devaluation and spending cuts adopted to bring this about. The fact that the reduction in consumption would have had to be greater but for the aid brought in by the structural adjustment programme often escapes notice.

Structral adjustment programmes suceed where policy ensures that activities involving irrationality and waste are cut, where they provide safety nets which reduce their impact on the poor and which enforce efficiency and accountability on institutions in all sectors. Current policy has been dominated by theorists in the World Bank and IMF, who emphasise the removal of price distortions, liberalization and privatization. This can conflict with the wishes of local regimes and lead to an adversarial process which makes policy agreement hard to reach and implement since this becomes the responsibility of the local state. Here failure may stem from the inadequacy of the policy theory imposed by donors, or from their inability to enforce it effectively because of administrative weakness or obstruction. Thus our evaluation of the reconstruction process in Uganda requires not only an assesment of the structure and role of local and international institutions, but also of the way in which they interact with each other.

In 1986 it was by no means certain that the NRM regime would be able to develop an effective relationship with the donor community. The central leadership supported socialist policies similar to those which had led the US into open conflict with the Sandinistas in Nicaragua, and which were clearly in conflict with the market-oriented thinking of the Bank and IMF. This could have held up support indefinitely, leading at worst to external aid for rebel groups in the north and long-term destabilization. Fortunately, however, the NRM leadership was more concerned with compromise than ideology and rapidly made sufficient concessions to maintain external support and incorporate conservative elements from local society. The donors began to respond, and, as the benfits of this support materialized the position of domestic policy-makers who also supported economic discipline and the market (notably in the Ministry of Planning) was strengthened. By the start of the 1990s the poor performance of parastatals and the state sector in general, growth in foreign support and the success of the overall pro-gramme had converted the President and key figures in the NRM to the new market-oriented policies, and relationships between donors and government had become extremely cordial.

There are no doubt important lessons for donors here about dealing with 'radical' regimes – a similar strategy in Nicaragua, Mozambique and Angola might well have prevented the devastating wars which reduced them to ruin.

While the relationship between external agencies and state has led to a positive growth process, there has also been much inertia and waste stemming from ineffective management on the part of the multilaterals. It took the Bank and IMF many years to get the government to remove the monopoly powers exercised by the Coffee and Cotton Marketing Boards, which have impoverished farmers, reduced exports and enriched a small clique of well-placed officials. A decision to privatize most parastatals was taken in 1988 and only implemented in 1994–5. Immense amounts of money have also been spent on consultancy reports and administration, while corrupt managements went on making losses at public expense. A new independent Revenue Authority was set up to improve tax collection, where officials were paid a 'living wage' in order to eliminate corruption. However the old staff were retained, so it is hardly surprising that the President is now claiming that little has changed.

While some donor programmes (notably the World Bank's trunk road programme) have been well-managed and completed on schedule, others have involved excessive overheads and had relatively little impact in the field. During the emergency the

16.4 *LWF ran a generally effective rehabilitation programme in northwest Uganda: a newly protected spring near Koboko, Arua district, 1990. (Tim Allen)*

multilaterals, with the exception of the World Food Programme, refused to allow their staff into the disturbed areas on security grounds although many NGOs were able to operate in less-disturbed parts of the region. Indeed the economic rationale for large-scale public food distributions in a country with a domestic food surplus and active private food marketing systems can be questioned. Had cash been given, local traders would have delivered food to them at much lower cost and beneficiaries would have transferred some of their income to other activities like education. In the northwest UNHCR has been accused of a high-handed and authoritarian approach, of persistent inefficiency and an inappropriate allocation of resources.

In some post-war situations large amounts of aid have been brought in by donors who cannot find viable local agencies to administer it. Much of it is then spent in the urban areas on immensely expensive and often not particularly effective expatriate personnel. The results are likely to be inflationary and socially damaging. In Uganda, on the other hand, the aid came in and built up gradually and there has been a relatively large supply of educated local people and an emphasis on rural development, strengthened by the existence of the RC system. This has reduced the share of the aid going to expatriates and spent on imports in Kampala. Development has been very uneven, but most areas which escaped the war have seen some of the benefits of the past few years. It seems probable that incomes of the rural poor from cash crops and wages have increased significantly since the late 1980s.[1]

International and local NGOs now play an increasingly important role in the most marginal areas. Agencies like the Lutheran World Federation, World Vision, Acord, Oxfam, Save the Children Fund, the main Churches and Médecins Sans Frontières have been prepared to operate in emergency situations which UN personnel have refused to enter on security grounds. They have provided emergency relief, health and education and are increasingly involved in long-term development programmes. While they

[1] *Uganda: growing out of poverty*, World Bank, Washington, DC, 1992.

provide a significant part of their resources from their own fund-raising activities, they are increasingly funded by large donors to manage long-term development programmes on their behalf. In many cases this involves them in managing large programmes with big staff, in others (as with Oxfam) it involves funding local partners, thus strengthening the local voluntary sector.

The use of NGOs for service delivery by donors is a reflection of their distrust of state agencies, and it further marginalizes state capacity, with negative consequences for long-term sustainability. Donors cannot afford to put all of their resources into the state sector, since supervision and accountability is so poor and capacity so weak that far less would reach the beneficiaries if they did. At the same time, it is critical that donors recognize that one of their most important responsibilities is to strengthen local institutional capacity in the state, voluntary and private sectors. This is something of which they are increasingly aware, and which takes the form of what amounts to a tutelary relationship between international NGO personnel and local institutions of all kinds – central and local state, voluntary and private.

The overall success of Uganda's development strategy has thus depended on the availability of aid (now increasingly threatened by the recession and debt servicing) and on the willingness of the government to maintain a benign regulatory environment which has allowed foreign agencies to operate without interference. This has given Uganda a greater share of the aid going to a region where political instability or intransigence in neighbouring countries is making it increasingly difficult for donors to function effectively. What is now essential is some attempt at the centre to establish a monitoring process which subjects the overall development programme to regular review and allows agencies and government to co-operate in the identification of new priorities, the elimination of waste and duplication, and the strengthening of local capacity.

The Private Sector

Institutional reform under structural adjustment emphasized the need to change the relationship between the state and the private, market-regulated sectors. This theory claims that monopoly power allocated by the state leads to inefficiency and corruption, while competition in the private sector ensures cost-effectiveness, accountability and innovation. Recent Ugandan history confirms this view, although the actual contribution to the growth of the private sector by donors has been relatively small and taken a long time to develop. A key element in the process of institutional change and development is, therefore, the way the private sector has responded to changes in the economic and regulatory environment in the recent past.

Past aid programmes mostly supported government projects; more recently they have tended to use voluntary agencies. However most services on offer in poor communities are actually provided by the private sector. Indeed, the official statistics underestimate its contribution since much of it goes unrecorded in the form of family production and activities in the illegal 'black' economy. It also encompasses activities ostensibly funded by the state, but actually paid for 'under the counter' by consumers. These enterprises have shown great resilience and enterprise in dangerous and difficult conditions. Traders continued to operate in Uganda in areas from which all outsiders were excluded; until the neighbouring economies collapsed they even operated an exchange process which linked importers in Mombasa with markets deep in Zaire and the Sudan.

Historically the private sector suffered from obstruction and neglect since the interventionist state created a regulatory regime which severely restricted its capacity to operate. It was excluded from profitable sectors (notably produce exporting) and suffered from restrictive licencing, regressive taxation, costly access to credit facilities and

16.5 *Job Taga, a local entrepreneur, outside his small shop located on the road between Adyumani town and the Nile, Moyo district, 1990. (Tim Allen)*

extortion by state agents. Price distortions (overvalued exchange rates, consumer subsidies, restrictive controls over wages and conditions of employment) marginalized and sometimes eliminated private producers where they could be effectively enforced. Indeed, the survival of the African business class has depended on the inability of the state to enforce many of the most restrictive and extractive aspects of its policy. Forex was traded on the parallel market, bribes to officials replaced taxation, smuggling broke the export monopolies of the Marketing Boards. The economic and political crisis in Uganda greatly impeded the levels of activity of small and large private producers. Output and consumption was cut by the collapse of roads, social services and law and order, the reduction in demand from urban and regional markets, and the increase in the real price of imported inputs. Yet the need to trade in order to survive produced

major changes in behaviour. The state no longer supported anyone other than the diminishing group able to manipulate official positions for personal benefit. The value of traditional export crops collapsed, and, with them the dominance of Marketing Boards and co-operatives. Farmers and traders diversified into new areas, and many of those with positions in the towns invested some of their resources in their home areas. Educated youths who would previously have joined the state went into the private sector instead. Local trade grew rapidly in all of the disturbed areas as soon as the worst threats from rebels had been removed. In 1990 cassava and sweet potatoes were being exported in large quantities to Kampala and neighbouring areas from Gulu and Teso – even as food relief was being brought into some of the latter areas by donors. A sharp rise in the international sesame price produced at the same time a rapid increase in exports from these areas.

By the late 1980s the business class had become the dominant social force in the country, and was strongly opposed to the maintenance of the interventionist system. This undoubtedly reduced political resistance to the liberalizing pressures from the donors, so many of the most restrictive aspects of policy were being reduced in the 1990s. The unofficial foreign exchange market had been legalized, export regulations had been reduced, incentives were being provided to foreign investors, the Marketing Board monopolies had been broken, and agreement had been reached on the privatization of all but a minority of parastatals. Improvements in law and order and in the road system had greatly reduced transaction and transport costs, leading to a rapid expansion in production and trade. Widespread access to land exists in all but the most crowded areas, so few people suffer from long-term food deprivation and most can obtain employment of some sort in rural labour markets. Thus real wages and welfare have almost certainly increased over the last six years, making a critical contribution to social and political stability.[2]

Too much must not be made of this, however. The productivity of local enterprises

[2] *District Management Study*, World Bank, Washington, DC, 1992.

16.6 *A co-operative group supported by LWF outside the building which houses their oil-pressing machine, near Yumbe, Arua district, 1988. (Tim Allen)*

is still abysmally low. Few firms have much capital or information so most operate with primitive equipment and produce low-valued products for saturated markets. Credit is not available to any but the small number of medium-sized firms, so activities requiring significant levels of skill and technology are excluded. Most economic growth is taking place in a very narrow area in the south (notably along the road between Iganga and Masaka), so regional inequalities are still growing. Aids and associated diseases are still spreading rapidly and claiming the lives of many of the best educated and most entrepreneurial people, leaving behind a growing army of economically dependent children. War, disease and social disruption has left many women without husbands and created a growing underclass of marginalized female-headed households. It will take many years of effective economic management to overcome these problems.

This growth in private sector activity, largely sustained by local enterprise with no external support, has made a greater contribution to the welfare of local communities than any external aid other than the repair of the trunk road system. This has restored a general belief in the possibility of progress and reduced social and political conflict. Provided the remaining legal obstacles to private sector activity can be removed and an effective credit, research and business information system be created, it seems likely that economic progress can continue, thus laying the foundation for a politically stable and socially equitable growth process.

Participatory Groups

Many participatory groups of diverse kinds have emerged in Uganda outside both the state and private sectors. Their role is widely supported as a way of mobilizing community action and enabling people to play a role in setting priorities and participating in project implementation. They are often supported by donors, notably by international

16.7 *Taking a break from distributing relief items, Luwero, 1986. (Ben Male/Oxfam)*

NGOs concerned to 'empower' the poor and increase cooperation and social solidarity. In Uganda their role has been particularly important in education, where elected parent teacher associations have become a critical factor in school management. They have also played an important role in the health sector where a large number of community based health care associations have been set up to provide primary health care, often in association with local mission hospitals. Local church management is also carried out on a voluntary basis, as are a wide range of social and developmental activities. Donors are now increasingly using them for income generation and rural credit provision and have preferred to support co-operative rather than private enterprise on the grounds that it produces more equitable results.

These processes are relatively new and it is only now that attempts are being made to evaluate their success and thus the effectiveness of the participatory approach as a whole. There is little doubt that the approach has drawn many people into collective activities, strengthened the capacity for social organization and provided cost-effective services which the state could no longer manage. However, the approach has not always produced the results expected of it, and its supporters need to take account of some serious problems which can arise if it is given uncritical support. Many income-generating projects fail because of ineffective management, lack of attention to markets, conflicts or corruption. Volunteers often lose their commitment because of the need to provide for their families, and projects collapse. Only the most active and best educated people in communities are able to take part, so programmes which depend on demo-cratic participation tend to exclude the poorest and worst educated, thus increasing rather than reducing inequalities.

Care therefore needs to be taken in the choice of projects, in developing effective management and incentive structures within groups, and to ensure that they are not given a 'soft budget constraint' by donors and thus allowed to use resources inefficiently. Where private 'one person management' is likely to provide more efficent services ideological resistance should not lead donors to support inefficient co-operatives instead. Ultimately we must recognize that an effective development strategy will depend on using the type of institution best fitted to perform particular tasks, rather than any one type to the exclusion of all others.

Conclusions

This rapid appraisal of recent Ugandan experience confirms the critical importance of 'getting the institutions right' if political conflict and economic decay is to be overcome. Thus we can now conclude by summarizing some of the key changes which have sustained the development process there, and which should be given careful consideration by other countries confronting similar problems.

The ending of civil war and development of a capacity to work for national unity has required a regime willing to negotiate with its enemies and incorporate as wide a range of interests into the central decision-making process as possible. It has also depended on the establishment of a local government system which has given local activists a strong focus for their energies.

A co-operative alliance between government, official donors, foreign and local NGOs has allowed a slow and incomplete, but nevertheless progressive process of reconciliation and reconstruction to be maintained despite an increasingly hostile external economic environment. Although this process has generated significant increases in output and in institutional capacity, it is not likely to be financially or administratively self-sustaining for many years given the weakness of international raw material prices and slow progress in restoring the integrity of the state apparatus. Thus progress will only continue if external funding can be sustained for many years, and for as long as no attempt is made to marginalize any significant social or political group.

Private enterprise has played a key role in sustaining services and generating incomes. This initially occurred despite official constraints designed to undermine these activities, but which were not effectively enforced. More recently the environment has been greatly improved with the elimination of some of the most restrictive regulations. However, the official privatization programme is only now achieving visible results and has been enormously costly. While constraints on private sector activities have been released, very little positive support, especially for small enterprises, has yet been made available.

Political and economic crisis followed by reconstruction has produced a great increase in social committment, with hundreds of thousands of people working voluntarily for social institutions of all kinds. Local government, schools, health care, churches, and some economic activities depend on this labour and provide communities with an array of services which would not be available if they had to be paid for on a full-cost basis. While the value of these services must be recognized, however, more effort needs to be devoted to ensuring that the agencies involved receive greater technical backing, and that those who perform them are provided with the incentives and training necessary to ensure effective performance.

While development theory in the past has tended to emphasise the value of one type of organization rather than another – state *versus* market, private *versus* collective – the Ugandan experience suggests that the best results occur when a combination of organizational forms are used. The problem is not to try to allow the state to take over the private sector, or to privatize all the activities now performed by the state. It is equally misleading to assume that voluntary groups will always produce more equitable results than private firms. The need is to recognize the different kinds of contributions which can be made by different kinds of organization, and to use those which perform particular functions best on the basis of a constant process of trial and error in the field.

17

TIM ALLEN
Incorporating Testimonies by Ronald Iya, Zacharia Eno & Others
A Flight from Refuge

The Return of Refugees from southern Sudan
to northwest Uganda in the late 1980s

Introduction

This chapter draws on some 20 months of fieldwork carried out in northwest Uganda over a five-year period (1987–92). It is concerned with the experiences of Ugandan returnees from southern Sudan, focussing in particular on what happened to those who repatriated between mid-1986 and early 1987. Virtually all of these people had been living to the east of the River Nile in Sudan since the early 1980s, and most of them subsequently settled in Uganda's Moyo District. Reference is also made to the repatriation of Ugandans who returned from the area to the west of the Nile in Sudan between 1987 and 1989, most of whom settled in Uganda's Arua District.

During the late 1980s, UNHCR became active in efforts to provide assistance to the returned population of northwest Uganda, running its own programmes as well as attempting to co-ordinate several international NGOs, most of which it partly funded. The fact that the UNHCR itself became an operational agency was unusual, but its role has been hailed as a notable achievement. In September 1988 a report on the repatriation exercise by the UNHCR Technical Support Service made the following assertion:

> By mid-1989, it is estimated that a cumulative total of almost 350,000 will have returned. The operation which amounted by end [of] 1988 to an estimated expenditure of almost US$15 million (i.e. US$40 per capita) over three years, will have been globally successfully implemented [sic] by UNHCR, LWF [Lutheran World Federation] and the local ministry of rehabilitation with maximum internal inputs in terms of human resources and minimum 'transit' infrastructure in reception centres. This success, due to a proper planning of the operation at [an] early stage and to an efficient management/monitoring on daily basis [sic], is all the more commendable as the working conditions were difficult (shortages of fuel, spare parts, insecurity etc.). *The strategy adopted in this operation should serve as a model for future similar operations subject, of course, to the appropriate adaptions to the local context.*
> (UNHCR Technical Support Services, Mission Report 55/88, Geneva: iii, emphasis added)

It is certainly true that a large number of refugees did move back into northwest Uganda in the late 1980s. It is also the case that, where investigation was attempted, the kinds of public health problems associated with sudden mass migrations in Africa were considered to have been contained. Thus I am concerned here with an instance of assisted repatriation which has been presented as a success story, even an example to emulate in comparable circumstances elsewhere.

However, in private some UNHCR and NGO staff were less enthusiastic about what had occurred. They recognized that the assistance effort had in fact been largely ineffective. Indeed, one senior staff member of the Lutheran World Federation (LWF) programme commented to me in 1988 that, 'if people have not starved, it has only been

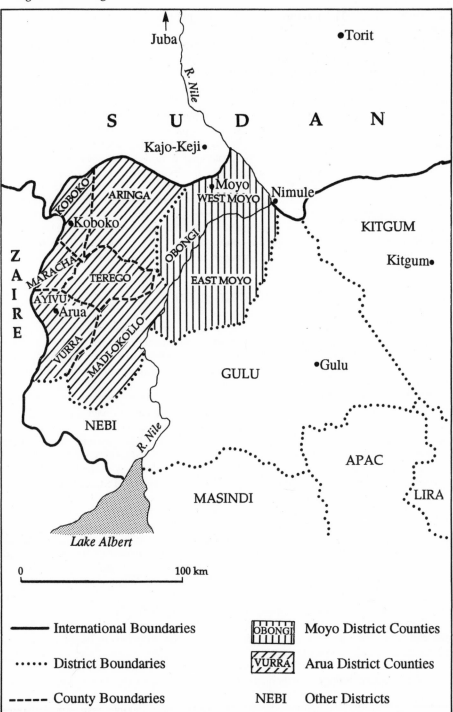

Map 17.1 *Northwest Uganda in the 1980s*

a matter of luck'. The interpretation of events presented here can be summarized as follows:

There was not much that was 'voluntary' about this repatriation. Most Ugandans remained refugees as long as they could, and only returned to Uganda when the war in Sudan made their continued residence impossible. Back in Uganda life was difficult. Economic activity was restricted (particularly in Moyo District), and the security situation has remained unpredictable into the 1990s. The relief effort mounted by UNHCR and other international aid agencies was of limited help, and Ugandan state services were inadequate. In Moyo District it took several years for agricultural production to reach a point whereby most families had enough to eat, and many people had to rely on gathered 'famine' foods for prolonged periods. That they survived as individuals and as groups reflected a remarkable capacity to make ends meet in sometimes extreme circumstances. From a local point of view, an important aspect of such circumstances was the fraught and sometimes violent business of allocating social accountability or, to put it another way, of creating and maintaining moral relationships within communities. These interpersonal tensions were poorly understood by relief and development workers, and rendered a considerable portion of their activities tangential to the everyday concerns of the supposed beneficiaries.

PART ONE: Flight and Repatriation

This part provides some historical background, as well as a general overview of the situation in the borderlands of northwest Uganda and southern Sudan during the 1980s. It is necessary to describe a confusing series of overlapping migrations, because it is the context within which people living in the region make decisions about their future. For the sake of brevity I resort to certain simplifications. These need to be noted at the outset.

I use the terms 'refugee' and 'returnee' for groups that have moved across the border in large numbers, and which have usually been recognized as 'refugees' or 'returnees' by aid agencies and governments. But the application of such labels may be more a matter of interpretation than is readily apparent. Although these are expressions which have taken on a local resonance, they are nevertheless introductions. Sometimes they may relate less to indigenous perceptions than to the formulations and strategies of outsiders.

For example, the head of the UNHCR operation in northwest Uganda in 1988 referred to self-settled Sudanese migrants as 'illegal immigrants'. There were several reasons for choosing to use this phrase: (1) refusing to recognize a group as refugees was a means of avoiding pressures form the Ugandan government to move them into official transit camps and regulated settlements (where they would have to be provided with food and water); (2) the UNHCR field office was fully occupied coping with the influxes of returnees; (3) it was suspected that some of those calling themselves 'refugees' were really 'returnees' trying to claim a special status; (4) using a provocative designation was a way of teasing young and inexperienced international NGO staff.

The categorization of people as 'refugees' and 'returnees' (and 'stayees') can also be misleading in that it deflects attention from the fact that populations have been moving about in this part of the upper Nile for a long time. As we shall see, migration has historically been an integral part of surviving, and of shaping collective identity – something which leads to further ambiguities. I have used the terms 'Ugandan' and 'Sudanese' here, and also employed conventional ethnic labels like 'Madi', 'Lugbara' and 'Acholi', but both nationality and ethnicity are far more flexible than outsiders often assume. I have met many individuals who have switched between these and other ascriptions in order to secure resources for themselves and their families. Where it seems

17.1 *There was not much that was 'voluntary' about this repatriation: returnees at Arinyapi reception centre, May 1986. (M. Barton/UNHCR)*

most relevant in the chapter, I draw attention to these complexities. However, I am unable to do them full justice in this context, and interested readers are directed to some of my other writings (Allen, 1991b, 1991c, 1994).

Historical Background

There is nothing new about mass movements in the border region between the modern states of Sudan and Uganda. When old people are asked to tell the stories of their lineage, they do not talk of ancestors buried since time began near the places their families now farm. Rather they describe the past in terms of movement from one place to another. Commonly these movements occurred to avoid fighting. Many tales mention attacks by Moslem raiders armed with guns, who stole cattle and took young women away as 'wives'. In the second half of the nineteenth century, the lands near the Nile were occupied successively by the marauding private armies of slave and ivory traders, by Turco-Egyptian forces, and finally by troops under Belgian or British employment. Local people either became clients or took refuge over mountain ranges, in deep forests or by crossing to whichever was the safer side of the river.

It is hard to ascertain what life was like before these violent incursions from outside the area. Ethnic identities and language groups had no doubt always been fluid, but by the turn of the century most groups living in the vicinity of the Nile were of diverse origin. They all appear to have been exogamous, patrilocal clans. Although a person would often need to trace descent through his or her mother's line, as a collectivity a clan or patrilineage recognized an eponymous male ancestor and traced descent from him in the male line from father to son. Male children were expected to remain in their father's village, while females left the parental home at marriage. In exchange for bridewealth, a

17.2 *Old people describe the past in terms of movement: a clan elder, Laropi, 1988. (Tim Allen)*

woman would go to live in the village of her husband, and would eventually be thought of as part of his clan, particularly after she had given birth to male children. A couple were not supposed to marry unless it could be shown that there was no close kinship link between any of their parents. The combination of population movements and this necessity to marry outside of clan groups meant that multi-lingualism was the norm.

Although ethnic labels were used by invading forces during the nineteenth century, they were applied in a vague way. It was not really until the time of the First World War that the present day 'tribal' identities began to be formalized and regulated. This was done partly by the creation of administrative districts which were supposed to have tribal boundaries. As part of a British colonial policy of indirect rule, populations were registered as belonging to a particular tribe, and placed under government controlled 'traditional' chiefs. Movement of lineages between chiefdoms was subsequently discouraged, and movement was further restricted by the boundary agreement of 1914. Following the withdrawal of Belgian forces from the territory to the west of the Nile in 1909, it was decided to adjust the border between what was at that time the British Protectorate of Uganda and the Anglo-Egyptian Condominium of the Sudan. The line eventually agreed upon was known to have divided closely related populations, including the various patrilineages which were being systematized into the tribal identities known as Acholi and Madi. Nonetheless, it was considered a necessary step for ease of administration, and as colonial government became more intensive, border crossing was controlled (partly as a means of limiting the spread of sleeping sickness). From this time the population on either side of the border found themselves on the receiving end of increasingly divergent colonial policies.

In northern Uganda from the 1920s, the original emphasis on indirect rule through supposedly 'traditional' chiefs was gradually set aside. Chiefs became local-level civil servants. Cotton and tobacco were introduced as cash crops, and young men were encouraged to migrate in search of work on the farms or in the industries of the south. Many others joined the army, police or prison services, and the educated looked for jobs as teachers or managers. By the time of independence in 1962, much of the population of northern Uganda was a commoditized peasantry. Families were concerned to raise money for manufactured goods, taxes and school fees, and depended on the provision of basic government services as part of their way of life.

In southern Sudan during the same period, events took a different course. Instead of being abandoned, indirect rule became a basic tenet of the condominium administration. In the 1920s fears of Moslem influence spreading up the Nile Valley prompted the government to introduce the so called 'Southern Policy'. This reinforced the authority of 'traditional' chiefs and discouraged movement and economic activity in the southern Sudan as a whole. Attempts were made to change the strategy in the last decade of Anglo-Egyptian rule, but at independence in 1956, southern Sudan still lacked even the basic infrastructure that had been built up in neighbouring territories. For example, the entire region had only one secondary school.

17.3 *'Why we fled our home' by Drale Thomas, a student at Metu secondary school.*

Such conservative administrative policies prompted some people living close to the border to travel south in search of work and other opportunities. Several years before Sudanese independence, migrants made their way into Uganda where most of them were readily absorbed into the economy. These movements increased from the mid-1950s following army mutinees in southern Sudan and the outbreak of the first Sudanese civil war. As fighting between southern Sudanese Anyanya guerrillas and the Sudanese national army escalated during the following decade, thousands more crossed the border as refugees. Many of these later migrants were located in refugee settlements such as the one at Onigo, near Obongi in Moyo District, which had a registered population of 4,845 in 1969.

In the early 1970s two events occurred causing population movements in the opposite direction. In 1971, Idi Amin seized power in Uganda and in 1972 the Addis Ababa Agreement ended the fighting in Sudan. Peace at home, combined with the hostility of Amin's regime to ethnic groups such as the Acholi, which had been linked with the ousted government of Milton Obote, prompted many of the Sudanese to re-patriate. Between 1972 and 1974 an estimated 78,000 Sudanese left Uganda. However, others, were associated with factions close to the Amin regime (Kuku, Kakwa, Madi and Bari speakers, and 'Nubian' Moslems), and some of these chose to remain behind. A few of them became prominent figures in Amin's administration and armed forces.

This second group of Sudanese in Uganda only returned to Sudan after the invasion of Uganda by Tanzanian forces together with the Uganda National Liberation Army (UNLA) in 1979. Their repatriation had a considerable impact on southern Sudanese politics, because many were relatively well educated and some had experience of senior positions. They tended to become antagonistic to less educated southern Sudanese who had established themselves in important posts in what had become Sudan's autonomous Southern Region (as a consequence of the Addis Ababa Agreement of 1972) (Allen, 1989a).

Various factions opened up in southern Sudanese politics, which increasingly became polarized between, on the one hand, the 'Nilotics' (including many of the prominent Dinka, the largest ethnic group in southern Sudan), and on the other hand the 'Equatorians', who sought to divide up the Southern Region so that the area in the far south could escape 'Dinka domination' and make better use of its supposedly more 'progressive' population. These antagonisms played a significant part in the drift back to full-scale war in Sudan.

The Flight of Ugandans to Sudan in 1980

When the Tanzanian army supported by the UNLA successfully overthrew Amin in 1979, thousands of Ugandans from northwest Uganda crossed the border into Sudan. They feared that the invading soldiers would go on the rampage because the northwest was Amin's home area. When this did not happen, most returned home. However, the security situation in northwest Uganda quickly deteriorated during 1980. Tanzanian troops were withdrawn, and former soldiers in Amin's army launched an offensive. The UNLA was displaced from Arua town in October 1980 and heavy fighting ensued.

In December, allegedly rigged elections brought Obote back to power and constraints on the activities of UNLA soldiers appear to have been lifted. Obote himself is supposed to have asserted that he would drive the population out of northwest Uganda and turn the region into a game reserve. Atrocities were perpetrated against civilians and people were forced to flee their homes. As in the 'Luwero Triangle' near Kampala, normal life became impossible. But the overall number of people who were killed was probably less than in Luwero, because it was possible for the population of the northwest to escape. Some people moved to the environs of the Catholic missions at the main towns (where their sanctuary seems to have been respected most of the time), or hid in the forests and hills, and perhaps a quarter of a million others became refugees, the vast majority in Sudan.

Many of the refugees were from the same ethnic groups as supporters of the 'Equatoria' faction in southern Sudanese politics, and they looked to influential 'Equatorians' for patronage and support. Joseph Lagu, the former Anyanya commander and now a leading 'Equatorian', was himself a Madi, the ethnic group of people from Moyo District, and publicly welcomed the Ugandans as his 'brothers'. Not surprisingly the influx of returnees and refugees from Uganda was a cause of concern for Lagu's political opponents, many of whom were associated with the so-called 'Dinka' or 'Nilotic' faction, which had tended to dominate southern Sudanese politics during the 1970s, and remained very important in the early 1980s.

The plethora of aid agencies that became involved in refugee assistance in southern Sudan found themselves in a political minefield. The Southern Region was being increasingly starved of funds by Khartoum, tensions were rising over the issue of administrative redivision, and the conflicts between southern politicians were being manipulated by northern Sudanese political groups. It soon became impossible to help refugees without appearing to make a statement of support for one faction, and provoking resentment, distrust and antagonism from the others. At the same time, it was rarely clear who an international aid agency's national implementing partner ought to be, and to a degree remarkable even in Africa, expatriate-run organizations became a law unto themselves.

The Ugandan Refugees in Sudan During the Early 1980s

Most of the Ugandan refugees settled to the west of the Nile in Sudan. 93,000 were settled in 29 camps and perhaps 70,000 were self-settled among the local Sudanese. I am

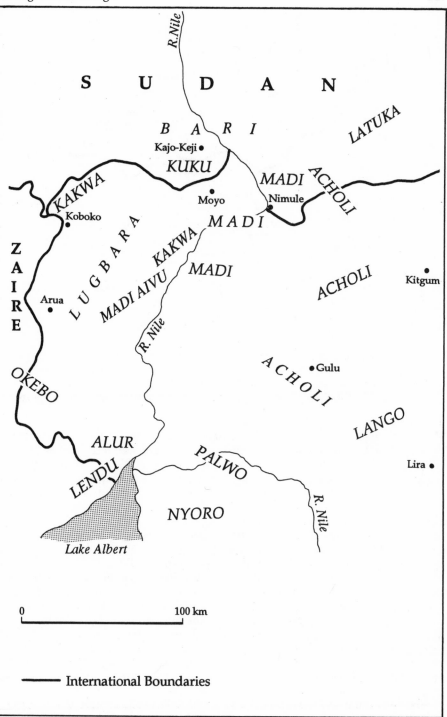

Map 17.2 *Ethnic groups of northwest Uganda*

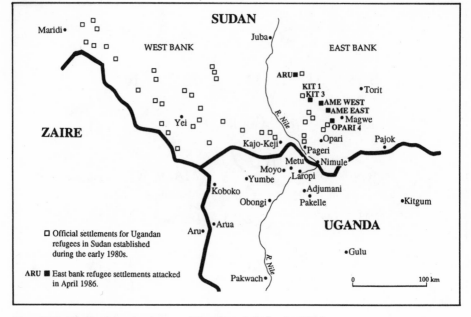

Map 17.3 *The border region between Uganda and Sudan in 1986*

going to refer to this group as the 'West Bank' refugees. A smaller population of Ugandans settled to the east of the Nile. I refer to these as the 'East Bank' refugees. There were about 33,500 living in 17 official camps, and up to 10,000 self-settled. Circumstances in exile for the West Bank and East Bank refugees differed in several respects.

West Bank Refugees

West Bank refugees were from all three of the main ethnic/tribal groups of northwest Uganda: Madi, Lugbara and Kakwa. Their experiences have been recounted by Harrell-Bond, based on research carried out in 1982–3 (Harrell-Bond, 1986). She argues that the efforts of international aid agencies to assist the Ugandans were implemented, or rather 'imposed', in an unprofessional manner, largely by expatriates who failed to draw upon the skills of the refugees or the Sudanese. She also highlights the counter-productive competition and ridiculous bickering that went on between aid agencies. In her view, the assumption that the vast majority of the refugees were going to subsist as farmers was a misconception, because 'many households were unlikely ever to be capable of supporting themselves through agriculture' (Harrell-Bond, 1986: xiv). She maintains that those refugees who had managed to make their lives reasonably comfortable at the time of her fieldwork had done so in spite of the relief effort rather than because of it.

If we accept this interpretation of the situation during the early 1980s, then it is clear that things subsequently improved. Whatever the limitations of the aid programmes, West Bank refugee families did become self-sufficient in food production and many began producing a surplus for sale in Yei or Kajo Keji markets. By the mid-1980s refugees living on the West Bank had so little interest in returning to Uganda that they remained in Sudan until fighting between guerrillas and government forces spread to the immediate vicinity of their farms and homesteads.

When they did finally leave, between 1987 and 1989, families tended to repatriate in stages. Reluctant to give up their well-established livelihoods in Sudan, and wary of the situation in Uganda, people kept their options open for as long as possible. Those with the opportunity to do so returned via official reception centres more than once. They did this in order to take advantage of UNHCR facilities in bringing back belongings and in order to receive multiple allocations of any available relief food and goods. Others travelled back to Uganda under their own devices, often after physically strong family members had first been to see what the situation was like, and had started to clear fields and rebuild homes. A large number used bicycles bought in Sudan to transport seeds, cuttings and valuables.

East Bank Refugees

Virtually all the East Bank refugees were Madis. Many of then fled in early 1980 and initially located themselves near the border town of Nimule, where the local people were also Madis. However, unlike many West Bank refugees, they did not remain self-settled for long. Most of them agreed to move to official refugee settlements. There were several reasons why they were willing to do so, including the fact that there were few unused places to farm in Sudan's Madi county which were close enough to a permanent water supply. The land was also generally less fertile than in parts of the West Bank. Perhaps another factor attracting the refugees to the official settlements was that some of the incompetence noted by Harrell-Bond in the activities of international aid agencies on the West Bank was avoided. The UNHCR entered into an agreement with Norwegian Church Aid (NCA), making this NGO its main implementing partner for the whole East Bank refugee programme. This meant that aid activities were not so affected by antagonisms between expatriate-run development agencies trying to run projects in the same place.

NCA was already running a huge integrated rural development programme, employing hundreds of local people, and scores of Norwegian nationals. Indeed it was sometimes referred to as 'the government of East Bank'. It tried to keep a balance between what was done in the refugee settlements and what was done in neighbouring locations, something which was important because the attitude of many locals towards the Ugandan Madis was quite hostile. The lack of available arable land in Sudanese Madi county meant that many of the refugees ended up being settled in previously un-cultivated places at the edge of Sudan's Acholi county. Here the population was more sympathetic to Obote and the UNLA than to refugees associated with Amin's administration.

Many of the Acholi in Sudan had returned from Uganda in the 1970s following the persecutions of Acholi speakers in Uganda under Amin. The Madi refugees of the East Bank were consequently quite isolated, dependent on NCA to maintain their pumped water supply and other services, and to buy their seeds via the Torit District Co-operative Union (which was in effect run by NCA). This situation made them very vulnerable when the security situation in southern Sudan deteriorated. Unlike the West Bank refugees, they were forced to repatriate suddenly *en masse* in 1986, leaving behind most of their crops, animals and other possessions.

The Repatriation of East Bank Refugees in 1986

Following the apparent success of the 'Equatoria' lobby and the division of Sudan's autonomous Southern Region in May 1983 into three smaller regions (Bahr-el-Ghazal, Upper Nile and Equatoria), the Sudan People's Liberation Army (SPLA) was formed by supporters of the 'Nilotic' or 'Dinka' faction. Although it subsequently sought to gain support in all parts of Sudan, antagonism continued with some groups in 'Equatoria'. The Madi were one of these groups, which explains why such a large proportion of the Sudanese Madi became refugees in Uganda when the SPLA managed to take control of their home area.

SPLA DISTARBING PEOPLE

17.4 *'The SPLA distarbing people' in the East bank refugee settlements, drawn by Itsara L, a primary school teacher working in Moyo district.*[1]

The activities of the SPLA began to affect the East Bank in 1984. The movements of expatriate aid agency staff were restricted due to the dangers of being kidnapped by the guerrillas, and it was no longer possible to travel freely between Juba and Torit without security clearance. Then in January 1985 the SPLA launched an offensive south of Torit. They met resistance from regular government forces and also from local militia which had been armed and persuaded that the SPLA incursions were in effect a Dinka invasion.

The fighting did not at this stage affect the refugee settlements directly, but the NCA expatriate staff were evacuated and, following an SPLA withdrawal, only a handful returned to maintain the programme, keeping their movements to a minimum. The refugees soon found themselves in a worryingly exposed position, without adequate monitoring by the NCA, let alone the UNHCR office in Juba. When Museveni's National Resistance Army (NRA) took power in Uganda the following year, individuals from the camps made visits to their former homes to establish what the situation was like. Having recognized that Uganda was safer than Sudan, some had decided to repatriate in 1986 once their crops had been harvested. But unfortunately they had to flee south before doing so.

It has been mentioned that several of the East Bank refugee settlements were located among the Sudanese Acholi. Like neighbouring East Bank ethnic/tribal groups, they had been encouraged by Equatorian political leaders to view the Dinka with distrust, and Acholi militia participated in the resistance to the SPLA in 1985. However, Acholi attitudes towards the Dinka were not straightforward. The Acholi language is itself a Nilotic tongue and a distant relationship is acknowledged with other Nilotic-speaking ethnic groups. Moreover, when the SPLA launched another offensive in 1986, some of the guerrillas had come from Lafon, a place located north of Torit where the population speaks Pari, a Nilotic language which is mutually intelligible with Acholi. This encouraged some Sudanese Acholi to join the SPLA, and collaborate in raids on the East Bank refugee settlements. In addition it is possible that Ugandan Acholi soldiers from the former UNLA, who crossed into Sudan following the ousting of Okello by Museveni's forces in January 1986 (see below), may have participated in the attacks.

During 1986, the SPLA's strategy seems to have been to remove the Ugandan refugees from Sudan's East Bank before they had harvested their crops. The aim was to secure a food supply for their operations close to the Uganda border without alienating the local Sudanese population. They therefore played upon the resentment of Sudanese living close to refugee camps who, in spite of NCA's efforts to be even-handed, felt that the Ugandans had received more than their fair share of foreign aid. Perhaps a score of refugees were killed, and the rest terrorised. Because of their lack of contact with the camps, UNHCR and NCA were not in a position to monitor the situation, let alone provide protection, and the refugees felt they had no option but to abandon their farms.

---

[1] It is interesting to note that the SPLA in this picture are shown wearing a kind of straw hat associated with supporters of the 'Equatoria' faction, some of whom had been armed by the Sudan government and employed as Militia. The artist seems to be making the point that one group of armed raiders is much the same as another.

Ronald Iya's Account of the East Bank Repatriation

Ronald Iya, a Ugandan who had been employed by UNHCR, has described events in a report he wrote in English. His story was corroborated by others, and explains why the repatriation from the East Bank was so disorganized.

> The [East Bank] refugees were preparing to repatriate towards the end of 1986, following the harvest, but these efforts were frustrated when the SPLA started attacking the settlements. Trouble started on 3rd April, when the SPLA were sighted around Ame East settlement. On 5th April, Joseph Kebulu a Sudanese national and a member of Parliament [the Regional Assembly in Juba] was killed and an NCA pickup was taken by the SPLA. On 16th April, Aru settlement was attacked by the SPLA. Nobody was killed but the property of refugees was looted. On 20th April, Kit 1 settlement was also attacked and from that day the Juba-Nimule road stopped being used. On 21st April, Ame East and Ame West settlements were attacked. Four refugees were killed and four children were lost and never found. On 23rd April, Opari 4 was also attacked. Properties were looted and houses burned, but nobody was killed. On the next day, Kit 3 settlement was attacked. Three refugees and a Sudanese national were killed, and another refugee disappeared.
>
> Each time these attacks occurred refugees sent a delegation to the Project Management of Refugee Affairs at Pageri. The Project Manager was a Sudanese national called Izakiel Walle. He refused to go to the settlements to assess the situation. I was at that time the Assistant Refugees Supervisor, and was sent to find out what was happening. I gave a full report, but the Project Manager would not take action, saying that I had exaggerated because I was a Ugandan. Yet he would not go to the scene himself. His real reason was that he realized that if the refugees repatriated he would loose his well paid job, which is actually what happened in the end.
>
> On 25th April, refugees from all the settlements arrived in Pageri on foot, demanding help to repatriate. The place quickly became congested, but the Project Manager still refused to inform the UNHCR office in Juba of what was happening. On the 28th April, he was forced to do so by the refugees, sending a radio message in their presence to Margaret, who was head of the UNHCR Sub-Office in Juba. She responded by sending Michael Kotevu, a refugee working as an accountant for UNHCR in Juba, to find out what was going on. Right from Aru, the first settlement on the way from Juba, he found the road filled by refugees walking to Pageri. He picked up a few children who could no longer walk in his landrover, and brought them to Pageri. He took back a full report to Margaret, who sent six lorries to help with transport on the 30th April. Two of these lorries were destroyed in a SPLA ambush on the way to Pageri. The others started to transport the refugees on the 1st May, and on the 2nd some more lorries arrived from Uganda to speed the exercise. Meanwhile many refugees decided not to wait for vehicles, but returned to Uganda on foot.

Northwest Uganda 1986–90

This section takes up the story from the Ugandan side of the border. The majority of the returnees from Sudan's East Bank set about establishing small family farms in Uganda's Moyo District. Part Two examines aspects of their lives following repatriation in some detail. Here I provide a background to that discussion. I outline political developments in Uganda during the late 1980s and discuss the security problems confronting the returnees. I also review the subsequent population movements in the region, both into Moyo District and into neighbouring Arua District, where most of the returnees from Sudan's West Bank eventually settled.

The Security Situation

In the year before the East Bank refugees fled back to Uganda, Obote had lost power in a coup to Okello, an Acholi army officer. But Okello never managed to establish himself, and Yoweri Museveni's National Resistance Army (NRA) took Kampala in January 1986. The Okello regime had sought reconciliation in northwestern Uganda, so when the NRA took over there was initially fear that the security situation would again deteriorate. However the subsequent occupation of the region took place peacefully with the compliance of the Uganda National Relief Front (the guerrilla organization which had been most active in West Nile against the UNLA).

Until locals were recruited, the NRA soldiers tended to be from the south of the country, and were not always well disposed towards the population. They were also very poorly paid, and were tempted to demand food and other commodities at cheap rates, as well as to become involved in informal border trading (sometimes in looted items). On several occasions NRA soldiers demanded resources from the international aid agencies which were trying to assist the returnees. In 1986 five UNHCR trucks were commandeered, which completely immobilized the relief effort for some time. Complaints were made at the highest level but, in the following year, attempts were again made to take over UNHCR trucks, and three trucks were taken from other agencies operating in Arua District. On more than one occasion development projects had to be stopped because of fears that the army would take equipment.

In addition, by the end of 1989, virtually every aid agency working in northwest Uganda had had at least one car stolen by 'bandits'. It became apparent that army officers had actually been involved in collaborating with these armed robbers to sell the vehicles in Zaire. The ambushes associated with this operation often involved the use of guns, and people were occasionally killed. Drunk soldiers also sometimes acted in extremely violent ways. On one occasion a grenade was thrown into a crowded dance at a community centre, and on another a man accused of stealing a chicken was tortured to death. However, attempts were made to stop such incidents, and in the last mentioned case the two culprits were publicly executed in Moyo town.

More worrying than the behaviour of NRA soldiers were the incursions from Gulu District by the Uganda People's Democratic Army (UPDA) and the so-called 'Holy Spirit Movement'. The latter was a kind of millenarian cult led by spirit mediums, the most prominent of whom were Alice Lakwena and Joseph Kony. These groups were in large part formed by disaffected Acholi soldiers who had fled from the south of the country when Museveni had taken power. They fought guerrilla war against the NRA in Gulu and Kitgum Districts during 1986 and 1987 (Allen, 1991a; Behrend, 1991). The UPDA eventually surrendered, but the Holy Spirit Movement continued to operate on a reduced scale following the defeat of Alice's army in late 1987. Attacks were made on Pakelle and Adjumani towns in East Moyo County in 1989, with the expatriate head of the UNHCR refugee programme being captured on one occasion (he was subsequently released unharmed). Joseph Kony remains at large, and occasional raids are still being launched into rural parts of the county. In the mid-1990s there have been rumours that Kony is receiving weapons from the Sudan government. There have, in addition, been numerous incursions from Sudan. Apart from small-scale raids, a large section of the SPLA crossed into Moyo District in December 1989 and Sudan government forces did so in January 1990. In November 1989 and again in February 1990, Moyo town was bombed from the air in apparent retaliation for alleged NRA support for the SPLA. Such incidents have continued in the 1990s.

Quite apart from fears about personal safety, these events have discouraged investment and have made trade difficult because the roads to Kampala have so often been closed. They have also hampered the work of the local administration just as much as they limited the effectiveness of international aid agencies. Under these circumstances, it is not entirely surprising that the UNHCR-run repatriation programme was sometimes chaotic. Attempts to register the Ugandans on arrival and provide a few relief items were largely unsuccesful.

Population Movements
At the end of 1986, the UNHCR had registered 109,771 returnees in Moyo District following the repatriation from Sudan's East Bank. This is an extraordinary figure, more

than double the East Bank refugee population. It is clear that some returnees had gained considerable experience in dealing with international agencies, and manipulated the registration system as much as possible in the hope of obtaining more assistance. Informants explained to me that it was easy to register children with different parents, and it was possible to purchase pre-stamped registration forms. It is unlikely that the actual number of Ugandans repatriating in 1986 was in excess of 40,000.

As has been noted above, the repatriation from Sudan's West Bank was a much slower process. This reflected the SPLA's more gradual advance to the west of the Nile, but it is also worth noting that there was considerable suspicion about any UNHCR encouragement to leave Sudan. The West Bank refugees were sceptical about reports that the situation had improved in Uganda. In the early 1980s, the Obote administration had tried to lure refugees back, and had received UNHCR support (Crisp, 1986; Harrell-Bond, 1986). Some of those who had returned from the West Bank had been killed. Now people were determined to stay where they were until they were sure that the situation in Uganda was at least safer than Sudan.

During a 30-month period between 1987 and 1989, most of the refugees living in official West Bank settlements were transported in convoys organized by the UNHCR. In the meantime, the large number of self-settled West Bank refugees found their own way home. UNHCR estimated that by June 1988 a cumulative total of almost 350,000 Ugandans had returned to Arua and Moyo Districts mainly from the West Bank (some also returned from Zaire). Again this is surely an overestimate. Based on house to house surveys I supervised in 1988 and the the 1991 Uganda census figures, it seems reasonable to guess that the total number of returnees to Arua and Moyo Districts between 1987 and 1989 was around 200,000.

However, the overall population movement was larger than this, because the activities of the SPLA also displaced a large number of Sudanese. Apart from escaping the fighting itself, Sudanese refugees arriving in Uganda during the late 1980s stated that they feared being persecuted by the guerrilla forces or being forcibly drafted into their ranks.

About 3,000 Sudanese refugees crossed the border in 1986 together with the Ugandan returnees from the East Bank. After months in transit camps, in March 1987 they were located at an official settlement in eastern Moyo District. These were the only formally recognized refugees at the time, but it was estimated that there were some 15,000 more self-settled close to the border in West Moyo County. In 1988 the number of self-settled refugees grew, and under Ugandan government pressure a transit camp was set up in East Moyo County to accommodate them. By 1989 it had a population of 30,000, but thousands of other Sudanese managed to avoid being rounded up, either by shifting back and forth across the border in relatively remote places, or by settling among Ugandan friends and relatives. There was an estimated refugee population of 60,000 in northwestern Uganda in mid-1991. In January 1992, 200 people per day were being officially registered, with this number dropping to around 150 people per day in March. The overall refugee population had risen to around 70,000 by the middle of the year and has subsequently remained at about the same level (although thousands more Sudanese refugees have crossed into Uganda further to the east).

PART TWO: The Returnees in Moyo District

This part of the chapter focusses on developments in one district of northwestern Uganda, Moyo District. Almost all the East Bank refugees who returned in 1986 and early 1987 settled in this district. For comparative purposes, some remarks are also made about the situation in Arua District, where most of the West Bank refugees settled following their return in 1987–9.

Moyo District

Uganda's Moyo District is an area of 5,006 sq km, of which about 4,668 sq km is land (the land area varies, depending on the level of the White Nile). It is divided into three counties: West Moyo, East Moyo and Obongi. Much of the population is concentrated in the first two. East Moyo County forms a plain to the east of the Nile. The other counties lie to the west of the river and are more mountainous. Mount Otzi, located to the north of Laropi rises to 1,565 metres.

According to a house to house survey I supervised in 1988, the total population up to the end of 1987 was 88,660, which compares with a figure of 106,492 from the official 1980 census. The 1987 figure includes 3,109 Sudanese refugees, and 25,650 Ugandans who returned from Sudan before 1986 or who had never left Uganda. Between 30,000 and 40,000 more Ugandans were repatriated to the district from Sudan's West Bank in 1988–9, and thousands of Sudanese refugees arrived in the district at the same time. Thus the population was well in excess of 150,000 by the end of 1989 and, although the overall density was still not high, pressures were felt in the cultivable parts of the Nile banks (such as at Laropi), and in the well-watered, but rocky, highlands. The official 1991 census indicated a total population including refugees of 178,500, giving a population density of 38 people per square kilometre. This compares with a 1991 figure of 82 people per square kilometre in Arua District to the west, and 29 in Gulu District to the east. The 1991 figure for the country as a whole was 84.

Moyo District used to be called Madi District, and most of the population speak Madi as a first language. There are, however, also groups speaking Lugbara- and Bari-related languages, and some 'Nubians'. In Uganda the term 'Nubian' refers to a category of Moslems tracing descent from people of Sudanese origin who were brought into what is now Uganda by invading armies during the nineteenth century. Under British Protectorate rule they were recognized as a distinct ethnic group by the government, and the men were commonly employed as soldiers. Under Amin, 'Nubian' ethnicity was expanded, to include virtually anyone who was a Ugandan Moslem, including the large number of Lugbara Moslems in Aringa County, but subsequently, this identity has become something of a liability. Lugbara Moslems now tend to call themselves Aringa, and in the 1991 census their ethnicity was registered together with other Lugbaras. According to the 1991 figures, of the population in Moyo District claiming Ugandan nationality, 82 per cent stated that they were Madi, 11 per cent stated that they were Aringa or Lugbara, 4 per cent stated that they were Kakwa, and 1 per cent stated that they were Acholi.

The Madi, and these other groups, recognize a traditional form of social organization in patrilineal clans. To a considerable extent these clans are still patrilocal. As explained above, this means that inheritance is normally (though not exclusively) traced through the male line, and that when a woman marries she leaves her father's home to live with her husband's lineage. A man living away from his patrilineal home may be considered to be an outsider, which can be disadvantageous. Sometimes men are forced into this position due to lack of land in their ancestral area. They may end up living with their wife's brothers, with their maternal uncles, or may move to previously unoccupied land in a remoter part of the district. This pattern of settlement has obviously been significant in the process of rebuilding communities since repatriation.

Under colonial rule Christian missionaries were very active in the region, and most Madi are now Roman Catholics, although local religious beliefs remain important. Ancestor veneration and spirit possession are common, but were not registered in the 1991 census, and in fact people tended to view such practices as part of daily life rather

17.5 Children in Laropi helping to rebuild the primary school, 1987. (Tim Allen)

than as a religion. In 1991 75 per cent of the population was classified as Catholic, 11 per cent Church of Uganda, and 11 per cent Moslem.

The Christian missionaries also introduced schools, and for various reasons the Madi proved very responsive to formal education. Great pride is taken in speaking English well, and levels of literacy in the vernacular are relatively high. According to the 1991 census, out of 118,750 people living in the district who were aged 10 or over, 53,827 were literate. The same census registered 31,763 school students, most of whom were between the ages of six and 24.

The International Aid Agencies

The publicity received by the 'West Nile Emergency' of 1986 in the international media prompted several foreign aid agencies to become involved in the relief and rehabilitation effort. Omitting those organizations which only worked with the Sudanese refugees in the district, or were only operational for brief periods, and also leaving aside the Catholic Church, which was not much involved in development work, the international agencies operational in Moyo District were the UNHCR, the Lutheran World Federation (LWF), Médecins Sans Frontières – France (MSF, France), and Swiss Disaster Relief, which was replaced in 1988 by Médecins Sans Frontières – Swiss (MSF, Swiss).

UNHCR

In May 1986, soon after the returnees from Sudan's East Bank began arriving in Moyo District, the UNHCR Technical Support Service was sent on a mission from Geneva to assess the situation. The LWF had been operational in northwest Uganda since 1984, and had taken responsibility for some immediate assistance to returnees. A small amount of food was quickly distributed to those gathered at reception centres in East Moyo County. Nevertheless the UNHCR mission from Geneva concluded that:

17.6 *Palm Sunday, Laropi, 1988.*
(Tim Allen)

The implementing capacity of LWF, UNHCR operational partner for returnee programmes, is at present rather insufficient and should be seriously strengthened to cater for managerial and technical requirements of an operation of this type, and for eventual new influxes (Technical Support services, UNHCR, Geneva, Mission to North-west Uganda Report, 86/08: 4).

On the basis of this report, the UNHCR funded the LWF, MSF and other international NGOs to work in the region, and also became an operational agency itself, theoretically in collaboration with the World Food Programme (WFP) and Ministry of Rehabilitation. In addition to having an overall co-ordinating role, the UNHCR programme was supposed to transport and register returnees, and procure and distribute food and other commodities (hoes, cooking utensils, pangas etc.). There followed a period of confusion. The UNHCR simply was not in a position to take on the role it assumed. Field staff had to refer so many issues to the Kampala office, or even to Geneva, that they were unable to respond flexibly to events on the ground. The agency's policy of restricting itself to the provision of relief and not becoming involved in anything that might be interpreted as development, made its co-ordination of LWF impossible. Indeed, there was a great deal of counter-productive antagonism between LWF and UNHCR field staff over areas of responsibility. Conflicts also arose within the Uganda office of the UNHCR, and between some of the field staff working in the northwest of the country and staff based in southern Sudan. There were rumours about embezzlement and accusations and counter-accusations of incompetence.

These problems compounded other difficulties, such as the commandeering of vehicles by the NRA. Registration was consequently chaotic, and most of the returnees in 1986 and 1987 received very little practical assistance. No WFP food was distributed from July 1986 until the third week of October, and no action was taken in response to an offer for funds to purchase food near Gulu before that area became insecure (Harrell-Bond and Kanyeihamba, 1986:9). According to UNHCR's own data, the total amount of food distributed up to the end of the year was only 10 per cent of expected cereals, 14 per cent of beans, 12.5 per cent of cooking oil, and 20 per cent of salt. This excludes the small amount of food distributed by the LWF in May, and the estimates of food required were based on the UNHCR's inflated figures for the repatriation. Nevertheless, it is clear that the returnees were left pretty much to their own devices. To make matters even worse, Swede Relief, an organization which was supposed to install 100 wells as part of the UNHCR operation, only succeeded in putting in three or four. In December 1986, about 7,000 people at a transit camp were having to use a single well. In a report written in March 1987, the UNHCR official responsible for the programme in Moyo District made no secret of how ineffective it had been, and commented that food distribution would have to improve quickly 'for the benefit of the good name of UNHCR'.

In 1987, attempts were made to improve UNHCR's relationship with the NGOs operating in Moyo and Arua Districts by holding regular meetings, but after a few months these were discontinued, and many of the basic problems remained unsolved. Efforts to assist returnees in 1988 and 1989 were somewhat more effective, the majority of Ugandan refugees resident in official West Bank settlements in Sudan being trans-

17.7 *Arriving at the UNHCR reception centre and receiving a 'speech' from an overweight official instead of being given relief items: drawn by Opi John of Metu secondary school.*

ported in convoys, and given a small amount of food relief and agricultural implements. There was also rudimentary health screening of some returnees, carried out on behalf of UNHCR by MSF (France) (see below). Nevertheless, it was symptomatic of the overall problems with the UNHCR programme that, in 1988, the head of the field office found himself being banned from even entering Moyo District for a period by the District Administrator. For most of the time it was difficult to see what purpose was served by the UNHCR presence, particularly since the organization lacked any mandate to protect returnees in the way it could claim to protect the rights of refugees. In fact, with the increase in the refugee population of northwest Uganda in 1989, the repatriation programme was formally ended, and the UNHCR office shifted into a new operation, running refuge transit camps and settlements (and continuing to employ many of the same staff).

LWF

To an extent the incapacities of the UNHCR were compensated for by the activities of LWF. Following the conflicts with UNHCR in 1986, LWF looked around for funding from other sources, notably the European Community, and implemented its own rehabilitation programme more or less independently. From 1986 the agency avoided any direct involvement in food distribution or returnee transportation, and concentrated on the reconstruction of buildings, particularly schools, the installation of bore-holes (LWF incorporated the former Swede Relief project), and longer term agricultural development. On a day-to-day basis it also assisted the local administration with service provision, informally lending equipment and staff for communication, road maintenance, and repair of the Nile ferry when it broke down.

Both a strength and a weakness of the LWF programme was its employment of experienced, international staff as section heads. The organization was run as an efficient, top-down bureaucracy. In part this was connected with the strong characters of the expatriates, as well as of some of the senior Ugandan staff. Most of these people were much more concerned with meeting agreement deadlines and doing a professional job, than eliciting local-level involvement. The consequence was that numerous bore-holes were drilled, but community maintenance schemes were often ineffective, and scores of schools were rebuilt without much local collaboration and without addressing the issue of how adequate education services were to be introduced and maintained.

To some extent the agriculture section was an exception. In contrast to the rest of the programme, staff promoted sustainable grassroots development, usually in collaboration with some kind of indigenous organization (such as a chapel council or women's club). As aims related to long-term goals, it is not easy to assess the effectiveness of such strategies. However, during the late 1980s, it seemed that participatory strategies were most difficult to implement where returnees had come back with almost nothing. In these places, it was often hard to locate well-organized local groups, and people were generally more mendicant, wanting seeds to plant and something to eat as quickly as possible. The more successful projects tended to be in Aringa County, immediately to the west of Moyo District, where many of the returnees had been self-settled in Sudan, had managed to bring back their belongings, and had experience in trading and the marketing of agricultural produce. Unlike Moyo District, much of the population of Aringa County is Moslem and, somewhat ironically, the LWF agricultural section's most effective local partner was a Moslem NGO.

There is of course a case for both grassroots strategies and rapid vertical interventions in a situation like that in Moyo District, but the power invested in LWF section heads resulted in each part of the programme going its own way. Sometimes there was competition between sections for resources, rather than flexible discussions about what was the most urgent need at any given time. This occasionally led to personal tensions, which became more of a problem as the life-style of one of the expatriates began to result in less efficient work and difficulties with the district administration. It is also the case that LWF staff played their part in the conflicts with the UNHCR. For example, the dilatory approach to the servicing of UNHCR vehicles in the LWF workshop (which had been funded by UNHCR) was not really to anyone's advantage. Attempts were made to deal with the situation by replacing some senior staff, and by setting up a new section for community development in 1989. However, a preference towards top-down interventions linked to simplistic notions of local ways of life remained an issue in the early 1990s.

The Medical NGOs
Of the medical NGOs, MSF (France) had been operational for the longest. Like the LWF, it began working in Moyo District in 1984 (initially in the whole district but withdrawing from East Moyo County in 1986). It was engaged in renovating Moyo Hospital and several dispensaries, and supplied additional medicines and equipment. There were usually about 10 expatriates based in Moyo town working on all wards of the hospital except the surgery wards, supervising building construction, and providing some in-service training of medical staff. They were also involved in child vaccination and sleeping-sickness control projects. In the latter they had some success in containing the spread of the disease.

The French staff were paid low salaries, were altruistic, and certainly saved lives, but the artificial introversion of compound life, poor English, short-term contracts, youth and lack of experience limited their efficacy. Moreover, the dependence on UNHCR for funding necessitated the involvement of MSF (France) in the near impossible task of

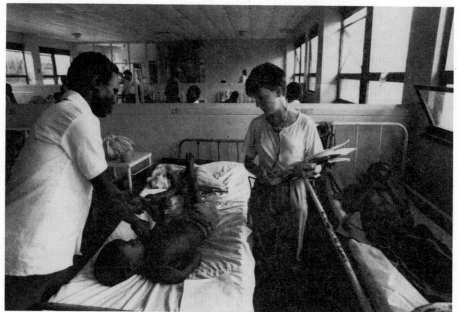

17.8 *A French, MSF nurse working with a Ugandan counterpart at Moyo hospital, 1988. (J. Cantin/UNHCR)*

screening those returnees transported on UNHCR vehicles. This required a medical team to stand by for days, then check hundreds of people in a matter of hours, and completely ignored all those who had been forced to make their own way back from Sudan. The raising of finance from other sources enabled the agency to become more flexible in its activities after 1988, but it still remained caught up in the provision of limited bio-medical health care on behalf of an over-stretched Ministry of Health. Although it was operational in the district for many years, it persisted in presenting its activities as short-term emergency relief, and made little effort to establish sustainable health programmes.

Similar points may be made about the Swiss NGOs, SDR and MSF (Swiss), which took over from MSF (France) in East Moyo County. SDR is not a semi-voluntary agency of the MSF variety, and did employ some more experienced expatriate staff, but the programme was persistently affected by squabbles between them, and was tied to an agreement to rehabilitate Adjumani Health Centre (designated a hospital in 1988) and several static dispensaries to 1960s levels, without a long-term training and support commitment. When it was time to leave, the only way of preventing these services from collapsing was to bring in MSF (Swiss) to maintain the operation at a less ambitious level.

International Aid Workers and Local People

All the international organizations operating in Moyo District were very concerned about ensuring a reasonable standard of living for their international staff. In order to operate in difficult circumstances, it was considered essential to cocoon them from what was happening to those they were trying to help. To an extent this could not be avoided, but isolation in well-stocked, fenced and patrolled compounds, limited an appreciation of what was actually going on. It also had the effect of depersonalizing relationships with the surrounding population. On the one hand, local people often ended up being perceived as amorphous recipients of things given out. On the other, the supposed beneficiaries of these interventions often found it impossible to distinguish one group of white faces in a car from another, and tended to view the aid agencies as a source of limited resources, something to 'get things out of before others manage to do so'. The end result was that, while the activities of the agencies were important in that they helped restore some of the district's destroyed infrastructure, much of what they attempted to do had only marginal impact on the realities of local people's daily lives.

The District Economy

On their return in 1986, the East Bank refugees found that their home area had been devastated. The situation was particularly bad in West Moyo County where there had been the most intense fighting between guerrillas and Obote's UNLA forces. But throughout the district, schools, dispensaries, shops, cotton stores and other permanent buildings had been destroyed. The cotton ginneries were broken down, bore-holes wrecked, and roads in a state of disrepair.

Before exile the majority of the returnees had been smallholders who cultivated cotton to sell to government buyers. With the money they earned, they would pay taxes and school fees and buy goods available in local shops, such as soap, radios, clothes, shoes and bicycles. In Sudan they had depended on Norwegian Church Aid to assist with schooling, water supply and crop marketing. Now they found themselves thrown back on themselves. Neither the state nor the international agencies were capable of providing much support. Perhaps even more so than in their first months in Sudan, they had to find their own means of winning a living in what were sometimes extreme circumstances.

In the years following repatriation, the district economy remained largely isolated from national markets. There were several reasons for this. To begin with, there was the problem of continuing insecurity which both discouraged investment and caused severe transport bottlenecks. Rebel groups operating from Gulu District made attacks into Moyo District, and ensured that the road to Kampala via Gulu was closed from late 1986 until 1988. The road was subsequently only open intermittently. The road to Kampala via Arua could take several days by truck, and was closed from time to time due to heavy rain, ambushes, armed incursions from Sudan, and NRA military activity. In addition, the route necessitated crossing the Nile at Pakwach, where there was a large NRA barracks and a notorious road block. If they did not have a special relationship with the soldiers involving a sharing of profits, merchants were often forced to donate part of their cargo in order to pass. The River Nile was not considered secure enough from rebel attacks to re-establish river transport by barge, and even the activities of fishermen was frequently restricted by the NRA. The Nile ferry at Laropi was permanently guarded by an NRA detachment.

All of this kept trade outside the district to a minimum. A limited amount of border trade became possible after the SPLA captured Nimule, but Ugandan Madis blamed the SPLA for forcing them to leave Sudan, and were nervous of trading across the border, where they might be viewed as Sudanese nationals and forcibly conscripted by the guerrillas. There were also few ways for families to generate money within the district. Cotton, government employment and money sent home by migrant workers had been the major sources of income in the past. None of these sources proved lucrative after returning.

The cotton ginnery at Adjumani was repaired in 1988, and was occasionally operational. But the seeds provided to farmers in 1988 failed to germinate, and the government cotton co-operative was not able to pay cash for much of the cotton grown in 1989 and 1990. Many people said that they wanted to grow cotton once the buying facilities were properly re-established, but the prices paid to farmers were low, and it was hard to see how cotton production could again become a mainstay of the district economy in the immediate future.

Most forms of waged employment were similarly unremunerative. Those who managed to find jobs as civil servants, medical staff, teachers or, increasingly, as NRA soldiers, received paltry salaries. A month's salary for a primary school teacher was barely enough to buy food to feed a family of five or six for three or four days, and long periods passed without any government salaries being paid in the district at all because of logistical difficulties in bringing money from Kampala. One of the highest-paid civil servants was the district agricultural officer. In July 1989 he had recently heard that he would receive a 40 per cent increase on his monthly salary. However he had not in fact been paid since May, when he had received 3,200 shillings. At that time the price of a large fish in Moyo market was 600 shillings, a large tin of cassava flour was between 850 and 900 shillings, a single sweet potato was 25 shillings, a bottle of beer was 550 shillings, and a new hoe was between 600 and 800 shillings. The cost of a reasonable meal for a family of five was between 200 and 300 shillings.

At the same time, the destruction of factories and agricultural estates and antagonism towards northerners meant that work in the south of the country was not forthcoming. Several young men from Laropi who made the journey returned complaining that it was just impossible to make ends meet. Unless they managed to find a job with one of the international aid agencies, the vast majority of men in Moyo District had no option other than to turn to small-scale agriculture, whatever their qualifications. In Laropi, 'peasant' farmers included a former jet-fighter pilot, a qualified accountant, and a mining engineer.

Lack of money within the district and transport problems also meant that there was little to buy in the markets other than local produce and a few cheap standard items, such as exercise books, pens, soap, mirrors and shoes made out of old car tyres. The only exceptions were when second-hand clothes arrived, sometimes in quite large quantities, and when there were sales of so-called 'essential commodities' at subsidized government prices, including sugar and soap.

Until the 1970s, there had been several businesses in the district run by Asians, but their shops were taken over following the expulsion of all Asians from the country under Amin. In the years before the population fled into Sudan, virtually all the larger permanent shops at the two main towns, Moyo and Adjumani, were owned by Moslem traders. These were either Moslem Lugbara from Aringa County in Arua District, or 'Nubians'.

This pattern was repeated after repatriation. A few Madis managed to open shops, but even at a small trading centre like Laropi, resident Aringa played an important role in the local market. They were part of large extended family networks, which enabled them to combine together with relatives living in other parts of Uganda to purchase basic commodities in bulk from Arua, Zaire or Kampala, and to find ways around the various logistical problems of transport. During the late 1980s profits were minimal, but the investment by Aringa families in their former business enterprises was expected to pay dividends over the long term. It placed them in a position to be able to benefit if more money did begin to be generated in the district.

Madi shopkeepers had no access to these networks, and had to brave the road to Kampala via Gulu in order to bring back a few things for sale. They barely seemed to break even, but trading offered an alternative to farming and some young men seemed to enjoy the excitement of travelling around. After 1988 they were joined by refugees, particularly Kukus from Kajo Keji area, who had been traders in Sudan. Many Kukus brought money or goods with them in order to set up shops while in exile, and an area of small wooden stalls was added to the market in Moyo town where the refugees could

17.9 *Madi shopkeepers barely made a profit: a new tea shop in Pakelle town, 1990. (Tim Allen)*

sell small items. Each stall sold much the same as the one next door, and again profits were almost insignificant. Virtually all the stallholders were young men. Some stated openly to me that they worked in the market in order to enjoy the town life and avoid being stuck in a rural refugee camp.

The relatively stagnant economy of Moyo District compounded the problems of the local administration. As government salaries remained inadequate, and since there were so few opportunities for earning money legally in the district, some form of 'corruption' was a virtual necessity for anyone who was prepared to turn up for work.

Partly as a means of compensating for the consequent limitations in the civil service, the NRM introduced local Resistance Councils (RCs), which were directly elected at village level and indirectly elected at parish, county, and district levels. Members of these councils often took their work very seriously, even though they were unpaid, and at least afforded people a voice and a capacity to mobilize which would otherwise have been impossible, given the chaos of recent years. But the lack of a clear demarcation of responsibility between RCs and the local administration led on many occasions to incapacitating confrontation, and the fact that the RCs were engaged in the distribution of 'essential commodities', when they were available, meant that they too were prone to 'corruption' as a way of making ends meet. Furthermore, as transport bottlenecks and cutbacks in state subsidies made the sale of these commodities less frequent, and it became apparent that there were few advantages and many difficulties involved in being an RC representative, many of the most able opted out. In any case, the acute limitations in government services could not be rectified by RC protests.

The lack of services affected every sector, but in the short term was perhaps most worrying in the sphere of public health. In spite of the presence of medical NGOs, health care services fell woefully short of needs. Some district medical staff were extraordinarily selfless, but resources were extremely limited and, like civil servants and teachers, it was impossible for them to turn up for work unless some additional income was available. Many had to maintain themselves by selling drugs that came their way to local shopkeepers.

The Public Health Situation

There was little monitoring of the population by either district health staff or aid agencies, so it is impossible to discuss issues of morbidity and mortality with much specificity. Reporting was very patchy. It was based on cases treated at dispensaries or the odd survey aimed at a particular disease. The following are notes about diseases and infections derived from the limited information available.

Large numbers of people were under-nourished. The UNHCR/WFP/Ministry of Rehabilitation food relief programme failed to provide much assistance, and low crop yields due to adverse weather conditions and pests in 1987, 1988 and 1989 meant that a large part of the population had to rely for many months each year on gathered 'famine' foods. Feeding centres for seriously malnourished children were set up at Moyo and Adjumani hospitals and remained full most of the time. But particularly in the hungry season between March and June this was an inadequate response to the problem. People had to manage as best they could. Eventually, in August 1989 quantities of relief food from the Food and Agriculture Organization (FAO) were allocated to the region in response to reports of widespread 'famine'. But by the time these resources became available some crops were being harvested and the immediate crisis had been averted.

17.10 *A family waiting to consult a local healer about their sick children, Laropi, 1989. (Tim Allen)*

The relief food was not distributed for fear of undermining local markets.

Under these circumstances, the nutritional surveys carried out since 1986 by Médecins Sans Frontières (France) and the Uganda Red Cross came up with what would seem to be surprisingly low figures for children under five years in the less than 80 per cent weight for height category (between 2 and 6 per cent and averaging at 4.8 per cent). But samples were very small (up to 500), and surveys were carried out infrequently (with gaps of six months to a year between them). They were also not linked to mortality rates, something which can lead to over-optimistic assessments, because low malnutrition rates may conceal the fact that many of those formerly registered as malnourished are now dead. Such misleading drops in malnutrition have been noted in Sudan and Nigeria (Keen, 1992: 30). Significantly, those surveys in Moyo District which registered borderline cases of malnutrition came up with much higher rates. In June 1989, for example, it was found that although only 5.4 per cent of the sample were less than 80 per cent weight for height, a further 14 per cent were between 80 and 85 per cent. In fact, it seems likely that the majority of children were sometimes very poorly nourished, and had a reduced resistance to disease. Diarrhoea was viewed as a normal condition unless it was particularly severe, and children that looked relatively healthy could waste away in a matter of days.

The most commonly diagnosed ailments at dispensaries included: malaria – which affected virtually everyone from time to time, bilharzia (infestation with *Schistosoma mansoni*) – which was so prevalent at Laropi that patients were not treated since they would quickly have been reinfected when returning to the river; other intestinal worms (mainly hookworm); 'eye infections' – mostly severe conjunctivitis; 'infected wounds' – often in the feet due to accidents occurring when hoeing without shoes; tropical ulcers; cerebrospinal meningitis; measles; tuberculosis; tetanus, and venereal diseases.

Because it was believed that local remedies were better for jaundice than biomedical ones, these cases were often not brought to dispensaries. They were nonetheless very numerous. Jaundice could be a symptom of various diseases, including hepatitis (perhaps caught from an unsterilized needle used at home) and alcohol-related liver problems.

Alcohol also causes morbidity and mortality in more immediate ways. Many men suffered regularly from the effects of severe hangovers, and during my stay in Laropi there were several fatalities arising from fights at drinking places, or as a result of drunks falling into the river at night. Other health problems not usually taken to dispensaries included pregnancy and labour complications. Occasionally women died in childbirth.

Aids was less of a problem than elsewhere in Uganda. A national survey in 1990 indicated that about 3 per cent of the sexually active population of the district were HIV positive. This relatively low level is a vivid illustration of the degree to which the area had been cut off from the rest of the country. There were correspondingly few recorded deaths from the disease.

Several of those who died were well-known individuals, something which has helped spread an awareness of the problem. In 1991 the recently retired head of the civil service in the district died of the disease. Copies of a letter he wrote on his death-bed warning others not to behave as he had done were circulated and read at church services. It was hoped that such publicity would do something to change sexual practices, but condoms were not widely available and there remained a considerable amount of sexual activity outside of marriage. If the area becomes more politically stable and integrated into the national economy, the number of cases can be expected to rise.

Of more immediate concern than Aids was the prevalence of trypanosomiasis (sleeping sickness), which is spread by the tsetse fly. Trypanosomiasis is a fatal disease which is difficult to treat, particularly when the infection has developed and symptoms have begun to appear (headache, fever, dizziness). By 1960, because of intensive treatment and vector control during the colonial period, the disease was almost eradicated in the area, but since that time control measures have become haphazard and many Ugandans were infected with the disease in Sudan. In 1989 the prevalence was estimated at 5 per cent in some parts of West Moyo and Obongi Counties, and as high as 30 per cent in one parish (Lomunga). Tests introduced and implemented by MSF (France) indicated an overall prevalence of 1.5 per cent for the two-year period from October 1987 (in West Moyo and Obongi Counties), and it was feared that this figure would rise as people continued to move across the Sudan border, and tsetse flies continued to infest the secondary forest which had grown up over much of the district while the population was in exile. Like tuberculosis, sleeping sickness requires a prolonged course of treatment, which needs to continue whether or not the patient actually feels ill. Patients with the so-called 'second stage' infection have to be administered with a highly toxic drug, which can itself be dangerous.

MSF (France) responded by collaborating with district medical staff in an attempt to limit the spread of the disease. Screening of the population, combined with hospital care for those infected kept the overall prevalence under 1.5 per cent. But a continuous effort for the foreseeable future will be needed to maintain this level, tying up a considerable part of the limited resources available for public health activities. It is still hard for people who feel well to understand why they should go to hospital for tests and treatment, particularly since some of those who do go die from the treatment itself. So long as the tsetse flies remain and there are people carrying the disease, reinfection for those who have been treated is always a risk.

Checking the spread of trypanosomiasis was a substantial achievement. But the overall health situation was only likely to improve if more adequate public health care programmes were established. Five years or more after returning people still found that when they went to a dispensary for treatment they were told that no drugs were available. There was also minimal primary care in the district, with immunization coverage remaining low compared with other parts of Uganda (in 1989 it was estimated that only 20 per cent of children had been inoculated for measles, tetanus, whooping cough, polio, diphtheria and tuberculosis). In addition there is evidence that the kind of selective interventions to control particular diseases adopted by MSF have little impact on overall morbidity and mortality rates. After all, if it was the case that diarrhoeal infections were the most widespread killer diseases, then the rehabilitation of hospitals and static dispensaries, and the provision of a small amount of bio-medicine, was never likely to have much impact.

Local Sources of Income

The limitation on economic activities in Moyo District forced people into a way of life which they had not lived before fleeing into Sudan, and many had avoided while living in exile. Almost all food had to be locally grown, caught or gathered. Village markets were quite lively places, but most of the buying and selling was an exchanging of products from within a small area. Fish from Laropi might be sold in Adjumani to buy finger millet from Pakelle, or a chicken might be sold to buy cassava flour.

Nevertheless, many families or individuals were unwilling to resort to subsistence agricultural production. Almost everyone wanted to send their children to school, and school fees seemed to rise every term. In theory school fees were not charged for primary education in the years following repatriation, but in practice contibutions had to be made through 'parents and teachers associations'. Money was also required for things like bridewealth payments, clothes, medicine and healing rituals. Moreover, the consumption of alcohol was a normal part of social life and it was difficult for a man to be accepted by his neighbours if he did not drink or occasionally provide visitors with waragi (the locally distilled liquor made mainly from cassava flour). The price of a bottle of waragi was the most commonly quoted local indicator of inflation, both because it was something which men had to buy and because selling it was the only source of regular income to many women. One very drunk teacher in Laropi once explained to me (tongue in cheek) that drinking every day in large quantities was the best way of assisting women and their children.

The amount a woman could make from brewing alcohol depended on whether or not she had her own distilling equipment (ideally a large metal fuel drum), and to what extent she could stop male relatives entertaining without paying her for what was drunk. Assuming she was able to sell all that she had made, and did not have to hire equipment, nor have to pay assistants to collect firewood and water, the following figures indicate the profit she could expect. In mid-1989, half a sack (three large tins) of cassava flour cost 3,000 shillings in Laropi. In Moyo or Adjumani towns it cost somewhat less, between 2,500 and 2,700 shillings. This would be enough to make one full drum of wiri, the strong beer which would then be distilled. The necessary amount of yeast would cost about 500 shillings. The waragi would be sold for 100 shillings per bottle in Laropi. 120 shillings could be charged in Moyo and Adjumani towns, or at the fishing camps located in remote places near the Nile. The number of bottles sold depended on how clever the woman could be at selling weaker liquor. Weak waragi could be made either by keeping the water used in the distillation process boiling for longer than necessary, or by directly mixing water in the bottles after distillation. If all went well, she might make 1,000 shillings profit. The price of feeding a family of five in Laropi in mid-1989 was about the same as mentioned for Moyo town, 250 to 300 shillings for a good meal (fish was cheaper than in Moyo, but flour was more expensive). But of course most rural families tried to feed themselves as much as possible with food they had gathered or grown.

Women could also sometimes earn small amounts of money by selling crops or gathered foods (like mangoes when they were in season), bundles of grass and poles for house building, grinding stones or grass mats. Often they would walk long distances with heavy loads in order to sell their produce at a place where the price was a little higher. Some of the money they earned might be given to their husbands, but most women I

17.11 *Making* waragi *and drinking it, by Maxwell of Pakelle.*

17.12 *Digging for gold, Metu, 1989.*
(Tim Allen)

spoke to tried to avoid pooling resources within their household as a whole. Often their menfolk were unable to contribute as much as they were, and it was anticipated that men would end up spending much of the money they received on alcohol. However, it was the men who 'owned' the land and who did much of the initial bush clearing and cultivation, therefore the issue of who should receive any income from the produce of the fields was often a cause of domestic arguments.

Sources of income for men varied in different parts of the district. In the hills around Metu, several individuals were involved in the back-breaking task of gold panning in the streams. Tiny amounts of gold were collected and sold to traders coming from Arua. People would listen to the BBC World Service to hear about fluctuations in the price on international markets, and sensitive scales were made using old tin cans with razor blades as weights. In July 1989, gold was sold in Metu for 60,000 shillings per tola. A tola was estimated as the weight of 12 razor blades, but most prospectors sold in much smaller quantities than this. The locally made scales were sensitive enough to be able to use just one razor blade as a weight.

Until 1989 gold panning had been a secret activity (although everyone knew it was going on). Panners complained that soldiers would sometimes come in the night and confiscate their gold. But in 1989 panning had been declared legal, and panners were hopeful that the Uganda Commercial Bank would eventually become involved in purchasing. However, two years later this had not yet happened. Moreover, parts of the mountains had become insecure, because there had been several incursions from Sudan by groups claiming to be part of the SPLA. Supposedly these guerrillas were searching for individuals working for the Sudan government, but it would appear that they also came with the intention of stealing gold.

Near to the Nile, men with fishing equipment would joke that the river was their own Uganda Commercial Bank, and certainly the availability of fish was something which compensated for the shortage of good farming soil and the swarms of mosquitos which made for sleepless nights. Those lucky enough to have canoes, nets and hooks could make quite a good living. They usually sold their catch in the early mornings to fishmongers, who would dry the fish and then take it on a bicycle to Moyo or Adjumani towns. Dried fish was a commodity in demand in both Arua and Gulu, so a small profit could almost always be made. The road to Gulu was often closed, so it was a common sight to see fishmongers pushing heavily laden bicycles up from Laropi over the Metu hills to Moyo. It was an exhausting four-hour trip, which the most hardworking might make several times each week.

In addition, both men and women could work as labourers for more affluent neighbours, an activity known as *leja leja*. Relatively well-off farmers would employ groups of people to open and cultivate fields or to help erect new houses. When food was particularly scarce, labourers might work for several hours in return for a couple of meals alone, but normally they could expect to receive the equivalent price of two or three bottles of *waragi*. Employing neighbours in this way was the means whereby the more affluent managed to establish farms quickly, setting themselves up as patrons. Some of them were in such a fortunate position because

17.13 *Fishermen, Laropi, 1988. (Tim Allen)*

they had earned money in Sudan and had managed to bring it with them, others were individuals who had inherited large fields in fertile locations. A few were just lucky. One man in Laropi, for example, planted large numbers of pumpkins close to the Nile and obtained a bumper harvest in 1987. By paying with pumpkins alone, he was able to employ some 20 people to re-establish all his family's fields, including those of his children living at his village. In mid-1989, payment for *leja leja* in Laropi was 100 shillings (or one bottle of *waragi*) to dig an area of about 2 x 50 metres of sandy soil. The area dug could be more than this if the soil was particularly light, while in places where the soil was richer and heavier, the area dug could drop to 2 x 30 metres.

Food and Survival

It has already been indicated that food supply for the returnees in Moyo District was inadequate. Those who came back to Uganda in 1986 left Sudan before harvesting their fields, and most of those who had stored food from the previous year were unable to transport it. Few people managed to return with chickens, goats, sheep or cattle. The food relief programme mounted under the auspices of the UNHCR and the WFP failed. For much of 1986 and 1987, many families had to depend on gathered 'famine' foods, including wild roots, which took several days to process before eating, and the seeds of a species of Nile water lily. There was an urgent need to establish farms, preferably with fast-yielding crops. Initially this meant engaging in the back-breaking task of removing secondary forest and bush cover with a few hand tools. But even once this had been done there proved to be several obstacles to achieving local food security.

Unless people settled in previously unoccupied parts of East Moyo County (where they risked attacks by the Holy Spirit rebels), or in previously unoccupied parts of West Moyo County (where they might be raided from Sudan and had to suffer the bites of tsetse flies), people mostly returned to their former ancestral locations. Only a few had registered claims over land, and there were numerous conflicts over farming rights. But these disputes were resolved relatively quickly by male elders deciding which family had cultivated a particular location in the past.

A consequence was that men who had received little formal education often obtained more land than those who had attended school. Families that had previously had a high status, producing civil servants, teachers and military officers, had tended to reduce their areas of cultivation, or had given up farming altogether. Fields had been passed on to the less 'progressive' members of the lineage. This meant that some of the best-educated returnees, including the sons of former government chiefs, were forced to 'borrow' land from uneducated relatives. It could be a galling reversal of accepted lines of patronage. 'Borrowing' allowed a man to open and cultivate a field for his family, but he recognized that the real 'owner' would eventually take it back. Men in this position were among the most frustrated and heavy drinking of the returnees.

Before fleeing to Sudan the men of a patrilineage living in the same village would occasionally cultivate a large field together, and their wives would often weed and harvest jointly as a group. In exile many of the Madi refugees had adopted a method of organizing formal reciprocal work parties known as *komponis* from nearby Sudanese farmers. *Komponis* had books of rules and committed each member to labour in the fields of all the other members on a rotating basis. They acted as a means of forging relationships between individuals who were not necessarily related to each other, and had played an important role in the establishing of rural communities in parts of southern Sudan following the return of refugees in the 1970s (for a detailed study of *komponis* in southern Sudan, see Allen, 1987).

But in the years following repatriation, agricultural production was usually done by immediate family members only, and even within a household group there might be little collaboration in agricultural work. Many families did not have 'a household budget', and financial income and even crop yields were often kept secret from other family members. (One of the funniest plays performed by the children at Laropi primary school at public functions was about a family in which different members tried to find food and eat it without the other members knowing.) Work groups were set up in a few locations, notably where new land was being opened up, such as previously forested areas near the Nile upstream of Laropi, or in East Moyo County where farms were sometimes quite large. Also, as has been explained, a farmer could call people for *leja leja*. But, by and large, each family (or part of a family) struggled separately to win a living by planting whatever was available.

There were several reasons for this degree of individualism, some of them linked to long-term processes, such as the replacing of finger millet by cassava as the basic staple during the 1950s. Cassava is not as nutritious as finger millet, but requires less farm labour and produces higher yields. Its adoption had freed more land for cotton cultivation and enabled many of the younger men to move away from home to take up salaried employment. Food crop production could be left largely to women cultivating the small plots allocated to them to feed their children. But men were not occupied with growing cotton following the return from Sudan, and cereals like finger millet and sorghum were quite widely planted in the 1980s.

It would seem that the basic reason for the lack of reciprocal work groups was the lack of food. When asked why they did not dig in their neighbours' fields, people would reply that it was because of hunger. A group could not be called without beer and something to eat, not as payment for the work done like *leja leja*, but for encouragement. Rotating work groups necessitated a basic degree of affluence. They made digging less of a chore, but were not an optimal use of resources and energy, because so much time was spent socializing. They also tended to make members responsible for each other and to act as a support network between families. Again people felt that they could not afford this kind of commitment. Speaking in the Madi language, one woman living at Laropi explained her situation in 1987 like this:

> In Sudan people had a lot of freedom. Things were nice and we were happy. But here in Uganda we are upset because of lack of food. You might have your mother with you, but what you have to eat is only enough for yourself and the children. You look at her suffering. It has brought too many problems. (translated from a taped interview made in mid-1987)

For those too weak to take care of themselves, life could be awful. Here a man of 67 describes his difficulties a few months before he finally wasted away and died. He also spoke in the Madi language.

> I am suffering so much. My wife and I are old now, but just assisting ourselves. There is no-one to help. In the refugee camp, Sudan Council of Churches helped us because I am disabled. Only one child is at home, and he is just eight. He is at Laropi primary school. My wife goes to collect water lilies. There is nothing else to eat. I have daughters who would help, but they are married in Metu, and bridewealth has been paid and consumed long ago. One of my daughters is already a grandmother. We have been given some things by the missionaries but it was only enough for a few days. My brothers' sons can do nothing for us. They have their own fathers to look after. In the past they would have done something, but today no-one has anything extra. My house was built by my daughters' husbands, who came with all the materials from Metu. But the children cannot stay long, they have their own homes. There is no-one to help my wife cultivate. We only have a small plot of sorghum, but it was all destroyed by pests. (translated from a taped interview made in mid-July, 1987)

In most parts of the district, farming was done by hand tools: hoes, pangas and axes. These tools were a considerable expense to families, because they wore out quickly when used for opening up land that had not been cultivated for several years. Fortunately they were usually available at reasonable prices due to the activities of international NGOs in the district. The LWF also encouraged ox-ploughing, and there was a positive response to this in parts of East Moyo County where the land is relatively flat and open. However, the prevalence of thin sandy soils in much of the district, as well as cattle diseases, limited the effectiveness of the project. In 1988 the government provided a tractor and ploughing equipment at subsidized prices to the 11 sub-county level RCs. But fuel was hard to obtain and very expensive. There was also no maintainance service provided for the machines and no spare parts. As a result, only a few larger farmers were able to afford to have their fields mechanically ploughed, and the tractors soon broke down.

Thus the livelihood, or rather the potential livelihood, of the great majority of people was based upon small-scale farming with hand tools. This was so almost irrespective of levels of formal education, let alone farming experience. It is not surprising that many people felt very frustrated about the lack of opportunities open to them, and also that cultivation knowledge and skills varied enormously. There were some spectacular mistakes, where highly educated people planted the wrong crop in the wrong soil at the wrong time of year, and harvested next to nothing. But even people who had been small-scale farmers in the district during the 1970s faced a new situation following repatriation. In the past they had cultivated cotton as a cash crop, and grown much of their food for household consumption in intensively farmed fields around their homes. Now there was no market for cotton, and the only chance of making money from agriculture was to produce a significant surplus of food crops. This was something most farmers had not attempted to do before fleeing to Sudan.

Zacharia Eno's Account
Zacharia Eno was a well-trained primary school teacher. He decided to settle at Laropi in 1986 because most of his male relatives had fled to the West Bank in Sudan and had not yet returned. Also it was possible to collect water lilies from the Nile, as well as roots and herbs from the nearby forest. He was appointed to teach at one of the two main primary schools in Laropi parish. This gave him some local status, but was of little assistance in feeding himself, his wife and their three children. The following description of his life in Laropi is taken from a detailed account he dictated to me in September 1989 (he spoke to me in English).

> When we arrived at Laropi, the trading centre was the only place which was not bushy. We started off by staying in the half-destroyed school buildings, but soon moved to a rough shelter

which we erected until a house could be built. There were many soldiers around, but they did not disturb people and were friendly. A bit more relief food was given: twice in May and once in June. But this was much less than had been given in Pakelle. It was only one or two kilos of beans and maize per person, and half a litre of oil. After that nothing more was distributed until October, when even smaller portions were given. People survived on water lily seeds collected from the River Nile, as well as gathered greens like *dodo* and *jiri*, and the leaves of cowpeas and cassava plants what were growing wild. Only a few people had fishnets and hooks, and could catch and sell fish. Sometimes I was able to buy fish with my small salary. There were in addition plenty of mangoes to eat in December, and in April and May [1987].

My salary was 24,000 old shillings per month. At that time a reasonable size mud-fish to feed the family cost 3,000 shillings, and a large cock cost about 10,000. Some money could also be earned by doing *leja leja*, that is agricultural labouring. I would do this with my whole family sometimes, the small children just doing what they could. I also started cultivating my own borrowed fields, and my wife collected materials to build a house. The roof was finished by the end of June (1986) and the walls were added in September (it was very small and the walls remained incomplete)...

Like most other returnees, Eno found it hard to find enough seeds and cuttings to plant in 1986 and 1987. Few families managed to bring enough back from exile, and most had to persuade friends and relatives who had not fled to give them some. Theft from fields was common. In addition, several of those crops which were more generally available for planting were prone to diseases and to destruction by pests. Virtually all the cassava planted became infected with leaf-mosaic disease, reducing yields by as much as half. The only way of dealing with the problem was to plant resistant varieties, but these were unavailable. At the same time, the sorghum was ruined by witchweed (*Striga hermontheca*), a semi-parasitic herb which attacks the roots of the host plants and can remain dormant in soils for many years. Witchweed had always been a cause of concern in the district, but had been held in check by the farming of cotton and groundnuts which inhibit its growth. Cotton was not widely planted following the repatriation for reasons already noted, and groundnut seeds were scarce until 1989. As a result, witch-weed spread rapidly. Other pests included weaver birds, locusts, and wild animals, such as baboons and bush rats which had multiplied in the absence of human inhabitation.

Lack of seeds and cuttings, and also the difficulties of clearing secondary forest, meant that Eno's family only planted small plots in 1986. However, the late rains were quite good, and some of the fields were more productive than he had anticipated:

The first crops planted were sorghum and maize, both planted in May. Pumpkins were planted around the homestead in June, and sweet potatoes in July. A field of simsim was dug in August, and beans and cowpeas were also planted in that month. We brought a few cuttings and seeds with us from Sudan, and planted a portion of the maize and beans distributed as relief food. Sweet potato cuttings were obtained from neighbours. The maize was ready at the end of August, but it was not a good yield due to lack of rain. In any case it was a small field, and was eaten from the field rather than harvested and stored. Sweet potatoes were ready at the end of October, however this was also a small field. Sorghum was harvested in December, but striga [ie. witchweed] and weaver birds depleted the yield. It amounted to one sack when threshed. The simsim field was small, but proved to be productive, two tins being harvested in December. Cowpeas were also ready at the end of the year, the harvest being one and a half sacks. The beans did poorly, not even one full bucket was collected at the end of December. The pumpkins were few, but a welcome change in a boring diet. During this period life was very hard, and the family often went hungry. It was tempting to forget problems by drinking *waragi*. Christmas 1986 was miserable.

The food grown in 1986 assisted the family until April 1987, when it ran out, and we again survived on water lilies and doing *leja leja*. We planted all the usual crops that year: cassava, maize, simsim, sorghum, cowpeas, potatoes, pumpkin, and vegetables. We cultivated in the same borrowed fields as 1986. There were three of these, each being 70 by 40 metres [field sizes were often known exactly by informants because they were measured with a two-metre pole]. In addition we had a small plot on an island in the Nile, which my wife cultivated because I am afraid of going in a canoe [he could not swim].

17.14 *Children helping to dig a sweet potato field, Laropi, 1989. (Tim Allen)*

Unfortunately the rains in 1987 were very late, and then were too heavy in May, destroying all the crops planted on the island. Also sorghum failed completely, again due to pests. Nevertheless, our main fields produced more than in 1986. Altogether one sack of maize seed was harvested, four large tins of simsim, one sack of cow peas and a reasonable amount of cassava and sweet potatoes which were stored in the field.

Other families in the district did not do so well, and in 1988 the rains were again erratic. Eno's family planted the same crops as in 1987, as well as rice and sugar cane in the dry bottom of a nearby stream.

The sorghum did better than the previous year, but was completely destroyed by grasshoppers in November before it was ready for harvest. Simsim yielded less than in 1987: about three buckets, because it had been planted too late in the year. The sweet potatoes produced many roots, but the tubers were small. The cassava planted was long-term, and only began to be ready in 1989. However it was lucky that the excessive rains which affected most other parts of Moyo District in late 1988 was not so much of a problem in Laropi…

Three years after returning many families were still confronting serious food shortages, and the arrival of large numbers of Sudanese refugees placed further pressure on limited local resources. The cassava was showing symptoms of leaf-mosaic, and the weather conditions were yet again poor. The early rains failed completely. As has been mentioned, there was talk of a major famine relief effort in August 1989, but this eventually came to nothing because the international aid agencies working in the district were worried about undermining markets.

By the early 1990s, the Sudanese refugees were receiving quantities of donated food, some of which found its way into local homes. Also seeds and cuttings had become more available, and farmers were able to plant a wider range of crops, including groundnuts. But in most respects, the problems of the 1980s remained. The district was still marginal to the national economy and neighbouring regions were intermittently insecure. Several farmers began to grow cotton in 1990 and some continued to do so in subsequent years, but cash was still not made available by the government to enable the buyers at

Adjumani ginnery to pay for all the harvest. Many farmers were sent away with credit notes which made no allowance for inflation. The fact that people still wanted to grow cotton in these circumstances was remarkable, revealing how strongly certain officially sanctioned ideas about progress had been propagated under British rule. It reflected a frequently articulated desire among the returned Madi population to return to the certainties of firm, paternal government. This was hardly a surprising sentiment given the upheavals of the post-colonial era.

The Difficulty of Establishing a Community

The basic struggle for survival in Moyo District during the late 1980s made it all the more difficult to establish communities. By establishing communities, I mean the business of creating and maintaining generally acceptable social relations between people living in close proximity to one another. Many aid workers seem to assume that Africans live in relatively cohesive societies, regulated by moral codes and guided by respected decision-makers. Most community development projects imply the existence of such local-level order, even when the country or region as a whole is in chaos. But often these supposed communities are little more than a diverse group of people struggling to find ways of living with each other in trying circumstance. Moral codes, decision-makers, and social order are unlikely to be things that are easily established following a period of upheaval. More commonly they are the focus of debate and conflict.

Life was hard for most of the returnees, and there was no safety net for those without close relatives nearby or for those whose relatives chose to ignore them. Small family groups had to manage as best as they could on their own, and were distrustful, even antagonistic to neighbours. The lack of co-operation in agriculture during the late 1980s meant that there was no routine forum for discussion and debate between neighbours, and resentments were prone to fester. There were in addition bitter conflicts within households. A home with a few resources would usually try to resist pressures to assist people outside the immediate family group, but even within the immediate family tensions could be acute. There were intense rivalries between co-wives, and between wives and sisters of the home who had returned to live with their brothers after a marriage had broken up.

Sometimes older people would attempt to assert notions of collective lineage responsibility, and male elders were usually recognized as having the right to resolve disputes over rights to fields. However, patrilineal authority had already been greatly weakened before the population fled as a consequence of labour migration, cash-cropping and commoditization. It was hard to see how it could be re-established, at least in the short term. In the late 1980s, most old people were dependent on their children for food and shelter. They had few resources to distribute. Cattle, sheep and goats had been lost, and male elders were therefore unable even to organize bridewealth exchange for women married into their lineages. There were a few relatively affluent men who managed to act as patrons, and they might help sort out conflicts within their clients' families, but they could not regulate social relations in any more general way. For much of the time I lived at Laropi, there was little sense of being in a community at all.

Taking a longer term view, a Madi collective identity is a relatively recent introduction. At the turn of the century, when the British colonial officers arrived in the area that eventually became Moyo District, the groups of diverse ethnic origin and linguistic background clustered near the Nile were living in constant fear of attacks by the armies of powerful chiefs to the east, who had obtained guns from ivory traders and Turco-Egyptian soldiers. In a sense, they were refugees. To British officers, they seemed bedraggled and rather pathetic. Their recent past had been disastrous. Their cattle had been stolen, or had died due to disease, and their numbers had been reduced by epidemics of sleeping sickness, polio, and meningitis (all introduced by invaders in the late nineteenth century). Under colonial rule, the Madi identity ascribed to the population took on a local meaning (the term 'Madi' itself was probably derived from a Sudanic word for 'a person', *ma'di*). The formulation of ethnicity was strongly influenced by restrictions imposed upon migration, and by the relationships between male lineage elders and male Europeans who worked in the area as administrators and missionaries. The local political power of selected genealogically important elders was enhanced under colonial patronage, and the patrilineal conceptions of tradition they promoted became the generally accepted version of a Madi tribal culture.

As time passed, competition with other 'tribes' also became important in the process. The tribal identities of the Madis' neighbours, the Acholi and the Lugbara, had emerged in much the same way, but were accorded a higher status in that their languages were systematized for administrative use. This issue of language proved to be very significant. Bibles were produced in the vernacular and in the case of the Acholi, so were books based on the oral histories of patrilineages. Such publications had the effect of giving some Ugandan tribal identities a degree of autonomy. But this was not the case for the Madi. It is no coincidence that during the late colonial period the Madi gained a reputation among British officials for being 'progressive'. Madis appeared to have an immense enthusiasm for formal education. But the reason was not hard to find. Madis had refused to accept administration or Christian evangelizing in the Lugbara or Acholi tongues. The language of administration had therefore become English, and speaking good English had evolved into an ethnic characteristic.

In the 1980s, this incorporation of values propagated under colonial rule remained an aspect of Madi culture. It was common to hear someone being called a 'true Madi' because he, or sometimes she, spoke fluent English. There was a tendency for people to look for external authority figures, who would expect them, or indeed require them, to pay taxes, grow cotton and send childern to school. In a sense, they needed to do these things in order to establish communities. Such acceptance of a role for local government was probably another reason why so many of the Ugandan Madi refugees accepted the regulations of official settlement life in Sudan. Not only were all the East Bank camps largely populated by Madis, but the vast majority of Madis who went to the West Bank also went to camps. Most of the self-settled refugees were either Lugbaras or Kakwas. The acute food shortages Madis faced following repatriation, the continued security problems and the inadequacies of state services tended to mean that life in the official settlements was remembered with nostalgia. The late colonial era and early independence period seemed like a Golden Age of social order and prosperity.

I do not want to push this interpretation too far. Idealizing the past is of course a common human response to declining living standards. Moreover, there was not a single Madi way of thinking about things, nor were the Madi a completely discrete group. But the argument I have presented is in essence a view that was quite frequently expressed. Madis did not have shared functional models of proper social life to fall back on. Or rather, the functional models which older people sometimes invoked required the existence of a relatively effective local government administration. This made it all the more significant that following repatriation government appointed chiefs and the new RCs had so few resources with which to back up decisions. Provided people did not antagonize the NRA soldiers, they were usually left to their own devices.

The state's incapacity in the late 1980s was preferable to the state's promotion of violent oppression under Obote, but it also meant that the local level judiciary could be ignored with impunity, and that there were few externally enforced controls on village-level social life. There was intense competition for scarce resources without clear behavioural rules or mechanisms for arbitration. Communal life was recognized as being

17.15 *An elder at a patrilineal shrine, Laropi, 1987. (Tim Allen)*

in crisis. Social accountability was not being enforced and people did not look after their relatives. For some, things were so desperate that they felt compelled to take the law into their own hands. To understand what this entailed, it is necessary to explain something about Madi conceptions of affliction and affliction causality.

Interpersonal tensions and social healing

There was a widespread belief in Moyo District that interpersonal tensions were not only the consequence of recent troubles, but were an underlying reason why these troubles had occurred. Although Madis would accept that things could just happen by coincidence, in some circumstances there was a tendency to ask why they happened to particular people and not to others, and occasionally there was a demand to know who was responsible.

In the past, illnesses or other problems were often interpreted as a manifestation of the influence patrilineal ghosts could have on the lives of their living descendants. Although such beliefs were not deliberately encouraged by the Protectorate administration (and were actively discouraged by Christian missionaries), this was one of the ways in which male authority retained local cultural resonances even though elders might in effect be acting as agents of the state.

Genealogically senior men were the guardians of patrilineal shrines. These were places that symbolized the unity of the extended family, and were the focus of healing rituals. In cases of affliction, therapy would involve a 'feeding' of the ancestral ghosts at the shrine. The ceremony would also allow for an extended discussion among relatives. Anti-social behaviour of individuals might be linked to the problem and the wrong-doer would be chastised. For example, the sickness of a child might be connected with the fact that her father drank too much *waragi*, or was working away from home and did not come to visit regularly enough, or had insulted one of his brothers' wives. Old people, both male and female, were believed to have a right to invoke ancestral ghosts to act on their behalf if they felt they were being treated badly. Senior males even had a duty to do so, because they were responsible for keeping their homes 'clean'.

In the 1980s affliction was still sometimes interpreted in this way. A libation at an ancestral shrine might be made in conjunction with other forms of therapy, such as a consultation with a herbalist or a trip to the dispensary. Some elders also argued that bad weather conditions, poor farm yields and the prevalence of bad behaviour were the consequence of not having perfomed rituals to placate the ancestors when people returned.

However the weakness in the elders' economic position meant that they relied on their sons for their own survival. It also limited their ability to constrain the actions of women married into their home through relationships maintained with other lineages by means of bridewealth transfers. Elders consequently found it difficult to persuade their relatives to take traditional moral explanations of affliction very seriously. Many people were willing to accept that when life was as it was in the 1950s and 1960s, the cult of ancestor veneration had been important. But it was hard to see how deceased relatives could be expressing their concerns about the living by means of the kinds of suffering people were now experiencing. If the spirit world was an influence, it did not appear to be a benign one.

Of more immediate concern were the activities of wild ghosts. The role of ancestral ghosts was clearly linked to lines of patrilineal authority. The manifestations of wild ghosts were equally clearly associated with the decline in male control over women. The domain of patrilineal ghosts was within the home. In contrast, wild ghosts inhabited streams and bushy places, and were rarely the deceased relatives of local people. Many of them were government soldiers, guerrillas or civilians who had died in the fighting during the 1980s. They were believed to seize women and make them ill or do strange things. Sometimes an affected woman would have headaches or would not be able to wake up in the morning, eat certain food or work in the fields. In other cases a woman would insist on sleeping in a tree away from her compound, would run into the forest screaming, or roll herself in dirt and tear her clothes. In the years following repatriation such occurences were very frequent and were said to be something new. Women had become possessed in the past, but much less often, and in a different way.

Therapy for women seized by wild ghosts involved expensive consultations with special female spirit mediums who organized dramatic seances. At these occasions the ghosts possessing the medium would speak through her in strange high-pitched voices, often in the Acholi language, and would enter into a discussion with the ghosts possessing the affected woman. The purpose was to discover what had to be done for the patient to be left alone. Usually her male relatives had to provide her with special food, clothes and sometimes other things like chairs or cooking utensils. Men would complain that dealing with their possessed wives or sisters always involved them buying presents. Nonetheless, they would usually contribute what was demanded, because they were genuinely fearful of what was going on.

The possession of women confirmed to men, but also to women too, that there was a dangerous quality to being female, a quality that was connected with the unpredictable violence of the realm outside of moral, patrilineally regulated social relations. This was a realm associated with things of the forest, and in recent years with the Acholi 'tribe'. Relationships with individual Acholi were not necessarily hostile, and the ethnic distinction between the Acholi and the Madi was much less clear than it appeared. But Acholi soldiers had killed people in 1980, Sudanese Acholi had helped attack the refugee camps in 1986, and in the late 1980s the Acholi-dominated Holy Spirit Movement launched raids into the district. A notion of 'the Acholi' had become closely connected with certain ideas about unpredictable powers and a setting aside of moral action. The fact that women were possessed by Acholi ghosts, and might speak the Acholi language at seances, could be interpreted as an attempt to come to terms with events. There is no doubt that some of the women who were said to be affected by wild spirits had been deeply disturbed by their experiences of war and displacement, and it seems likely that they were suffering from what could be defined in psychiatric terms as mental disorders.

For their part, the spirit mediums took pains to present themselves as good people. They stressed their work as healers, and claimed that their powers came from God or the Virgin Mary. In this way they attempted to assert a socially acceptable basis for their activities. Obviously they could not present themselves as reinforcing patrilineal conceptions of moral action, so they sought an alternative form of moral probity by linking themselves with the Catholic Church. It was essential for them to do this, because they were taking a considerable risk. Their seances demonstrated that they had knowledge of things men could not deal with, and they also confirmed that women were bringing unruly forces into the home.

17.16 & 17.17 *Santina, a spirit-medium,*
performing a seance (above) and later posing
with a rosary and Christian prayer books
(below), Metu, 1989. (Tim Allen)

When men talked about the problems involved in establishing communities, they almost invariably complained about women. Frequent possession by wild ghosts was an aspect of this, but female behaviour was out of their control in other ways too, most seriously with respect to sorcery. Few families could afford to make bride-wealth payments, and this contributed to making marriages unstable. It meant that a married woman did not really become incorporated into her husband's patrilineage and there were even doubts about her children. If she had a fight with her in-laws, she might run away to her father's home, where she would be protected by her brothers. She would be given land to farm and might take her children with her, claiming that they belonged to her father's patrilineage and not to her husband's. She might also try to secure some of the resources which were being allocated to her brothers' wives, and could argue that she was known in the home, whereas women married in from outside ought to be treated with suspicion. Such competition within household groups meant that women often spread rumours and openly squabbled with each other. When accusations and counter accusations were made, women might remind relatives of tragedies that had happened and ask them why they thought these things had occurred. The implication was that someone was a sorcerer who was using *inyinya* (magical poison) to cause harm in the home.

There were various kinds of *inyinya*. Sometimes a sorcerer was believed to have buried a substance in the ground, causing animals to die and crops to wither. On other occasions it was claimed that a sorcerer was putting something in food and killing people. Numerous deaths of children and the sudden deaths of apparently healthy adults were evidence that *inyinya* was at work. Such ideas were by no means something restricted to rural people with little formal education. The district magistrate became so worried that she asked the LWF to seal her office so that there was no possibility of anyone putting things in it while she was out. A Madi

Catholic priest once told me that he had actually seen a sorcerer hurt a victim just by touching. To deny that *inyinya* existed was said to be foolhardy, a provocative invitation for sorcerers to demonstrate their powers.

Although it was possible for anyone to be a sorcerer secretly, it was usually thought to be something inherited. Suspicion was therefore directed at individuals who were not of the patrilineage, notably wives who had no children from a man of the home or for whom no bridewealth had been paid. The prevalence of deaths, illnesses and other afflictions in the late 1980s was taken as evidence that women coming to settle in their husbands' villages were not being properly vetted. Some of them must have come from families of sorcerers!

Talk of sorcery was common at funerals, and if the mourners became drunk, specific accusations might be made. Usually things would calm down after a good deal of shouting, but occasionally there was a consensus about who was to blame. On such occasions confirmation might be sought from one of the female spirit mediums, and extreme action could be taken. During the time I lived at Laropi some dozen cases came to my notice where accused sorcerers were tortured to death. For example, in mid-1988 a small child died and his mother suggested that the new wife of her husband's father might be responsible. Other people confirmed that the accused woman had been suspected of sorcery when she had been in the refugee camp in Sudan. Although she was pregnant at the time, she was tied up and beaten until she admitted her guilt. Then she was killed, and so were her two children from a previous marriage (to a man of a different patrilineage).

Many people were shocked by the brutality of these killings, but those who carried them out were not punished. It seemed to be accepted that the accused had been guilty, and several informants suggested that these deaths might discourage other sorcerers in the neighbourhood from using their evil skills. Some of the subsequent executions of individuals accused of using *inyinya* in Laropi area were implemented by RCs, and on one occasion by the NRA soldiers stationed near the Nile ferry. By and large such occurrences were viewed as a distressing but necessary response to an extreme situation. A basic level of trust between people living together had to be established, and that meant 'cleansing' the neighbourhood of sorcerers. In 1989, some parish-level RCs even lobbied the district committee to seek official approval to try *inyinya* cases and implement sentences on the convicted. They were unsuccessful, but their efforts reflected a general concern to involve the government in dealing with the problem, and thereby assist more effectively in the difficult task of forming and maintaining local communities.[2]

A Brief Comparison with Arua District

Ugandan refugees settled on Sudan's West Bank began repatriating several months after the East Bank refugees. Most of them (about 150,000) settled in Arua District. Although the rural security situation was often worse than in Moyo District, there were several factors which enabled many of these later returnees to establish reasonably comfortable lives.

First, some areas of Arua District are very fertile and well watered. In these places, farmers were able to cultivate tobacco, for which a relatively high price was paid by the British and American Tobacco Company (BAT), based in Kampala. They could also grow food crops for sale in the large market at Arua town.

Second, although sections of the road from Arua to Kampala were poorly maintained and were sometimes impassable, when the route was open the return journey took

[2] A more detailed discussion of social healing in Moyo District can be found in Allen (1991a) and Allen (1992).

betwen two and four days less by truck than the journey between Moyo and Kampala. For more wealthy merchants, there was also the option of fairly regular weekly flights between Arua and Entebbe.

Third, traders could cross into Zaire where there was a huge informal market at Ariwara, just over the border. According to Meagher, in 1988 some informants claimed this was the largest market in Africa. In addition to traders from Sudan, Zaire and Uganda, others came from as far away as Somalia, Senegal, and Ghana to do business. The most important commodities exchanged were gold, US dollars, coffee, clothes, imported consumer goods and foodstuffs (Meagher, 1988). Profits here were much higher than in Arua market itself, and in fact many of the enterprises in Arua town seem to have been little more than a front for what were officially illegal activities going on behind the scenes. Little attempt was made to disguise these activities, and the district authorities appear to have been involved in promoting them.

Fourth, the returning Ugandans from Sudan's West Bank repatriated in stages. Perhaps half of the West Bank refugees had been self-settled, and many had become quite well off in Sudan's fertile Yei River District. Even those in UNHCR-run official settlements had become self-sufficient in food production, and were very active in Yei market during the mid-1980s. Most families appear to have had at least a few resources to return home with, and because the security situation on the West Bank deteriorated gradually, they were able to bring property back with them.

Fifth, in part because there was more to build upon in the way of markets, communications and local resources, aid agencies found it easier to obtain village-level participation for their projects. In Aringa County, for example, the agricultural section of the LWF was able to work closely with a local Moslem NGO which had the capacity to mobilize farmers. The need to produce quick results meant that expatriate-run development schemes tended to concentrate efforts in relatively better-off locations, and parts of Arua District were much more fertile ground for 'grassroots' collaboration with 'communities' than places like Laropi in Moyo District.

It needs to be stressed, however, that these advantages did not lead to an adequate standard of living for everyone. In 1989, when the FAO was considering food relief in northwest Uganda, nutritional surveys indicated that some populations in Arua District were in a worse position than people in Moyo District. Where farmers grew tobacco on a large scale, there was correspondingly less cheap food in the rural markets, and the border trading opportunities near Arua town led to rapid social stratification, intense local antagonisms, banditry and theft. I was unable to undertake long-term village level research in Arua District, but it would appear that the kinds of violent incidents described above in Laropi were quite common. In 1989 the Catholic newsletter of Arua Diocese and the government-run national paper carried stories of RC involvement in the persecution of families using 'witchcraft'. In one of the counties of the district, several people were reported to have been tortured and killed (Allen, 1991a: 158–9).

PART THREE: Issues for Consideration in Aid Work

I have given an outline of the repatriation to Moyo District during the late 1980s, commented on the activities of the international aid agencies, and tried to show what life was like for the returnees. I have also looked at ways in which a range of cultural values have been relevant in what has occurred at the local level, and have emphasized how complex and fraught the continuous process of establishing communities with minimal external support can be. It would be misleading to derive from this analysis a series of clear policy prescriptions, because a great deal of the information that is important for those implementing assistance programmes is always likely to be location-specific.

Nevertheless, many parallels could be drawn with situations elsewhere – the extremities I have described are sadly not exceptional. It may, therefore, be useful to end by drawing attention to some of the issues underlined by this particular case study which seem most relevant for practitioners.

- The differences between refugee and returnee migrations relate to internationally recognized conceptions about nation states. It is however important to be aware that the differences between such categories may be less clear for the actors themselves. This is particularly so in marginal areas where people have frequently moved back and forth across international borders. In these locations nationalism, like ethnicity, may be asserted differently in different circumstances. People who attempt to obtain things from aid agencies by registering themselves in a way that manipulates the system are not necessarily 'cheating'.

- There is a serious problem with aid agency staffing. For various reasons, some of them to do with funding, it seems to be inevitable that the senior field staff of international agencies working in Africa are mostly expatriates. This is bad enough in itself, but the situation is often made worse by the choice of people appointed. Much has been written about the unprofessional approach of international aid agencies. It is often pointed out that staff are on short-term contracts and inexperienced, and that there is little institutional back-up to compensate. This is certainly true in some instances, notably that of the medical NGOs, but in others the opposite is the case, with equally damaging results. Some aid agency staff are over-professional and highly experienced in the wrong way. A construction engineer or car mechanic trained to deal with sophisticated equipment may have inappropriate concerns about particular standards, and may secure resources which could be better used for other purposes. Moreover, some experienced international aid workers have attitudes which local people find overbearing, and which tend to cause friction both within and between organizations. In 'hardship' posts like northern Uganda, a kind of 'frontier' or 'cowboy' mentality too easily becomes prevalent, and needs to be controlled. There were international aid workers in Moyo District who should not have been allowed to remain as long as they did.

- Contrary to the claims of the 1988 UNHCR report quoted at the start of the chapter, the relief operation in Moyo District was not a success. In retrospect it was surely a mistake for the UNHCR to have acted as an operational agency, and rather than serving as a model for future operations, the strategy adopted should probably be avoided. Certainly the tensions among UNHCR field staff, and between the UNHCR office and both the local government administration and representatives of international NGOs, were unhelpful. The UNHCR was not in a position to protect returned refugees and resisted involvement in essential development work. A great deal of time was taken up with ineffective numeration at official reception centres. The organization also proved to be inflexible, and only adapted slowly to changing circumstances.

- Although the relief operation in Moyo District was inadequate, there had certainly been a good case for a rapid, efficient, top-down intervention in response to the situation. However, emergencies need to be treated as relatively short-term events. When they are not, administrative structures are put in place, and service provision is attempted in a manner which, in the long run, cannot be sustained. Unsustainable projects are, or course, a general problem. This is partly because both international NGOs and UN organizations operate by setting up their own bureaucracies, often by-passing local structures. But when they do so as a response to an emergency, as it was in Moyo District, it can result in the emergency itself becoming institutionalized.

When asked why their organization had not become seriously involved in primary health care schemes, MSF medics would respond that they were not working for a development programme. Similarly UNHCR officers would maintain that longer term problems were for UNDP to deal with, since they did not fall into the category of emergency needs. Yet, paradoxically, by continuously linking repatriation with the idea of an emergency, it seemed that when a real one did occur, there were delays in dealing with it. Thus agencies already operational in the area on an 'emergency' basis were sluggish in responding to the refugee influxes of 1988–9. It was perceived as a different emergency from the one they had funding to deal with.

• There is a need for more adequate monitoring of relief and development operations. In Moyo District the relief effort failed, but because there was no publicity about what was going on, and because most senior staff in the aid agencies lived a life so divorced from the surrounding population, many seem to have genuinely believed that it had succeeded. The medical NGOs had no effective means of assessing the overall impact of their activities, and UNHCR made little attempt to discover what life was actually like for the mass of returnees. Some form of ongoing social research should be an integral part of programmes.

• Another reason why research is so important, particularly in relief work, is that viable community life cannot be assumed. Returnees may be coming home, but they may have had little previous contact with people they find to be their neighbours. In social upheaval, local-level mutuality is something grappled with, sometimes violently. Relief workers need to know who the losers are in order to provide assistance effectively, and development projects which call for community participation are unlikely to succeed unless considerable efforts are made to establish the community which might participate.

• There is an especially urgent need for community-level studies of health, understood as well-being rather than the absence of disease. Research documenting the prevalence of diseases is obviously valuable, but it sets aside investigation into how people themselves engage in a struggle for a healthy life. Given the spread of civil wars in Africa, research has to be attempted on collective and individual trauma. Occurrences of spirit possession and the killing of sorcerers cannot simply be set aside as cultural survivals from a supposed traditional past. As in Moyo District, they are more likely to be an aspect of dynamic local responses to upheaval and suffering. It is also worth bearing in mind that if there are insights to be derived from work among people who have been severely abused in the West, then it might be anticipated that without help, some of those who have been traumatized will eventually end up becoming the traumatizers of others.

Note

Fieldwork in Uganda was funded by the University of Manchester, the European Community and UNRISD. Logistical support was provided by LWF. The views expressed in this paper do not necessarily represent those of these organizations. A great deal of support and encouragement was received during and after fieldwork from Paul Baxter, Melissa Parker, Hans Martin Fisher, Hubert Morsink and Dan Mudoola.

References

Allen, T. (1987) 'Kwete and kweri: Acholi farm work groups in Southern Sudan', *Manchester papers on Development*, Vol. 3, No. 2: 60–92.
— (1989a) 'Full circle?: an overview of Sudan's "southern problem" since independence', *Northeast African Studies*, Vol. 11, No. 2: 41–66.

— (1991a) 'The quest for therapy in Moyo District', in H. Bernt Hansen and M.Twaddle (eds), *Changing Uganda*, James Currey, London
— (1991b) 'Understanding Alice: Uganda's Holy Spirit Movement in context', *Africa*, Vol. 61, No. 3: 370–99
— (1991c) 'Histories and contexts: using pasts in the present on the Sudan/Uganda border', *Bulletin of the John Rylands University Library of Manchester*, Vol. 73, No. 3: 63–91.
— (1992) 'Upheaval, affliction and health: a Ugandan case study', in H.Bernstein, B.Crow and H. Johnson (eds), *Rural livelihoods: crises and responses*, Oxford University Press, Oxford.
— (1994) 'Ethicity and tribalism on the Sudan–Uganda border', in K.Fukui and J.Markakis (eds), *Ethnicity and conflict in the Horn of Africa*, James Currey, London.
Behrend, H. (1991) 'Is Alice Lakwena a witch? The Holy Spirit Movement and its fight against evil in the north', in H. Bernt Hansen and M.Twaddle (eds), *Changing Uganda*, James Currey, London.
Crisp, J. (1986) 'Ugandan refugees in Sudan and Zaire: the problem of repatriation', *African Affairs*, Vol. 86, No. 339: 163–80.
Harrell-Bond, B.E. (1986) *Imposing aid*, Oxford University Press, Oxford.
Harrell-Bond, B.E. and G. Kanyeihamba (1986), 'Returnees and refugees – EEC mission to Uganda', mimeo, Refugee Studies Programme, University of Oxford, Oxford.
Keen, D. (1992) *Refugees: rationing the right to life*, Zed Books, London.
Meagher, K. (1988) 'The Market in the lived economy: a report on the dynamic of official and parallel market activities in Arua District, Uganda', mimeo, Institute of Development Studies, University of Sussex, Sussex.
UNHCR Technical Support Services (1986) 'Mission to north-west Uganda report', mimeo, UNHCR, Geneva, Switzerland.
— (1988) 'Mission report 55/88', UNHCR, Geneva, Switzerland.

18 MELISSA PARKER
Social Devastation & Mental Health in Northeast Africa

Some Reflections on an Absent Literature

Introduction

There is a great deal of psychiatric and psychoanalytic research exploring the psychological consequences of war and upheaval in the Western world. This research suggests that a large proportion of people suffer long-term impairment to their mental health as a consequence of the traumatic events they have had to endure. It seems reasonable to suppose that many of the refugees in northeast Africa who are reported to have returned 'home' may also be distressed and troubled by the experiences they have had at times of war and upheaval. Unfortunately, there have been very few attempts by psychiatrists and psychoanalysts to document the longer term consequences of war among non-Western populations in clinical settings; and psychiatric epidemiological research is virtually non-existent. A few social anthropologists have addressed issues of social well-being among refugees who have returned home but much of their work is imbued with notions of cultural relativism and it is difficult to see how governments and international agencies can act on the information which has been presented.

This chapter, therefore, raises the following two questions (with a view to helping research workers describe and understand traumas among populations in northeast Africa): to what extent can psychiatric and psychoanalytic approaches to the study of trauma shed light on the individual and collective difficulties which refugees face when they return 'home'? Is it appropriate to assume that returnee refugees who have experienced war-related traumas will face similar difficulties as those Europeans and North Americans who have struggled to reconcile losses and accept the traumas they have witnessed, experienced or perpetrated at times of war? The chapter is divided into three sections. The first section assesses psychiatric contributions to the study of trauma and upheaval and particular emphasis is given to the study of post-traumatic stress disorder. The second section focuses on psychoanalytic contributions to the study of trauma, drawing upon case material generated by the Holocaust; and the third summarizes the key points. This chapter raises more questions than it answers. This reflects the dearth of information about the psychological and social consequences of mass movement; and there is clearly an urgent need for more research.

Psychiatric Approaches to the Study of Trauma

Psychiatrists practising in North America, Europe and many other parts of the world increasingly rely on the most recent edition of the American Psychiatric Association's

(APA's) *Diagnostic and Statistical Manual of Mental Disorders* (currently DSM-111-R, 1987) to make their diagnoses.[1] The manual indicates that individuals respond to severely traumatic events in a multitude of ways. These include the development of depression and a variety of anxiety disorders. Post-traumatic stress disorder (or PTSD) is one of the most commonly cited anxiety disorders and this section focusses on PTSD to illustrate the strengths and weaknesses of comparative psychiatric approaches to the study of trauma.

PTSD was first classified in DSM-111 (1980) and its identification emerged from the work on 'shell shock' towards the end of the First World War as well as psychiatric work with survivors of concentration camps and Vietnam war veterans. It is usually diagnosed if the individual has experienced an event that is outside the range of usual human experience and the traumatic event is persistently re-experienced by recurrent and intrusive recollections of the events (in dreams, nightmares or daytime 'flashbacks'). These occurrences may be so intense that the individual feels as if s/he is reliving the event. Post-traumatic stress disorder is also characterized by reduced involvement with the external world (diminished interest, detachment or estrangement, or constricted affect); and at least two of the

18.1 *There have been very few attempts by psychiatrists and psychoanalysts to document the longer term consequences of war among non-Western populations in clinical settings; and psychiatric epidemiological research is virtually non-existent: Mozambican refugee in Malawi, 1988. (UNHCR/1810/A. Hollmann)*

following symptoms: sleep disturbances, hypervigilance (often manifested by a tendency to startle easily); inability to concentrate; survivor guilt; avoidance of activities that arouse recollection of the trauma; and intensification of symptoms by exposure to events that symbolize or resemble the traumatic event. The primary symptoms are listed in Table 18.1 but a variety of secondary symptoms have also been associated with PTSD. These include depression, 'death anxiety', impulsive behaviour, substance abuse and somatization.

Until 1980, stress disorders were generally seen as acute, time-limited phenomena which diminished with time unless some pre-existing character pathology was present which enabled symptoms to be maintained. DSM-1 (1952), for example, contained a diagnosis called 'gross stress reaction', which was thought to diminish rapidly unless maintained by pre-morbid personality traits. That is, prolonged responses to stress were assumed to have their roots in individual history. The idea that severely traumatic events occurring in adulthood might have psychological consequences which are prolonged, irrespective of an individual's vulnerability, is thus a relatively recent formal conceptualization.

---

[1] This manual is available in 13 languages and its shortened form – the *Quick Reference to Diagnostic Criteria* (the 'mini' D) – has become virtually a textbook in many Third World countries where funds are limited (see Littlewood, 1992).

Table 18.1: *Diagnostic criteria for post-traumatic stress disorder*

A The individual has experienced an event that is outside the range of usual human experience and that would be markedly distressing to almost anyone, e.g.: serious threat to one's life or physical integrity; serious threat or harm to one's children, spouse or other close relatives or friends; sudden destruction of one's home or community; or seeing another person who has been, is being (or has recently been) seriously injured or killed as the result of an accident or physical violence.

B The traumatic event is persistently re-experienced in at least one of the following ways:
   1 Recurrent and intrusive distressing recollections of the event (in young children, repetitive play in which themes or aspects of the trauma are expressed)
   2 Recurrent distressing dreams of the event
   3 Sudden acting or feeling as if the traumatic event were recurring (includes a sense of reliving the experience, illusions, hallucinations, and dissociative [flashback] episodes, even those that occur upon waking or when intoxicated
   4 Intense psychological distress at exposure to events that symbolize or resemble an aspect of the traumatic event, including anniversaries of trauma.

C Persistent avoidance of stimuli associated with the trauma or general responsiveness (not present before the trauma), as indicated by at least three of the following:
   1 Deliberate efforts to avoid thoughts or feelings associated with the trauma
   2 Deliberate efforts to avoid activities or situations that arouse recollections of the trauma
   3 Inability to recall an important aspect of the trauma (psychogenic amnesia)
   4 Markedly diminished interest in significant activities (in young children, loss of recently acquired developmental skills such as toilet training or language skills)
   5 Feeling of detachment or estrangement from others
   6 Restricted range of affect, e.g. unable to have loving feelings
   7 Sense of foreshortened future e.g. child does not expect to have a career, marriage, or children, or a long life

D Persistent symptoms of increased arousal (not present before the trauma) as indicated by at least two of the following:
   1 Difficulty falling or staying asleep
   2 Irritability or outbursts of anger
   3 Difficulty concentrating
   4 Hypervigilance
   5 Exaggerated startle response
   6 Physiologic reactivity at exposure to events that symbolize or resemble an aspect of the traumatic event (e.g. a woman who was raped in an elevator breaks out into a sweat when entering an elevator).

E Duration of the disturbance of at least one month. Specify delayed onset if the onset of the symptoms was at least six months after the trauma.

Source: APA:DSM-III-R, 1987: 250-1

Current application of PTSD

A great deal of research has been undertaken on PTSD since its official recognition in 1980. Most of this work has taken place in Western countries among American soldiers returning from Vietnam (e.g.: Helzer *et al.*, 1987; Snow *et al.*, 1988; Pitman *et al* 1989; Speed *et al.*, 1989); British soldiers returning from the Falklands war (e.g.: O'Brien *et al.*, 1991) and men, women or children who have witnessed civilian catastrophes as diverse as the King's Cross Underground fire of 1987 (Sturgeon *et al.*, 1991); a sniper attack in a school playground (Nader *et al.*, 1990); the capsize of the *Herald of Free Enterprise* ferry at Zeebrugger Harbour; and ritual abuse in childhood (Young *et al* 1991). All this research draws attention to the fact that traumatic events may impair an individual's social and psychological functioning for many months and years after the incident and the consequences can be fatal. For example, American soldiers returning from Vietnam found it difficult to resume their pre-war roles as husbands, fathers and stable employees, and self-destructive behaviour is common. Indeed, Summerfield (1990) cites some research which suggests that the number of veterans who subsequently died from suicide, drug and alcohol abuse, and shoot-outs with police exceeds the 50,000 who died at war.

Research workers have also diagnosed PTSD among southeast Asian refugees attending clinics in North America (Kinzie *et al* 1984; Kinzie *et al.*, 1986; Kinzie *et al.*, 1990, Sack *et al.*, 1986; and Moore *et al.*, 1991). This work suggests that PTSD often occurs among children and adults who have experienced or witnessed distressing events in violent environments. Kinzie *et al.*, (1986a), for example, worked with 40 Cambodian schoolchildren in the USA who had lived through four years of concentration camp-like conditions. They found that 50 per cent had developed PTSD; and mild, but prolonged depressive symptoms were also common.

Research documenting the proportion of civilians who have developed PTSD or other so-called disorders in violent environments is meagre. The small amount of work which has been done suggests that the longer term consequences of witnessing or experiencing appalling acts of violence may be serious. Summerfield's pilot study in Nicaragua (1990), for example, suggested that 25–50 per cent of the adult population experienced PTSD. Straker *et al's* (1988) work with youth in a South African township also indicated a high but unspecified occurrence of PTSD; and Richman's (1991) work with children in Mozambique noted symptoms associated with PTSD.

The increasing tendency to diagnose PTSD among refugees from Southeast Asia and people who have been exposed to war traumas in South America and sub-Saharan Africa raises some difficult and important questions. Are there universal responses to extremely traumatic situations which can be accurately described by making psychiatric diagnoses such as depression and PTSD? Or, to put it another way, is it possible to describe and understand the impact of war-related traumas among non-Western patients by employing psychiatric categories which have emerged from the experiences of Western patients in clinical settings? What is the most appropriate way for psychiatric epidemiologists to contribute to the study of war-related traumas?

With reference to the first question, it is increasingly acknowledged by psychiatrists that it is extremely difficult to diagnose PTSD and other psychiatrically defined diseases detailed in DSM-111-R among non-Western individuals. For example, the introduction to the revised edition of DSM-111-R states: 'caution should be exercised in the application of DSM-111-R diagnostic criteria to assure that their use is culturally valid. It is important that the clinician not employ DSM-111-R in a mechanical fashion, insensitive to differences in language, values, behavioural norms, and idiomatic expressions of distress' (APA, 1987: *xxvi*). That said, the manual does not explain how or when the clinician's understanding of the patient's values, behavioural norms and idioms of distress, etc. should be incorporated into their diagnoses and therapy. It is not surprising, therefore, that this cautionary note has not been heeded and that psychiatric research and therapy is rarely informed by a detailed knowledge of the patient's cultural background and their idioms of distress.

The designation of events as 'traumatic' and the interpretation of their social and psychological sequelae present a number of theoretical, methodological and practical problems. One of the most important issues which requires attention includes the following: PTSD is imbued with culturally specific conceptions of normality and deviance and it is thus difficult to make appropriate diagnoses. The following two examples illustrate this point. First, an essential feature of PTSD is the development of characteristic symptoms following a psychologically distressing event that is outside the range of usual human experience. The DSM-111-R manual excludes 'common experiences as simple bereavement, chronic illness, business losses, and marital conflict' (1987: 247) but while this may be appropriate for middle-class North Americans it is not clear how to interpret distressing events that are outside the range of usual human experience among populations where it is usual to witness a great deal of murder and torture (Jenkins, 1991; Littlewood, 1992). Second, the name PTSD implies that the traumas are finite events which gradually recede into the past and the diagnostic criteria discount the fact that many people actually live with prolonged warfare, economic insecurity and sustained states of terror and fear. It is clearly difficult to diagnose PTSD against this background – especially as some of the primary symptoms of PTSD may be adaptive responses to particularly awful circumstances. To quote Summerfield: '[i]t is hard for a mother to mourn a murdered child whilst her other children continue to be at risk of the same fate. And while threat continues, hypervigilance, a core element of PTSD, is adaptive' (1990: 5).

The above two examples draw attention to some of the limitations of the current conceptualization of PTSD. Indeed, several investigators have suggested that the diagnostic category of PTSD should be reformulated to allow for the fact that many people in war-torn environments experience continuous trauma (Summerfield, 1990; Straker, 1988; Turner and Gorst-Unsworth, 1990).

But, to my mind, it is not clear whether the notion of PTSD needs to be reformulated or whether it is inappropriate to seek to describe war-related traumas in terms of American psychiatric categories among people in northeast Africa and other parts of the non-Western world. The reasons are many and include the following: first, cross-cultural psychiatric research assumes a model of pathogenecity/pathoplasticity whereby 'biology is presumed to "determine" the cause and structure of the disorder, while cultural and social factors, at most, shape or "influence" the content of disorder'. (Kleinman 1987: 450). Psychiatric diagnosis thus entails eliciting the signs and symptoms of ill-health to identify the hidden disorder. There is a growing body of research which suggests, however, that biological and cultural factors dialectically interact. There may be times when biological factors have a greater influence on outcome than social factors (and vice versa) but most of the time it is the interaction between the two which affects the nature and extent of ill-health. Indeed, there are times when the interaction between biological and social factors transforms the biology just as it alters social relationships (Kleinman, 1987: 450).

A second problem which is associated with the way in which psychiatric disorders (such as PTSD) are conceptualized concerns the way in which 'the disorder' is identified. Generally speaking, a questionnaire is employed which enquires about the presence or absence of a variety of clear-cut, specific and unambiguous signs and symptoms which together constitute the disorder. Epidemiologists investigating the prevalence of a particular disorder will thus translate their questions into the local language (adjusting them for semantic difference, where necessary); and administer the questionnaire to a stratified sample of the population. This approach enables the most vulnerable sectors of a population to be identified. A survey carried out in region x, for example, may indicate an overall prevalence of PTSD of 30 per cent but show that 80 per cent of children between the ages of 5–10 years have PTSD compared with a prevalence of 20 per cent among adults.

However, this approach ignores the hazards associated with interpreting signs and symptoms out of their cultural context. Obeyesekere, among others, has illustrated some of the difficulties associated with decontextualizing signs and symptoms. To quote:

> Take the case of a South Asian male who has the following symptoms: drastic weight loss, sexual fantasies, and night emissions and urine discolouration. In South Asia the patient may be diagnosed as suffering from a disease, 'semen loss'. But on the operational level I can find this constellation of symptoms in every society .... If I were to say, however, that I know plenty of Americans suffering from the disease 'semen loss', I would be laughed out of court even though I could prove that this disease is universal. The trouble with my formulation is that while the symptoms exist at random everywhere, they have not been 'fused into a conception' (as semen loss) in American society. Yet if I were to employ the methodological norms implicit in the several Diagnostic and Statistical manuals and apply them from a South Asian perspective to the rest of the world (as Western psychiatrists do for depression), then it is incontrovertible that 'semen loss' is a disease and is universally found in human populations' (1985: 136–37).

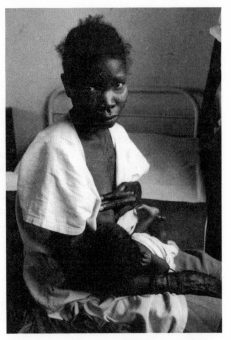

18.2 *Figures relating to PTSD convey little about the impact of social upheavals on people's capacities to manage daily life and personal relationships: Mozambican mother and child in Tanzania. (UNHCR 949/Jean Mohr)*

Guarnaccia *et al.* (1990) have also drawn attention to the difficulties of diagnosing and assessing the prevalence of psychiatrically defined disorders across cultures. Their paper reviews epidemiological research on the mental health of Puerto Ricans and other Hispanics in North American cities. According to surveys using standardized symptom check lists and diagnostic interviews, this research suggests that Puerto Ricans have consistently experienced more symptoms than other ethnic groups. It is difficult to interpret this finding as Puerto Ricans appear to respond positively to items on a symptom check list. In fact, Guarnaccia *et al.* (1990) suggest that the constellation of symptoms covered by these surveys matches a locally defined and socially acceptable illness (*nervios*). The fact that other ethnic groups do not acknowledge and/or articulate distress in the same way as Puerto Ricans does not, of course, mean they are not distressed – although epidemiological research may suggest otherwise.

There are many other difficulties associated with collecting and interpreting psychiatric epidemiological data. With reference to PTSD, research conducted in a number of different countries may suggest that the prevalence of this disorder varies a great deal within and between populations. Assuming survey figures reflect, however partially, variations in the experience of distress it is far from clear how these types of figures should be interpreted, as PTSD (and other disorders) convey very little about how daily life is affected and altered by the manifestation of a variety of signs and symptoms. The impact on relationships such as a mother's ability to care for her children; a man's motivation to sow seeds for the coming year; a child's ability to pass school exams, etc. is not conveyed by these types of figures. The symptoms associated with PTSD are not, of course, pleasant but epidemiological data does not help us to understand why certain experiences are so devastating and distressing. Moreover, they convey very little about the conflicts and difficulties people face in their daily lives as they struggle to accept the traumas they have witnessed, experienced and/or perpetrated.

Finally, the following question requires attention: in so far as it is possible to diagnose psychiatrically defined disorders in different cultural settings, it is far from clear whether the development of these disorders is an appropriate response to appalling occurrences. Should we be more or equally concerned about the people who experience, witness or perpetrate appalling acts of violence and do not become depressed or develop anxiety disorders such as PTSD? To the best of my knowledge we do not have any epidemiological information conveying the nature and extent of responses to severely traumatic events (PTSD or otherwise) and it is not known whether some disorders are more common than others and whether some people experience a particular disorder more severely than others. Indeed, it is not clear whether it is possible for some people to remain unscathed by violent events while others who have experienced similar events struggle to accept these occurrences for years and even decades after their cessation. It will not be possible to address these questions without conducting interdisciplinary research with a longitudinal dimension.

Psychoanalytic Approaches to the Study of Trauma

Psychoanalytic approaches to the study of trauma are very different from psychiatric approaches to trauma. There are a multitude of theories about appropriate ways to interpret traumatic occurrences and their consequences for individual well-being. This section does not attempt to assess the relative merits of these different theories. Instead, salient issues emerging from the psychoanalytic literature on trauma are raised to alert research workers in the field of mental health to issues which may be relevant to their work among populations who have experienced considerable trauma in northeast Africa.

In contrast to the psychiatric literature there has been a great deal of discussion in the psychoanalytic literature about how to define trauma and distinguish between partial trauma and cumulative trauma. These discussions have been greatly influenced by psychoanalytic work with patients who survived the Holocaust but struggled to adjust to life thereafter. They have also been influenced by Freud's work on trauma. Krystal has summarized some of this work and tells us that 'it is the subjective experience of helplessness which determines whether a situation is traumatic as distinguished from one of danger ... The essence of recognized and admitted helplessness is the surrender to the inevitable peril ... Helplessly surrendering to the peril changes the affective state from the hyperalert and hyperactive response (anxiety) to one of the blocking of emotions and progressive inhibition (1978:92).[2]

Jucovy (1992) recently reviewed the psychoanalytic literature on the Holocaust and shows, among other things, that more than a decade lapsed before clinical reports about patients who survived the Holocaust appeared in the psychoanalytic literature. A curtain of silence descended shortly after liberation; and it seems that temporal and emotional distance were necessary before survivors were able to deal with their repressed memories and therapists were able to respond to their needs.

However, there is now a large body of work which shows that psychic suffering

---

[2] Krystal, among others, has built on Freud's work and he describes the following responses as typically associated with traumatized occurences among patients: '... a paralysed, overwhelmed state, with immobilization, withdrawal, possible depersonalization, evidence of disorganization. There may be regression in any and all spheres and aspects of mental function and affect expression. This regression is followed by characteristic recuperative attempts through repetition, typical dreams, and eventually by long-term neurotic, psychosomatic, or other syndromes' (1978: 95). The so-called traumatic neurosis is just one of many possible sequelae of traumatization.

among survivors persisted after liberation, in spite of a gradual return to normal daily routine. In common with the psychiatric literature, a great variety of clinical pictures have been identified and these range from psychosis to neurosis. The following responses are often involved in the development of these different syndromes: first, defence mechanisms such as denial appear to have helped prisoners to survive imprisonment. Indeed, it has been suggested that prisoners able to combine 'psychic closing off' of an unbearable external reality with an intense remembering of an idealized past and magical fantasizing of an alternative world – without becoming psychotic – did relatively well. In addition, 'automization of the ego' or 'robotization' (which involves an automatic functioning of the ego, without accompanying affect); and identification with the aggressor, who was seen to be omnipotent, are phenomena which are frequently cited in the literature. Unfortunately, some of these psychic 'adaptations' which appear to have been necessary for survival during imprisonment were later found to have resulted in irreversible psychological damage and to impair daily life a great deal.

18.3 *There has been a great deal of discussion about how to define trauma and distinguish between partial and cumulative trauma: an old man living at a refugee camp in Hararghe region, Ethiopia. (UNHCR/17056/S. Lamb)*

Second, there is widespread agreement that a clear-cut 'survivor syndrome' can be identified. Niederland (1968), for example, observed more than 800 survivors and describes the syndrome as being composed of the following symptoms and signs: anxiety (which is associated with fears, sleep disturbances, multiple phobias and 're-run' phobias); disturbances of cognition and memory; chronic depressive states; tendency to isolation, withdrawal and brooding seclusion; alterations of personal identity, of the body and self-image, and of the perceptions of time and space; psychosomatic manifestations; and a 'living corpse appearance'.[3]

Reflecting on the psychiatric literature, there appears to be considerable overlap between the so-called 'survivor syndrome' and 'post-traumatic stress disorder'. This is intriguing as psychoanalytic and psychiatric theories and practices are so different from each other. Indeed, it draws attention to an interesting point made by Summerfield (1990): human beings appear to have a relatively limited repertoire of responses to major trauma.

[3] Grubrich-Simitis suggests that one of the reasons a survivor syndrome can be identified is due to a certain uniformity in the extreme traumatization in the camps. To quote: '...I do not mean that even in this utmost horror, shades of difference did not exist. It made a difference whether one was imprisoned in Theresienstadt or in one of the extermination camps such as Auschwitz or Treblinka, or whether, within the camp, one had to exist in the death area or, for example, in the workman's barrracks. However, it is the combination of the extreme traumatic conditions in all concentration camps, the realization of a psychotic universe, that constitutes the essential difference between this and other forms of massive traumatization: the disruption of family ties and the loss of a familiar sociocultural environment; continuous separation anxiety; the witnessing of torture and murder; the perpetual helpless expectation of one's own violent death ... persistent experiences of debasement and degradation through being regarded as a member of a minority to be wiped out, as 'vermin fit only to be exterminated'; being the object of systematic genocide (1981:422).

18.4 *'Remove seeds of war': Ugandans in Arua district, 1989. (Tim Allen)*

A third theme to emerge from the psychoanalytic literature on trauma concerns the effects of the Holocaust on the second generation. Observations reveal some character-istic conflicts and recurrent patterns in children of survivor families who sought treat-ment for varied emotional problems. These include the following: survivors' children often lived their lives in a way where the reality of the past seemed to intrude excessively into the reality of the present. This phenomenon of 'transposition' or living in a 'time tunnel' may be illustrated by the following example: '... a Holocaust survivor, seeing a uniformed police officer in an American city approach her car, however coincidentally, [may] have a panic attack. A scene such as this, witnessed by a child [sitting next to her mother], can only foster the illusion of how precarious life can be' (Jucovy,1992: 271).

In addition, survivors' children were found to have an intense need to act as redeem-ers for their parents, whose unbearable suffering during the Holocaust continued in the form of unresolved mourning. The children of the second generation were often over-valued and overprotected, but they had to tread softly, as their parents could not easily tolerate aggressive behaviour and were apt to call them 'little Hitlers', utilizing a deriva-tive of their own need to identify with the aggressor, often called projective identification.

However, identification with the aggressor takes many forms and the literature is replete with different examples illustrating the types of difficulties children experienced as a result. A young man, for instance, told his therapist that '... when he misbehaved during his childhood, his mother placed his head in the kitchen oven, warning him that this is what Nazis did to Jews in concentration and death camps' (Jucovy, 1992: 274).

It should be stressed, however, that not all survivors became ill after liberation and survivors' children have not necessarily suffered from their violent experiences. Unfortunately, there is very little psychoanalytic writing which sheds light on why some people caught up in the Holocaust remain able to function while others break down. This is partly due to the fact that observations and theories about trauma have been generated from small, self-selected samples in very specific clinical settings created by psychoanalysts. Indeed, the unusual relationship which develops between psychoanalysts and their analysands in clinical settings has tended to generate questions about the extent to which the pre-traumatic personality, its tolerance for stress and post-traumatic life experiences influence the nature and extent of distress subsequently experienced. That said, Grubich-Simitis has suggested that one of the most traumatizing factors in the Holocaust was experienced by adults whose children were taken away from them and murdered (thereby violently reversing the natural order of dying); and she posits that experiences such as these will break any psychic structure.

At this point I would like to draw your attention to an important difference between the psychiatric and psychoanalytic literature on trauma. The psychiatric literature on PTSD (and other disorders) does not convey any sense of whether the traumas experienced in southeast Asia are different from those experienced in Central America. It is not clear, for example, whether a nightmare endured by a Cambodian child has the same resonances as a nightmare endured by a child from El Salvador. This is inevitable as the context and meanings are never explicitly addressed in psychiatric research. By contrast, the psychoanalytic literature demonstrates that each tragedy has its special qualities. The clinical material has far more depth and the reader is spared little as examples of 'acting out' are cited again and again. It is easy to see how traumatic events are relived and experienced, albeit in a diluted form. The psychoanalytic literature also highlights the fact that individual responses to similarly awful events often vary by age, gender, family circumstances, psychological vulnerability prior to the traumatic events, etc. Psychiatrists are also interested in documenting and responding to this variability but the discipline is far less able to shed light on how people respond and live with trauma and why it is that some experiences are so devastating.

That said, there are probably just as many questions about the application of psycho-analytic ideas to non-Western settings as there are about the application of psychiatric ideas to non-Western settings. This point was brought home to me in conversations I have had with researchers who have spent time with war-damaged populations in Africa. It appears that, while it is common for people to display symptoms of trauma, sometimes in locally specific ways. it is rare for anyone to express feelings which might be rendered in English as 'guilt' (personal communication with T. Allen and A. Brett). This observation raises the question of whether we should assume that 'survivor guilt' is always going to be present among the traumatized (even though it may be repressed). It has been docu-mented that in African communities guilt-type feelings can be interpreted as a motive for witchcraft, so there may be good reasons for denial. However, it is just as likely that local conceptions of individuality and ideas about being a person throw up a different range of emotions and behaviours to those noted by psychoanalysts in the West. There is growing anthropological literature related to such issues but analysis remains largely speculative (Heald and Deluz, 1994; Heelas and Lock, 1981; Kareem and Littlewood, 1992; Marsella and White, 1982; Littlewood 1990; Schwartz, White and Lutz, 1992).

Conclusion

This chapter has focussed on psychiatric and psychoanalytic approaches to the study of trauma. The emphasis has been on individual rather than collective responses to trauma and without wishing to belittle individual experiences there are inherent limitations to this approach – namely, the danger of medicalizing awful social problems and deflecting attention from national and international responsibilities (Kleinman, 1987; Higgen-bottom and Marsella, 1988).

In addition, a number of difficult and awkward questions have been put to one side. The psychiatric and psychoanalytic literature assumes a mind/body dualism and a notion of self that is inextricably intertwined with Western notions of autonomy and individual responsibility. Research undertaken by social anthropologists in northeast Africa (and

18.5 *Mengistu's ex-soldiers, Addis Ababa, Ethiopia, July 1991. (Dario Mitidieri/CAFOD)*

other parts of the non-Western world) highlights these assumptions by continually drawing attention to the different ways in which health, illness and the notion of self for example, are culturally constructed. There are innumerable examples illustrating the different ways in which individual and collective distress may be expressed and it is far from clear whether psychiatric and psychoanalytic approaches to trauma can be usefully applied in some of these regions.

In spite of the fact that anthropologists have shed light on the limitations of Western understandings of trauma and demonstrated the need for more research to be undertaken at a local level, they have not shown that psychiatric and psychoanalytic approaches to trauma are useless. It is possible that some of these ideas are helpful but it is currently unclear which of these ideas can be deployed to understand and respond to suffering.

One possible way to resolve some of the issues raised in this chapter would be to undertake some epidemiological research in an area where refugees have returned 'home'. This research could document the prevalence of psychiatrically defined disorders (such as PTSD, depression etc.) among a random sample of the population. The investigators could then be encouraged to live and work in the area for a couple of years and to spend extensive periods of time with a sub-sample of the population. The ethnographic information generated by a protracted stay in the region could then be used to examine the concepts employed in the survey and, where appropriate, to interpret the data which had been collected.

Acknowledgements
The London School of Hygiene and Tropical Medicine and the Health and Population Division of the UK Overseas Development Administration covered the costs incurred in the writing of this chapter.

References

American Psychiatric Association (APA). (1980). *Diagnostic and statistical manual 111* (DSM-111). American Psychiatric Association, Washington, DC.

— (1987) *Diagnostic and Statistical Manual 111–Revised*. American Psychiatric Association, Washington, DC.

Grubrich-Simitis,I. (1981) 'Extreme traumatization as cumulative trauma. Psychoanalytic investigations of the effects of concentration camp experiences on survivors and their children'. *The Psychoanalytic Study of the Child*, 36: 415–50.

Guarnaccia, P.J., Good, B.J., Kleinman, A. (1990) 'A critical review of epidemiological studies of Puerto Rican mental health', *American Journal of Psychiatry*, 147: 1449–56.

Heald, S. Deluz, A. (ed.) (1994) *Anthropology and psychoanalysis: an encounter through culture*, Routledge, London.

Heelas, P., Lock, A. (1981) *Indigenous Psychologies: the anthropology of the self*, Academic Press, London.

Helzer, J.E., Robin, L., McEvoy, C. (1987) 'Post-traumatic stress disorders in the general population', *New England Journal of Medicine*, 317: 1630–4.

Higgenbottom, N., Marsella, A.J., (1988) 'International consultation and the homogenization of psychiatry in southeast Asia'. *Social Science and Medicine*, 27: 553–61.

Jenkins, J.H. (1991) 'The state construction of affect: political ethos and mental health among Salvadoran refugees', *Culture, Medicine and Psychiatry*, 15: 139–65.

Jucovy, M.E., (1992) 'Psychoanalytic contributions to Holocaust studies', *International Journal of Psycho-Analysis*, 73: 267–82.

Kareem, J., Littlewood, R. (ed.) (1992) *Intercultural therapy: themes, interpretations and practice*, Blackwell Scientific Publications, Oxford.

Kinzie, J.D., Fredrickson, R.H., Ben, R., Fleck, J., Karls, W. (1984) 'Post-traumatic stress disorders among survivors of Cambodian concentration camps', *American Journal of Psychiatry*, 141: 645–50.

Kinzie, J.D., Sack, W.H., Angell, R.H., Manson, S., Rath, B. (1986) 'The psychiatric effects of massive trauma on Cambodian children: 1. The children', *Journal of the American Academy of Child Psychiatry*, 25: 370–76.

Kinzie, J.D., Boehnlein, J.K., Leung, P.K., Laurie, J.M., Riley, C., Smith, D. (1990). 'The prevalence of post-traumatic stress disorder and its clinical significance among Southeast Asian refugees', *American Journal of Psychiatry*, 147: 913–17.

Klein, M. (1975) *Love, guilt and reparation and other works*, Volume 1. Hogarth Press, London.

Kleinman, A. (1987) 'Anthropology and psychiatry: the role of culture in cross-cultural research on illness' *British Journal of Psychiatry*, 151: 447–54.

Krystal, H. (1978) 'Trauma and affects. The Psychoanalytic Study of the Child', 33: 81–116.

Littlewood, R. (1990) 'From categories to contexts: a decade of the "new cross-cultural psychiatry"'. *British Journal of Psychiatry*, 156: 308–27.

— (1992) 'DSM-1V and culture: is the classification internationally valid?' *Psychiatric Bulletin*, 16: 257–61.

Marsella, A.S., White, G.M. (1982) *Cultural conceptions of mental health and therapy*, Kluwer Academic Press, Dor.

Moore, L.J., Boehnlein, J.K. (1991) 'Treating psychiatric disorders among Mien refugees from Highland Laos' *Social Science and Medicine*, 32: 1029–36.

Nader, K., Pynoos, R., Fairbanks, L., Frederick, C. (1990) 'Children's PTSD reactions one year after a sniper attack at their school' *American Journal of Psychiatry*, 147: 1526–30.

Niederland, W.G. (1968) 'Clinical observations on the "survivor syndrome": symposium on psychic traumatization through social catastrophe', *International Journal of Psycho-analysis*, 49: 313–15.

Obeyesekere, G. (1985) 'Depression, Buddhism, and the work of culture', in A. Kleinman and B. Good (eds) *Culture and depression: studies in the anthropology and cross-cultural psychiatry of affect and disorder*, University of California Press, Berkeley.

O'Brien, L.S., Hughes, S.J. (1991) 'Symptoms of post-traumatic stress disorder in Falklands veterans five years after the conflict', *British Journal of Psychiatry*, 159: 135–41.

Pitman, R.K., Altman, B., Macklin, M.L. (1989) 'Prevalence of post-traumatic stress disorder in wounded Vietnam veterans', *American Journal of Psychiatry*, 146: 667–69.

Richman, N. (1991) 'Children in Mozambique: towards an understanding of strategies for survival', paper presented in Namibia at a workshop on healing the social wounds of war.

Sack, W.H., Angell, R.H., Kinzie, J.D., Rath, B. (1986) 'The psychiatric effects of massive trauma on Cambodian children: II. The family, the home and the school', *Journal of the American Academy of Child Psychiatry*, 25: 377–83.

Schwartz, T., White, G.M., Lutz, C.A. (1992) *New directions in psychological anthropology*, Cambridge University Press.

Snow, B.R., Stellman, J.M., Stellman, S.D., Sommer, J.F. (1988) 'Post-traumatic stress disorder among American legionnaires in relation to combat experience in Vietnam: associated and contributing factors', *Environmental Research*, 42: 175–92.

Speed, N., Engdahl, B., Schwartz, J. et al. (1989) 'Post-traumatic stress disorder as a consequence of POW experience', *Journal of Nervous and Mental Diseases*, 177: 147–53.

Straker et al. (1988) 'PTSD: a reaction to state-supported child abuse and neglect', *Child Abuse and Neglect*, 12(3) 383–95.

Sturgeon, D., Rosser, R., Shoenberg, P. (1991) 'The King's Cross fire. Part 2: the psychological injuries', *Burns*, 17: 10–30.

Summerfield, D.A. (1990) 'The psychosocial effects of conflict in the third world', Oxfam House, Oxford.

Turner, S., Gorst-Unsworth, C. (1990) 'Psychological sequelae of torture', *British Journal of Psychiatry*, 157: 475–80.

Young, W.C., Sachs, R.G., Braun, B.G., Watkins, R.T. (1991) 'Patients reporting ritual abuse in childhood: a clinical syndrome', *Child Abuse and Neglect*, 15: 181–9.

19 YONAS ENDALE
Ethiopia's Mental Health
Trampled by Armed Conflicts

Introduction

Ethiopia's experience of epidemics, famine and war are much better known to the to the world than the colours of its tricoloured flag. They have caused appalling suffering, often manifested in acute psycho-social stress.

The country has just emerged from the longest civil war in Africa. During the past 30 years, and especially during the 17-year rule of the Mengistu regime, various contending groups have utilized all forms of struggle, ranging from the exchange of vitriolic rhetoric to the use of napalm bombs. The fighting has been extremely costly both in terms of human lives and materials.

The defence minister of the present transitional government has estimated, on the basis of official records of the Derg regime, that about 500,000 soldiers of Mengistu's armed forces, 150,000 fighters of the Eritrean People's Liberation Front (EPLF), Tigray People's Liberation Front (TPLF) and other rebel groups, and at least 500,000 civilians, died between 1974 and 1990. Other estimates are even higher. A figure of 1.5 million has been suggested as the number of Ethiopians killed in the war in Eritrea, a figure which excludes Eritrean casualties. Military expenditures increased from 106.5 million birr in 1974 to 2.3 billion birr in 1990–91. In 1989 Mengistu himself admitted that military expenditure covered 50 per cent of recurrent state expenditure. In contrast the health budget declined from 6.1 per cent in 1973–74 to 3.2 per cent in 1990–92.

Mengistu is said to have had a harsh upbringing and a bitter life experience. He displayed rigid and hypersensitive behaviour in his years of rule. He declared war on 'counter-revolutionaries' at the centre, 'secessionists' in the north, 'feudal remnants' in the west and 'Somali expansionists' in the east. He was at his most eloquent when talking of an 'international conspiracy' against his regime, whereas his speeches were quite boring when he talked about issues relating to economic development.

It was not only the government but also the opposition forces that were engaged in multiple warfronts. As well as fighting government forces, the EPLF fought against the Eritrean Liberation Front (ELF), and the TPLF against a variety of other guerrilla outfits. Government and opposition hit squads frequently killed each other in the streets or in people's own homes. The various factions widely used the 'splitting' ego defence mechanism, openly declaring that everyone had to choose between revolutionary or counter-revolutionary camps – being neutral was inadmissible to both. They forced independent thinkers to take sides.

19.1 *Yonas Endale with one of his patients at the Armed Forces General Hospital in Addis Ababa, 1992. (Tim Allen)*

Mental Health Services in the Armed Forces

The Armed Forces General Hospital is located in the capital city, Addis Ababa. It has 600 beds, making it the largest in the country. The hospital evolved to its present status from a small clinic of the imperial bodyguard. Currently it provides 11 specialized services, one of which is psychiatric care.

Mental health care is virtually non-existent in Ethiopia. Up to the 1980s there was only one psychiatrist for the whole country. At present there are only nine psychiatrists to serve Ethiopia's 52 million people. Ethiopia's WHO representative has recently stated that out of 400 million Africans about 8 million people are estimated to suffer from mental disorders, and that one million of these are estimated to come from Ethiopia.

Up to February 1992 there was one Yugoslav-educated Ethiopian neuro-psychiatrist working at our hospital, together with expatriate psychiatrists from the Soviet Union and Bulgaria. Currently there is one full-time psychiatrist (the author) and two psychiatric nurses. We run a daily out-patient and a 30 bed in-patient service. As well as soldiers in the Derg army, since May 1991 the hospital has served the army of the Ethiopian People's Revolutionary Democratic Front (EPRDF) (which the council of representatives declared to be the army of the Transitional Government of Ethiopia in April 1992).

Every week we see 20–25 new patients as out-patients, of which about 80 per cent are diagnosed to have post-traumatic stress disorder. The rest suffer from bodily disorders, adjustment disorders, dissociative conversion disorders, organic brain syndromes and others. The most common complaints are undue generalized fatigue, persistent dissatisfaction, and re-experiencing war trauma in the form of nightmares. Almost all the patients present symptoms related to war and conflict stress.

A typical afflicted soldier will come to the out-patient service, walk into the examination room and sit in a very informal way. He is likely to show visible self-neglect in the form of long unkept hair and poor hygiene. He may ask for an interpreter if he speaks Tigrinya (i.e. the local language where the TPLF army comes from). He will then proceed to narrate detailed stories about his life, and will talk at length about his headache, intolerance of auditory stimuli, disturbed bowel habits, disturbed sleep pattern, decreased concentration, etc. Although he will appear fatigued, he will jump from his chair if the door is banged. He will not only explain his problems but he will also tell you the causes, such as the hot weather in his area of assignment. He has an impressive interest in discussion and is ready to listen to any other possible causes, but will nevertheless persist in his attributions. In the end he expects to be given a quick solution, and will say that he has no time to waste making endless appointments with doctors. He is likely to complain if he is disappointed, and will draw attention to the fast decisions that were made by medical staff in the field during the war.

Out of the patients we see in the out-patient department we select psychotics, those with self-destructive behaviour and those with homicidal tendencies to be managed as in-patients. Both ex-service men of the Derg army and soldiers of the EPRDF forces are treated in the same ward. Although they have been fighting each other for years, we are amazed to find that they get on very well with each other. The ideological wall created by politicians is set aside. Patients are managed with anti-psychotics, anti-depressants, symptomatic treatment for insomniacs, etc. They are encouraged to discuss their traumatic war experiences with each other and health workers. Aggressive and acutely disturbed patients are kept in the ward, the others are encouraged to socialize with patients in other wards. Patients are not stigmatized by wearing a different uniform nor is there a barbed-wire fence separating the psychiatry ward from medical and surgical wards.

In order to establish correct diagnoses, the norms of behaviour in the area that the new army comes from need to be known. I have therefore contacted social scientists, i.e. psychologists and sociologists, and this contact has now matured into a steering committee that is working towards the establishment of an institute of community mental health promotion – the first of its kind in our country.

The hospital has accepted the proposal that the mental health problems of conflict can best be handled by an intersectoral approach. Thus psychiatrists, psychologists, social workers and psychiatric nurses will be grouped together, and the department renamed. Instead of the Department of Psychiatry, it will be called the Department of Mental Health Services.

Examples of Particular Cases

S is a 30-year-old male patient who came to our department in July 1991 complaining of disturbing nightmares that were getting worse, three months prior to arrival. About eight years ago, while crossing River Tekeze (one of the largest rivers in Ethiopia) with his platoon, a sudden surge in the current swept away almost all his colleagues. He was one of the few survivors. The images of his beloved comrades keep on recurring with varying intensity. He has associated sad feelings of not being drowned with his friends.

Patient A, who is a 28-year-old EPRDF soldier, complains that, while in the day-time he is in Addis Ababa, at night he is on the battlefronts of Tigray and Eritrea. He wakes up from his sleep drenched in sweat and panicking.

19.2 *Politicians must learn to love their countrymen rather than their ambitions of power: a young man photographed in the mountains north of Addis Ababa, 1992. (Tim Allen)*

M, a 38-year old male, has a similar sleep disturbance ever since his sister was killed in front of him. He avoids seeing her pictures.

TA is a 33-year-old male patient who was brought to us by his friends in June 1991. On arrival he talked incoherently of various unrelated matters with quick shifts from one topic to another. His personal history revealed that he had shown behavioural changes after he sustained a blast injury to his head on 10 May 1991. A skull X-ray showed multiple small foreign bodies in the brain tissue. A mental status examination was made and a diagnosis of organic brain syndrome with maniac manifestation was made. He was admitted and put on haloperidol (an anti-psychotic drug) and made a rapid improvement and was discharged. Following treatment he had swings of emotions between being energetic and withdrawn, uninterested in life. On one occasion he tried alcohol which gave him a temporary relief from mental disturbance. He quit alcohol after being told of its consequences. He now lives with his wife and a four-year-child who was born amidst war. The child is hyperactive and once shot his left hand by pulling the trigger of his father's pistol which he took from where it was kept.

Appeal

As a former political prisoner of seven years and torture survivor, I have the background to appeal on my own and on my patients' behalf to the politicians of my country. You must accept responsibility for your policies, which can have far-reaching consequences. Much of the damage you cause may not be as easily seen as dead bodies, burned fields, destroyed schools and ruined roads. You have undermined the mental health of hundreds of thousands of people, many of whom may never fully recover. You should exercise self restraint, and should learn to love your countrymen more than your ambitions of power.

20 AMELIA BRETT
Testimonies of War Trauma in Uganda

In March 1991, I returned to Uganda after a gap of 16 years. During those years much of the country had been involved in protracted civil wars, and thousands of people had undergone appalling experiences. As a social worker based in the United Kingdom, working with women and children who had survived episodes of traumatic physical, emotional and sexual abuse, I had expected to find evidence of psychological damage. However, what struck me most was the energy, positiveness and will to rebuild shattered lives.

At one point during my visit I was privileged to attend a conference on post-war reconstruction. This took place in the east of the country, and was organised by Teso women. Many of the participants had suffered terribly during the fighting. They had only recently been released from government concentration camps, where they had been located for 'protection' from Holy Spirit Movement guerrillas. Hundreds had died in the horrendous conditions. The rest had emerged to find their farms overgrown, with only the remaining bitter cassava to harvest. Virtually all livestock in this previously cattle-dominated agricultural system had been plundered, so meat and milk were unavailable and the land had to be broken by hand instead of by the plough. Schools and health care facilities were ruined, and the road system had fallen into disrepair.

Amidst this chaos and privation these women had organized the conference. Accomodation, communal meals and refreshments were prepared for some hundred participants – a remarkable feat given the circumstances, and the discussion was full of optimism for a better future. I hesitated in this positive atmosphere to enquire about post-traumatic distress, but many questions came to mind. How had they coped? What resources did they draw upon? What gave them strength? How had their lives and those of their children been affected by what had happened? How were they able psychologically to accommodate their experiences? Were there latent and unresolved emotional issues biding their time to emerge at times of further stress, or perhaps when time allowed a psychological breathing-space? Would their lives be haunted by their memories, as are the lives of many survivors of the Holocaust, and those of survivors of the deliberate sadism of rape or of childhood experiences of abuse?

Back in England I reflected on these issues, and searched for publications which might provide me with insights. Somewhat to my surprise I found that the literature on post-traumatic distress in non-Western settings was very thin. Having obtained a small grant from the Maternal and Child Epidemiology Unit of the London School of Hygiene and Tropical Medicine, I decided to revisited Uganda again in the following year (May/June 1992). My intention was to gain some sense of the social and psychological impact of war on Ugandan populations by collecting life histories and narratives.

I focussed particularly on women and children. A selection of testimonies are presented here. They are more or less verbatim accounts, which were written down at the time of the interview. I worked with local interpreters chosen for their interpersonal skills, and the interviews were conducted very slowly and gently.[1]

The account of woman A

Subject A is in her early thirties, and lives in Luwero. The area of the Luwero Triangle in central Uganda achieved universal notoriety in the 1980s when the plight of the Baganda countryfolk, who had been killed and tortured in their hundreds of thousands as 'soft targets' by government troops during a guerrilla war, was exposed by the media. The war in this area took place between the Uganda National Liberation Army (UNLA), the army of Obote's [later Okello's] government, and the National Resistance Army (NRA) lead by Y. Museveni.

A was brought up in her parents' house, being the last-born of her mother, the twentieth child. Only she and one sister survived into adulthood. A was educated to Primary 5 (i.e. she went to primary school for five years). Her father and his brothers had built houses together, so life was easy- she had freedom to visit anyone and eat anywhere. She had a secure and happy childhood playing games like 'mothers and fathers' and hide-and-seek, which she loved, as well as helping out with cooking and digging. She left school and married at 14 years, giving birth to five children: two girls and three boys. Two of the boys died of measles.

When war broke out in her home area during the time of 'Obote 2' [i.e. the mid-eighties] she was still married and living in K District. Her family had to flee to Lukola area and hide in the bush. They had to remain in hiding for three years, wearing only one small cloth to keep decent. They had to search for food constantly. She witnessed many people being killed and she had many times to crawl away like a snake on her belly. At one point she became accidentally separated from her husband and children and only met up again with them by sheer chance. Insecurity would force many moves in a day. They used to get sick and she developed huge sores on her legs. During these years the Museveni Youth [members of the NRA] would patrol, find out who needed treatment and take them to small bush clinics.

When they came back from the bush they found that their house was still standing and only doors and contents had been taken [i.e. the wall and roof survived]. So they settled into digging, clearing the banana plantation, planting coffee and returning to normal life. They worked very hard and raised money to send the children to school. The NRA soldiers were well disciplined and deployed locally for security. All was well, except for friction with her husband who began drinking. She had had enough of him, she had no interest in sex, and did not want to become pregnant. She did not seek another partner, she had had enough. She left him and her children and moved away to live with her maternal grandmother where she remains to this day

She suffers from 'palpitations' and this worries her. (I was told that many people who had had to flee and live in the bush suffer with this symptom, which is said to indicate a nervous condition). Even the slightest bang will immediately bring back those days, but this reaction has lessened as time goes by. She used to have regular dreams of her frightening experiences, but has not done so for two years now, and says that God assisted her. She prays often, and her Catholicism sustains her.

---

[1] Pictures illustrating this chapter were collected at the same time as the interviews. They are all drawings by schoolchildren. Their names have not been included in captions at their request.

20.1 *'Widows suffering in certain homes in Teso, while others enjoy themselves': drawn by a 14-year-old boy in Kumi district.*

20.2 *'The unhappy family': drawn by a 13-year-old boy in Kitgum.*

20.3 *'They are suffering from diarrhoea': drawn by a 13-year-old boy in Kumi district, to show what life was like in government concentration camps.*

Comment

Despite her years of near starvation, displacement and trauma, the outcome for A has been relatively positive. She was initially able to reconstruct her life and cultivate without fear of robbery, and was able to send her children to school (education is highly valued and prioritized by parents). She has had the support of her extended family to turn to on leaving her husband and children. A did not state that she had been raped. However, it is likely that she was, or at least witnessed it happening to others. The work of the Medical Foundation for the Care of Victims of Torture in Luwero indicates that it is quite common for women who had suffered rape to lose interest in sex and maternity, thus turning away from the role of wife and mother in a society in which it is considered almost obligatory (interview with Stella Kabaganda, Medication foundation case worker, Kampala, 1992). It may also be noted that A displayed both somatic symptoms and memory-triggered responses, both indications of post-traumatic stress. The drinking problem which her husband developed after his experiences is also a typical indicator. The life of this small peasant family has been distorted and curtailed, and it is possible that the destruction of the family unit might have been prevented had some form of therapeutic help been available to them.

The account of woman B

Subject B lives in Teso in eastern Uganda. This is an area of land shortage where the climate of instability created by the war led to violence and opportunism and the settling of old scores. She is a mother aged 32, married with seven children of her own and caring for a further six orphans, with some responsibility for her three young brothers' school fees. B was born in a neighbouring county, one of seven children, six of whom were boys. Life was good, but she only had schooling until Primary 4. She married at the age of 17, and the family got cattle (i.e. her marriage brought cattle into her father's home as a bridewealth payment).

Her husband earned money by labouring in the fields, but their relationship was violent and only changed when she was 'saved' in 1987 (i.e. became a born-again Christian). This changed her behaviour, and life improved.

Then, during the insecurity of 1989, her problems increased when her husband was falsely accused of complicity with guerrilla forces by their neighbours, who hoped to lay claims to his land when he was imprisoned. He was accused time after time, and repeatedly sent to prison where he was severely beaten. Her neighbours were happy when they saw her suffer, especially when she was forced to buy food instead of growing it all herself.

One night, at a time when her husband was in prison, she was preparing the family for bed, when the neighbours came with guns. She did not hear them approach. They ordered everyone outside, and began firing. She had taken in an 18-year-old orphan lad whose work she had become dependent upon. As he tried to run away he was shot dead, next to the granary. She escaped with her children. She could only bury him the following day without ceremony, and without dignity, as she lacked resources. She feels worried by this omission.

During the time of insecurity it was very difficult to care for all the children, and food was short. Blankets from the Red Cross had to be cut in two to cover the children. They had to sleep in a nearby school at night for many months and everyone was very fearful.

She developed problems with her heart, which the doctor at the hospital said were caused by 'too much thinking'. He said that she should try to relax ... she saw that this made sense and was encouraged by his advice. She prayed and had faith that God would look after her. She has waist pains because she has to carry the small children to the

20.4 *'Fighting with rebels': drawn by a 12-year-old boy in Kitgum district, showing how his family was caught in the cross-fire.*

garden when she goes to cultivate. The severe beatings whilst in prison have ruined her husband's health, and he suffers from chest pain and needs hospitalization if he is strained physically, so he cannot help her. Even the small children have to work in the fields.

After the 18-year-old lad was killed, she had numbness in her arms and legs which took one and a half months to go away. She explained to me that a lot of thinking had almost made her mad. The fact that no ceremony was conducted to mark the young man's death continues to trouble her. She used to see his body in dreams, and would also dream of people coming again with guns. She is startled even by chickens, and the older children are also frightened. She tries to please them and comfort them and advise them saying, 'God will look after us'. She stopped dreaming when her husband was released from prison.

She has no male relatives to help her. Her cousin-brothers (i.e. her father's brothers sons) who she would customarily turn to are dead. Three of her own brothers are dead as well and she cares for their children plus those of her cousin-sisters. As she was 'the only girl in the womb', she also tries to help her three surviving young brothers who are at senior school locally. She repeated stoically that she has no relations to help her. She tries to pay school fees for all the children hopelessly. Two of the orphans are paid for by charity. She feels overwhelmed by her responsibilities for so many children, without the help of an active man.

Comment

In the case of B, she has had to take on the burden of caring for many children with little support and this has forced her to put her own needs for rest and recouperation, both psychological and physical, to one side. Many of her needs are material, and even her spiritual need to lay to rest the spirit of the murdered lad depends upon funding for an appropriate ceremony, which is beyond her means. B is barely coping, and although the

20.5 *'The rebels stealing [from] a poor family': drawn by a 13-year-old boy in Kumi district.*

predatory neighbours cannot take the land she subsists on whilst her husband lives, her situation is most precarious, and she clearly needs social support in her parenting tasks. Her Christian faith sustains and comforts her and the Church network is her only source of help. In the face of such admirable fortitude, one is tempted to cite the need for the inclusion of a further category to the UN Declaration of Human Rights, that of the right to emotional wellbeing to justify therapeutic intervention to help resolve such suffering and the incalculable effects on children and future generations.

B's story indicates that a system of mediation and compensation is needed, to help resolve problems in situations where the former mechanisms of conflict resolution are no longer viable. In addition it appears that some kind of intervention is necessary to give women rights to land in event of the demise of the male head of the home. It is no longer possible to rely with much confidence upon the resources of the extended family in times of hardship.

The account of boy C

Subject C is a schoolboy aged 14, living in Acholi, northern Uganda. This area was badly affected by warfare following the NRA takeover in Kampala in 1986. Guerrilla groups, mainly composed of ex-soldiers, resisted Museveni's forces. The best known of them was the Holy Spirit Movement, led by a female prophetess and spirit medium, Alice Lakwena. She seems to have captured the hearts and minds of the defeated fighting men, and inspired a blind faith in her abilities to invoke supernatural powers. During this period of instability there were also numerous incidents of banditry and theft. Thousands of families were forced to flee their homes, losing everything. The raiders were known locally as the Olum, i.e. 'men of the grass'. As in Teso the disruption to civil society plus

20.6 *'Thieves burning and stealing a home': drawn by a 12-year-old boy.*

wholesale cattle-rustling have left the country economically ruined and with the social fabric worn thin.

C was born locally, the last of nine children. There was only one girl. His natural father died when he was a baby, and his father's brother accordingly took responsibility for the family. However, he was abducted by the Olum and taken to the nearby river where he was killed. His corpse was recovered, and it was possible to bury him correctly, according to custom.

C's memories of his childhood are dominated by the need to cultivate, but there were times during the dry season when people were joyful and sang. The family would cultivate and sell the harvest for cash. C went to school up to Primary 3. His mother paid his school fees.

Then, in January 1991, he himself was abducted by the Olum. At that time he was 13 years old. He was with seven friends playing cards at home, enjoying himself, when three strangers appeared. Some of the adults were at a funeral, others were drinking alcohol nearby and did not notice what was happening. The Olum left the older boys, but took away the three youngest.

They crossed the river to Gulu and from there were led to the National Park at Paraa. Here the NRA attacked the Olum and their prisoners from the air (February 1991). They were forced to disperse, and ran even deeper into the bush towards the Nile River. They stayed there for some time, and then another attack was staged by the NRA, this time on the ground. All Olum were in camouflage uniform, and all were ex-soldiers with guns, apart from the recruits. The unit numbered more than 100. He and his two friends were the only abducted youths without uniforms.

There were many rites involved in the (Holy Spirit) cult. On crossing a road they would kill one member. They would remove his uniform and shoot him. The choice appeared to be at random, but the choice was made by the leader. He would select the

20.7 *Heavy fighting in Kitgum district, drawn by a 14-year-old boy. The text in the picture reads: 'stranded children whose parents have escaped have been killed in crossfire or by Olum'.*

sacrificial victim from 'those who cook for themselves' (i.e. those men not allowed to travel with a kidnapped woman who would cook for him). There were about 40 of these men. Sometimes the 'victim of the road' was stripped of his uniform and beaten to death instead. The leaders could have as many as four women travelling with them. The leaders were well-armed and had bodyguards. When going into battle with the NRA they rubbed shea nut oil onto their bodies, believing that this would deflect bullets, and would sprinkle water around the perimeter of their camp in a rite of protection. They would also sing special songs and blow animal horns. Members of the Olum would wear a chain around the neck with a coloured plastic coil keyring attached. Whenever they needed food they would take it from villagers.

One night in February 1991, they were surrounded by the NRA at night. The NRA shone a searchlight and began firing. The Olum were caught unawares. The Olum lost many men. Those who escaped scattered and regrouped again to return towards Gulu. As they wandered, C's feet were cut by the burnt grass stubble and his legs cut by the remaining long grass. Many fell sick but were forced to go on by the Olum, as 'pretence' of sickness was punished by shooting. C witnessed a killing of this sort too. Any prisoners they took had to keep up with the band or perish.

C saw attacks on villages which involved people being chopped to death if they refused to show the way, the torching of houses and the rape of girls. Sometimes women would be pushed into a hut and the hut would then be fired. He was not made to perform these atrocities. They were done by the uniformed soldiers. People who had been abducted were graded, those serving longest would be brought into the unit with the 'gift' of a uniform. It was not possible to refuse. People managed to escape at times. The worst rule in his eyes was one that said that if you had a brother in the unit and he was killed in battle, then you would also be killed by the unit.

20.8 *A drawing by a 16-year-old girl in Kitgum district. Her brother became a soldier in the NRA.*

The unit continued to travel many hundred of miles through difficult terrain, first around Gulu then around Lira and then they made for Kitgum via Adilang. One night, they had camped and were cooking. He had been sent for water. He threw down the jerrycan and fled. He recognized his home! As membership of the group had changed over time nobody in it knew that he came from the area. The group were said to have travelled back to the vicinity of Gulu, where they continued their campaign of terrorism.

Then came the NRA operation to pacify the area, which was viewed as a trouble spot. Villagers were told to stay at home, and were only allowed to travel in order to fetch water or to bathe. If they did otherwise they were deemed to be supporters of the Olum. The villagers were told to arm themselves with old-fashioned bows and arrows only, guns were forbidden. This left them exposed and vulnerable to attack. One day (29 May 1991), four of them decided to go to bathe. On the way home they saw a file of soldiers coming towards them. They assumed they were NRA. On meeting them on the path they made way for them to pass, but realized with shock that these were not regular soldiers but were the Olum! Their carrying of bows and arrows infuriated the Olum who identified them as allies of the NRA. They were captured and tied 'like chickens' with their elbows behind their backs. They were marched from the capture point whilst the band argued about their fate. The men wanted to kill them but their leader objected, ordering instead the amputation of their right hands. His reason was that they would then not be able to fire their bows and arrows, and would themselves feel the pain that they would have caused the Olum had they injured them with the arrows!

The captives were hit on the chest with gun butts, and pricked with knives and arrowheads, drawing blood to stop them struggling. They crossed the river still bound, and walked to an abandoned homestead where they were ordered to sit whilst one of the 'soldiers' was sent to find a hoe handle upon which to amputate the hands. They were

20.9 *A drawing by a 13-year-old boy in Kitgum district.*

asked to choose between death and amputation, and all chose life, naturally. C did not plead for mercy because of his knowledge of the Olum – pleading could make things worse. He witnessed the other amputations, his being the last.

He was numbed almost insensible and remembers clearly this feeling of 'not feeling'. Two people held his arm and the third struck with his *lokela*, a small axe. It was cut six times before it was cut through. They were unbound and told to return home. They were instructed to tell the NRA to follow the Olum if they could. The messengers being wounded made this a most insulting gesture.

As they approached the village they met the NRA who gave chase unsucessfully. The NRA treated them with injections and dressed their stumps. They spent the night in the village, then were given food and a note to go to the hospital.

C's mother came with them, and remained to look after them until they left the hospital. His brothers brought food to the hospital. He was in hospital for eight months. The stump remained healthy and he was the first to heal. His worst experience was the loss of a hand – not the pain, but being handicapped. Whilst in hospital a Malokali (a person who has been 'saved') gave them all much encouragement, staying with them. They all prayed together. He prayed to God for help to make the medicine cure him.

After his time with the Olum, C dreamt about what took place in the bush, the shooting, the fighting, everything. He now only dreams if he is lonely, because this reminds him of all the travelling and other experiences. He does not dream about his amputation, and never has (however, he sweated heavily when describing the event). He finds that he is jerked back to memories at times. During the interview he nearly jumped up from his chair when an airplane took off from the nearby airstrip. He said that he was immediately reminded of the NRA bombing attack. He is now back at school and enjoys this. His fees are paid because he is an 'orphan' (i.e. he is fatherless). He is doing

20.10 *A Karamajong cattle raid in Kitgum district, drawn by a 15-year-old boy.*

well and comes sixth out of his class of 20. He says that his future will be difficult. He fears for his future.

Comment

Again the overwhelming nature of physical difficulties obscures to some extent the psychological distress engendered by C's experiences. This young lad was one of three amputees interviewed who had all suffered at the hands of the Olum. All could foresee lives without the possibility of wife and family because of their disability. The ability to cultivate is essential for all but the wealthiest. The stoicism of the three amputees was remarkable – the deeply scarred flesh of their inner arms testimony to their attempts to dig with hoes strapped to their mutilated limbs. Should scarce resources be devoted to psychological rehabilitation when physical needs are so clearly paramount and survival and quality of life so dependent on the provision of a prosthesis? In my own professional work I had never encountered anyone who had both witnessed such a range of horrors and been subject in turn to a personal traumatic experience of such a deliberately crippling nature. How could treatment be prioritized and what psychological therapies would be acceptable? Are our Western 'talking' therapies appropriate?

The account of women D and E

Subjects D, age 30, and E, age 33, are both women from Acholi area. Before the terrible event of April 1990, life was good in their clan village. There were over 200 inhabitants in this collection of homesteads scattered over a square mile of very fertile and productive land. They had had more than 100 cattle before the raids of the Karamajong rustlers.

20.11 *'A sorrow full home': drawn by a 12-year-old boy in Kumi district.*

On Sunday, 1 April 1990, everyone was at home preparing to go to Mass, so no-one was in the fields. Without warning and in broad daylight, the Olum struck. It was 10 am. There were 60 Olum, all armed, plus about 100 captives travelling with them. In their small homestead it was clear that there was no escape, and nobody panicked or ran off, as this was useless. The Olum camped, cooked and made off without doing any harm.

However, at midnight they returned. All were sleeping indoors. The Olum started gathering people together. There was no moon, and it was very dark. The Olum claimed that one of their prisoners had escaped with a gun, and this boy who had escaped was said to be from the village (he was). After they made this allegation they took D and E and six of their children and forced them into a hut, saying that the Holy Spirit had told them to do this. One of the children was kept outside. D and E were numbed with fear. Were they to die? What was to happen to them? They did not know what to do. They could not even cry out they were so terrified. They appealed to the Olum, asking what would happen. The Olum said they would be spared for the present, but the rest of the villagers were to be killed! They were guarded, but the door of the hut was kept open so that they should watch.

The people of the village were packed into a nearby hut, and the killing began. Nine men were hacked to death with axes – D and E's husbands and grandfathers. Then four women and four children were pushed into another hut which was set on fire. Two of the women attempted to escape and were axed to death. Two children also struggled out, but were spared because the Olum said they had become 'angels'. Because of this, the rest of the villagers were also spared.

After this, all the buildings were set alight, including the graineries and the chickens in their coops were destroyed. The two 'angels' joined D and E in their hut, and the whole group of the Olum withdrew, leaving them behind. The women felt very bad. They lost their bearings in the shock. They did not know where they were. They tried to control themselves because of the children. Their instinct was to protect the little ones. Everything was aflame. They left the hut for a nearby field so that the children would not see th horrors of the scene. The children were told to keep silent because of the Olum. The oldest child was especially worried. The attack had lasted from midnight until past one. They sheltered in the fields until dawn.

E decided to leave the village and seek safety in the nearest town with the children, whilst D remained to inform the other families of what had happened, and to ask for assistance with the huge task of burying the dead. D then caught sight of the Olum who, to her horror, were still in the area! On seeing this she started to run from household to household to warn the others of the threat. Some did not believe her and remained to be slaughtered. She tried so hard to convince them. She escaped with five people who believed her. They headed towards town – herself, three men and two other women. The neighbours living closest to her household were behind a small ridge and so could not see the burning huts, whereas those farther away could see the flames! Her story was so terrible that people seemed unable to believe it. Those who would not flee were later killed.

D and E were reunited at the town. She arrived as the townspeople were preparing a search party to try to find her, and she was able to tell them of the fresh attack. Father Valentino (a Catholic priest) was very brave and went to check their village. He returned to get male relatives for burials at 3 pm. The Olum had left the area. There were 42 burials, and it took three days. Only adults went to the burials. The children did not attend because of the horrible mutilation of the bodies, and also because people were afraid that the Olum might return. When the burials were completed, people remained in the town. They had nothing. No food or goods remained. But they were welcomed, all 10 of them by a Catholic family.

The two widows have since accrued responsibility for 12 children because of the killings within their extended families. In order to have a man to take on the role of head of the home, they have linked themselves with a man who has has a wife and only one child. They are as mothers to him, he is a son to them (i.e. they have not become his wives). One of their husbands' brothers joined them, but subsequntly died of malaria. There are no more brothers, all are dead. The children have fallen sick too and so has D.

D and E want to go back to their own home, and do not know what to do as widows. It is difficult to attract partners because of the great burden of children. They feel at a loss. The children are a problem, because of education fees, medicines, etc. The elders have tried to seek out some appropriate men for them but nobody wants to take on big responsibilities when life is so difficult. There is enough good land, but the children are very young. The oldest son was killed with his father, and the oldest girls are 13 and will soon marry and leave. Where they are now staying, they are reliant on others and can plant only a little. They want to cultivate their own fields but cannot bear to move back home. They both feel that they cannot afford to give in to their sorrows as, if once they did, they would crack.

D suffers from many bad dreams which she believes come from her terrible experiences. She sees those she used to know alive and then they gesture towards their mutilated corpses. At night, and sometimes even in daylight she feels chilled, and begins to shake and then she sees these figures appear before her. She was taken to hospital for this sickness, and was examined. The diagnosis was given as a reaction to stress and she was given Panadol and aspirin for sleeping and for her bad headaches. She has to rest a lot, and everyone respects this need.

E is reminded of the incidents every time she is working hard. When she becomes tired she remembers being helped before. She says that she is now recovered, but she has nightmares every night and will quarrel with the Olum in her dreams.

Both the women feel much heartache, their loss is always in their minds. They have feelings of panic when a child is ill as they feel so alone and without resources. Both used to love to dance and sing, now neither can bear to. They are both excluded from the consoling rites of the elderly women as they are too young. In the past their condition would have not come to pass, as a husband's brother would have had to take responsibility for them. There are thus no consoling rituals for this totally exceptional modern circumstance. They had chosen marriage as their lives, without a husband life is very sad. They are becoming resigned to their lot, there is no end to their struggle. Both are terribly disappointed that an attempt by the elders to wed them to younger men has failed.

The women with whom they have taken refuge help to discipline the children, and organize digging for them as well. So they have some help. They are also able to talk to others who listen patiently and with great sympathy. A Catholic Sister, 'Mary', is a great help to them and supports them. She is an inspiration, keeping them to their beliefs despite pressures to take easy paths.

Comment

There is no land shortage in this area, and community ties are powerful and supportive. The two able and articulate women are close and also have Sister 'Mary' to inspire them and to maintain their self-esteem. Despite the horrors of their experience and their lively stress-reactions, they are coping, although D's hallucinations and feelings of lethargy indicate a deep malaise. There is a sympathetic local attitude towards post-traumatic distress, and sufferers are viewed as reacting quite naturally to an extraordinary personal experience. Stigma is thus absent.

D is the only survivor who spoke of a feeling of guilt to me, and that was in terms of her personal failure to convince fellow villagers of the consequences of remaining in their homesteads. She feels guilty that they were subsequently killed by the Olum, but not guilt that she survived an attack (i.e. not the so called 'survivor guilt' noted among trauma victims in the West). The people I interviewed were all puzzled by my enquiry as to whether they felt any sense of guilt at surviving when others died. They replied consistently that you should only feel guilt if you have sinned. Surely the killers must feel guilt, rather than themselves. Perhaps the question was clumsily formulated and a different phrase might have elicited a different response?

The exclusion of the two women from the rituals of the older female mourners seems to me to be of significance in that the communal singing and dancing (for which the Acholi are justly famous) perhaps generates a catharsis, consolidating a common feeling of sorrow and allowing public, acceptable and lengthy expression of feelings. Their exclusion denies them a socially acceptable form of emotional expression, in a society where feelings are by convention not always openly displayed. As a therapist I wondered what could become a substitute for such a rite in times of social dislocation.

As in all the survivors' reports, a psychological reworking of the terrible experience is occuring, sometimes on an hourly basis, to enable the survivor to comprehend and distance herself from it, until terror fades and a conviction that it is possible to live a life in security returns. How much more difficult to do this when the Olum have gone but food insecurity and ill health threaten themselves and their many children!

The special tragedy of the two women which adds to their forebodings about the future is the loss of their cohort of marriageable men, so many of whom were killed in the troubles. In normal circumstances, the women would be 'inherited' by a brother of their husband, and their future children would continue to be recognized as his (i.e. the dead husband's) offspring.

From a professional viewpoint it was clear that therapeutic strategies need to be evolved to help survivors to recover from their post-trauma distress. What form these take in order to be culturally congruent and appropriate has still to be determined.

Meanwhile the fostering of the tolerant attitude, which links somatization to manifestations of post-trauma distress and normalizes nightmares and flashbacks as part of the search for comprehension, should be encouraged.

The impact of the kinds of experiences described here upon children can be gauged from the drawings collected from those who had survived attacks. On discussing their needs with their teachers, it seemed to me that a school-based programme of play and drama therapy could usefully enable the children to explore their feelings without challenging any cultural norms. To some extent the drawing of appalling events, which the children could link to specific incidents, also seemed to be having this effect. Perhaps it helped them, in a small way, to objecify and distance their most painful memories.

I had the feeling that a similar point could be made about the people I interviewed. Telling someone what had happened, perhaps particularly a stranger, seemed to help. Possibly the way forward for those concerned about therapy, at least in the short term, is just to listen, and to provide people with the space to bear witness.

21 MICHAEL M. CERNEA
Bridging the Research Divide:
Studying Refugees & Development Oustees

Countries in a post-war situation, and the processes of war-to-peace transition, place the social problems of relocating war refugees and displaced population high on the world's agenda, with increasing visibility and urgency. At the same time, problems with a strikingly similar socio-economic content are brought up by the very numerous instances of 'planned' population displacement caused by development policies and programmes. Within the social science literature dealing with displaced populations, however, there exists an excessive separation between, on the one hand, the study of post-war and disaster-related refugees and, on the other hand, the study of populations uprooted by development projects. Separation entails weak communication. Indeed, these two bodies of social science research virtually do not 'speak to each other'.

Following up on my earlier attempt to bring this issue into discussion (Cernea, 1990), the present chapter argues that the dichotomy must be overcome. Both bodies of literature stand to gain from breaking out of their relative isolation. *Empirically*, they could enrich each other by comparing their factual findings. *Theoretically*, they could broaden and refine their generalizations by integrating their sets of concepts. *Methodologically*, they could sharpen their enquiry by exchanging research techniques and approaches. And in the *public arena*, they could more effectively help displaced populations of all sorts by mutually reinforcing their policy and operational recommendations.

The reasons for overcoming this persisting dichotomy are intrinsic to the situation of displaced populations. In this chapter I will discuss some *commonalities and differences* between situations where populations flee from wars, natural disasters or political events, and situations in which groups of people are forcibly displaced by planned developments. Since both categories are displaced populations, for the purposes of this article I will generally use the term *refugees* to describe the first category and the term *oustees*[1] to describe the second.

The chapter first considers the different causes that lead to the creation of either refugees or oustees, and distinguishes sub-categories within these two broad groups; second, it considers the magnitude of refugee and oustee flows, their human rights implications and the impoverishment they cause; third, it examines the different types of assistance provided through international aid to refugees and oustees; and fourth, it explores the similarities or differences that make the comparative analysis between refugees and oustees relevant. The chapter also discusses the policy principles that

[1] The term *oustees* is borrowed from the Indian literature on involuntary population displacement, where it is commonly used to describe people forcibly 'ousted' from their habitat through government intervention, generally for the purpose of some development-required change in land or water use; it may not be the best concept, and it is rarely used in other countries, but it is employed here as a convenient abbreviation instead of 'development-displaced people'.

development programmes must follow to reduce forced displacements and provide for the social reinsertion of the people they displace.

When discussing refugees, the focus of the present chapter is on *internal* rather than on *international* refugees. The sharp increase in the number of internally displaced people worldwide during the last two decades, especially in Africa and Asia, has brought these issues into the limelight. Particularly in post-war situations in Africa and recently in eastern Europe, the refugee problem has taken the dimension of a human and political disaster with vast international implications.

A Questionable Research Dichotomy

Social science research on displaced people has grown faster over the last decade than during any other comparable period. Yet its findings are far from being integrated theoretically or practically. Analytical specialization has also led to a rather rigid research dichotomy: namely, the literature on 'refugees' coexists side by side with a literature on 'oustees' or on 'development-caused involuntary resettlement.' There is little communication and mutual enrichment between them. Concepts and propositions are not interlinked, and empirical findings are rarely compared and integrated. For instance, most of the writings on refugees omit oustee groups from the typology of displaced populations. In turn research on oustees foregoes the opportunity of doing comparative analysis by studying refugees. As a result, the chance for more in-depth treatment is being missed.

The split among these related research fields is not the only one. We can speak, in fact, of a *three-way split*, rather than a dichotomy. Indeed, another distinct research field dealing more or less with the same processes is the one known as disaster-research. I do not propose to expand here on this 'third domain', which has certainly built an impressive body of research on its own. Yet, the victims of disasters, the populations upon which the disaster research literature bears, are partly the same as in the case of the two other bodies of research literature. The disaster research literature typically centres on people affected by natural catastrophes, many of whom become refugees. It deals comparatively less with refugees from political events such as civil wars or ethnic persecution. Even more seldom does it study oustees from man-made disasters, such as failed resettlement from development programmes.[2] This additional split is another ground for an integrative effort, particularly for integrating research findings.

The reasons for distinguishing between various populations – refugees and oustees – are certainly valid, and will be emphasized further in this chapter. But do these reasons also justify the absence of comparative analysis, or the lack of overarching concepts and theories encompassing both (and perhaps other) categories of populations? In my view, certainly not.

To take an example: as a discipline, anthropology owes a large part of its general knowledge about resettlement to African early experiences with displacements caused by high dams (Brokensha, 1963–4; Cernea, 1994). The Volta resettlement from Ghana's Akosombo and Kpong reservoirs, the resettlement of the Gwembe Tonga in Zambia, or the relocation of the Egyptian Nubians from the Aswan dams, are the best known cases and, alone, have yielded a sizeable body of social science research and publications. Several African scholars have dedicated multi-sided research to the resettlement of the people from the Kainji Lake Basin in Nigeria (Oyedipe, 1983). Social geographers and other researchers have focussed on the Niger River displacements. Recent studies on involuntary resettlement in Africa have brought up new issues, such as the impact of

---

[2] The limiting effect of this orientation on the disaster research itself are worth a separate analysis.

reservoirs not only through displacement but also through the dramatic modifications they cause to the traditional recessional agriculture downstream (Horowitz, *et al.* 1993; Horowitz and Salem-Murdock, 1990). Yet, research on Africa's refugees from wars, ethnic persecution or natural disasters seldom reaches back towards the early literature on development-related displacements on the same continent, for the comparative analysis of distinctions, similarities, or lessons about coping strategies.

The fact that books and conferences on refugees usually overlook development-related displacement, and conversely that students of the latter leave refugees out of their research horizon, has a threefold weakening effect. First, it is weakening the political influence of such research on governments; second, it is weakening the design of operational programmes to assist these populations; and finally, it is weakening the effort to build social theory by generalizing larger bodies of empirical findings that result by aggregating what has been called 'contiguous problem analysis' (Dubin, 1978).

What makes the comparison between refugees and oustees possible and useful? Both populations undergo a major disruption in their patterns of social organization and culture. They are facing the same task of physically and culturally surviving this disruption by reorganizing their economy and their ways of life. This makes their situations eminently comparable and apt to reveal diverse, innovative, and largely yet unresearched social mechanisms for absorbing disruption shock, for coping, and for re-establishment. Moreover, comparing the response strategies and behaviours adopted spontaneously by refugees and oustees to regain normalcy can yield lessons for assistance approaches.

Stepping stones towards this goal have been laid through some scholarly contributions within sociology, particularly by Drabek (1987) and Kreps (1983, 1987). Drabek constructed an inventory of sociological findings about human responses to disasters. The inventory clarifies and codifies responses by type of social group and phase of the disaster's cycle. This scholarly tool is useful to both researchers and planners: it can help either model building or developing operational approaches for prevention or mitigation. However, this inventory is limited to *natural* disasters and some aspects of technological hazards. By design Drabek's inventory does not incorporate findings about responses to such man-made, planned events as reservoir submergence. An inventory of the latter category of human responses, facilitating comparisons with responses to natural calamities, would be extraordinarily useful.

Another factor favouring such a bridging of the research divide is the recent rapid expansion of the literature on development-caused displacement and relocation, particularly over the last eight to 10 years. This rapid expansion has changed, in my view, the state of the art.[3] The expansion itself also embodies this new state of the art. Three features characterize this expansion and stand out: first, the growth of resettlement research by researchers from developing nations; second, the operational bent of most of this literature, its proactive stand and interest in the practical aspects of how resettlement should or should not be done; last, but not least, the policy debate, the transition from description and analysis prescribing solutions and to policy formulation, including the 'translation' of research findings from anthropology and sociology on resettlement into recommended approaches and institutional policies on resettlement (for details, see Cernea 1993a). Developing a systematized inventory of human and institutional responses to development-caused displacement is now an endeavour waiting for a challenge-tempted author. An intellectually stimulating step in this direction is the annotated bibliography on development-caused population displacement by Guggenheim (1994). This bibliography lists some 700 titles, a surprising number which mirrors research expansion in this area.

Other stepping stones towards integrating the study of both 'refugee relocation' and

---

[3] The last review of the state of the art was done about 20 years ago (Scudder 1973); taking it as a point of reference would allow for an interesting stock-taking assessment of the vast recent progress.

'development relocation' have been laid by some scholarly attempts to develop a single analytical framework for both. For instance, Scudder and Colson (1982) delineated such an anthropological framework around the concept of stress and proposed to distinguish among successive temporal stages of the process of dislocation–relocation (see also Scudder, 1991; Scudder reconsidered and amended this framework in his 1993 study, in which he addressed also the refugee-oustee question). In a less formal elaboration, Oliver-Smith and Hansen (1982) suggested that such population movements might be treated as degrees on a continuum of *migration* processes, ranging from voluntary to involuntary migration – although attributing the concept of 'migration' to planned dislocations might be a bit of an overstretch. By and large, however, the positive appeal launched by these integrative approaches has still not triggered systematic comparative research. Such investigation still remains to be done. A recent excellent monograph on the resettlement programmes in Ethiopia (Pankhurst, 1992) is one of the few exceptions in the way it attempts to capture the linkages and real-life overlaps between state-induced resettlement and refugee-causing natural circumstances.

Causal Agents of Population Dislocation

Any examination of commonalities and differences between refugees and oustees should start with the causes that account for such processes of social disintegration. Explaining causality is essential for understanding the origin, identity and composition of various displaced populations, their basic needs, and the ways in which they can be assisted. Among the circumstances leading to forced displacements, we generally distinguish four main types or clusters of causal agents:

a   natural environmental disasters: droughts, famines, floods, earthquakes, etc.;

b   wars/political turmoil;

c   persecution: ethnic/racial/religious; and

d   development policies and programmes causing major changes in land/water use.

Events belonging to the first three types trigger massive *refugee* flows. Conversely, the fourth type listed above – purposive change processes – often results in the creation of *oustee* populations. This typically occurs when major infrastructure construction programmes demand compulsory population displacement for acquiring 'right of way'. Such displacements are being carried out through state authority. For want of a more adequate concept, populations forced to move by development programmes are described under a variety of terms: as 'oustees' – the term used in this chapter – or 'evictees', 'displacees', 'resettlers', 'relocatees', 'project affected persons', etc. *Within* these large groups – refugees and oustees – further conceptual and practical distinctions can be made.

Distinctions within refugee populations

A distinction made between refugees displaced by one of the first three types of causal agents ('a', 'b' or 'c') is whether or not they have crossed an international border, or have remained in their country of origin. This is a circumstantial distinction rather than a theoretical one, but it is quite important in its practical consequences.

Internal refugees are those who, having abandoned their houses and lands, still remain within the borders of their country. International refugees are those who have crossed an international border. Indeed, in the case of racial persecution or civil war, the 'push' factors are much the same for the refugees who cross a national border and seek shelter elsewhere, as for those who leave their shelter but cannot or choose not to leave their countries and thus become 'internal' refugees.[4] The trauma of being an 'internal refugee', a refugee in one's own land, is not necessarily less than being a refugee on foreign soil.

The distinction between internal and trans-border refugees is consequential, however, for *resource allocation and assistance strategies*. While there are established international structures mandated to assist international refugees, much less institutionalized support is available for internal refugees. The Georgetown Declaration (1988) correctly called attention to the fact that, despite the huge number of internal refugees, 'at present no international agency has responsibility for ensuring the adequacy of protection and assistance, including health care, for *internally* displaced persons'.

Cross-border refugees are recognized by international agencies as refugees. However, the same agencies tend not to recognize as 'refugees' those displaced people who do not cross borders, namely the *internally displaced people*, even though both the triggers and the consequences of their displacement may be identical. In practical terms, this difference in formal recognition results in huge disparities in the levels of public and private assistance provided to such groups. These circumstances have prompted refugee experts to state that in the area of refugee assistance 'the challenge for the future is presented by internally displaced people, [where] roles and mandates are unclear' (Keely, 1988).

Distinctions within oustee populations

Returning to *oustee* populations, we can make a different kind of distinction among them. According to the degree to which they endure losses, populations displaced by infrastructure construction (or comparable programmes) can be subdivided into the following sub-categories:

a people who lose their houses;

b people who lose land (in full or in significant part), but not their houses; and

c people who lose both houses *and* farm land or other productive assets.

Compensation and other rights and economic entitlements are often denied to some of the people displaced by government-sponsored development plans through a 'simple' device: they are omitted from oustee statistics and, implicitly, from resettlement planning. This happens more often to people in the sub-category (b) above. Technical and planning agencies tend to ignore them on the grounds that their houses are not destroyed and therefore they are not technically displaced. In practice, however, the loss of even one significant part of a household's farmland (e.g., some 25 per cent of the total holding) may make that farm economically unviable and thus compel the family to move away; it may cause marginalization and the sliding of a family from barely above to below the poverty threshold (Cernea, 1990b). For instance, this happens to many people when vast networks of irrigation canals are constructed: the 'right of way' swallows part of a family's cultivated land, but leaves untouched its house, located farther away (Morse et al., 1992). Those who lose only their houses but not their lands (category 'a') may sometimes avoid becoming oustees if alternative house plots can be secured nearby, in the vicinity of their lands and kin.

Labelling (designation of status) is a powerful tool of practical policy used by governments for allocating or withholding resources from certain groups, as was correctly argued in the case of refugees (Zetter 1988, 1990). *Mutatis mutandis*, the denial of oustee status to those in sub-group (b) above, (e.g., as is happening in some programmes in Indonesia or India) is another case of labelling manipulation. This is not just an

---

[4] In certain regions, particularly in Africa where boundaries often split areas inhabited by the same ethnic group, some refugees may not even be initially aware of whether or not they have crossed a border.

innocuous semantic matter, but a matter of recognizing rights. Mislabelling is a way to belittle the adverse effects of projects through the device of refusing to recognize the losses, rights, and legitimate entitlements of part of the population affected.

Under the provisions of the World Bank's policy regarding involuntary resettlement (see World Bank 1990; Cernea 1988, 1995), all three subgroups [listed in (a), (b), and (c)] are defined as project-dislocated populations, and their socioeconomic re-establishment must be carried out by the same projects that displace them. There are differences in the degree to which one or another category is affected by specific losses and this is to be reflected in their overall compensation packages, but without entailing a denial of their status as development affected oustees.

The Magnitude of Forced Displacements

The magnitude of forced displacement is often not fully realized. Although in some post-war countries large return movements have occurred, the total number of affected people continues to increase. In the early 1980s there were about 11 million cross-border refugees. In 1993, the UNHCR estimated that the figure had risen to 18.2 million (UNHCR, 1993: iii). Subsequently there have been further huge cross-border movements, particularly in Africa. Figures are less easy to obtain for internally displaced populations, but these too seem to be rising. It is now increasingly being recognized that they are even higher than for those displaced internationally. In 1993, the UNHCR estimated that there were about 24 million internally displaced people worldwide, and this figure excludes those forcibly displaced by development programmes. There are, in fact, no readily obtainable aggregate estimates for this latter group. Lack of information about development-induced displacement is partly a consequence of countries not publishing official statistics about those affected – something which partly explains the insufficient public awareness of the issue. Nevertheless, extrapolated information from recent research makes it clear that such displacement occurs on a very large scale.

Some of the most massive and visible individual cases of development related displacement are those associated with dam and reservoir construction. Table 21.1 shows the size of displacements caused, or expected to be caused, by the construction of some major dams in various countries. But these projects are not the only significant causes of development displacement. A recent study of all World Bank-assisted projects entailing resettlement during 1986–1993 has found that the transportation, water supply and urban infrastructure sector now has the largest number of projects involving resettlement in the Bank's project portfolio, representing above 51 per cent (World Bank, 1994). This compares with agricultural projects (14 per cent) and energy and industry projects (about 29 per cent). While these proportions refer to the Bank's project portfolio, they reflect the overall world trend of rapidly increasing urban population displacements (Cernea, 1993b). In addition, massive forced dislocations are entailed by other types of development projects, such as thermal power plants or open-strip mines. Quite often, seemingly innocuous projects such as establishing an agricultural research centre or a national park, building a hospital complex in a city or constructing a drinking water storage basin, involve land expropriation which deprives many families of their habitats or productive assets.

In the absence of country-based statistics, the only way to assess the magnitude of worldwide development-caused displacement is to develop an estimate based on (i) available displacement information from the better known projects, and (ii) investment trends in infrastructure. With respect to the former, it needs to be born in mind that project-constructing agencies commonly underestimate the number of people adversely

Table 21.1 *People affected by dam-caused displacement*

Dam	Country	Number of People
Already Built		
Dongpinghu	China	278,000
Sanmenxia	China	319,000
Srisailam	India	100,000
Assad	Syria	60,000
Keban	Turkey	30,000
Portile de Fier	Romania/Yugoslavia	23,000
Victoria	Sri Lanka	31,500
Akosombo	Ghana	84,000
Kossou	Côte d'Ivoire	85,000
Kainji	Nigeria	50,000
High Aswan	Egypt	100,000
Nangbeto	Togo/Benin	12,000
Saguling	Indonesia	55,000
Danjiangkou	China	383,000
Sobradinho	Brazil	60,000
Itaparica	Brazil	50,000
Mangla	Pakistan	90,000
Currently under Construction		
Three Gorges	China	1.1 million
Xiaolangdi	China	181,000
Shuikou	China	70,000
Ertan	China	30,000
Tehri	India	105,000
Narmada Sardar Sarovar	India	250,000*
Almatti	India	160,000
Narayanpur	India	60,000
Yacyreta	Argentina/Paraguay	50,000
Kayraktepe	Turkey	20,000
Under Design		
Kalabagh	Pakistan	80,000
Gandhi Sagar	India	100,000
Soubré	Côte d'Ivoire	40,000
Komati	Swaziland	20,000
Karnali (Chisapani)	Nepal	50,000

Note: This table is based on data from project documents and/or public sources. Some of these projects were co-financed by the World Bank, while others were financed entirely from domestic or other international sources. For most irrigation dams already built, data refer to reservoir displacements, without including the number of people displaced by the canal/road networks in the irrigation command areas.

* This number includes 127,000 people displaced by the reservoir, reported in 1993 by the Narmada Control Authority, and people affected by significant loss of land to the canal and road networks downstream, as documented by the Sardar Sarovar Independent Review (see Morse, *et al.*, 1992).

affected by their activities. As a rule, the real numbers of displaced people are likely to be more accurate for internationally assisted projects than for domestically financed ones, which tend to be less scrutinized (and more haphazard when it comes to resettlement operations). Nevertheless, it is essential to include domestic projects because they undoubtedly account for the bulk of forced displacements. Therefore, an estimate of the aggregate magnitude of development displacement worldwide needs to be based on the better verified final counts of people displaced by projects receiving international assistance, combined with an assessment of how that data relates to data on other infra-structural investments.

The study of World Bank-financed projects causing displacement, mentioned above, has made possible such an estimate of the overall displacements taking place in the developing world because of dam construction and urban and transportation projects. The study found that in the early 1990s about 300 new high dams (above 15 m) are entering construction every year and that they entail the displacement of some 4 million people. If dams with a height of less than 15 m are included, the total would be considerably greater. In addition, the projects for urban and transportation infrastructure being started every year entail the displacement of some 6 million people, on average. Thus, in both sectors at least 10 million people are being displaced by every year's new cohort of development programmes. The overall total for all sectors is certainly greater because it should include the oustees from other projects such as thermal plants, open-strip mining, parks and forest reserves, etc., for which overall estimates are not yet available.[5]

These aggregate numbers are staggering. Over the last decade, at least 80 to 90 million people have been displaced by programmes in only two development sectors. *Population displacement by development programmes is now a worldwide problem, of a magnitude previously unsuspected.* Moreover, ongoing industrialization, electrification and urbanization processes are likely to increase, rather than decrease, the number of programmes causing involuntary population displacement over the next 10 years. Particularly in countries engaged in large hydropower programmes, there are annual 'waves' of newly displaced people. Recent statistics from China, for instance, show that over the last three decades, from the late 1950s to 1989, the number of people displaced by water conservation projects alone exceeded 10 million (Chao, 1990). For India, a 1989 study by Fernandes, Das and Rao estimated that during the last four decades some 15.5 million people were displaced by projects (dams, mines, industries, wildlife reserves, etc.); most of them still have to be 'rehabilitated'. In a follow-up analysis (1991), Fernandes revised upward that initial assessment to about 18.5 million people.

Massive displacements also occur under another category of state-sponsored programme aimed at large-scale population redistribution. Such resettlements – many compulsory, and some voluntary but state-promoted – are allegedly initiated to improve the condition of those relocated. Whether or not they actually improve it is a matter to be assessed *ex-post* in each case. Lassailly-Jacob (1994) has pointed out that three major reasons are typically advanced for such massive population redistribution programmes: (i) maximized utilization of a nation's resources; (ii) strategic considerations and counter-

---

[5] In the methodology for making this estimate we took into account all available information on dam construction in the developing world provided by the International Commission on Large Dams (ICOLD) and the World Register of Dams (see ICOLD 1988, 1993; also Mermel 1990). The ICOLD statistics indicate that from 1951 to 1982 an average of 340 dams entered the construction stage every year. During the early 1990s worldwide construction of high dams has averaged about 300 new dams per year. China alone has been starting construction of about 150 dams a year in the early 1990s. Because ICOLD statistics are silent on population displacements, affected populations were taken from World Bank statistics for the projects it finances. Weighted averages by classes of dam height were used in extrapolating population data from the universe of Bank-financed dam projects to the overall number of dams reported by ICOLD statistics.

insurgency measures; and (iii) apartheid policies. There have been numerous examples of such programmes, some of them dating back to colonial times. Openly recognizing strategic and counter-insurgency reasons, the French army undertook a massive policy of population *regroupement* (regrouping) during the 1954–61 Algerian War of Independence, to prevent the rural population from actively assisting the guerrillas or from being exposed to fighting. Apartheid policies in South Africa were accompanied by forced mass population relocation into areas knows as homelands (de Wet 1993). The Bulusu of East Kalimantan (Indonesia) and other interior Dayak groups have been forcibly relocated to government-established resettlement centres, with the stated purpose of providing them with services unavailable in their area of origin (Appell, 1985).

Other population redistribution programmes have claimed to have agricultural development goals. Examples include the relocation of the Azande population in Sudan (1946–50), the mostly coerced villagization programme in Tanzania that brought some 5 million scattered peasants into nucleated settlements, or the involuntary relocation of farmers in Ethiopia away from drought-prone and famine areas (Dieci and Viezzoli, 1992). The evidence from such schemes is often mixed and controversial. Some of the social scientists who conducted empirical studies have concluded that, in fact, these relocations were politically motivated operations disguised by authorities under a 'development' rhetoric (Clay, 1986, 1988; Kesmanee, 1988; De Mars, 1992). Other researchers contend that more complex economic, social and ecological factors may be at work in such situations. In his subtle analysis of the Ethiopian resettlement programmes, Pankhurst argues that the 'stereotypes of resettlement as either purely induced by famine or enforced by the government [are] equally misleading simplifications' (Pankhurst, 1992: 9) .

In conclusion, the displacement of oustees from development programmes fully invites comparative analysis with the displacement of refugees *by sheer magnitude and not only by the nature of the social problems engendered.* The fact that planned programmes often produce long-term benefits (usually for other people) does not make the disruptions any less, or the hardship any lighter, for those who have the misfortune to be uprooted.

Human Rights, Entitlements, and Impoverishment

Situations engendering refugees, as well as planned displacements caused by development raise important issues of human rights. Both types of situations cause the impoverishment of populations which often are already marginal or poor. It is important to at least briefly define the main legal points involved, particularly as they regard the oustees – because the discussion of refugees' human rights and poverty conditions has already a large literature supporting it (Zolberg *et al.*, 1989; Downing and Kushner, 1988; Zetter, 1988; Harrell-Bond, 1986).

The magnitude and disastrous impacts of displacements worldwide, and the increased visibility of these impacts, have gradually contributed (not alone, obviously) to the significant trends observable in international policy and in aid-flows: one is the advent of the human rights argument more to the forefront of the policy dialogue; another is increased concern about the secondary impoverishment effects of programmes that are primarily supposed to help reduce poverty.

Human rights and development
Legal scholars, anthropologists, and sociologists increasingly explore the ethical, economic and juridical links between human rights and policies for inducing development (see Shihata 1988, 1993; Paul, 1988, 1989 and 1992; Downing and Kushner, 1988). Anticipating the direction in which the international situation is evolving, it can be predicted that the formulation of future development policies and programmes will

21.1 *The building of the Kariba dam in the late 1950s has provided electricity and has afforded opportunities for commercial fishing: boats arriving at the dock of a fishing company located on the Zimbabwean shore, after a night on the lake, 1992. (Tim Allen)*

21.2 *Many people have benefited from the electric power produced by the Kariba project, the vast majority of them living in urban centres: downtown Harare, 1992. (Tim Allen)*

increasingly have to take into account the protection of basic human rights, including the rights and entitlements of oustees.

Three distinct sets of human rights issues are pertinent to the design and implementation of development projects:

a issues regarding general economic rights, particularly those pertaining to sharing equitably to the benefits of development;

b issues related to protecting the basic human rights of, and providing emergency assistance for, people affected by civil war, ethnic persecution, or natural disasters; and

c issues arising when development programmes adversely affect the rights and welfare of some population segments.

The legal questions regarding the definition of rights and entitlements are central to how displacement and resettlement take place. The very decision by the state to expropriate and displace people raises issues regarding people's right to self-determination and the right to control one's own life and fate. Such decisions are based on the state's right of eminent domain, which is to take away private property for the purpose of public use even without the consent of the property owner. The state is normally required by law to pay just compensation to the property owner. Practice shows, however, in case after case, that only a small portion of the losses suffered by displaced persons are recognized in the formal economic and legal systems, or procedures, of most developing countries. Loss of usufruct rights, rights of way, customary rights to land, etc., are poorly or not at all recognized in many national legal systems. In addition, the perception of what should be defined as basic human rights is not just a legal matter. It is dependent on culture as well and on the development of a mature civil society. As Downing correctly pointed out, the 'precise content of human rights logics varies between and within the same culture at different times. Yet, the logics also tend to share critical, perhaps universal dimensions' (Downing, 1988: 9). For instance, customary rights of indigenous and tribal people, including their access to common property resources (forests, grazing lands, etc.), are recognized in a few countries but not recognized in others. Moreover, even a recognized right to compensation for lost assets may not by itself constitute an adequate means to re-establish the standard of living of the affected population (Shihata, 1993). Under certain circumstances, the denial by the state of displaced peoples' rights and entitlements in situations of forced displacement has led to active resistance against resettlement and to sharp political conflicts (Oliver-Smith, 1994). Legal experts and human rights activists are exploring the possibilities of a 'charter' to define and help secure human rights in development processes when it appears that people are put at risk (Paul, 1992 and personal communication).

The state resorts to the exercise of eminent domain law when it constructs new infrastructure that is essential for national development, satisfies the needs of many beneficiaries, and generates gains unobtainable in any other way. Because such constructions entail the forced displacement of those 'in the way', the state voids the right of private individuals to hold on to their land and residences, compelling them to move elsewhere. Such conflicts, however, are not between private right and public wrong, or between public right and private wrong. Most often, this is a conflict between right and right, when the public sector acts on behalf of the rights of the larger numbers of people that expect to benefit from a certain development, while those adversely affected oppose it on the grounds of their own legitimate right to the place where they live and work. Thus, the fulfillment of the needs of the many[6] clashes with the rightful entitlements of the few.

This conflict between right and right is not insoluble. It can be negotiated and over-

---

[6] Assuming that the given development will indeed benefit many and not only the selfish interests of a powerful minority.

come if the public sector, the state, is prepared to fully recognize the losses and pains inflicted on those called to make the immediate sacrifice and to accept uprooting. In practical terms the problem is not that the conflict is irreconcilable under any circumstances, but that the premisses for resolution are often not equitably provided by the public sector. These premisses consist not only of financial compensation. They also include democratic consultation; provision of options to those affected through information, participation, and the building up of consent; recognition of local customs and traditions; and fair legal protection. Of course, these premisses also consist of considerable material resources necessary to reconstruct what is being lost – resources that must be contributed by the public sector and by the project's beneficiaries. Each real development that requires displacement usually does generate gains, but the problem is that the gains are only rarely shared by those who bear the pains. The core demand is to ensure that those who are the temporary victims of such projects are also enabled to have their basic rights to socio-economic progress equitably satisfied.

Impoverishment through displacement

Like becoming a refugee, being forcibly ousted from one's land and habitat by a dam, reservoir or highway is not only immediately disruptive and painful, it is also fraught with serious long-term risks of becoming poorer than before displacement, more vulnerable economically, and distintegrated socially. Most of the research to date – both refugee research and oustee research – has vividly documented the adverse effects of forced dislocation. The most pervasive consequence is that many displaced people remain unable to reconstruct their income generation capacity. While it is easy to see why this happens in the case of refugees, the process is more complex and even more unacceptable in the case of oustees. They are supposed to receive compensation for their lost assets, and effective assistance to re-establish themselves productively; yet, this does not happen for a large portion of oustees.

The empirical research evidence reveals a set of recurrent characteristics when the resettlement of oustees does not amount to income restoration and people are left worse off. While each of these characteristics is irreducible to the others, they have a common denominator: they converge into a process of impoverishment. Data from many empirical studies has been synthesized into a model of impoverishment risks resulting from forced displacements (see Cernea, 1990b; 1991). This model shows that development-caused displacements, if not mitigated by policies and approaches that restore oustees to their previous living standards, tend to lead to impoverishment by the following eight typical processes:

a landlessness;
b homelessness;
c joblessness;
d marginalization;
e loss of access to common property resources;
f food insecurity;
g increased mortality and morbidity; and
h social disintegration.

Such adverse effects of development should not be denied or belittled, but must be acknowledged from the outset and addressed with appropriate mitigatory means. The evidence that substantiates these trends is massive, and the above features are derived from the factual descriptions of many cases, notwithstanding the variability of individual displacement situations (Scudder 1981, 1991, 1993; Appell 1985, 1991; Salem-Murdock, 1989; Horowitz, 1991; Ganguly Thukral, 1992; Partridge et al., 1982; Christensen, 1982; Areeparompil, 1989; Fahim, 1988; Rew and Driver, 1986; de Wet, 1991; and many others).

A more detailed review of this evidence (see Cernea, 1990b) showed that one unavoidable process in displacement, whose far-reaching pernicious effects are not yet sufficiently recognized, is the one listed last – *social disintegration*. Established integrated communities as well as social support networks territorial or kinship based, are dismantled through displacement. Anthropological and economic research in developing societies have demonstrated how important the informal networks among households are as a *social support system*, partly substituting for insufficient cash income and for other resources. Informal social networks among households and families help cope with poverty through informal loans, exchanges of labour, food, clothing, durable goods, gifts, etc.; they help in house-building, in caring for children, in emergencies, etc. The dismantling of these networks through the dispersion of their members causes direct *economic* losses, in addition to *social* and *cultural* ones. This is a loss of *social capital* – of patterns of social organization able to mobilize individuals in collective actions for common interests, which, if dismantled, are hardest to rebuild. Such loss of already existing social integration and social capital is compounded in development projects which relocate people in a dispersed manner, rather than in groups and social units.

Taken together, the eight key dimensions of impoverishment through displacement provide a warning model that can inform policies and plans for dislocation, and thus help prevent and mitigate such consequences. It is crucial to emphasize that impoverishment through involuntary displacement is not inevitable. But avoiding it, as will be discussed in the last section of this chapter, requires a convergence of policy, planning, financial resources, and social-technical expertise.

Emergency Assistance to Refugees

Growing public recognition of the human rights issues, of the impoverishment processes,

21.3 *As the waters rose following the building of the Kariba dam, thousands of Tonga were forced to leave their land, and were displaced into less fertile locations. In many places they have been denied access to the lake shore, which has become a tourist playground, and their crops are vulnerable to destruction by protected animals, notably elephants and buffalos. The time before displacement is recalled with longing: a Tonga elder, Zimbabwe, 1992. (Tim Allen)*

21.4 *Since the displacement, many Tonga have had to farm in locations unsuitable for agriculture: among the stalks of her dehydrated millet, a Tonga woman picks the leaves of wild shrubs to cook for supper, Zimbabwe, 1992. (Tim Allen)*

and of the political and ethical implications of the drama of both refugee and oustee populations, have led over the last two decades to increased financial and other assistance to displaced populations.

Despite the essential differences in the causes of refugees' and oustees' uprooting, there are significant similarities in the consequences. Refugees and oustees resemble each other in that they are both victimized by events for which, as individuals, they cannot be held responsible. Both lose their houses and households; they temporarily or permanently lose their lands, water wells, workshops, vending stalls, or other assets.[7] In both cases, their production systems are dismantled, their ways of making a living are disrupted and their very livelihood critically jeopardized. The supporting social networks in which their existence was embedded are unravelled. Both relocate in previously unknown places, among host populations often suspicious or directly hostile.

Two new trends became manifest in the assistance to displaced populations, particularly during the 1980s. These trends were little analysed by the research community. The first trend is a considerable *increase in the number and diversity of international aid projects* targeted to disaster victims – refugees and non-refugees; the other is a significant *orientation towards distinct project components geared to assist development oustees* in their re-establishment.

As 'vehicles' for such assistance, governments and aid agencies largely use two categories of interventions: (a) emergency assistance projects, for immediate and temporary help to refugees; and (b) resettlement projects (or project components) aimed at permanently relocating the people displaced by planned change. These trends open up new possibilities: on the one hand, refugee relief aid can be better informed with the experience of approaches that pursue not just short-term relief, but redevelopment, as do some projects for oustee resettlement; on the other hand, assistance given to oustees can be improved by learning from the coping mechanisms used by refugees to survive under harsh conditions (Christensen, 1982) and to regain self-sufficiency.

The new trends are quite visible in the lending patterns of the World Bank, which are indicative of the presence of refugee and oustee issues on the international aid agenda. After its establishment in 1945, all the Bank's loans from 1947 to 1953 were given for post-war *reconstruction projects*. Europe was then home to about 6 million refugees, and those emergency operations were addressed to a wide spectrum of needs and populations, including refugees. As these problems started to subside, however, in 1953 the World Bank ceased this type of operation. It replaced them with investment lending. Only after almost two decades, and because of a serious aggravation of the worldwide problem of refugees, did the World Bank resume emergency assistance operations in 1970. By this time, the refugee problems had shifted dramatically to developing countries, where the bulk of the refugees existed then and now. This assistance is primarily financial and technical. It provides an immediate response to disasters and has benefited large numbers of refugees fleeing natural or socio-political catastrophes (as well as people living in adjacent areas).

Especially in the 1980s, the frequency of emergency loans and the amount of resources they channelled have risen sharply. For instance, 76 emergency projects were approved between 1974 and 1991, out of which 19 between 1989 and 1991. The resources channelled through such Bank-assisted projects between 1984 and 1988 were 3.5 times larger than in the prior five years (see Table 21.2). The diversity of these activities is significant: during 1989 alone, 18 loans were approved for post-disaster

---

[7] Yet even in this respect there are some differences. Compared to other refugee-causing circumstances, development-related displacements inflict upon the uprooted population material losses that often are greater, or definitive. For instance, refugees fleeing their homelands because of civil war, persecution, or flooding may in some cases at least return to their farming land; those displaced by dam reservoirs, however, will never get the same lands back, and simply cannot return to their prior homes. The compensation most receive for expropriation is supposed to help them regain substitute assets.

Table 21.2 *Emergency projects by type of disaster: 1969–91**

	FY69-73		FY74-78		FY79-83		FY84-88		FY89-91	
	No.	US$m	No.	US$m	No.	US$m	No.	US$m	No.	US$m
Civil war	4	165.6	2	60.7	7	257.5	2	123.0	5	245.0
Cyclone/hurricane	1	25.0	–	–	5	76.2	3	25.6	3	254.0
Drought	–	–	8**	35.0	–	–	3	400.0	1	16.0
Flood	–	–	3	135.0	1	7.0	5	345.5	5	301.1
Earthquake	2	50.0	2	86.5	3	85.0	4	580.0	5	469.3
Forest fire	–	–	–	–	–	–	1	56.9	–	–
Volcanic eruption	–	–	1	7.0	–	–	–	–	–	–
Total	7	240.6	16	324.2	16	425.7	18	1,531.0	19	1,285.4

Notes: * No emergency assistance loans were made by the Bank between Financial Year (FY) 1954 and (FY) 1969. For the period subsequent to FY69, this table includes only the Bank loans and projects labelled 'emergency operations', but, in addition, many other Bank projects also provided assistance to refugee populations. For instance, two important refugee assistance projects were targeted to Afghani refugees in Pakistan, but these are not included in the table. The emergency interventions reflected in this table have benefited, of course, also those disaster victims who did not become refugees. This table includes only new projects and new full scale loans/credits, which were additional to the emergency assistance provided through the speedy re-allocation of unused proceeds from other on-going Bank operations.

** Includes six loans to the Sahelian countries in FY74 for a series of inter-related drought relief projects.

reconstruction projects; of these, one was a post-civil war reconstruction project in Mozambique (urban rehabilitation); two were drought-assistance projects (India); five were post-hurricane projects (one in Costa Rica, one in Mexico, and three in Jamaica); two were post-earthquake projects (both in Nepal) and eight were post-flood assistance.

Post-war reconstruction issues have received increasing attention in the Bank's work during the 1990s, particularly during 1993–1995. This has included experiments with new approaches in assistance projects, as well as in-depth field analysis of the demobiliza-tion and reintegration experiences in post-war countries such as Ethiopia, Namibia, Uganda (World Bank, 1995). A strategy discussion paper on 'post-conflict reconstruction' is currently preparing the grounds for broadening Bank lending and technical assistance to countries undergoing war-to-peace transition processes (Holtzman, 1995, draft).

Strategy Alternatives in Assisting Refugees

A key strategy issue in refugee assistance is always the trade-off between short-term relief needed immediately and investments for long-term redevelopment. The World Bank emphasizes the latter type of measures. Particularly after war or civil war periods – during which production activities and trade lines had been disrupted – Bank projects primarily aim to restore production and productivity and to rebuild the transportation systems required for recovery. This approach also creates employment. The Bank's 1984 policy guidelines on emergency lending, revised and improved in 1989 (World Bank, 1989), formally recommended to use, during post-disaster assistance, what is being called the 'window of opportunity' for preventing/mitigating future disasters: namely, financing certain preventive measures which tend not to be seen as a priority in normal times, yet are likely to be adopted in addition to immediate relief.[8] In such situations, resources are provided both for the reconstruction of damaged physical infrastructure and for building additional preventive physical and organizational protection systems.

Africa is the continent where most refugee-assisted projects have been carried out. An

[8] Weighing and deciding on trade-offs in such situations is vulnerable to imperfect initial information. Built-in flexibility for midstream adjustments is needed. This is why World Bank assistance usually needs to be complemented by short-term relief programmes by other agencies, including non-governmental organizations.

21.5 *In Mozambique, the World Bank has provided emergency assistance to support the government's immediate rehabilitation efforts through quickly disbursed hard currency to meet priority needs: returnees to Mozambique, 1990. (S. Errington/UNHCR)*

example of a recovery programme after war and civil disturbance is the Bank's Reconstruction Credit to Uganda (FY80) given immediately after the overthrow of the military government in 1979. At that time Uganda's domestic economy was devastated, following large-scale physical destruction. Reconstruction was also complicated by social disruption, administrative disarray and continued political strife. In response to the urgent situation, the Bank approved a quick disbursing project to rapidly supply inputs for the productive sectors and to meet short-term foreign exchange needs. Unfortunately, however, policies carried out subsequently by the new government caused, in turn, other waves of refugees from political and ethnic oppression and appalling atrocities. Other comparable cases include projects in Mozambique (FY85), Ghana (FY83) and Zimbabwe (FY81), where the Bank has financed recovery programmes and imports critical to begin a long-term process of rehabilitation and reform.

When Mozambique joined the World Bank in 1984, its economy was suffering from the effects of the civil war with its refugees, inappropriate policies, natural calamities and structural imbalances of long standing. Against this backdrop, the government developed a policy and a two-year Economic Action Programme designed to stem the economic decline. The Bank's emergency assistance supported the government's immediate rehabilitation efforts through quickly disbursed hard currency to meet priority needs as the government began the process of rehabilitation. The initial project made possible imports of equipment, spare parts and raw materials for the key sectors of industry, agriculture and transport, and directly helped the reintegration of war-displaced people into productive activities. This approach has been replicated and validated in other, smaller scale projects assisted in Mozambique by bilateral donors, like the Italian-sponsored project near Gondola (Manica province) and the Swedish-sponsored seed production unit in Chimoio. Results from these two projects confirm (see Morna, 1990) that production-oriented aid (inputs, seeds, etc.) enables former war-refugees to shake-off their dependency upon relief-aid, re-establish themselves on a productive basis and become again self-sustaining.

More recently, in 1992 and 1993, the World Bank started work on a large-scale, long-term programme to assist Mozambique in addressing its gigantic current problem: reintegrating productively the 4 or 5 million of post-war refugees and internally displaced people now returning (or already returned) to their sites of origin. This programme may well be the largest ever undertaken refugee resettlement assistance strategy.

In many cases, internationally assisted programmes for refugees have made the difference between life and death for uncounted numbers of people. Emergency programmes have, however, a limited scope, their implementation is often less than fully satisfactory, and what is needed is long-term resettlement-cum-development assistance. The least addressed dimensions in such programmes are usually the cultural and psychological ones, including the patient social engineering work necessary to re-establish the refugee population in new, viable settlements, with access to productive activities, some employment, and services. Indeed, as Harrell-Bond observed (1986: 2), 'establishing a rural settlement involves social engineering: the reading of the literature produced by agencies responsible for refugee work suggested that the full implications of this reality has escaped attention'; these guidelines re-focus the Bank-provided assistance on restoring the self-sufficiency and autonomy of the affected population through redressing its productive capacity.

Similarities and Differences: Oustees and Refugees

The previous sections discussed several substantive matters about refugees and oustees such as causality, magnitude, impoverishment processes, rights and entitlements, assistance strategies which, each and all, offer the 'territory' for comparative research on refugees and oustees, identifying similarities and differences. These far from exhaust the possibilities for such comparative research, but point to fertile directions, and also allow for a few additional comments.

Overstatements of similarities between refugees and oustees can sometimes be found in the literature, oversimplifying the differences. For instance, some social scientists describe communities displaced by development programmes as 'development refugees'. Without appropriate analysis, this description risks becoming more a metaphorical label than a rigorous concept, and is not helpful for practical purposes. Applying it wholesale to define all those displaced by development programmes would blur certain essential differences between oustees and refugees, and would be misleading. There are sharp dissimilarities between refugees and oustees in legal status and entitlements to assistance.

One key difference between the situation of oustees compared with refugees is the responsibility of the state *vis-à-vis* development-displaced people. This responsibility is of a different nature to the state's responsibility towards refugees: the first is assumed deliberately through the state's decision to enforce the legal principle of eminent domain.

Asserting this difference is a cornerstone in the argument about the material entitlements of those uprooted by state-pursued change. When people are displaced by a public development project, it is incumbent upon the government to ensure that the oustees are fully compensated and enabled to reconstruct their productive livelihood. However, if such assistance is not provided, development-displaced people are likely to become destitute, landless or homeless. Their situation becomes, in essence, similar to that of refugees.

This is not an abstract possibility: in many cases, people displaced through government-sponsored development programmes, who have not been adequately assisted to re-establish themselves economically, have actually fallen into a refugee-like situation. An example of people transformed into refugees by government-sponsored intervention comes recently from Uganda, from a 'forest management and conservation project' funded in part by European donors with an environmental justification. Under this project, about 35,000 people inhabiting the Kibale Game Corridor area were brutally expelled; in 1992, to accelerate that expulsion from certain areas, people's houses were burned down and food stores were destroyed or looted. They became refugees; some were 'relocated' into camps in the Bugangaizi area, while the whereabouts of many thousands, forced to flee, are not known.

A 'sliding process' whereby established inhabitants become oustees and soon refugees, happened, for instance, to many people displaced by the Srisailam dam in India, to people displaced by the Danjiangkou dam in China, or to many of the oustees from the Hirakud multi-purpose dam project in Orissa, India (Baboo, 1992). A paper prepared by Oxfam (1993) about the Hirakud dam oustees shows how 30 years after the initial displacement and inadequate resettlement of people from the Hirakud reservoir, some of the same families have not fully recovered, and are facing eviction once again, this time because of the construction of some thermal plants in the same area.

It is, therefore, conceptually and practically useful to point out explicitly, rather than blur, both similarities and differences between the status of refugees (from war, ethnic persecution, drought, etc.) and the status of oustees from planned programmes. This permits highlighting the circumstances in which the use of violence, or bad planning, or other forms of *abdication of government responsibility*, convert oustees into refugees. The purpose of resettlement policies must be to prevent absolutely the sliding of development-displaced people (oustees) into a refugee-like condition.

The definitions currently accepted internationally for the term *refugees* tend to be fairly restrictive. They are (on purpose) not open to encompass either voluntary migrants or people dislocated by planned projects (see, for instance, the definitions discussed in Zolberg et al., 1989; or the definition used by the United Nations). This is under-standable for both practical and conceptual reasons. Since many countries and inter-national organizations grant special entitlements to refugees, every attempt to define the term is underlined by the concern to avoid confusing, for instance, a voluntary economic migrant with a genuine refugee.[9]

From Research to Practice: Reducing Displacements

A consequential difference between refugees and oustees consists in how their condition sets in: sudden onset, rarely anticipated, versus slow, planned, well-in-advance-known onset. This provides options for assistance strategies to development oustees that range on a broad spectrum: from effective ways to sometimes *avoid* development-induced dis-placement, to other ways to *reduce* its size, and in most cases, to *mitigate* its negative impacts.

[9] Zolberg's discussion (in Zolberg et al. 1989) of the refugee definition highlights the element of violence. He proposes a sociological distinction between three 'prototypes' under which refugees can be conceptually clustered, depending on the circumstances that led to their becoming refugees. These are the *activist*; the *target*; and the *victim*. All three prototypes represent people uprooted from their habitat. The circumstances of their uprooting are different for each category, but one common characteristic of their situation is '*fear of violence*'. 'All three types of refugees have in common the fear of immediate violence – violence resulting from conflict between state and civil society, between opposing armies, or conflict among ethnic groups or class formations that the state is unable or unwilling to control' (Zolberg, et al. 1989: 269). If the consequences of their situation are considered these three types all share similar refugee characteristics: abrupt destitution; residence loss; loss of economic self-sufficiency; cultural separation; identity deprivation; socio-psychological stress; and others. If adopted for practical purposes, this typology has potential implications regarding the forms and amounts of assistance to be given to refugees who can be identified with one or another 'type'.

Drawing on the experience of projects causing such displacements, I will briefly refer to four important issues concerning means and solutions in addressing development-induced displacement: (a) avoidability of displacement through technical optimization and/or correct financial costing; (b) the need for national policies and legal frameworks governing forced displacement operations; (c) development-oriented strategies *vis-à-vis* relief approaches; and (d) resource allocation for reconstruction and the responsibility of national governments.

Avoidability of displacement

While development projects are and will be necessary, there are approaches and techniques apt to avoid, or often reduce, forced displacement. Development is not in itself a blind legitimizer of any displacement, regardless of size and consequence. On the contrary, induced development programmes must seek every opportunity to minimize disruption. For instance, experience has demonstrated that if planners carefully weigh trade-offs between dam height, power generating capacity, and the size of population dislocation, they may be able to reduce the latter. Small decreases in reservoir elevation may significantly cut down the number of people affected by submergence, with relatively little loss of power or irrigation benefits. This was demonstrated by the designers of the Saguling dam in Indonesia, who ultimately selected a reservoir elevation of 645 metres instead of the initially envisaged elevation of 650 thereby reducing population displacement of some 90,000 people to 55,000 (Soepartomo and Tjiptohandojo, 1988). In the same way, optimization studies for road trajectories in Shanghai (China) under the Bank-assisted urban improvement project have resulted in alternative routing which avoided the displacement of several thousand families. Correct costing of resettling (both people and infrastructure) and the inclusion of the estimated costs in the new project, may also show from the outset that one or another project causing displacement is too costly and therefore should not be started. It is necessary to avoid engineering biases in the justification of such technical projects by opposing the fatalistic treatment of displacement as always unavoidable.

Filling policy and legal vacuums

The government's political and moral responsibility *vis-à-vis* development-dislocated people is higher, in all respects, than it is in the case of refugees from natural calamities, because the former displacement is initiated by the government and enforced through the state's power of eminent domain (Shihata, 1988). However, this responsibility is often not assumed through explicit policies. Indeed, many countries have laws permitting expropriation by the government, but do not have formal regulations or policies guaranteeing full resettlement and rehabilitation of oustees. The absence of such domestic policy frameworks allows many abuses and infringements of peoples' socio-economic rights to happen and remain uncorrected. The eminent domain laws and their prescriptions for compensation, which usually were crafted for situations of a limited expropriations, are utterly unfit in cases of massive expropriations.

Until recently, even some international donor agencies, such as the regional development banks for Africa, Asia and Latin America, and many bilateral donor agencies, did not have formal policy guidelines for projects that cause displacement. As a result, when these agencies financed projects entailing displacement, they funded the new physical infrastructure and hardware but only seldom provided equal guidance and financial support for resettling the oustees. Resettlement was being left to the local/territorial agency alone, which definitely has less resources and less overall responsibility. The practical consequence of this policy vacuum was that relocation tended to remain largely unplanned, underfunded, and poorly implemented.

The first time when an explicit policy for addressing the socio-economic and cultural issues of involuntary resettlement was enunciated by an international development agency was in 1980, when the World Bank issued its formal policy guidelines on social issues in resettlement, a policy grounded in social science knowledge about resettlement (see World Bank, 1980, 1994; Cernea, 1988, 1990a, 1993a, 1995; Qureshi 1989). This policy is protective of the interests of those displaced and is regarded even by severe critics of the World Bank as promoting the highest standards in resettlement.[10] This institutionalized policy requires Bank staff and borrowing agencies to pursue resettlement standards of higher quality than would be pursued in the absence of such a policy. The two most important effects of this policy to date have been more systematic *planning* for relocation and more adequate *resource allocation* to the resettlers in a broad spectrum of projects in Africa, Asia and Latin America.

Adequate implementation of this policy in projects, however, does not result automatically from just the adoption of sound policy. Departures from policy norms occur for various reasons, sometimes related to inadequate performance of Bank staff, yet more often because of disregard of project provisions or legal agreements by implementation agencies and borrowing governments. The Bank-assisted Narmada Sardar Sarovar dam project is only the most known case of departure from policy guidelines and poor implementation, but definitely not the only one in India (Morse *et al.*, 1992). For instance, resettlement implementation has fallen below the standards established for resettlement in the Narayanpur and Almatti reservoirs in Karnataka state under the Upper Krishna II project; the provisions of the resettlement action plan, legally agreed upon between the Bank and the country, have been disregarded during implementation, so that twice – in November 1992 and again in September 1995 – the Bank had to suspend the disbursement of its loan for this project. Also in India the Bank had to decline extension of the credits for other projects (e.g., for Upper Indravati and for Subernarekha dams) also because of the borrowing agencies' failures in carrying out resettlement. Similar examples exist in other countries as well – Indonesia, Turkey, Brazil, Madagascar. This demonstrates that a good policy alone – and even a good plan alone – are not enough, if the political will, organizational capacity and financial resources are not adequate. Consistency of resettlement *implementation* with policy must be constantly enforced, and also monitored with the direct participation in such monitoring by the people affected and their organizations.

There is a considerable gap between the resettlement policy norms adopted by the Bank, on the one hand, and the rather weak domestic norms (or sometimes complete policy vacuums) regarding displacement in many developing countries, on the other. For instance, it appears surprising that India and Indonesia two countries with many major on-going development programmes that cause large scale displacements – do not have a national policy regulating involuntary resettlement caused by public sector investments.

The same can be said for many countries in Africa, such as Kenya, Côte d'Ivoire, Togo and others, in which the state is promoting major projects causing displacement yet is not adopting adequate policies to regulate it and address its consequences. The weak (or absent) political commitment of governments to income restoration of those displaced is one of the root causes of the formidable problems created and perpetuated

[10] For instance, the by-now famous Morse review commission, which severely criticized the design, appraisal, and implementation of the Sardar Sarovar projects in India, concluded at the same time that '...*the Bank had, in its 1990 and 1991 directives, set the highest standards of any aid or lending organization in the world for mitigating adverse consequences to human well-being caused by "involuntary resettlement"'* (Morse et al., 1992: 37). Over the last few years (early 1990s) other international donors have followed suit. Significant, in this respect is the adoption by all the Organization for Economic Cooperation and Development (OECD) member countries, in December 1991, of unified policy guidelines for their aid agencies on involuntary displacement and resettlement in projects assisted by these countries (OECD, 1991). The OECD guidelines are virtually the same as the Bank's resettlement policy, taken as their model. The adoption by all major donors of similar resettlement guidelines reflects the broader trend towards recognizing that international aid flows should contribute to the protection of basic human rights.

for decades by forced displacements. In most African countries, compulsory resettlement, including the growing urban developments for infrastructural improvements, are carried out by government agencies in a policy vacuum. Certainly, laws and guidelines to empower the state to take away land 'needed for the public good' do exist. But sorely missing in the majority of African countries are explicit policies and legal frameworks to compel relevant state agencies to effectively address the vital issues of livelihood restoration and productive re-establishment of those displaced (Okidi, 1993). The expropriation laws generally lay down rules for the type of compensation that must be paid for the expropriated land. However, the notion of 'compensation' – payment for land taken for public use – is a narrow concept that differs in substance from the more exacting principle that the state has the obligation to restore people's economic well-being and capacities as productive agents. This distinction between mere compensation, on the one hand, and resettlement on a productive basis, on the other hand, is a critical one, yet it is conspicuously absent from the African policy literature.

In some countries, the Bank–Borrower policy dialogue and the lessons derived from Bank-assisted projects have already led to the elaboration of improved or new domestic legislation. Yet at the same time other states and governments are clearly not willing to commit themselves to issuing binding policies. They offer only ad-hoc and limited improvements confined to one or another project. Furthermore, certain states deliberately go to great lengths to circumscribe the validity of such improvements only to internationally assisted projects, exempting the domestic projects from the improved rules at the expense of the people affected by these domestic projects.

The Bank holds that the projects it finances should not engage in practices which violate universally recognized rights. In order to strengthen the legal guarantees in that respect, it actively encourages the enactment of domestic legal and policy frameworks in borrowing countries that would apply to resettlement *under all projects*, and not only under the few projects that receive international financial assistance. Researchers, legal experts, NGO activists and many others involved in resettlement have concluded that policy and institutional changes are widely needed in many developing countries (see Ganguly Thukral 1992; Shihata, 1991; Paul 1988, 1991; Dhagamwar, 1989). Independent legal scholars have noted that it cannot be said to be improper 'interference' for the Bank or International Development Association to insist, as a formal condition of a project loan, that project-consistent state law be adopted in borrowing countries to secure recognized rights for the people affected by the project; on the contrary, it would be inconsistent and 'unlawful to fail to insist on such protection' (Paul, 1988: 118). The independent adoption of national resettlement policies by governments of developing countries will go a long way towards safeguarding people's human and economic rights and speeding up the productive re-establishment of oustees. Some principles and elements of the Bank's resettlement policy might be used also as a guide in assisting refugees who return to their places of origin.

Development versus relief

Relief assistance to internally displaced populations is necessary, but not sufficient. On the 'development versus relief' issue, the debate has been going on for a long time. But the problem has not been resolved partly because humanitarian agencies are better at relief than development, partly because funders want operations to appear to be short-term interventions, and partly also because some specific situations are such that immediate relief is imperative and the only practical possibility.

The issue of development versus relief is not only a matter of resources, however, although the resources needed for the former are higher: it is also a matter of approach and strategy, a matter of how resources are deployed. Scarce assistance resources must be deployed as a leverage to elicit the capacities, energy and initiatives of those assisted, to strengthen their propensity to self-organization, and meet their basic interests in socio-economic re-establishment.

The key policy objective in resettlement is restoring the income-generating capacity of resettlers. Therefore, *because involuntary displacement dismantles a previous production system and way of life, all resettlement programmes must be development programmes as well.* Indeed, when resettlement is unavoidable, what is most needed is to ensure that the oustees' productive base and income-earning ability are reconstructed, that is, restored to the level they would have achieved without relocation, and improved whenever possible.[11] Reaching this basic objective is largely dependent on the allocation of adequate resources for the re-establishment of people's productive capacity and on the participation of those affected in creating the new socioeconomic arrangements.

Reconstruction and Resource Allocation

The crafting of reconstruction strategies may improve through experience transfers between projects for resettling development oustees and for post-war refugee reinsertion. Specialists have signalled that 'too often the kind of agencies involved in the relief activity [for refugees] simply do not know much about longer term, developmental approaches' (Clark 1989: 10). Relief workers are asking pertinent questions about 'how can assistance be provided in ways that are as developmental as possible?'; or what ways can be found 'to build some kind of economic activity into the lives of refugees?' (Clark 1989: 10–11).

In resettlement projects, the *core of the resettlement plan is a development package.* It must consist of provisions centred either on land-based strategies or on employment-based strategies. The most effective, and relatively less costly, are the land-based strategies. They often involve land reclamation, small-scale irrigation, tree-crops development, fisheries, social forestry and similar kinds of income-generating activities. Sometimes, land scarcity is a major limiting factor, given high population densities. Vocational training for jobs outside agriculture is used in employment-based strategies, but this avenue also requires investments in job creation. Vocational training alone, without actual employment in the newly acquired skills, does not restore the livelihood of those displaced.

In all such activities, it is essential to stimulate the initiative of those to be resettled and assist their own efforts for self-resettlement among the host population at the new location. In fact, research on refugees has documented the effectiveness of self-resettlement, under certain circumstances. Hansen's research among Angolan refugees in Zambia found that self-resettled people achieved greater autonomy and integration in the long term than refugees that have spent an equal period of time in government-controlled refugee schemes (Hansen, 1990). Similarly, an IDRC research in Tanzania, led by A. Chol and M. Mbago, among Burundi refugees from ethnic persecution suggests that self-settled refugee villages achieve better and more durable integration within the surrounding local host population than government-established refugee centres – this assessment being based on productive status, intermarriage with citizens of the host country, interpersonal relationships, education and stability (cf. Harris, 1991). Such findings suggest that more encouragement given to the initiative, energy, and self-organizing capacity of oustees may unlock a potential insufficiently used in resettlement programmes.

[11] This policy objective was formulated clearly in the Bank's 1990 operational directives: 'All involuntary resettlement should be conceived and executed as *development programs*, with resettlers provided sufficient investment resources and opportunities to *share in project benefits.* The displaced should be (i) compensated for their losses at full replacement cost prior to the actual move; (ii) assisted with the move and supported during the transition period in the resettlement site; and (iii) assisted in their efforts to improve their former living standards, income earning capacity, and production levels, or at least to restore them. Particular attention needs to be paid to the needs of the poorest groups' (World Bank, 1990: 3(b)).

Philanthropy from the private sector and the public, which is crucial for refugee assistance, cannot be counted upon as a resource in programme-caused dislocation. The government bears the primary financial and institutional responsibility for relocation in a manner that will restore the economic autonomy of those uprooted. The participation of NGOs in the planning and implementation of relocation is essential because NGOs are apt to express the needs and defend the rights of those displaced. Some NGOs are better placed than government agencies to mobilize and organize the energies of those displaced for reconstructive activities. In turn, bilateral donor agencies should never finance only the construction of new physical structures without also assisting the reconstruction of sustainable livelihoods for those displaced.

In sum, there is much to explore about the similarities and differences between the condition of refugees and development oustees, and about how their needs can be addressed. The very nature of these similarities and differences offers the basis for more comparative analysis and for a better dialogue between the bodies of social science literatures devoted to the study of these populations. Their findings can complement and reinforce each other. Most important is the benefit for social action: comparative research will not only serve for in-depth conceptual developments, but will also inform policy and operational assistance more comprehensively and effectively.

Acknowledgement

This study was started as part of the author's research while a Visiting Scholar at Harvard University, Department of Anthropology, on leave from the World Bank. An abbreviated version, submitted to the refugee research seminar organized by UNRISD in Addis Ababa, Ethiopia, (1992), was expanded for this volume. The author expresses grateful thanks to D. Maybury-Lewis, I. Shihata, James C.N. Paul, Ruth Cernea, S. Guggenheim, B. Harrell-Bond, J. Clay, N. Yalman, R. Zetter, A. Hansen and Tim Allen, for comments or discussions that have benefited the study. Special thanks are due to Camille Weithers, who helped in the final editing of this paper. The views, findings and interpretations contained in this study are those of the author and should not necessarily be attributed to the institutions with which he is associated.

References

Appell, G.N. (1985) 'The Bulusu' of East Kalimantan: the consequences of resettlement', in G.N. Appell (ed.) *Modernization and the emergency of a landless peasantry, studies in third world societies*, Vol. 33, Williamsburg: College of William and Mary.

Appell, G. N. (1994) 'Our vision of human rights is too small: anthropological perspective on fundamental human rights', in Hitchcock, R.K. and Morris, (eds.) *International Human Rights and Indigenous People*, forthcoming.

Areeparampil, Matthew (1989) 'Industries, mines and dispossession of indigenous people: the case of Chotariapur', in W. Fernandes and E.G. Thukral (eds.) *Development, Displacement and Rehabilitation*, New Delhi: Indian Social Institute.

Baboo, Balgobind (1992) *Technology and social transformation. The case of the Hirakud multi-purpose dam project in Orissa*, Concept Publishing Company, New Delhi, India.

Brokensha, David W (1963–4). 'Volta resettlement and anthropological research', in *Human Organization*, Vol. 22, No. 4, 286–90.

Cernea, Michael M. (1988) *Involuntary resettlement in development projects. policy guidelines in World Bank Financed Projects*, World Bank, Washington, DC.

— (1990a) *From unused social knowledge to policy creation*, Development Discussion Paper No. 342, May, HIID, Harvard University, Cambridge, MA.

— (1990b) *Poverty risks from population displacement in water resource projects*, Development Discussion Paper No. 355, HIID, Harvard University, Cambridge, MA.

— (1990c) 'Internal refugee flows and development-induced population displacement', *Journal of Refugee Studies*, Vol. 3, No. 4: 320–39.

— (1991) 'Involuntary resettlement: social research, policy and planning', in Cernea, M.M. (ed.), *Putting people first. Sociological variables in rural development*, 2nd ed., revised and enlarged, New York-Oxford: Oxford University Press.

— (1993a) 'Anthropological and sociological research for policy formulation on involuntary resettlement', in M. M. Cernea and S. Guggenheim (eds), *Anthropological approaches to resettlement: policy, practice and theory*, Westview Press, Boulder, CO.

— (1993b) *Urban environment and population resettlement*, World Bank, Washington, DC.

— (1994) 'African population resettlement in a global context', in C. Cook (ed.) *Involuntary resettlement in*

Africa, World Bank, Washington, DC.

— (1995) 'Social integration and population displacement: the contribution of social sciences' in *International Social Science Journal*, Mouton, No. 143.

Chao, Liang (1990) 'State plans new rules for dam resettlement, *China Daily*, No. 2632, 4 January.

Christensen, Hanne (1982) *Survival strategies for and by camp refugees: report on an exploratory sociological field study in Somalia*, UNRISD Report No. 82: 3, Geneva: United Nations.

Clay, Jason W. (1986) Research Report: 'Refugees flee Ethiopia's collectivization', *Cultural Survival Quarterly*, Vol. 10 No. 2: 80–5.

Clay, Jason W. (1988). In J.W. Clay, S. Steingraber and P. Niggli (eds) *The spoils of famine. Ethiopian policy and peasant agriculture*, Cambridge, MA: Cultural Survival.

Clark, Lance (1989) *Internally displaced persons: framing the issues*, Center for Policy Analysis and Research on Refugee Issues, Washington, DC.

de Mars, William (1992) *Decade of displacement in Ethiopia: internally displaced persons and humanitarian response*, Refugee Policy Group, Washington, DC.

de Wet, Chris (1993) 'Involuntary resettlement as imposed transformation' in M. Cernea and S. Guggenheim (eds.) *Anthropological Approaches to Resettlement: Policy, Practice, and Theory*, Westview Press, Boulder, CO.

Dhagamwar, Vasuda (1989) 'Rehabilitation: policy and institutional changes required', in W. Fernandes and E.G. Thukral (eds) *Development, Displacement and Rehabilitation*, Indian Social Institute, New Delhi.

Dieci, Paolo and Claudio Viezolli (eds) (1992) *Resettlement and rural development in Ethiopia*, Milan: Franco Angeli.

Downing, Theodore (1988) *Human rights research: The challenge for the anthropologist*, in T. Downing and G. Kushner (eds), *Human rights and tribal people*, Cultural Survival, Cambridge, MA.

Downing, Theodore and G. Kushner (eds.) (1988) *Human rights and tribal people*, Cultural Survival, Cambridge MA.

Drabek, Thomas E. (1987) *Human systems responses to disasters. An inventory of sociological findings*, Springer Verlag, New York, Berlin and Heidelberg.

Dubin, R. (1978) *Theory building*, Free Press, New York.

Fahim, Hussein (1988). *Egyptian Nubians: resettlement and years of coping*, Salt Lake City: University of Utah Press.

Fernandes, W. (1991) 'Power and powerlessness: development projects and displacement of tribals', in *Social Action*, Vol. 41, No. 3, July.

Fernandes, W., J.C. Das, Sam Rao (1989) 'Displacement and rehabilitation: an estimate of extent and prospects', in Fernandes, W. and E. Ganguly Thukral (eds) *Development, displacement and rehabilitation*, Indian Social Institute, New Delhi.

Ganguly-Thukral, E., (ed.) (1992) *Big dams, displaced people, rivers of sorrow, rivers of change*, Sage Publications, New Delhi and London.

The Georgetown declaration on health care for displaced persons and refugees (1988) Georgetown University, Washington, DC

Guggenheim, Scott (1994) *Involuntary resettlement: an annotated reference bibliography for development research*, processed.

Hansen, Art (1990) 'Long-term consequences of two African refugee settlement strategies', paper presented at the meetings of the Society for Applied Anthropology, York, UK.

Harrell-Bond, Barbara E. (1986) *Imposing aid: emergency assistance to refugees*, New York: Oxford University Press.

Harris, Craig (1991) *Integrating refugees into host countries*, IDRC Reports, Vol. 19, No. 3, Ottawa, Canada, October.

Holtzman, Sreven (1995) 'Post-conflict reconstruction', World Bank, Social Policy and Resettlement Division, draft.

Horowitz, Michael M., D. Loenig, C. Grimm and Y. Konate (1993) 'Resettlement at Manantali, Mali: short term success, long-term problems', in M. M. Cernea and S. Guggenheim (eds), *Anthropological Approaches to Resettlement: Policy, Theory, and Practice*, Boulder, Colorado: Westview Press.

Horowitz, Michael M. (1991) 'Victims upstream and down', in *Journal of Refugee Studies*, Vol. 4, No. 2, Oxford University Press.

Horowitz, Michael M. and Muneera Salem-Murdock (1990). *Senegal River Basin monitoring activity: synthesis report*, Institute for Development Anthropology, Binghamton, New York.

Keely, Charles B. (1988) Foreword to *The Georgetown Declaration of healthcare for displaced persons and refugees*, Georgetown University, Washington, DC.

Kesmanee, Chupinit (1988) 'Hill tribe relocation policy in Thailand', *Cultural Survival Quarterly*, 12(4).

Kreps, Gary A. (1983) 'The organization of disaster response: core concepts and processes', *International Journal of Mass Emergencies and Disasters*, Vol. 1: 439-67.

— (1987) 'Classical themes, structural sociology, and disaster research', in Russell R. Dynes, De Marchi, and C. Pelanda (eds) *Sociology of Disasters: Contribution of Sociology to Disaster Research*, Franco Angeli, Milan.

Lassailly-Jacob, Veronique (1994) 'Government-sponsored agricultural schemes for involuntary migrants in Africa: some key obstacles to their economic viability', in Adelman, H. and J. Sorenson (eds) *Refugees: Development Aid and Repatriation*, Westview Press, Boulder and York Lanes Press, New York.

Mahapatra, L.K. (1983) 'Development for whom?' paper presented at the International Congress for Anthropological and Ethnographic Sciences, Vancouver.

McColm, R. Bruce (1989) 'The world's unwanted', *The Wall Street Journal*, 28 September.

Mermel, T.W. (1990) 'World Bank's share of worldwide dam construction', in G. Le Moigne, S. Barghouti and H. Plusquellec (eds) *Dam Safety and the Environment*, World Bank Technical Paper No. 115, Washington, DC.

Morna, Colleen Lowe (1990) 'Refugees return to the farm', *African Farmer,*, 4, July.

Morse, Bradford, J. Berger, D. Gamble, H. Brody (1992) *Sardar Sarovar. The report of the independent review*, Resources Futures International (RFI) Inc., Ottawa, Canada.

OECD (1991) 'Guidelines for aid agencies on involuntary displacement and resettlement in development projects', OECD/GD(91)201, Paris, December.

Okidi, C.O. (1993) *Policy and legal framework on development driven involuntary resettlement in African countries* (draft), Moi University, School of Environmental Studies, Eldoret, Kenya.

Oliver-Smith, Anthony (1994) 'Resistance to resettlement: the formation and evolution of movements', in *Research in Social Movements, Conflicts and Change*, Greenwich, CON: JAI Press.

Oliver-Smith, A. and Art Hansen (1982) 'Involuntary migration and resettlement; causes and contexts', in A. Hansen and A. Oliver-Smith (eds) *Involuntary migration and resettlement*, Boulder, Colorado, Westview Press.

Oxfam (1993) 'The Hirakud dam project', Public Policy Department, processed.

Oyedipe, F.P.A. (1983) *Adjustment to resettlement: a study of the resettled peopled in the Kainji Lake basin*, University Press Limited, Ibadan, Nigeria.

Pankhurst, Alula (1992) 'Resettlement and famine in Ethiopia. The villagers' experience', Manchester University Press, Manchester.

Partridge, W.L., A.B. Brown and J.B. Nugent (1982) 'The Papaloapan dam and resettlement project: human ecology and health impacts'. In A. Oliver-Smith and A. Hansen (eds.) *Involuntary Migration and Resettlement*, Westview Press, Boulder, CO.

Paul, James C.N. (1988) 'International development agencies, human rights and humane development projects' in *Denver Journal of International Law and Politics*, Vol. 17, No. 1.

— (1989) 'Rural development, human rights and constitutional orders in sub-Saharan Africa', in *Third world legal studies – 1989: pluralism, participation and decentralization in sub-Saharan Africa*, Valparaiso University, Indiana.

— (1992) 'The human right to development: its meaning and importance', in the *John Marshall Law Review*, Vol. 25: 235.

Qureshi, Moeen (1989) 'Resettlement, development and the World Bank' in *The Bank's World*, No. 5, May.

Refugee Policy Group (1992) *Internally displaced persons in Africa: assistance challenges and opportunities*, Center for Policy, Analysis and Research on Refugee Issues, Washington, DC.

Rew, Alan and P.A. Driver (1986) *Evaluation of the social and environmental impact of the Victoria Dam Project*, Overseas Development Administration (ODA EV392), London.

Salem-Murdock, Muneera (1989) *Arabs and Nubians in New Halfa*, Salt Lake City: University of Utah Press.

Scudder, Thayer (1981) 'What it means to be dammed', *Engineering and Science*, Vol. 54, No. 4. Pasadena.

— (1991) 'A sociological framework for the analysis of new land settlements, in Cernea M.M. (ed.), *Putting people first. sociological variables in rural development*, New York, Oxford University Press.

— (1993) 'Development-induced relocation and refugee studies: 37 years of change and continuity among Zambia's Gwembe Tonga', *Journal of Refugee Studies*, Vol. 6, (forthcoming).

Scudder, Thayer and Elisabeth Colson (1982) 'From welfare to development: a conceptual framework for the analysis of dislocated people', in A. Hansen and A. Oliver-Smith (eds.), *Involuntary Migration and Resettlement*, Westview Press, Boulder, Colorado.

Scudder, Thayer (1973) 'The human ecology of big projects: river basin development and resettlement', *Annual Review of Anthropology*, 2.

Shihata, Ibrahim F.I. (1988) 'The World Bank and human rights: an analysis of the legal issues and the record of achievements', *Denver Journal of International Law and Politics*, Vol. 17, No. 1, 39–66.

Shihata, Ibrahim F.I. (1991) 'Some legal aspects of involuntary population displacement', in Michael M. Cernea and Scott E. Guggenheim (eds), 'Anthropological approaches to resettlement: policy, practice and theory', Westview Press, Boulder, CO.

Soepartomo and P. Tjiptohandojo (1988) 'Comparison between predicted and observed environmental impacts in Saguling Reserve', in CIGB-ICOLD, *Sixteenth International Congress on Large Dams*, Vol. 1, San Francisco, June.

UNHCR (1993) *The state of the world's refugees*. Penguin, New York.

World Bank (1980) Operational Manual Statement 2.33, *Social issues associated with involuntary resettlement in bank-financed projects*, Washington, DC, February.

— (1989) Operational Directive 8.50: *Emergency recovery assistance*, Washington, DC, November.

— (1990) Operational Directives 4.30: *Involuntary resettlement,* Washington, DC, June.

— (1994) *Resettlement and development: the bankwide review of projets involving involuntary resettlement 1986–1993*, World Bank, Environment Department, Washington, DC.

— (1995) 'From emergency to development: the demobilization and reintegration of ex-combatants in Ethiopia'; 'Beyond repatriation: the demobilization and reintegration of ex-combatants in Namibia'; 'From swords to ploughshares: the demobilization and reintegration of ex-combatants in Uganda'; 'War-to-peace transition in Sub-Saharan Africa: lessons from the Horn, the Heart and the Cape'; Poverty and Human Resources Division, Technical Department, Africa Region, The World Bank. (These first three case studies, and the last study, a synthesis paper, were prepared by a core team led by Nat J. Colletta, with support from several Bank staff and consultants).

Zetter, Roger W. (1988) 'Refugees and refugee studies: a label and an agenda', *Journal of Refugee Studies*, Vol. 1, No. 1.

— (1990) 'Labeling refugees: forming and transforming an identity', paper given to the Program in International Cooperation in Africa, Illinois: Northwestern University.

Zolberg, Aristide R., A. Suhrke, and S. Aguayo (1989) *Escape from violence. Conflict and the refugee crisis in the developing world*, New York: Oxford University Press.

22 TERENCE RANGER
Concluding Reflections on Cross-Mandates

I was invited to this symposium not because I know anything about the current situation in the Horn but because I attended the UNRISD Harare seminar on voluntary repatriation and gave the closing summary there. So I find myself again summing up today after a week in which I have learnt a great deal – much of it relevant far beyond the Horn – and during which I have often been stimulated to make comparisons with southern Africa. In what follows I have no doubt that some references to Zimbabwe and Mozambique will creep in.

Yet the experience of this week has been very different from Harare. In that symposium there were clashes between government and agency spokesmen on the one hand and researchers on the other. The methods, findings and legitimacy of research on 'refugees' and 'returnees' were all called into question. So when I summed up in Harare I found myself speaking – to the accompaniment of apocalyptic thunder and lightning – about refugee research, its essential links with the general study of African rural societies, the responsibility of researchers to refugees or to peasants even before the managerial state.

This week researchers have been listened to respectfully – perhaps too respectfully. My task today is to address content rather than method. And here, too, it seems an easier task than in Harare. At first sight there seems to have been remarkable common ground both in our approach – the *questioning* of protocols, mandates, boundaries, identities – and in our aspiration towards one or other form of a 'cross-mandate' which transcends definitional frontiers, whether that cross-mandate be disciplinary, regional, organizational. There has been little to choose between academics, practitioners, agencies and governments in the vigour of the questioning and the ardour of the aspiration.

But while I shall summarize this apparent consensus, I do not want to rest there. It seems to me that the implications of our questioning challenge – and perhaps subvert – our aspirations. I shall seek to draw out this challenge.

Questioning Definitions

Attacks on the definitions with which both researchers and administrators have worked in the past came from every angle. They have been attacked from 'above' as in Enoch Opondo's overview paper and from 'below' in a series of case-studies. You will remember that His Excellency Abdul Meijid Hussein, Minister for External Economic Co-operation, told us in his opening address that he had been waited on by a 'returnee' just as he was setting out for the symposium and that his visitor had rebuked him for coming to yet another talking shop. He would do better, the returnee told him, by 'listening to people like us'. Well, some of our paper-givers *have* listened to the people in the groups among whom they have worked – Wendy James to the 'Uduk', David Turton to the 'Mursi', Tim Allen to the 'Madi'. Work on such small groups, as we were warned by Richard Hogg, can obscure wider regional dynamics, and it can irritate policy-makers because of its emphasis on the need to study every particular case. But, as we have seen, it can bring to bear the real experience of people on the often deadly effect of enclosing definitions. Yet it also became clear that one does not have to work on a small scale or follow one group for years in order to question definitions. In this symposium officials and agency representatives have challenged them too and chafed against their limitations.

Out of all this questioning have come a number of different critiques of the notions of 'refugee', 'returnee' and 'voluntary repatriation'. It is worth setting them out in turn:

1 *Errors of fact or plain misrepresentation.* The detailed case studies have made it plain that so far as individual and group experience is concerned the terms 'refugee', 'returnee' and 'voluntary' carry little meaning. As Tim Allen told us, 'at the local level there may be no clear distinction between a "refugee", a "returnee", a migrant and a "stayee"'. People were aware that agencies made such distinctions and they would themselves variously claim such identities where it was advantageous to do so. But their own experience made nonsense of the definitions, as they moved to and fro across boundaries, always partly pushed and partly pulled, finding themselves in more or less the same situation wherever they ended up. Wendy James, whose 'Uduk' have now returned to Ethiopia in the latest stage of their astonishing wanderings, have crossed and recrossed international boundaries five times. Their 'original' home in the Sudan has now become almost as much an imaginary community as their successive stopping places; however much they may be defined as 'refugees' in Ethiopia, they are at least as much 'returnees'. She urged that they not be allowed to fall between the stools of definition. And David Turton reminded us that for the 'Mursi' – whose identity lay in their self-perceived capacity to move on – the act of 'return' constituted a failure rather than a success. In all these cases rapidly imposed categories did violence to the facts of both experience and perception.

2 *Errors of lumping.* The notions of 'refugee', 'returnee', 'stayee', of 'voluntary' and 'compelled', not only conflict with individual experience, they also impose a misleading generality upon an infinitely complex situation. People have been on the move in the Horn for a great variety of reasons; movement has meant quite different things in different societies. As Tim Allen remarked, 'we are imposing simplistic categories on highly complex social situations'.

3 *Errors of stereotyping and dehumanizing.* The definitions not only oversimplified and overgeneralized, they also demeaned. As Enoch Opondo remarked, '*labelling* is a persistent danger in assistance programmes' and 'a vehicle for promoting non-participation and control'. The label 'returnee' could be a perpetuation of the powerlessness of the refugee: 'returnee is a label which has the potential of isolating the returning refugees as helpless individuals who need outsiders to plan for them.' Enoch proclaimed an objective with which all participants agreed – that the aim was to transform refugees and returnees into 'ordinary people', with all their extraordinary variety of identity and agency.

4 *Errors of separation from the poor as a whole.* But if 'returnees' could be stigmatized, they could also be invidiously favoured. Thus the UNHCR chief in Ethiopia, Cecil

22.1 *Zimbabwean refugees in Mozambique, 1976. (UNHCR/S. Viera de Mello)*

22.2 *Mozambican refugees in Malawi, 1988. (UNHCR/18018/A. Hollmann)*

Kpenou, called in his eloquent oral statement for a focus on all the needy poor rather than only upon returnees with ration cards. He reminded us of the complaint of the unassisted 'stayees' — 'We have nothing to eat but the dust of the trucks which relieve them'. He called for an agenda not only to respond to disasters but 'to break the vicious circle of permanent emergency'.

Moving beyond the inadequacy of definitional categories, some papers drew attention to deeper *conceptual* limitations. We were accustomed to a language created by nineteenth-century nationalism; to concepts which had come to seem natural and unquestionable. Such language and concepts now exercised a tyranny over the imagination. Thus Richard Hogg attacked the idea of frontiers and borders as naturally separating one 'patria' from another so that 'repatriation' was seen as a cure-all. Bounded territories were taken as given units of reconstruction and development. By contrast, he himself stressed the interdependence and linkages which exist between different neighbouring territories, which need to be developed and strengthened in any rehabilitation-cum-development programme.' Writing in particular of the Ogaden, he stressed the importance of focussing on 'the single economic zone' rather than a bounded district, and of the 'revitalization of the regional economy as a whole'.

David Turton pointed out the 'powerful sedentarism in our thinking' which makes us pathologize 'up-rootedness' and migration and which makes permanent settlement seem the natural order of things. Hence we always hear of 'the nomad problem'. But he called for us to problematize what he called 'sedentism' as well.

Now, if I may comment as well as summarize, these are all challenges which resonate with me as a southern Africanist and whose importance extends beyond the Horn to Africa as a whole. The recent research on Mozambican Zambesia reveals a pattern similar to Tim Allen's account of the Sudan/Ugandan border, with constant crossings and recrossings of the frontier; within Mozambique itself internally 'displaced people' are at least as numerous as external 'refugees'; it is far from clear that the repatriation of these refugees — for which the Mozambican and Zimbabwean authorities are now preparing — will be straightforwardly 'voluntary' even though it will not be coerced. Evidence from the camps for Mozambican refugees in neighbouring territories shows that they have come to think of themselves as disregarded and voiceless and that they have no confidence that this will change when they become 'returnees'. But there has also been remarked for southern Africa the same contrast made during this symposium between the politically educated and mobilized Eritrean refugees, eager to return within the framework of a national development plan, and the bewildered refugees of the southern Sudan and northwestern Uganda. At the Harare symposium Stella Makanya argued that the relatively painless return and reintgration of Zimbabwean refugees from Mozambique after 1980 was the product of political consciousness rather than of superior agency planning.[1] The contrast with the alienated Mozambican refugees of today was sharp.

Moreover, the conceptual barriers constituted by the idea of frontiers and the bias in our thinking about pastoralism and sedentism certainly operate in southern Africa too. I supervise several doctoral students who are working in various districts in eastern Zimbabwe, right up against the border with Mozambique. Their work inexorably carries them towards the border but their research is just as inexorably closed off by it; the detailed maps with which they work end their detail at the frontier and show the Mozambican side as blank; although researchers know perfectly well that in pre-colonial times their areas were part of a regional economy which linked them with the Mozambican coast, it is almost impossible to think of them as anything other than 'remote'.

---

[1] S.T. Makanya, 'The desire to return', in T. Allen and H. Morsink (eds) *When Refugees Go Home*, James Currey, 1994.

Moreover, as I said in my summing up at the Harare conference, the border has come to assume a greater reality since 1980 than before it. Whereas once Mozambicans regularly crossed the border to take up waged employment on commercial farms, state plantations and in the communal areas, so that the agrarian economy of the eastern half of Zimbabwe depended upon their low-cost labour, now every Mozambican entering Zimbabwe must either accept classification and encampment as a 'refugee' or be regarded as a spy. Clearly it is imperative for both intellectual and economic reasons to de-mystify the border.

So far as the 'problem of sedentism' is concerned, I have been thinking throughout the symposium of a contrast drawn by Tim Allen during the workshop day which preceded it. Speaking about 'Madi' ideas of identity, he made the point that these did not derive from any sense of place or territory and he contrasted this with the ideas of the 'Shona' peoples of Zimbabwe, who assert the central significance of the ancestral lands in which their heroic and holy dead lie buried. The contrast is real. Yet the most authoritative historian of the Shona-speaking peoples[2] shows that before colonialism they constantly moved from one area to another, leaving one zone to lie fallow and recover while they moved on to exploit more fertile land. Shona oral traditions are designed not so much to reflect the antiquity of continuous occupation as repeatedly to reassert spiritual ownership of freshly occupied territory. After colonial conquest, of course, the Shona people were confined to demarcated Reserves of poor soils; the twentieth-century problem of sedentism and its effect on the environment had begun.

We can see in Zimbabwe, too, a confirmation of David Turton's point that return to previously occupied land may not be what people wish. In Matabeleland during the twentieth century there has been constant eviction and removal of Africans from their lands. Now that 'European' farms and ranches have been acquired by the government for resettlement, there is a debate between the state and the people of Matabeleland. The state wants at least some people to 'return' and to resettle the land in one or other planned model; the people themselves say that they have been moved about quite enough. They wish to remain close to schools and clinics and bore-holes and to use the resettlement land for relief grazing. They want the cattle to return but not the people.

Towards the Cross-Mandate

The final definitional barrier eroded during this symposium was that between 'Relief' and 'Development'. Everyone agreed that the human problems of the Horn could not sensibly be treated as a series of emergencies, by agencies operating on a short-term basis. One way of putting this was to define the recent history of the Horn as one permanent emergency; another way was to say that only by achieving sustainable development could the cycle of emergency be ended. Sustainable development could not be achieved by separating people out into arbitrary categories; it had to be based on the participation of all the 'ordinary people' of the Horn.

So the symposium moved towards the collapse of conventional definitions, towards the recognition of process, towards the expansion of mandates, whether scholarly or administrative. There were calls for cross-discplinary research; Wendy James invited relief-workers to do linguistic research on African ideas of affliction and causation; Douglas Johnson described how he, as a historian, had nevertheless become an adminis-trator of relief; every Ethiopian or Eritrean speaker, as they introduced themselves, revealed spectacular cross-mandate careers, moving between scholarship, politics, relief administration, prison.

But, of course, the main cross-mandate that the symposium discussed was the one

[2] D.N. Beach (1980) *The Shona and Zimbabwe, 1800–1850*, Heinemann Educational Books, London.

recently pioneered in northeast Africa by the UNHCR and presented to us in a series of interventions by Cecil Kpenou of UNHCR's Ethiopian office. Kpenou's exposition of the cross-mandate collaboration of United Nations agencies, together with the NGOs, and within the framework of Ethiopan Government development planning, was the major reason for the appearance of consensus at the symposium. After all, a breakaway from UNHCR's restrictive mandate only to protect and relieve refugees had been called for in papers written for the symposium before their authors knew about the initiative in Ethiopia; it was welcomed in papers written by authors who did know about it; Wendy James appealed to it as a way of overriding the definitional rigidities which imperil the 'Uduk'. Cecil Kpenou's moving fervour in presenting a future in which relief gives way to reintegration and reintegration takes place within a systematic plan for development; in which the focus switches from assisting those with formally defined entitlements to assisting all the poor; in which rural society and economy is reconstructed – all this won him a well merited round of applause.

Nevertheless, there remain some reservations. At the level of aspiration, calls for new ways of thought and life on the part of the agencies sounded so utopian that I began to think of the cross-mandate as belonging to what Turton called 'the land of dreams' to which there is no returning rather than to his 'actual terrain' to which migrants move. At the level of implementation, it was hard to see how the cross-mandate is going to work. Even in Ethiopia the draft statement of inter-agency collaboration (which the government has asked UNHCR to produce) had not yet been circulated. Richard Hogg told us that in the Ogaden, where the idea of the cross-mandate is being invoked, there is much confusion about its implications. It isn't clear at the moment whether the cross-mandate will allow the various UN agencies to go on being separate – indeed by means of the collaboration of all to allow each to be *more* distinctly focussed – or whether there will be some sort of fusion. (Someone invoked the vision of a single UN flag flying in Addis instead of the banners of all the different agencies.)

No doubt these and other uncertainties will be clarified as the cross-mandate begins to operate. But I want to raise here a more fundamental question. It has seemed to me to be odd that when we have discussed this week the artificial dichotomy between 'Relief' and 'Development', it has been the idea of development which has seemed the less problematic. It has been as if it would be a great release to be freed from emergency relief and enabled to participate in development work. Yet we all know that in other conferences in other places the whole idea of 'Development' has itself been questioned and deconstructed. Development is no longer – in the words of the Pope – the new term for Peace. We all know of the failings both of Commandist and of Liberal development planning, united despite their other ideological differences by their arrogance and top-down authoritarianism. We know that African intellectuals like Professor Issa Shivji are rejecting a definition of Human Rights in Africa which derives from the ideology of developmentalism.

Plainly, we cannot link the idea of development at all straightforwardly with the concern for the environment voiced here by Gaim Kibreab and other speakers. For one thing, so many African development plans have intensified the problems of sedentism by insisting on regrouping or villagization, and even Kpenou spoke of doing away with all 'unnecessary movement'. For another thing, it is clear that development projects have often been counter to the interests of the poor. We heard this morning from Elias Habte-Sellassie about 'development' schemes in the Awash Valley which *created* refugees. In Mozambique today, where much land is being leased to multinational corporations or to white commercial farmers, 'returnees' may find themselves coming back as a labour-tenantry. Plainly the UNHCR does not intend such consequences, but the ambiguities of development make one anxious about the speed with which the cross-mandate strategy is designed to operate.

Now, you might say – and I would myself be very sympathetic – that UNHCR-led development would be bottom up. The two formulations we have had this week have been – restore agricultural production and 'normal markets', and general development will follow; and aim at a minimum of adequate food, adequate water, adequate health provision and adequate education. It sounds marvellous, an echo of the rural welfarism which characterized Zimbabwean development planning in the early 1980s. Yet, there are immediately vast problems. Zimbabwe and other African countries have found this minimum strategy vastly expensive. Zimbabwe is currently striving to provide water and food at the expense of charging for health and education. One has to ask where the huge sums necessary for such a strategy in Ethiopia are likely to come from in an era where, as we have been told by Mandefro Tegegne, all the world applauds the idea of voluntary repatriation but no-one is anxious to pay for it. Surely the costs in Ethiopia would far exceed the US$250 million sought by the Eritrean Government and stigmatized by UNHCR and the United States as a grotesquely inflated demand. If funds cannot be found for Eritrean repatriation, in a seemingly ideal situation where we are told that the government wants the refugees back, the refugees want to come back, and there is an overall rehabilitation plan, then they will not be found for the more ambiguous situations in Ethiopia and the Sudan. And if enough money is not available, will there not be a concentration of development in the core areas of countries, leaving those very border regions which have generated refugees still neglected? Will there not be a focus on the sedentary and a neglect of the nomadic? Can the UNHCR persuade governments not only to tolerate but to exploit the profits of unofficial cross-border trade?

And then there are the political problems of the cross-mandate. In the Ethiopian case the national government is to be the 'lead' agency; but there is no state in the southern Sudan; and as Hubert Morsink reminded us insistently, national regimes are not the best 'leads' for *regional* development plans. In any case, African states themselves are profoundly problematic. Mohamed Salih insisted to us that states must *always* play the lead role, stressing the unrepresentativeness and lack of accountability of UN agencies and NGOs. Yet in pondering his dictum that 'A bad state is better than no state at all', one is compelled to remember the contribution of 'bad states' to the permanent crisis of the Horn. And even 'good states', as I personally take Julius Nyerere's Tanzania to have been, have initiated development plans and had them backed with huge international grants and loans, which in the end have been very far from achieving sustainable participatory development.

Getting Institutions Right

This is, of course, where we turn to Teddy Brett's paper on 'Recreating war-damaged communities in Uganda: the institutional dimension', and to the discussion initiated by him and Gaim Kibreab this morning. You will remember that Brett detected three phases in African development thinking since political independence – a phase in which the slogan was 'Get Ideologies Right', a phase in which it was 'Get Prices Right', and now a phase in which it has become 'Get Institutions Right'. It was now widely recognized, he told us, that the decay of Africa's institutions was the most fundamental dimension of the African crisis.

From the perspective of this symposium it was what Brett had to say about local government institutions which was most relevant. It has often been the collapse of the legitimacy of local government which has led to factionalism, war and flight; today, successful repatriation and rural development from below will clearly depend upon people being drawn in to credible local institutions of participation and representation.

In the general discussion, Brett remarked upon the difficulty of achieving democratic accountability when a majority of a state's population was illiterate and cut off from information. I want now to make some comments on his model, on his Uganda case-study and on the question of local institutions in general drawn from the southern African experience.

1 It seems to me that in a democratic system the most crucial role for people in the rural areas is not really to demand accountability for management at the centre. As Gaim Kibreab said, people know what they want, and their role is to demand the resources to achieve it. The role of the state in a democratic system is to balance such demands. One of the major deficiencies in supposed African democracies has been failure to construct institutional means for the expression of local interests. In Zimbabwe development plans theoretically proceed from the bottom up. In practice, however, they always descend from the top. Local institutions – such as village development committees – either act as the instruments of the state

22.3 *Everyone knew that no-one had ever paid any attention to them and that no-one ever would: refugees from Mozambique.* *(UNHCR/19068/A. Hollman)*

or at best share in silent obstruction of central development plans. In Mozambique it is now recognized that a critical element in Frelimo's loss of much of the rural population was its refusal to allow that rural people might understand their own interests. In both Zimbabwe and Mozambique the result has been the revival of so-called 'traditional' authorities, whose legitimacy and accountability is both more understandable and more enforceable.

Now, of course, there is a particular refugee/returnee dimension here. If rural 'ordinary people' have been voiceless, refugees have been yet more so. I was told this year of a visit to a Mozambican refugee camp by various NGO workers and by representatives of the Mozambican churches. Refugees were asked to express their grievances and their desires. At this point an old man rose and in tears protested. Everyone knew that no-one had ever paid any attention to them and that no-one ever would. To ask them was both a waste of time and adding insult to injury. A Mozambican bishop replied, invoking the need for courtesy to guests and pointing out that the refugees had plenty of time. Let us pretend, he said, that someone *may* pay attention. So the day was spent recording the views of the refugees and consolidating them – and in the end the refugees agreed that cables be sent to Rome, where Frelimo and Renamo were negotiating, expressing their demands. I don't know whether the Rome negotiators paid any attention to these cables but with an election coming up there is certainly a new sensitivity to rural opinion. Refugees and returnees are now being instructed by 'animation' teams in the arts of plural electoral politics where once they were instructed in Socialist mobilization. Elections are blunt instruments for ensuring that every so often regimes have to pay attention to local demands but they are better than nothing. And these are considerations which will certainly have to be taken into account in the Horn. Can the patriotic mobilization of Eritrean refugees and returnees, for example, give way to the flexibilities of pluralism, or will its development plan display the commandist arrogance of past revolutionary regimes ?

2 As I have implied above, at local level rural people have very clear ideas of account-ability even if their ideas cannot be enforced at the centre. And certainly if one defines Civil Society in the way Brett does as the 'sphere of reciprocity' then the rural areas are the zone *par excellence* of Civil Society. I stress this because much of the discussion of democracy by African intellectuals is dominated by the assumptions of the 'modern' urban classes; in Mozambique it has been explicitly asserted that African rural areas cannot be democratic nor constitute any part of Civil Society, and in Zimbabwe those who wish to see 'the peasantry' play a key role in politics are frustrated by its apparent inability to do so. It needs to be said that if the idea of Civil Society *cannot* include local, rural democratic institutions then it will have to be jettisoned as yet another irrelevant European notion of political modernization. The democrats of northeast Africa must learn to understand and respect rural societies.

3 Gaim Kibreab raised in particular the question of 'traditional' authorities and the environment. There was sharp debate between those who held that there had been significant traditional constraints on abuse of the land and those who held that rural ignorance was the greatest environmental threat. Here I would like to draw some lessons from my work over the past five or six years on the environmental history of the Matopos in southern Matabeleland. In the Matopos mountains there exist today influential shrines of a High God cult which articulates an ideology of relationship with the land. Rhodesian scientific conservationism, ignoring this ideology, imposed itself upon the hills, evicting most families and policing the cultivation of those who remained. But the lesson is not so much the superiority of indigenous tradition over colonial science. It is more that neither form of knowledge is adequate in itself. So-called 'tradition' had to change so as to take account of greatly increased population pressure and the other effects of sedentism. Scientific conservationism was often less sensitive to ecological realities than indigenous practice, but it also had much to offer to peasant agriculture and stock-rearing. So, like the other false dichotomies des-troyed at the symposium, we must reject the sterile dichotomy of 'traditional' and 'modern'. Cultivators and pastoralists deserve the best of agricultural and veterinary expertise, offered to them in the spirit of democratic voluntarism. Certainly the alleged ignorance of rural populations and the threat it poses to the environment must never be allowed to abort the development of local democratic institutions.

4 My research in the Matopos also relates to the very important discussion on healing initiated by Tim Allen and Melissa Parker. You will remember that that discussion posed several problems. What did one do if local ideas of 'healing' resulted in the killing of old women as witches? Could one focus on individual post-traumatic stress or might one aim at societal healing? Could this be done by provision for mental health in rural clinics or by means of understanding and harnessing indigenous concepts? These questions are central to the process of return and of rebuilding local societies of legitimacy.

The southern African data illustrates both what not to do and also the potentials for collective healing from violence. In Mozambique, it seems to me, there has been a swing from total contempt for indigenous ideas of healing to a too-great readiness to endorse whatever is locally demanded. I was told this summer by a Mozambican researcher about the first two points in a memorandum written by a local administrator on how to win support. These were, first, 'to build palaces for the diviners', and second, 'to build prisons for the witches'. 'I admire the work done on African religions in Zimbabwe', he added, 'but don't you think this is going too far?' Well, yes, I do, just as I think that the 'Madi' witch-killings described by Tim Allen are repugnant to any system of legitimate rural democracy. Their social cost, quite apart from their moral cost, is too great.

In any case, witchcraft explanations duck the real issue of collective cleansing of guilt and collective re-establishment of peace and right relationship with the land. In Zimbabwe since 1980 there has been a fascinating development within every religious system – mainline Christianity, African independency, so-called African Traditional Religion – of healing rituals which relate individual guilt and suffering to collective experience and to the violent history of 100 years of war and state oppression. Perhaps because of these rituals, witch-killings (once abundant during the guerrilla war) have ceased in rural Zimbabwe; the possibility has been offered for the re-establishment of a rural Pax Africana. I certainly believe that Yonas Endale, the very impressive Ethiopian doctor who told us of his experience with the post-traumatic depression of Ethiopian soldiers, needs to explore not only the international literature of psycho-therapy and psychiatry but also the range of collective rituals available in Ethiopia itself.

Ethnicity, Representation and Legitimacy

There remains one critical issue. Brett's paper on Uganda took for granted, without dis-cussing it, that local government must have an ethnic base. 'Ethnicities' hitherto excluded must be made to feel part of the political system. Yet as many of the papers and dis-cussions of this symposium show, ethnicity must be problematized as rigorously as all the other terms we challenged. All the detailed case-study papers showed the recency, fluidity and relativity of ethnic identity. That is why I have insisted on placing ethnic names in quotation marks throughout this summary. David Turton shows that 'Mursi' identity, though valued, is perceived as conditional on particular circumstances and as less funda-mental than clan membership. Tim Allen shows that 'Madi' identity has been constructed in response to the practices of the colonial state. Wendy James offers in her paper a superb case study of how the 'Uduk' have first been perceived and now perceive themselves as an ethnicity. But her paper also shows how other groupings have been fragmented and lost all identity in the upheavals which have created the 'Uduk'. As she remarks, the 'Uduk' are not a historic people with a problem, but a people created by the problem.

Now, of course, the achievement of 'Uduk' group identity has been in many ways a heroic enterprise and one which will not be lightly given up. It has come to mean something even to be 'Madi' and on occasion something worth fighting and killing for. But it is plain that in northeast and southern Africa ethnicity is not something primordial, something given, something which defines identity exclusive of all other factors. I found myself in great sympathy with Julius Holt when he protested against the constant enumeration of 'those bloody Somali clans' as though to know a person's clan was to know everything essential about them. One might say that in many cases ethnicity is another dimension of the problem of sedentism and that there still exist wider networks of interaction and culture.

From all this I draw two conclusions for the re-establishment of local political institutions in northeast Africa:

1 Given that the state has played so great a role in creating modern 'ethnicity' and tribalism in the first place, there is no way out of destabilizing 'tribal conflict' by

means of *further* definition and reification by the state. What needs rather to be done is to separate wherever possible the political and the ethnic, so that, for example, whole populations are not purged as part of the attack on this or that faction leader. We can learn from events in the Soviet Union and in Yugoslavia the dangers of an official 'nationality' theory. Commentators write as if ancient ethnic hostilities have erupted from the ruins of the centralizing state. In fact, Stalinist nationality theory created many new ethnic entities and reified old ones, leaving ethnicity as the sole principle of organization available when the central state collapsed. It seems most unfortunate that the new regime in Ethiopia has maintained its predecessor's interest in the enumeration and mapping of 'nationalities' and that its plans for regional government are based on the idea of the dominant ethnicities. As Alula Pankhurst pointed out, the census shows northerners scattered all over Ethiopia; as Richard Hogg pointed out, minority ethnicities in regions fear domination and every local faction can ally itself to one of the new ethnic parties. Unless Ethiopia is very lucky, or changes its policy in time, there must be danger of secession movements and even of 'ethnic cleansing'. So, like Richard Hogg, I would greatly prefer a federal system based on pan-ethnic regionalism rather than on dominant ethnicity.

2 In other situations, of course, it may prove impossible to implement a regionalism which is not expressed in ethnic terms – western Kenya is bound to be 'Luo', central Kenya bound to be 'Kikuyu'. But here I strongly recommend a reading of volume two of John Lonsdale and Bruce Berman's *Unhappy Valley*.[3] Here Lonsdale gives a masterly analysis of the difference between what he calls moral ethnicity and political tribalism. The first is his short-hand for the processes which have ensured in Kenya that debates about values and relationships have taken place within ethnicities rather than at the centre of the state; the second his short-hand for the political manipulation by the state of tribal clientages. The trick for a democratic state is to seek to generalize moral debate and to abstain from tribal manipulation. Unfortunately, President Moi seems to be doing exactly the opposite.

In short, and to summarize, to show the sort of respect for the culture of ordinary people which is necessary to re-establish communities and to bring returnees and stayees into legitimate democratic politics, it is *not* necessary to privilege ethnicity. In so far as debates about legitimacy and accountability have taken place within the disputed definition of ethnicity these can be given expression within a wider and more diffused system of local government.

Conclusion

Perhaps I should declare two 'interests' in conclusion. Teddy Brett remarked that during the period when states tried to get the ideologies right, there was a suppressed debate between 'anarchists', who disliked either state or market interventions in rural society, and both Socialist and Liberal advocates of state modernization. I guess I speak today as a repentant or born-again anarchist. I have disliked and do dislike expressions of state arrogance towards the masses; it has often been tempting to see the state simply, in the current terminology, as 'stomach' or 'vampire'. However, in the contemporary Africa of the retreating state it is possible to see that local rural people need the state. The trick is for the state to be adequately responsive to local demands, and for that one needs not academic but African agrarian anarchists. I think that once they have broken away from

[3] Bruce Berman and John Lonsdale (1992) *Unhappy Valley: conflict in Kenya and Africa*, James Currey, London.

22.4 *Ethiopia has been given a rare second chance: children near Addis Ababa, 1992.*
(Tim Allen)

the impotent anonymity of the refugee camp, 'returnees' can make pretty good anarchists. That makes me optimistic about their contribution to democratic reconstruction.

And that is my second declaration of interest. I am by nature an optimist about Africa. I expected that the realities of the northeast part of the continent would be the strongest possible test of such optimism. And yet I have found a good deal to be optimistic about. Abdul Meijid Hussein said that Ethiopia has been given a rare second chance, 'not something that happens often in history'. In Brett's account, Uganda has a second chance too. Eritrea has a first chance. Maybe, if the various cross-mandates really work, and the definitional and conceptual rigidities are abandoned, and the delicate balances of democratic development are achieved, northeast Africa can break the cycle of permanent crisis and turn refugees and returnees into ordinary people.

Index

330